HIPPOCRENE U.S.A. Guide to

America's South

Other Books by Tom Weil

A Clearing in the Jungle (1979)

A Balance of Power (1981)

Last at the Fair: A Book of Travel (1986)

America's Heartland: A Travel Guide to the
  Back Roads of Illinois, Indiana, Iowa and
  Missouri (1989)

America's South: A Travel Guide to the
  Eleven Southern States (1990)

The Cemetery Book: Graveyards, Catacombs
  and Other Travel Haunts Around the World (1992)

The Mississippi River: Nature, Culture and
  Travel Sites Along the "Mighty Mississip" (1992)

America's Heartland: A Travel Guide to the
  Back Roads of Illinois, Indiana, Iowa, Missouri
  and Kansas (2nd edition, 1992)

America's South: The Atlantic States
  (2nd edition, 1993)

to

AMERICA'S SOUTH:

The Gulf and the Mississippi States

The States of Alabama, Mississippi,
Louisiana, Kentucky, Tennessee
and Arkansas

TOM WEIL

HIPPOCRENE BOOKS
New York

For Ruby and Mike Stern
and
In Memory of William K. Jacobs, Jr.

This guide is based on *America's South*, published in 1990 by Hippocrene Books. *America's South: The Gulf and the Mississippi States* covers six states which border the Gulf of Mexico and the Mississippi River and includes an extensive new chapter on the Civil War sites. The first volume of the new editions, *America's South: The Atlantic States*, which also includes a guide to Civil War sites, was published in 1993.

Photos courtesy of Alabama Bureau of Tourism and Travel, Arkansas Department of Parks and Tourism, Kentucky Department of Travel Development, Louisiana Office of Tourism, Mississippi Division of Tourism, and Tennessee Tourist Development (State Photo Services).

For information, address:
Hippocrene Books, Inc.
171 Madison Ave.
New York, NY 10016

Library of Congress Cataloging-in-Publication Data
Weil, Tom.
    Hippocrene U.S.A. guide to America's South: the Gulf and the Mississippi states: the states of Alabama, Mississippi, Louisiana, Kentucky, Tennessee, and Arkansas.
    p.   cm.
Includes index.
ISBN 0-7818-0171-0
    1. Southern States—Guidebooks.   I. Title.   II. Title: Hippocrene USA guide to America's South.
F207.3.W395   1994
917.604'43--dc20
                                        93-49645
                                           CIP

Contents

"For peregrination charms our senses with such un-speakable and sweet variety, that some count him un-happy that never travelled."
—*Robert Burton,* The Anatomy of Melancholy

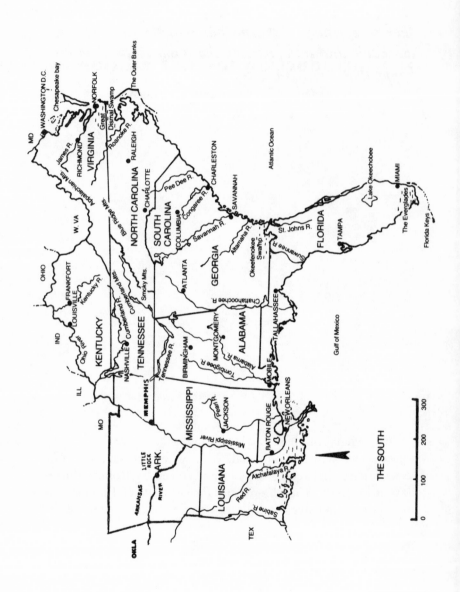

THE SOUTH

Introduction to First Edition

A Welcome to the Reader

This book is a guide to the eleven Southern states. Although *America's South* serves as a complete guide to the entire region, including the cities and the better-known places, the book emphasizes the area's back-road, off-the-beaten-track attractions—the pleasant villages, scenic rural areas, picturesque corners of the countryside, unusual historical enclaves and other such places that typify the small-town old-time South. Many of these sights are delightful; some of them the traveler will find unusual; while a few present a certain eccentricity that recalls the caution voiced by Robert Beverley in his 1705 *The History and Present State of Virginia*, the first comprehensive work on the South's leading state in the early days:

> 'Tis agreed that travelers are of all men the most suspected of insincerity. This does not only hold in their private conversations, but likewise in the grand tours and travels with which

they pester the public and break the bookseller. There are no books (the legends of the saints always excepted) so stuffed with poetical stories as voyages, and the more distant the countries lie which they pretend to describe, the greater the license those privileged authors take in imposing upon the world.

My reason for "imposing upon the world" and "pestering" the public—but, hopefully, not breaking the bookseller— with *America's South* arises from my belief that back-road roamings in the United States provide one of the most delightful travel experiences available anywhere. This book will guide you to the region's unusual and little-known areas, places filled with the flavor and feel of the South where you can gather your own collection of "poetical stories," as Beverley put it, about this historically rich and colorful region of America.

The book presents a series of itineraries. Although all arrangements of guidebooks are arbitrary—apart from the alphabetic, favored by some guides, which lacks all coherence except the purely mechanical—I have tried to devise routings with a certain geographic logic to them, itineraries that make sense and which are convenient to follow. Of course, rarely, if ever, does the traveler follow on the road a path identical to the one on the printed page. So as you wander off the suggested routes, both the index and the section headings will help you locate material on the places you visit. Those headings provide a general idea of the cities included, but the text also contains many other attractions located between those cities not listed at the beginning of each section. Areas such as the Natchez Trace, Cumberland Gap, the Great Dismal Swamp and others that spread across more than one state are usually covered in the chapters on each state whose territory they occupy.

Although it's impossible to include every worthwhile attraction in a region as vast as the South, and equally impossible to know the interests of any particular reader, I've tried to mention at least in passing virtually all of the places that "the unbiased traveler seeking information," as Mark Twain described the ideal tourist, might enjoy. This diverse and comprehensive compilation of sights includes a complete range of subjects so that readers or roamers who favor culture, history, the arts, the outdoors, scenery, food, wineries, recreation, museums, factory tours, festivals, water sports, ethnic enclaves and any number of other interests will find those topics covered.

America's South, however, features those back-road, out-of-the-way and lesser-known attractions—often so difficult to ferret out—that afford unexpected delights and unusual experiences. The text attempts to steer travelers to corners of the South which, in my view, the visitor will find especially colorful, interesting, historic or otherwise rewarding, and I have devoted relatively more space to those less obvious but no less alluring places. Even the city sections usually include some of the offbeat attractions. My presumption, and hope, is that the independent and resourceful traveler will, once introduced to a particular place, by inquiry and exploration find there additional attractions too numerous to list in the text. Whole books could be and have been written about any one of the sights included in *America's South.* So please realize that once you arrive at a certain place, it most likely offers attractions in addition to those mentioned in the text. On the theory that any traveler interested in back-road off-the-beaten-track attractions savors in his soul a certain sense of adventure, I've included bed and breakfast establishments, places that lack the predictability of the chain motels but which offer the delights of individualized and personalized accommodations. Also mentioned are inns and hotels of historic interest or which boast an especially attractive setting or ambiance, as well as restaurants that serve typical regional food or, like the hotels, offer interesting or historic features.

The narrative also includes unusual or typical festivals, fairs and similar such celebrations. These are mentioned not only so the traveler might attend such festive events but also to indicate what a community finds worth commemorating, a facet of a locality that suggests the area's flavor. This conforms with my intention to present to the reader not only the South's attractions but also its ambiance. With a view to that end, I have laced the narrative with a scattering of anecdotes, quotations, historical references, minibiographies of colorful characters and other such vignettes that suggest something of the South's flavor, culture and background. This added dimension hopefully makes *America's South* suitable not only for the sightseer but also for the armchair traveler who wants to read about the region.

Frequent references in the text to sights listed on the National Register of Historic Places (referred to in the book as the National Register) arise because Register listing, although not infallible, seems to me to indicate the probable merit of an attraction. Criteria for Register designation include "significance in American history, architecture, archaeology, engineering, and culture" of places

> that possess integrity of location, design, setting, materials, workmanship, feeling, association, and: A. are associated with events that have made a significant contribution to the broad patterns of our history; or B. are associated with the lives of significant persons in our past; or C. embody the distinctive characteristics of a type, period, or method of construction; represent the work of a master; possess high artistic values; or represent a significant and distinguishable entity whose components may lack individual distinction; or D. have yielded, or may be likely to yield, information important in prehistory or history.

The inclusion of Historic Register references and brief historical comments, it is hoped, will enrich the travel experience by integrating place and time: the text puts into the context of the past the sight you see. As for the past, many places in the South boast that they are the "oldest" or "first" of their kind and I have recorded such claims even though localities elsewhere in the region may put forth the same boast of antiquity or longevity, a competition I leave to the different claimants to sort out.

America's South is a companion volume to *America's Heartland,* a guide to and evocation of the Middle West, also published by Hippocrene. In the course of my travels to collect material for these two books, which cover nearly one third of the states, both the remarkable openness of the American people and the fascinating variety offered by the United States have greatly impressed me. Those who complain that the country has become standardized and homogeneous need only leave the interstates and the airports to roam the inner states and back roads, where travelers will find an extraordinary mix of cultures, ethnic groups, religions, societies, customs, attitudes, sights and traditions as interesting as anywhere in the world.

For me, and I hope for you as well, there is something alluring about starting not only a trip but also a travel book. Anticipation sharpens the senses and whets one's appetite for the world that lies before us, either on the road or on the printed page. In 1857 Sir Richard Burton, the greatest traveler of modern times, wrote:

The gladdest moment in human life methinks is the departure on a distant journey. Shaking off with one mighty effort the fetters of habit, the leaden weight of routine, the cloak of many cares, the slavery of home, man feels once more happy. The blood flows with the fast circulation of childhood. Excitement lends unwonted freedom to the muscle, and the sudden sense of freedom adds a cubit to the mental stature. . . . A journey, in fact, appeals to the imagination, to memory, to hope—the sister Graces of our mortal being.

So I welcome you to *America's South*—both the book and the region—with the wish that your hopes, memory and imagination will all be filled and fulfilled by that historic, colorful and often eccentric corner of the country.

Travel in America's South

The American South has always exerted a fascination for outsiders as well as Southerners. From the very earliest days of the continent's exploration, the region attracted travelers. The first extended expedition through the North American interior included much of the South when Hernando de Soto and his six hundred soldiers trekked across an area comprising some three hundred and fifty thousand square miles starting in western Florida, where the adventurers landed in October 1539. From there the Spaniards proceeded to the Blue Ridge Mountains, then southwest across Alabama to the Mobile Bay area, on to Mississippi and over to Arkansas. So began organized tours through the South. Soon additional groups—not quite yet on a Cook's Tour or an American Express jaunt—traveled from Europe to visit the region, and before long the French, the Spanish and the English each established in the South their first North American colonies. From 1861 to 1865 a number of Northerners—not exactly tourists—journeyed through all parts of Dixie, a veritable invasion of Yankees, and about a century later, not far from where de Soto departed on the first group travel excursion through the region, Walt Disney colonized a corner of Florida, an outpost that stimulated a new invasion of visitors into the South.

The entire South is a theme park of sorts. If the region didn't exist, someone would have to invent it. Because the South does exist, many observers have tried to reinvent it. Library shelves—and perhaps readers—groan under weighty tomes about the fabled region, books that examine, analyze, interpret and misinterpret the area. What other American region could supply such fertile ground for all the legends and lore, speculations, studies, introspections, inspections and dissections, factions and fictions—not to mention novels and other fiction—that stem from the South? And what other corner of the country affords the traveler such a colorful array of people and traditions—white and blue collar, blue bloods and redskins and red-neck types, blacks and the blues, the Blue Ridge Mountains, Kentucky's Bluegrass country and Alabama's Black Belt region, the Navy's Blue Angels and the Army's Green Berets, the Green and the Red rivers, a Greeneville and Greenvilles, Greensboros and Greenwoods, Baton Rouge, oranges and lemons, yellow fever memorials, white columns and white cotton, an Auburn University and a Scarlett O'Hara plus many other hues across the South's spectrum? Such familiar staples as cotton fields and columned antebellum plantation houses typify the image of the region most outsiders hold. Travelers to the South carry with them mental baggage heavy with accumulated perceptions, myths even, that seem to define the area, one of Faulknerian complexity—so the mythology goes—permeated with a not yet *Gone with the Wind* romanticism, a land garnished with moss-draped oaks, irrigated with mint juleps, embellished with those stately mansions and oozing with antebellum charm.

As America's most self-conscious region, the South seemingly likes to cultivate its myriad mythologies—the soil there nurtures myths as readily as it does cotton or tobacco—just as outsiders apparently enjoy being beguiled by them. Familiarity breeds content, making it comforting to view the South through Scarlett-colored glasses. When the Hachette publishing house in Paris wanted to define the region for French readers it issued a book entitled *Le Sud au temps de Scarlett*— "The South of the Scarlett Era." *Gone with the Wind*'s Scarlett O'Hara, the forward affirms, symbolizes the South much as Don Quixote does Spain, a comparison the region's first tourists, the Spaniard de Soto and his men, might not appreciate. Americans as well as foreigners tend to see the South in those myth-laden antebellum terms. "The average American thinks of the old South as a unit," says the evocatively named Thomas Jefferson Wertenbaker in *The Old South*. "To him the region below the Mason and Dixon Line was a land of wealthy planters who built stately mansions, filled their broad acres with the labor of scores of slaves, [and] lived luxuriously." This quintessential image of the South conforms with the 1823 description by John A. Quitman, later Mississippi governor, of daily life in the great houses of Natchez: "Mint juleps in the morning are sent to our rooms, and then follows a delightful breakfast in the open veranda. We hunt, ride, fish, pay morning visits, play chess, read or lounge until dinner, which is served at two p.m. in great variety." These strenuous exertions demanded an afternoon nap, after which "the tea table is always set before sunset, and then, until bedtime, we stroll, sing, play whist, or croquet. It is an indolent, yet charming life, and one quits thinking and takes to dreaming." This sort of dreamy routine at least one latter-day observer described as *The Lazy South*, the title of David Bertelson's study of Southern attitudes toward work—an X-rated four letter word in the region, he claims.

Back in those lazy days long before Martin Luther King, cotton was king and blacks the monarch's vassals. The South, so myth had it, enjoyed in those days an idyllic existence. "Plenty was the rule; want was a stranger to the humblest. Life was prolonged by the feeblest exertion," maintained W. Brewer in his 1872 history of Alabama. "Her citizens were hospitable, her officials were faithful, her slaves contented and happy." So seemed the South in the antebellum era, a time doomed to end but destined to survive in the region's mythology. An early precursor of future frictions occurred in April 1830 when—to President Andrew Jackson's Jefferson Day dinner toast, "Our Federal Union—it must be preserved!"—Vice-president John C. Calhoun of South Carolina tellingly replied, "The Union—next to our liberty, the most dear!" This succinct response, which cost Calhoun Jackson's support for the 1836 Presidential nomination, speaks volumes about the attitudes of the two antagonists, as does the Civil War battlefield colloquy between the Confederate trooper who shouted across the lines to a Union soldier, "Why don't you come over to our side? We're fighting for honor and you're only fighting for money," to which the Yankee retorted, "Well, I reckon each of us is fighting for what we need the most."

Tourist bureaus in the South can thank the Civil War for creating throughout the region a countless number of attractions—museums, monuments, mementos, memorials, and even myths, all of which travelers in the Southern states will find in abundance. You could muster an entire army with all the soldiers' statues that stand in courthouse squares in Dixie. To this day the War Between the States, as Southerners call the conflict, survives as one of the regions overriding myths. Who in the North, or elsewhere, ever thinks about the war? In the South, however, the conflict which so split families, the nation and even the South itself serves, ironically, as a kind of unifying force, a historical trauma and drama whose impact still lingers in the former Confederate states.

These archetypical elements—the columned mansions, a *Gone with the Wind*ism, the laid-back and perhaps even lazy way of life, the war's lingering influence—and others have all contributed to the South's image and to the mythology that the region remains a land apart, different in its essence from other areas of the nation. "Myths about slavery, plantations, poor whites, Secession, the Civil War, Reconstruction, black-white relations and a host of other topics envelop the South," notes Grady McWhiney in *Southerners and Other Americans*. "One of the great myths of American history is that when the Civil War began Southerners were fundamentally different from the Northerners." As the visitor to the South will learn in the course of his travels, the myths— the antebellum atmosphere and all the rest—are true in the sense that they define certain aspects of the South. But those myths, viewed alone, present a false image of the area, for they reflect only a small portion of the South's culture and thus fall far short of defining the Southern states as they are today. As for differences, the South, to be sure, is different, but so in their own way are the Middle West, New England, the cowboy West and other American regions, each of which boasts its own distinctive characteristics. Although the South likes to fancy itself as a distinct sort of place—an area defined by its seemingly unique quirks, eccentricities, grotesqueries, folklore, legends and mythologies—taken as a whole today's South, much as it might like to be different, "is really just another region," as Edmund Fawcett and Tony Thomas conclude in *The American Condition*.

It is the South's remarkable and unexpected variety, rather than its unique traits as represented by the myths, which characterizes the region. Although the South, like any section of the nation, does in some ways offer a different and distinctive flavor, the area contains many attractions which visitors might not expect to find in that part of the country. A traveler who spends any length of time in the Southern states may well be surprised at the wide range of sights there. Much of the South, in fact, seems quite un-South-like. Even the old South didn't always operate true to its conventional image. Before the Civil War, to take just one example, Virginia opposed secession, North Carolina never officially seceded but only repealed its 1789 legislation authorizing it to join the Union, and Kentucky never seceded at all. All this is just not Southern-like behavior. As for today's South, it may well be the nation's most varied region, for Dixie boasts examples of features found elsewhere, along with many attractions unique to the Southern states. This combination of home-grown and outside characteristics lends the area its variety and a richness travelers will find appealing.

The South's geographical variety—its characteristics typical of other regions—includes elements more commonly associated with the North, the East and the West. As Fletcher M. Green asserts in *The Role of the Yankee in the Old South,* Northern influences and institutions abound in the South, phenomena which belie "the myth that the people of the Northern and Southern states constituted two distinct and irreconcilable social and cultural groups." Around the South a traveler will encounter such New England-like attributes as covered bridges, ski resorts (in North Carolina, Tennessee and Kentucky), colonial architecture, Elizabethan-era gardens and accents and a British burial ground (all in North Carolina), Revolutionary War monuments and battlefields, fishing villages, Atheneum-like cultural societies (Charleston and Louisville boast such institutions), and a Boston Route 128-type high-tech enclave at North Carolina's Research Triangle Park. Middle Western touches in the South include such Wrights and wrongs as structures built by Illinois' Frank Lloyd Wright (in Frankfort, Kentucky and many in Lakeland, Florida) and monuments to Ohio's Orville and Wilbur Wright and a bank (in Russellville, Kentucky) robbed by Missourian Jesse James's gang, while Missourian Mark Twain's ancestral town (in Tennessee) and Abe Lincoln of Illinois's birthplace (in Kentucky) recall those two figures associated with mid-America.

In the nineteenth century the South was the West, the American frontier. Wild West traces still survive there with any number of exhibits, memorials, houses and historic sites that recall Daniel Boone, Davy Crockett, George Rogers Clark, Jim Bowie and other such pioneers. Rodeos and buffalo herds bring Western touches to two Southern states (Florida and Kentucky), South Carolina's town of Cowpens recalls where America's first wranglers tended cattle herds, and, to go with the cowboys, Indians still reside in their own settlements in North Carolina (Cherokee), South Carolina (Catawba), Mississippi (Choctaw) and Florida (Miccosukee and Seminole). On view in North Carolina and Georgia are mines where the nation's earliest gold deposits surfaced there in the South, not in the mineral-rich West, and in Louisiana and Arkansas gushes oil, a commodity more commonly associated with the Southwest. Heavy industry, a far cry from the cotton-dominated plantation culture, operates at Birmingham's steel factories and at shipbuilding facilities in Mississippi and Virginia, while in the Washington, D.C. area, a corner of Virginia so permeated with outsiders a Southern atmosphere barely survives, functions the government industry, including the Pentagon and other installations of the once-hated Federals.

One of the South's most pronounced traits, the drawl, sounds forth less and less, giving way to the crisp tones of the SUPPY—Southern-based Urban Professional, Probably Yankee. During the Carter years drawl-tongued Southerners observed how nice it was to have a person in the

White House who didn't speak with an accent. Thanks, or no thanks, to modernization some Southern cities resemble those glossy high-rise high-energy places common elsewhere around the land, light–years away from John Quitman's slow-paced, or no-paced, Natchez way of life. "When I asked a Columbia, South Carolina, banker what he wanted his city to become," recounts John Syelton Reed in an essay in *The American South: Portrait of a Culture,* edited by Louis D. Rubin, "he expressed his admiration for Charlotte. Charlotte, meanwhile, wants to look like Atlanta; and Atlanta, it seems, wants to look like Tokyo." If Atlanta resembles Tokyo, then the new South even includes a touch of the Far East as well as the Northeast, Wild West, Middle West and other regions.

In addition to the South's variety of place—those attractions reminiscent of other regions' cultures—a varied temporal mix exists in Dixie. The Southern states encompass areas of different eras, places that reflect the region's stages of development. Still today survive primeval lands—or waters—such as the Everglades and the Great Dismal Swamp, which contain corners believed never yet explored. Here exists the true "deep" South—places hidden deep in the countryside and in time preserved in their pristine pre-exploration state. Indian settlements recall the days before the palefaces arrived, while at Bradenton, Florida, a National Historical Site commemorates where Hernando de Soto landed in the New World in 1539. Dozens of re-created or restored colonial and pioneer settlements—like Virginia's Jamestown and Williamsburg, Fort Boonesborough in Kentucky and many others—recall the region's early days. In addition to those reconstructions the South offers any number of original settlements which, tiered in time, trace the area's evolution. These include eighteenth-century showplaces like Charleston and Savannah and the lesser known Old Maryland Settlement in Mississippi, remote villages founded during and reminiscent of the earliest pioneer days, once frontier but now back-tier towns that seem to have strayed into the wrong century, isolated Appalachian enclaves of another era, self-contained cultures like the Melungeons in Tennessee and the Cajuns (not connected with the Louisiana culture of that name) near Mobile who live a hundred years behind the times, and a wide variety of other attractions that exist contemporaneously but which originated in and represent different epochs. Those time capsules range from prehistory through the colonial, pioneer, Revolutionary and Civil War eras—preserved pockets of the past—and up to the present day and even tomorrow, with such modernisms and (for the South) newfangled phenomena as Republicans, the Wal-Mart (of Arkansas) retailing revolution, Miami's state of the art social problems, up–to–the–minute Japanese factories and the General Motors futuristic Saturn plant in Tennessee, Saturn and other planetary probes at Cape Canaveral and other NASA bases which send rockets to the stars, other sorts of stars of the universe at the brand new high-tech 1990s Universal Studios in Florida, and Disney's EPCOT "community of tomorrow." With this wide range of past and present, a temporal spectrum, the South's entire history coexists simultaneously: In the Southern states you can travel in time as well as place.

So deeply ingrained in the nation's consciousness has the South's traditional antebellum image become, travelers may not expect such a wide variety of attractions—geographical, featuring those which recall other regions, and temporal, with those that represent all the area's eras. Perhaps only in the Southern states can the visitor find such a rich mix of cultural variety and historical continuity. Along with this breadth of tone and time goes a depth rooted in the familiar, including both family and locale—a deep attachment, among Southerners, to place. A sense of place is one of the South's most characteristic traits. In an article on "Place and Time:

The Southern Writer's Inheritance," the *Times Literary Supplement* of London commented: "If one thing stands out in all these writers, all quite different from another, it is that each feels passionately about place. And not merely in the historical and prideful meaning of the word, but in the sensory meaning, the breathing world of sight and smell and sound."

The much commented on agricultural orientation of the South reflects this deeply rooted sense of place. Unlike the North, where plants meant factories, in the South plants stemmed from the land and produced foods, not goods. Walt Whitman's poem on the region, "O Magnet-South," sings the praise of "the cotton plant! the growing fields of rice, sugar, hemp!" So central was cotton to the South's economy, and the very fabric of the region, that back in 1861 Mississippi used the commodity—a kind of white gold—to back paper money, a development which prompted a plantation owner (as quoted in *Confederate Mississippi*, by John K. Bettersworth) to comment that such notes were "safer than that of the Bank of England, which is based on credit, while this is based on a staple commodity indispensable to the commerce of all Christendom." The Founding Fathers, in their day, seemed happily married to Mother Earth. So attached was Patrick Henry to his Virginia plantation that in the 1790s he turned down offers to serve as U.S. senator, Secretary of State, U.S. Supreme Court Chief Justice, and Ambassador to France. In 1794 Thomas Jefferson wrote John Adams: "No occupation is so delightful to me as the culture of the earth," while George Washington, as Philip Alexander Bruce notes in *The Virginia Plutarch,* was constantly drawn back to Mount Vernon for "his interest in the operations of his plantation; the allurement of his own fields, forests, and streams; the excitement of the fox hunt."

This sense of place, along with the South's strong interest in kin and clan—the familiar and the family—perhaps explains why the region boasts hundreds of show houses, family homesteads that recall the generations which, each in its time, occupied the property, as well as dozens of pageants, shows and theatrical presentations which dramatize a locale's characters and history. Homey houses, filled with family furnishings and portraits, and stage plays filled with local dramas and people, seem to evidence the South's orientation toward place and personalities. What Thomas D. Clark wrote about families in his native state, in *Agrarian Kentucky,* describes much of the South: "For most Kentuckians their history is translated into the personal terms of revered ancestors, political and military heroes, self-sacrificing pioneers, unforgivable family enemies, and uninhibited scoundrels who have furnished them moments of vicarious enjoyment." Southern clans—and even the racists chose to organize themselves into a Klan—remain tied by a web of associations, memories, domestic dramas and family lore, connections that link generations as well as contemporaries. Still common in the region are family reunions such as the one described by Ben Robertson in *Red Hills and Cotton:* "During the morning we would sit in the shade of the trees and Cousin Unity and our Great-Aunt Narcissa and Cousin Ella would begin at the beginning of time, long before the Revolution, and trace the kinfolks from then until the moment of that reunion. They would tell us who had married whom, who had gone where, and what had happened."

Of course, as Jefferson once wrote: "The earth belongs always to the living generation. . . . The dead have no rights. They are nothing; and nothing cannot own something. . . . This corporeal globe, and everything upon it, belongs to its present corporeal inhabitants during their generation." But in the South the past—with its vanished but remembered generations, history-filled show homes, lingering Civil War memories, age-old oak trees and ever growing family trees— somehow seems more of a presence than elsewhere. A tonality of time suffuses the South, along with a sense of place and family. The irresistibly human account (in *Bluegrass Craftsman*) of Ebenezer Stedman, returning to his Kentucky home one autumn afternoon after spending the summer of 1822 in Ohio, preserves a moment in past time, an evocation of place and family that seems to summarize some of the south's underlying traits:

> Jest at this Moment . . . he put his hand on the Gate To open & the next few Steps to nock on the Dore & then to hear once more the voice of Dear Mother. I Rap. Then i hear, "Who is thare?" That is Mother. I Speak. She new my Voice. But didn't She get up quick & the Dor open quick & Didnt She have me in hur arms quick.

A traveler's journey through the Southern states will, in time, hopefully afford the visitor a feel for the land's texture—its sense of place and past, the ties of kin and clan, the stereotypical antebellum attractions interwoven with varied elements reminiscent of other regions and with varied places from all eras, for such are some of the characteristics which typify the eleven states that comprise America's South.

I

The Deep South

1. Alabama

A pronounced small-town and rural flavor dominates Alabama. A few cities—Birmingham, Huntsville, Mobile and Montgomery, the state capital—lend an urban touch to the state, but such metropolitan areas are few and far between, the "between" filled with woods, fields, valleys, and an occasional settlement. The small towns, seemingly self-contained and remote from the greater world beyond, live in a sort of sleepy isolation. "By late afternoon, heat has formed a haze behind which the sun disappears with a final, ferocious glare," writes Virginia Van der Veer Hamilton in *Alabama: A Bicentennial History*. "Bullfrogs along the Alabama River and tree frogs in the pines set up their evening clatter. Night in the [rural areas], when the last drugstore within twenty-eight miles has extinguished its lights, exudes a special kind of loneliness." And by night those villages scattered across Alabama seem fragile, vulnerable, as pictured by James Agee in his famous *Let Us Now Praise Famous Men:* "All over Alabama the lights are out. . . . The little towns, the county seats, house by house white-painted and elaborately sawn among their heavy and dark-lighted leaves, in the spaced protections of their mineral light they stand so prim, so voided, so undefended upon starlight."

Starlight forms part of the state's folklore, for "stars fell on Alabama" back on the night of November 12–13, 1833, when celestial showers flashed through the skies, a display described by the Florence *Gazette:* "Thousands of luminous meteors were shooting across the firmament in every direction; their course was from the center of the concave toward

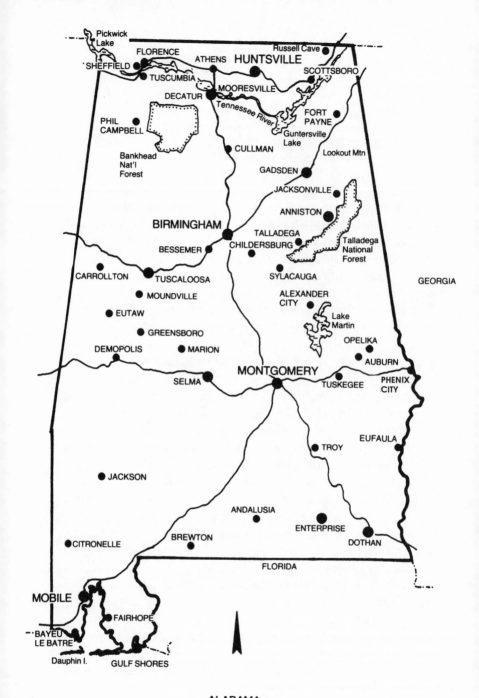

Pickwick Lake
FLORENCE
SHEFFIELD
TUSCUMBIA
DECATUR
PHIL CAMPBELL
Bankhead Nat'l Forest
ATHENS
HUNTSVILLE
Russell Cave
SCOTTSBORO
MOORESVILLE
Tennessee River
FORT PAYNE
Guntersville Lake
CULLMAN
Lookout Mtn
GADSDEN
JACKSONVILLE
ANNISTON
BIRMINGHAM
TALLADEGA
CHILDERSBURG
BESSEMER
Talladega National Forest
CARROLLTON
TUSCALOOSA
SYLACAUGA
MOUNDVILLE
ALEXANDER CITY
Lake Martin
EUTAW
GREENSBORO
OPELIKA
DEMOPOLIS
MARION
AUBURN
MONTGOMERY
SELMA
TUSKEGEE
PHENIX CITY
GEORGIA
EUFAULA
TROY
JACKSON
ANDALUSIA
ENTERPRISE
CITRONELLE
BREWTON
DOTHAN
FLORIDA
MOBILE
FAIRHOPE
BAYEU LE BATRE
Dauphin I.
GULF SHORES

ALABAMA

0   50   100m.

the horizon, and then they seemed to burst as if explosion. The scene was as magnificent as it was wonderful. To the eye it appeared to be in reality a 'falling' of the stars . . . presenting a scene of nocturnal grandeur." Many rural folk took the unusual heavenly display as a warning the day of judgment was nigh or as an ominous portent. But the state's main celestial connection since the "stars fell on Alabama" has been beneficial—the huge National Aeronautics and Space Administration facility at Huntsville where scientists develop star-bound rockets.

Alabama has been less starstruck than earthbound. In the state's Black Belt—a stretch of rich dark clay soil some thirty-five miles wide that cuts across Alabama's central section—remains a touch of the Old South, rooted in the soil, with antebellum architecture and cotton plantations. Back in the old days the roads in such rural areas kept the locals truly earthbound: by one muddy way some wit posted a sign that read, "This road is not passable/Not even jackassable./So when you travel/Take your own gravel." Even after the Civil War "the life of the State was its soil," noted William Warren Rogers in *The One-Gallused Rebellion*, that quaint title referring to the late nineteenth-century Alabama agrarian movement grounded in the rural folk who clung "to the Old South need that farming was the proper and desirable way of life."

Country and rural though the state may be, it is not by any means uniformly "Old South." Thanks to the ravages of the Mexican boll weevil, commemorated in a statue at Enterprise, the so-called Wiregrass section of Alabama in the southeast was forced to diversify out of cotton to other crops, and the antebellum flavor is largely lacking there. Similarly, the northern part of the state, which extends into the southern edges of the Appalachians, includes a rugged terrain of craggy canyons, mountains, hardwood forests, rivers and caves, while along the Gulf Coast, with its long white sand beach, perch Florida-like resorts.

Even politically the state's regions varied. Rumor had it that over the courthouse at the northern town of Huntsville, center of Union sympathizers, the American flag remained flying even after adoption of Alabama's Secession Ordinance. On January 13, 1861, two days after the Ordinance passed, L. R. Davis, a state legislator from northern Alabama, wrote a friend from Montgomery, that Confederate stronghold: "Here I sit & from my window see the nasty little thing [the Confederate flag] flaunting in the breeze which has taken the place of that glorious banner which has been the pride of millions of Americans and the boast of freemen the wide world over. I look upon the old banner as I do or would the dead body of a friend and I would scream one loud shout of joy could I now see it waving in the breeze although I know the scream would be my last." Such was the lament by one Alabama northerner for the disappearance of the stars and stripes. Poor Alabama always seems to be losing or gaining too many stars. Davis's fellow north Alabama citizens threatened to secede and form a state to be named Nickajack, but this came to nothing, and just as well for "stars fell on Nickajack" somehow doesn't sound quite the same as the original phrase.

Alabama, then, offers a wide range of primarily back-country small-town sights, with a few urban areas thrown in for good measure. The state's variety will surprise you: the hilly factory city of Birmingham is light years away in ambiance from the gracious coastal city of Mobile, and the Black Belt's antebellum tone seems a world apart from the less genteel texture of the northern part of the state. A visit to Alabama will introduce you to a wide range of Southern cultures, customs and countryside.

Northern Alabama

Tuscumbia and
Florence—Huntsville—Cullman—Scottsboro—
Gadsden—Birmingham

Alabama is more earthy than the other Southern states. Apart from Mobile and some areas in the cotton belt, Alabama for the most part lacks that Old South magnolia-sweet antebellum atmosphere found in such states as Mississippi and South Carolina. Of Alabama's estimated two thousand still surviving pre-Civil War mansions, only a relatively few are true showplaces. Ralph Hammond's 1951 *Ante-Bellum Mansions of Alabama* included only sixty-four such houses, fewer than in the small town of Natchez, Mississippi. Apart from one early mansion, Birmingham offers no antebellum buildings, for the simple reason that the state's largest city was founded after the Civil War. A strong populist rural strain, exploited by such Alabama politicians as James "Big Jim" Folsom and George Wallace, pervades the state. The six-foot eight-inch tall Folsom campaigned accompanied by "The Strawberry Pickers" band against such supposedly entrenched economic interests as plantation owners and industry, which he labelled "Big Mules," better known elsewhere as "fat cats." A "strawberry" band and "mules"—that sort of country language appealed to the voters, who elected "Big Jim" to two terms as governor (1947–51, 1955–59).

Typifying that outdoorsy, rural turf Folsom so fruitfully plowed in a political way is the unusual dog cemetery in northwestern Alabama, where a tour of the northern part of the state might conveniently begin. If you ever hankered to see a coon dog graveyard, Alabama is definitely the place to go. When Key Underwood's favorite such dog, Troop, died in 1937 the grieving owner buried the animal at a site that soon became a cemetery for other such hunting hounds. Now some one hundred canines, their graves marked with touching epitaphs, repose at the Key Underwood Coon Dog Memorial Graveyard, located west of route 247 about twelve miles south of Cherokee on U.S. highway 72. On U.S. 72 near Cherokee rises Barton Hall, an 1840s Greek Revival mansion, listed on the National Register, while six miles north of town stand seven structures that comprise the Old Natchez Trace Historic District, also listed on the Register. At Colbert Ferry, on the banks of the Tennessee River near the Trace, once operated a ferry established there in 1790 by George Colbert, who supposedly made as much as twenty thousand dollars a year carrying people—a dollar a head plus a fee for livestock—across the river. Colbert, who served as head chief of the Chickasaw Indian Nation for twelve years, was said to have charged Andrew Jackson $75,000 to ferry his army across the Tennessee there.

About twenty miles east of Cherokee you'll come to the turnoff for the Tuscumbia-Muscle Shoals-Florence area a few miles north. This is one of Alabama's most interesting corners. It was at Muscle Shoals, not in Tennessee, where the Tennessee Valley Authority started operations. As long ago as the early nineteenth century area settlers asked the federal government to help tame the shoals, an impediment to navigation. Not until 1880 were locks begun there, a project undertaken by Alabama engineer George Goethals, who later engineered a rather more renowned waterway—the Panama Canal. During World War I workmen began construction on the Wilson Dam and Lock, established to supply power for a munitions plant. In 1933 the nearly mile-long dam was turned over to TVA as the first of that agency's hydroelectric installations. The Wilson Lock, the world's highest single lift lock, raises and lowers river traffic about one hundred feet and requires fifty million gallons of water to fill. Both the Wilson Dam and Lock, as well as the Wilson Hydro Plant there, are open (free) for tours (for information: 205-386-2442). A rather different sort of local attraction are Muscle Shoals' thirteen music studios, which make the town the nation's third-largest recording center. Several studios let visitors see the pop music production process (for information: 205-383-0783 or 205-764-4661).

One of America's most famous music personalities was born in Florence, just across the Tennessee River from Muscle Shoals. In a rough-hewn cabin on the west side of town W. C. Handy first saw the light of day on November 16, 1873. The area back then was called Handy's Hill after W. C.'s grandfather, a Methodist minister, a profession Handy's father also followed. The family hoped the boy would also join the clergy, so when young Handy came home one day with a guitar, his father told him to trade it for a dictionary. The restored cabin and attached museum (Tu.–Sat., 9–12; Sun., 1–4, adm.) contain period furnishings and memorabilia that trace the famous blues composer's early years in Florence and his later career, which took him to the Delta area in Mississippi, to Memphis and to New York City. Handy's library and his beloved "golden trumpet" are on display, as is the piano said to be the one he used to compose "St. Louis Blues" and other classics. During the second week in August every year Florence mounts a week-long Handy Festival, featuring a musical review, jazz jam sessions, dancing and other noteworthy entertainments. Florence is an attractive, tree-shaded town perched above "where the Tennessee River, like a silver snake, winds her way through the red clay hills of Alabama," as Handy wrote in his 1941 autobiography, *Father of the Blues*. Near the waterway rises a forty-three-foot Indian mound, the largest in the Tennessee River Valley. A museum at the site (Tu.–Sat., 9–12; 1–4, adm.) contains Indian objects, exhibits on the culture of the mound builders and some prehistoric artifacts dating back ten thousand years.

At the north end of town stretches the pleasant well-wooded campus of the University of North Alabama, the South's first coeducational college. General William Tecumseh Sherman used 1855 Wesleyan Hall on campus—listed on the National Register and one of the Tennessee Valley's few surviving Gothic Revival-style buildings—as his headquarters while en route to reinforce Union troops in Tennessee. Also on campus is a lion's lair where Leo, a five-hundred-pound African lion that serves as the school's mascot, resides. The big cat consumes ten pounds of meat daily. A block from campus stands Pope's Tavern, built as a stagecoach stop and tavern in 1811 (Tu.–Sat., 9–12, 1–4, adm.). A historical museum now occupies this house, where Andrew Jackson stopped in 1814 on his march to engage the British in what turned out to be the Battle of New Orleans. During the Civil War the inn served as a hospital for both Confederate and Union soldiers. The nearby National Register-listed Karsner House, 301 North Pine (M.–F., 8–5, free), built by Maryland native Benjamin Karsner in 1831 to resemble townhouses in the east, is north Alabama's only surviving Federal-style residence.

At Tuscumbia, a few miles south of Florence, stands the attractive two-story white wooden, green-shutter house known as Ivy Green (M.–Sat., 8:30–4:30; Sun., 1–4:30, adm.), also listed on the National Register. Here Helen Keller, the blind and deaf girl who became a world-famous figure of vision and insight, spent her childhood. Helen was born in 1880 not in the house itself, built by her grandparents in 1820, but in a cottage on the ten-acre grounds, well garnished with magnolias, oaks, honeysuckle and century-and-a-half-old English boxwood. Her very early childhood was normal: "During the first nineteen months of my life," she wrote in her autobiography, "I had caught glimpses of broad green fields, a luminous sky, trees and flowers." But, she went on, those "happy days did not last long. One brief spring, musical with the song of the robin and mockingbird, one summer rich in fruit and roses, one autumn of gold and crimson sped by and left their gifts at the feet of an eager, delighted child." Then, silence and darkness—what Helen called "the valley of twofold solitude." An illness, believed to have been scarlet fever, struck Helen, leaving her deaf, blind and mute. Ivy Green remains today much as it was when young Helen lived there. Downstairs, original Keller family furniture and old photos fill the bedroom, parlor and dining room. A one-room museum installed in the back bedroom occupied by Helen's Aunt Eveline contains exhibits on the girl's early days at Ivy Green and on her early life out in the world. Photos picture her with Alexander Graham Bell, Eleanor Roosevelt and President Dwight D. Eisenhower, her left hand exploring his face. Behind the house stands the famous water pump where Helen—then "only a little mass of possibilities," as she described herself—learned her first word, "water." At the nearby outdoor theater scenes from Helen's early life come alive every summer when *The Miracle Worker* is performed on weekends in June and July; for information: 205-383-4066.

Although more compelling sights lie to the east of Tuscumbia, if you're heading south you'll find two privately owned natural areas: the Dismals, a canyon filled with flora, caves, waterfalls, rock formations and phosphorescent worms called "dismalites" that glow at night; and the Natural Bridge, a sixty-foot high sandstone span, supposedly the longest such natural feature east of the Rockies. On route 253 south of U.S. 278, a few miles west of the bridge lies the hamlet of Pearces Mill, where eleven early 1870s structures, listed on the National Register, offer examples of Ala-

bama's Reconstruction period architecture. To the east of
the bridge spreads William B. Bankhead National Forest,
which occupies most of Winston County. During the Civil
War the county, one of Alabama's most pro-Union areas,
threatened to secede from the Confederacy and form the
"free state of Winston," an event (or nonevent) recalled every
year at the Winston Festival. The 180,000-acre Bankhead
Forest takes its name from a member of one of Alabama's
most prominent political families, whose neoclassical style
National Register-listed homestead stands in the town of Jasper to the south. The Bankhead clan supplied two U.S. senators and a congressman who became Speaker of the House,
as well as actress Tallulah Bankhead, the Congressman's
daughter. Tallulah answered a movie magazine ad promising
"You can be a star" and, indeed, she became one, proving
that there can be truth in advertising.

On highway 20 to the east of Tuscumbia stands the house
of "Fighting Joe" Wheeler (8–6 during the summer, adm.),
the only Confederate general later to attain that rank in the
U.S. Army. A West Point graduate, Wheeler participated
in more than five hundred skirmishes during the Civil War,
commanded in one hundred and twenty-seven full-scale encounters, and had horses shot out from under him eighteen
times. He served in the U.S. Congress from 1882 to 1898,
and when the Spanish-American War broke out he volun-
teered for duty at age sixty-two and was commissioned to
command troops in Cuba.

Overlooking the Tennessee River in Joe Wheeler State Park
to the north is an especially attractive redwood and stone
lodge with seventy-four guest rooms (205-247-5461, 800-
544-5639). The Wheeler National Wildlife Refuge, where
you can view migrating waterfowl (the peak season is late
December and January) and other birds and visit the Givens
Interpretive Center (Tu.–Sun., 10–5, free) is just south of
Decatur, originally called Rhodes Ferry but renamed by di-

rection of President James Monroe for Commodore Stephen Decatur who, known for his affirmation "our country, right or wrong," commanded the fleet at the Battle of New Orleans in the War of 1812. For recreation Decatur offers Point Mallard Park, a huge (seven hundred and forty-nine-acre) publicly owned complex just by the Tennessee River with such facilities as an ice rink, golf course and the nation's first wave swimming pool. For education, Cook's Natural Science Museum in Decatur (M.–Sat., 9–12, 1–5; Sun., 2–5, free) contains displays of insects, mounted birds and animals, live animals, minerals, shells and other objects from the world around us. The museum is unusual in that it is privately owned, started as part of an employee training program by Cook's Pest Control Company. The old Decatur and Albany residential districts contain some attractive Victorian-era homes, while the restored Old State Bank (M.–F., 9:30–4:30, free), opened in 1833 as a branch of the State of Alabama Bank, stands proudly as one of the few structures in Decatur that survived the Civil War. Another building from that period is 1842 Founder's Hall, centerpiece of Athens State College, Alabama's oldest institution of higher learning, at Athens twelve miles north of Decatur. The chapel in the hall (M.–F., 8–4:30, free), saved from burning by Union troops when a college official produced a letter supposedly written by President Lincoln, houses wood carvings that illustrate New Testament stories. Just east of Decatur nestles the hamlet of Mooresville, one of Alabama's most picturesque settlements. Founded in 1818, the village is older than the state of Alabama and is its oldest incorporated town. The antique rough-hewn wooden post office is just one of Mooresville's dozen or so early to mid-nineteenth-century structures listed on the National Register.

Before proceeding east to Huntsville, the metropolis of north Alabama, you may want to swing south to Cullman, on the way glancing at the former Morgan County Courthouse in Somerville on highway 67 southeast of Decatur. The Federal-style structure, built in 1838 and listed on the National Register, is the oldest courthouse building still standing in Alabama. Cullman was established in 1873 by Colonel John G. Cullman, a German who acquired from the L & N Railroad (the 1913 Spanish Colonial-style depot is listed on the National Register) a huge swath of land where he founded a colony for German immigrants. Cullman advertised the settlement's attractions in the Northern press: "No malaria, no swamps, no grasshoppers, no hurricanes, and no blizzards." Unfortunately the colonel forgot to mention that there was no fertile land either. But Cullman was a great promoter, and thousands of Germans moved to the area. Although a German-language newspaper was published in Cullman until 1942, today few remnants remain of the German presence there, apart from a replica of the founder's Bavarian-style mansion that houses the local museum, by which stands a splendid statue of the city father himself shown with a walking stick in his right hand and a thick beard on his chin. The four-acre Ave Maria Grotto (7-sunset, adm.), listed on the National Register, displays more than one hundred and fifty miniature replicas carved by a local Benedictine monk from 1910 to 1934 of many of the world's holy shrines. Cullman being the only town in the U.S. with that name, a local lad once saved himself twenty-five cents by sending a wire from Germany that omitted the state, listing only his father's name and "Cullman, U.S.A."

Alabama's covered bridge country lies to the southeast in Blount County, but one of the state's most impressive such spans stands on county road 11 northwest of Cullman. There stretches the irresistably photogenic 1904 Clarkson Covered Bridge, a two hundred and fifty-foot long two-span construction, listed on the National Register, perched in a park with a working grist mill, log cabins and hiking trails.

Blount County boasts one-third of Alabama's surviving dozen covered bridges, and all four are still in use. Three hundred and eighty-five-foot Nectar Bridge, one of the country's longest, spans the Locust Fork branch of the Warrior River a mile east of Nectar off highway 160; Swann Bridge, three hundred and twenty-four feet, lies a mile and a half west of Cleveland off highway 79; tin-roofed Easley Bridge leaps Dub Creek three miles northwest of Oneonta a mile and a half northwest of U.S. highway 231; and lattice-sided Horton Mill Bridge, the country's highest covered bridge above water, is five miles north of Oneonta on highway 75. Every October Blount County hosts a covered bridge festival.

On the way back north you'll pass through Arab, thirty miles south of Huntsville, where Stamps Inn, converted to a bed and breakfast establishment in 1988, offers lunch (M.–F.) and overnight accommodations in antique-furnished rooms (205-586-7038). Car-clogged, construction-frenzied Huntsville, once a quiet, laid-back Alabama town, took off like a rocket in the 1950s when the U.S. located there the Redstone Arsenal where Wernher von Braun directed the American missile and space program from 1950 to 1970. Apart from a few remnants of the old days, Huntsville is a rather unattractive, congested "nouveau" city filled with latter-day buildings. But it's worth braving the traffic to visit the Alabama Space and Rocket Center (June–August, 8–6; Sept.–May, 9–5, adm.). The Center offers a fascinating and unique look at America's space program—past, present and future. Demonstrations, hands-on exhibits, rides simulating a moon flight and space shuttle trips, and a film shown on a huge screen in a tilted-seat theater give you a feel for outer space. Also on offer is a tour of the Marshall Space Flight Center, the National Aeronautics and Space Administration's largest facility, which takes you to four NASA labs where scientists carry out research on twenty-first-century projects.

Old Huntsville—what's left of it—can be found in the Twick-enham Historic District, Alabama's largest group of antebel-lum homes, listed on the National Register, and downtown at Constitution Hall Park (March–Oct., Tu.–Sat., 10–3:30; Sun. from 1; Nov.–Feb., 10–2:30, Sun. from 1, adm.) where costumed guides take you around to a group of reconstructed 1819 buildings from the time Alabama's Constitutional Con-vention was held there. The Huntsville Museum of Art, housed in the Von Braun Civic Center, offers a good collec-tion of American artwork by painters such as Reginald Marsh, Thomas Hart Benton, Jasper Johns and James Mc-Neill Whistler (Tu.–F., 11–7; Sat., 9–5; Sun., 1–5, free). An attractive place to stay in Huntsville is Monte Sano State Park high above town where fourteen cottages perch on a cliff overlooking the city (205-534-3757).

From Huntsville, highway 72 winds east through attractive hilly countryside to Scottsboro. For more than half a century the town has been inextricably connected with the famous "Scottsboro Boys" case in which nine black teenagers were accused of raping two white women on a train heading to-ward Scottsboro. The conviction of the accused—the last of whom died in 1989—caused a worldwide furor. After the initial conviction the defendants were freed, then Ala-bama reconvicted them, then they again gained freedom and were then once more reconvicted. In 1935 the Alabama legis-lature appropriated thirty-five thousand dollars for a "Scotts-boro case fund" to relieve Jackson County of debts incurred to prosecute the case, which had become ruinously expensive for the county. The Jackson County/Scottsboro Heritage Center (Tu.–Sat., 9–4, adm.) occupies an 1880s Greek Revival-style house, next to which stands the original court-house and some pioneer log structures. Scottsboro offers two unusual shopping opportunities. From the horse and buggy days originates the "First Monday Trade Day," a nearly century-and-a-half-old tradition of bartering, haggling and swapping all manner of merchandise. This up-scale flea market—perhaps it should be called a fly market—takes place the first Monday of each month and the Sunday before. From the jet age began a true fly market—the Unclaimed Baggage Center, an emporium founded in Scottsboro in 1970 to sell the contents of luggage lost during air travel. True bargains are to be found if you don't mind buying someone else's hand-me-downs or, rather, fly-me-downs. The Scottsboro store is at 509 West Willow; Unclaimed Baggage also operates three other stores, all in Alabama, at Albertville, Boaz and Decatur; for information: 800-274-5753. Northeast of Scottsboro, in the far upper corner of the state, lie the transportation towns of Stevenson—with a history museum installed in the old train depot (M.–Sat., 9–5; Sun., 1–4, free) that recalls the Civil War when the settlement served as an important rail junction—and Bridgeport, where one of Alabama's few remaining ferries operates. From Bridgeport it's an eight-mile drive west to Russell Cave National Monument (8–5, free) where, starting in 1953, relics of Indians who lived in the cave nine thousand years ago were discovered. Excavations by the Smithsonian Institution in collaboration with the National Geographic Society uncovered the remains of successive bands of Indians who occupied the cavern until A.D. 1000. Some of the excavated artifacts are on display in the visitor center, while the cave itself houses an exhibit of the excavations.

South of Russell Cave along the eastern edge of the state, near the Alabama-Georgia line, nestles the rustic hilltop village of Mentone, with the unusual Sally Howard Memorial Chapel, its rear wall formed by a huge boulder, built by Congressman Milford Howard in 1937 as a memorial to his wife. Nearby lies the town of Fort Payne, with two National Register-listed relics, the Opera House, the state's oldest theater (1889) still in use, and the 1891 pink limestone train depot. Fort Payne also boasts a more contemporary attraction—the Alabama Fan Club and Museum, a recently opened facility with displays pertaining to the country music group "Alabama." East of Fort Payne lies Little River Canyon, a scenic area with the deepest gorge east of the Mississippi. The Little River is America's only waterway that forms and flows on the top of a mountain. Gadsden, to the southwest, nestles in the foothills of the Appalachian mountains. The town was named for James Gadsden, who in 1853 negotiated the Gadsden Purchase, the acquisition by the U.S. of parts of Arizona and New Mexico from the Mexican government.

At the Broad Street entrance to the Coosa River Bridge stands a monument to fifteen-year-old Emma Sansom who led the forces of Confederate General Nathan Bedford Forrest in pursuit of Union troops, while at Noccalula Falls Park is the reconstructed Gilliland-Reese Covered Bridge, moved in 1967 to a pioneer village near the ninety-foot falls. Not far from Gadsden, to the west, lie the Blount County covered bridge country and the unusual Horse Pens 40 (March 15–Nov. 15, adm.), a forty-acre enclave of natural stone formations so named because the barriers once served to corral horses. Five miles southeast of nearby Ashville stands the Looney House, an 1820 two-story log "dogtrot" house that contains period furnishings and a local history museum (Sat.–Sun., 12–5, adm.).

Before heading on to Birmingham you might want to detour to the east where you'll find some attractions of historic interest. At Jacksonville, north of Anniston, is the Dr. Francis Medical Museum (open by appointment: 205-435-7203, free), with medical items used by area doctors in the nineteenth century. Between Jacksonville and Anniston lies Fort McClellan, where you'll find three military museums: the U.S. Army Military Police and the Chemical Corps museums as well as an entire building devoted to displays on the Women's Army Corps (M.–F., 8–5, free) tracing the history of WACs starting in May 1942. Busts of Pallas Athene, the Corps' insignia, stand inside the entrance, while a collection of WAC hats hangs on a mirror fixture beneath a sign that invites visitors to "Try on a hat for history." In Anniston stands a statue of Samuel Noble, the town's founder, whose careful arrangement of the city's streets, water supply, sewer lines, schools and other services led to the settlement's nickname, "the Model City." Anniston's Museum of Natural History (Tu.–F., 9–5; Sat., 10–5; Sun., 1–5) houses a colorful menagerie of stuffed African animals, birds and other wildlife as well as a display called "Underground Worlds," a manmade "cave" formed out of a mile of steel, fifteen-hundred plastic drinking straws (the stalagtites), papier mâché, sand and a vivid imagination. St. Michael and All Angels Church, built in 1888 for foundry workers, is a splendid Romanesque-style structure, and the nearby Victoria mansion an equally impressive late 1880s Victorian-style house, listed on the National Register, now functioning as an unusually attractive restaurant and inn (205-236-0503).

In Talladega National Forest south of Anniston rises Cheaha Mountain, at 2,407 feet Alabama's highest point. The peak stands in a state park within the forest. Cheaha Park is an isolated mountain enclave with an inn, a lodge, stone cottages, camping facilities and a restaurant (for information on these facilities: 205-488-5111). To the east of the forest, near the Alabama-Georgia line four miles west of Graham, stands the 1881 two-story frame Butler's Mill (F.–Sat., 8–4, free) which originally functioned as a saw-, feed- and gristmill as well as a cotton gin, these days serving simply as a gristmill. At the town of Ashland, closer to the forest to the south, stands the modest story-and-a-half frame house, listed on the National Register, where U.S. Supreme Court Justice Hugo Black grew up. West of the forest, toward Talladega, is the International Motor Speedway, where daredevil drivers race at speeds of more than two hundred miles an hour. Adjacent to the Speedway rises the International Motor Sports Hall of Fame (9–5, adm.), filled with car exhibits. The museum's prize is the low-slung streamlined "Bluebird," the car Malcolm Campbell drove to set a world speed record (276 m.p.h.) at Daytona Beach in 1935. Other items on display include stock cars, racers and antique autos.

When you reach Birmingham, Alabama's commercial and industrial center, the very first thing you'll see is the towering statue of Vulcan, Roman god of the forge, which crowns the crest of a hill overlooking the city. Vulcan, the world's largest cast-iron figure, represented Birmingham at the St. Louis World's Fair in 1904, and was later emplaced in its present perch to symbolize the city's iron and steel industry. From the Vulcan statue—whose torch glows green unless an automobile fatality occurs, in which case a cautionary red color appears—high atop Red Mountain the young city of Birmingham spreads out before you. Little more than a century ago the city below didn't exist. In 1871 promoters organized the Elyton Land Company to develop the area. Colonel James R. Powell, the president of the firm, so praised his new town he became known as "the Duke of Birmingham." Iron, coal and limestone deposits fed the city's steel mills which prospered until the Depression, a slump that hit Birmingham so hard the Communist Party, sensing easy pickings among the unemployed, established its Southern headquarters in the city. In the 1950s Birmingham was thought by some observers to be the nation's most segregated large city: theaters, restaurants, elevators, cemeteries, water fountains, rest rooms and virtually all other areas were separated by race. When Eugene "Bull" Connor ordered fire hoses and police dogs used against black demonstrators on May 3, 1963, the city, embarassed by its nation-

ally publicized image, finally took steps to ease the seeth-
ing racial tension. Although Birmingham voters defeated
Connor in his next bid for reelection as public safety commissioner, the citizens of Alabama proceeded to elect him
to the office of state public service commissioner.

Birmingham, having been founded so recently, lacks that
antebellum magnolia-scented sort of atmosphere found in
so many Southern cities, so visitors must content themselves
with more prosaic attractions. Museums include the Alabama Sports Hall of Fame (W.–Sat., 10–5; Tu. and Sun.,
1–5, adm.) with exhibits on such figures as one-time University of Alabama football coach Paul "Bear" Bryant and boxer
Joe Louis; the Museum of Art (Tu.–Sat., 10–5; Th., to 9;
Sun., 2–6, free), including Italian Renaissance works from
the Kress Collection and the Rives Collection of ancient Near
East objects; Red Mountain Museum (Tu.–Sat., 10–4:30;
Sun. 1–4:30, free), featuring natural history exhibits; The
Southern Museum of Flight (Tu.–Sat., 9:30–5:30; Sun., 1–5,
adm.), an excellent collection of old planes, mementos and
aviation-related exhibits; the Alabama Museum of the Health
Sciences (M.–F., 8–12, 1–5, free) and the adjacent Reynolds
Historic Library (including rare medical books), featuring
displays on the history of medicine in Alabama; the Sloss
Furnaces (Tu.–Sat., 10–4; Sun., 12–4, free), two huge blast
furnaces, listed on the National Register, with displays on
the iron-making process and the city's industrial heritage;
and a similar museum, recently opened, at Tennehill Historic
State Park (7–9, adm.), thirty miles west of Birmingham,
with displays that recall the area's iron and steel industry
at the site where the iron-producing furnaces that began that
industry in the Birmingham area stand. At Bessemer, southwest of Birmingham, are the Historic Pioneer Homes area
(May 1–Sep. 1, Sun., 1–4, adm.), with three houses dating
from the 1830s, and the Bessemer Hall of History Museum

(Tu.–Sat., 10–4:30, free), where you'll find not only displays on local history but also an oddly varied collection of other items, including a mummy and also a typewriter that belonged to Adolf Hitler. For overnight accommodations in the area, Bed and Breakfast Birmingham (P.O. Box 31328, Birmingham, AL 35222, 205-933-2487) offers rooms in forty private homes.

Southern Alabama

*Tuscaloosa—Demopolis—Marion—Selma—
Montgomery—Tuskegee—
Opelika—Eufaula*

Southern Alabama's attractions, ranging from ghostly remnants of events of the past to civil rights and Civil War landmarks, lie at widely scattered points in the lower part of the state so a certain amount of zig-zagging is necessary if you want to see the most interesting places. At the village of Carrollton, near the Alabama-Mississippi line at the western edge of the state, one of those ghostly remnants of the past spooks the two-story brick Pickens County Courthouse—the image of the face of Henry Wells imprinted on a pane when a bolt of lightning struck as the prisoner peered out an upstairs window at a lynch mob below. Perched on the shores of Lake Aliceville at Pickensville, eleven miles west, is one of the South's most attractive visitor centers (May 1–Sep. 30, M.–F., 10–6; Sat., 11–7; Sun., 1–7; Oct. 1–April 30, M.–F., 9–5; Sat., 10–6; Sun., 1–6, free), this one devoted to the Tennessee-Tombigbee Waterway, the two hundred and thirty-four-mile long link, completed in 1985, connecting the Gulf of Mexico with the country's inland river system. A twenty-two-foot relief map in the center's Greek Revival-style building traces the waterway's course through its ten locks and dams, while aboard the "U.S. Montgomery," a National Register-listed ship that saw service from 1927 to 1982 as a snagboat used to clear river channels, are displays on old days on the rivers.

Tuscaloosa, as the name of the city and its Black Warrior River suggest, was once Indian country: in the Choctaw and Creek language "tuska" means warrior, "lusa" black. Before white settlers pushed the Indians out the Creek and Choctaw once staged an Indian ball game in the area to determine which tribe would get hunting rights there. As at many cities with state universities, the institution fairly well dominates the town. On the campus stands the 1829 Gorgas House (M.–Sat., 10–12, 2–5; Sun., 3–5, free), originally built as a dining hall, one of the nation's oldest college structures. The house now contains a Spanish colonial silver collection and memorabilia of William Crawford Gorgas, Surgeon General of the U.S. Army, whose efforts to eliminate yellow fever in parts of Panama enabled workers to complete construction of the Canal. Other historic structures in Tuscaloosa include the Battle-Friedman House (Tu.–F., 10–12, 1–4; Sun., 1–4, adm.), a Greek Revival-style mansion built in 1835; the Mildred Warner House (Sat., 10–6; Sun., 1–6, free), embellished with beautiful period furnishings and paintings by such artists as Edward Hopper, Mary Cassatt and John Singer Sargent; and the 1820s-vintage Old Tavern Museum (Tu.–F., 10–12, 1–4; Sat. and Sun., 1–4, adm.) in Capital Park, site of the former state capital. At the Oriental-style headquarters complex of Gulf States Paper Corporation is a collection of more than one hundred and fifty modern American artworks (tours on the hour, M.–F., 5–7; Sat., 10–7; Sun., 1–7, free). On the other side of the Black Warrior River, beyond Northport—called Kentuck shortly after being settled in 1813—lies Lake Lurleen State Park, named

for Governor George Wallace's wife, herself a governor of
Alabama.

From Tuscaloosa you can proceed either to the east or
head south and swing your way around to Montgomery.
The southern route is covered starting in the third paragraph
below. If you're driving east you'll come to Montevallo, located in the exact geographical center of the state, where
the attractive Alabama College campus, with its 1823
Federal-style National Register-listed King House, embellishes the town. At Brierfield, south of Montevallo, is
Ironworks Park where ruins of a mid-nineteenth-century
iron-producing furnace, listed on the National Register, recall the Civil War era, and the childhood home, also listed
on the Register, of William Gorgas, the conqueror of yellow
fever whose Tuscaloosa house is mentioned earlier. Farther
east lies the marble-rich town of Sylacauga, that mouthful-
of-a-name derived from Indian words meaning "place of the
Chaluka tribe." Part of what was once the town's terrain
now adorns the U.S. Supreme Court Building in Washington, Detroit's General Motors Building and other renowned
structures, constructed of blocks extracted from what's considered to be the world's finest white marble deposit, a seam
some thirty-two miles long, a mile and a half wide and
about four hundred feet deep. One of the hardest, densest
substances known, the cream white marble at Sylacauga has
been quarried since 1840. The town's Isabel Anderson
Comer Museum and Art Center (Tu.–Sat., 1–4; Sun., 2–5,
free) houses a collection of artworks.

Southeast of Montevallo and southwest of Sylacauga lies
the village of Verbena, a late nineteenth-century settlement
listed on the National Register, that served as a haven for
families fleeing yellow fever epidemics. In Confederate Memorial Park at Mountain Creek, just to the south, is a Civil
War museum and Confederate cemetery with the grave of
the Confederate Unknown Soldier. If you ever wondered

where sports team uniforms come from the answer is: Alexander City, Alabama, a town southeast of Sylacauga. The Russell Company there, the nation's largest athletic uniform maker, which employs some two-thirds of the town's thirteen thousand residents, furnishes uniforms to the National Football League, Little League and almost every other league, except the Junior League. Just east of Alexander City lies Horseshoe Bend National Military Park, an unusually interesting historical area. It was here where Andrew Jackson broke the power of the Creek Indians and started on the road to the White House. In July 1813 the Red Sticks, a Creek clan, led by High Head Jim, encountered American troops at the Battle of Burnt Corn in Baldwin County northeast of Mobile. Frightened settlers in the area swarmed to Fort Mims, which the Indians attacked on August 30th, executing (literally) what's been called the bloodiest massacre in American frontier history, Word of the slaughter reached Andrew Jackson in Nashville, then confined to bed with a bullet in his left arm from a duel. On hearing the news, Jackson immediately vowed to lead troops in retaliation. "Jackson was too weak to leave his bed, but he was strong enough to make war," Marquis James wryly observed in his *The Life of Andrew Jackson*. Hoping to protect themselves by the encircling river, the Creek gathered inside the horseshoe bend on the Tallapoosa. On March 27, 1814, Jackson's forces attacked the Indians' position and after what he later called "a very obstinate contest" defeated the Creek. Jackson, moved by the sight of an Indian boy clinging to his dead mother's breast, took the child to Nashville and raised the youngster as his son Lincoyer. After its defeat, the Creek Nation ceded to the U.S. some twenty million acres of land, out of which was carved the state of Alabama. Nine months after Horseshoe Bend, Jackson defeated the British in the Battle of New Orleans. These two encounters are considered the most important pre-Civil War military campaigns ever fought in the (then) southwestern part of the nation. Jackson's two victories made him a national hero and led to his later election as President. Such are the attractions to the east of Tuscaloosa.

The itinerary south from Tuscaloosa and then east to Montgomery, the state capital, takes you first to Mound State Monument (9–4:45, adm.) where more Indian history is preserved. Located on the Black Warrior River, the monument includes twenty millenium-old Indian mounds, six facsimile reconstructions of prehistoric buildings and a museum with artifacts excavated at several hundred archeological sites. Eutaw, to the south, is an especially attractive town, with a large group of old houses dating back to antebellum times when cotton brought prosperity to the area. Main Street, lined with nineteenth-century mansions, curves west from the square and is joined by side streets filled with large oak trees. The two-story brick Greek Revival-style Greene County Courthouse (1869) sports a nicely designed iron balcony, while such other structures as the Coleman-Banks Home (1850), First Presbyterian Church (1851), Kirkwood (1860), topped by a curious cottage-like superstructure—all listed on the National Register—and the Dunlap House, with an especially attractive yard, all add their charms to Eutaw, originally named Mesopotamia.

South of Eutaw lies Demopolis, founded in 1818 as the so-called "vine and olive colony" by French Bonapartists who left France after Napoleon's fall from power. Hoping to grow grapevines and olive trees in the area, the French acquired nearly 100,000 acres along the Tombigbee River, but the project quickly failed. Among the pioneers were the officer who accompanied Napoleon to Elba, a former member of the French National Assembly, and Count Charles Lefebre-Desnouettes, a cavalry major-general who rode in Napoleon's carriage during the French army's retreat from Moscow and who, in a log cabin near his Demopolis house, installed a bronze statue of the famous leader. Demopolis lies in Alabama's Black Belt, not a racial designation but a reference to the rich black soil in the south-central part of the state where cotton plantations once thrived. Two antebellum showplaces in Demopolis recall those old days—1832 Bluff Hall (Tu.–Sat., 10–5; Sun., 2–5, adm.), fronted by huge square columns of a type peculiar to the region; and Gaineswood, one of the best places in Alabama and, for that matter, in the entire South, to visit a vividly evocative pre-Civil War plantation house (M.–Sat., 8–5; Sun., 1–5, adm.). It took nearly twenty years to build the twenty-room mansion, a meticulously constructed and beautifully maintained property filled with its original furniture, family portraits and such elegant touches as silver hardware on the doors. A visit to Gaineswood is truly a unique look at the splendors of a vanished yet not forgotten age.

Northeast of Demopolis, at Greensboro, is 1835 Magnolia Grove (Tu.–Sat., 10–4; Sun., 1–4, adm.), another antebellum mansion that also contains original family furnishings. Glencairn—an 1837 Greek Revival-style house and, like Magnolia Grove, listed on the National Register—bears at its entrance notably fine woodwork. Other old houses line the oak- and magnolia-shaded sleepy streets of this Black Belt town, whose Main Street, with more than a hundred such antique structures, comprises the Register-listed Greensboro Historic District. Marion, east of Greensboro, is another of those small Black Belt towns—one of Alabama's oldest, dating from 1817—with a rich stock of attractive vintage houses, among them Carlisle Hall (c. 1857), one of the South's finest Italianate-style residences; the Peters Home (c. 1860), laden with frilly woodwork; the Lea-Collins Home (c. 1830), where in 1840 Republic of Texas President Sam Houston married Margaret Lea; and the beguilingly named Reverie (1860). By the main entrance walk at the Perry County Courthouse is a monument to Nicola

Marschall, who designed the Confederate flag, the original
of which she presented to the Marion Light Infantry at Confederate Oak near the entrance of Judson College's Jewett
Hall, named for founder Milo P. Jewett, who later established Vassar College. An 1852 Baptist church report proudly
noted of Judson, one of America's oldest women's colleges,
that "all jewelry, even ear-rings and finger-rings, is prohibited; and every temptation to extravagance is removed." It
was at another local women's school, Marion Female Seminary, listed on the National Register, where Nicola Marschall
designed the Confederate flag and uniform. Those venerable
female educational institutions failed to help latter-day Marion resident Coretta Scott, who was forced to attend a "colored" school she had to walk three miles to reach. Scott
later studied at Antioch College in Ohio and then at the
New England Conservatory in Boston where she met and
married a young man named Martin Luther King, Jr.

Nearby Selma became nationally known when King led
the famous civil rights march along U.S. highway 80 from
that town to the state capital at Montgomery, nearly fifty
miles east. In March 1965 gracefully arched Edmund Pettus
Bridge in Selma was the scene of a not-so-graceful confrontation between civil rights demonstrators and police, an encounter that provoked the march to Montgomery. This
focused national attention on the civil rights cause and led
to passage of the Voting Rights Act of 1965, prompting
one historian to call Pettus "the most significant bridge in
American history since Concord." From early days Selma
was a city of encounters. The city is said to have been where
Hernando de Soto met the great Indian chief Tuskaloosa.
Three centuries later the North and South clashed at Selma
when Union forces devastated the city, site of the Confederacy's second-largest arsenal (after Richmond). In 1820 the
town's promoter, William Rufus King—who served as a senator and as Vice-president of the U.S.—named the settlement

"Selma" from the Greek word meaning "high seat" or "throne," as the city occupied the high north bank of the Alabama River. Selma's first famous King reposes in the Old Live Oak Cemetery, a garden of a graveyard filled with moss-draped oaks and, in the spring, a rainbow of white dogwood, azaleas and other blossoms. For more than ten years Selma furnished both of Alabama's U.S. senators, John Tyler Morgan, known as the Father of the Panama Canal, and Edmund W. Pettus, after whom that "most significant bridge" is named. Pettus Bridge is just one of Selma's many sights that recall the area's rich history. Ten-room Sturdivant Hall (1853)—designed by Thomas Helm Lee, cousin of General Robert E. Lee—one of Alabama's few mansions with Corinthian-style columns, shows the pre-Civil War way of life (Tu.–Sat., 9–4; Sun., 2–4, adm.), while Brown Chapel, used by Martin Luther King, Jr., as headquarters during his time in Selma, recalls a later phase of the city's history. The Old Town Historic District—with five hundred and sixty-seven structures, Alabama's largest such area—contains a variety of architectural styles, and the Water Avenue Historic District includes twenty-one commercial buildings that comprise one of the South's few antebellum riverfront streets. Both Districts are listed on the National Register, as is the 1840s Greek Revival-style Selma Historic and Civic Building, formerly the Dallas County Courthouse. It was there where court clerk Sanford Blann poetically recorded the January 1841 marriage—in the Deep South seldom referred to as a union—of one John Chestnut and Elizabeth G. Craig: "I rode through wet and stormy weather/To join these loving folks together. . . . Let no man interfere betwixed 'em,/And let them stay as I fixed 'em/And whether it be for woe or weal/This I certify under hand and seal/The twentieth day of this first moon,/Eighteen hundred and forty-one." Also Register-listed and poetic are the scanty but haunting remains—old cemeteries and a few forlorn red-brick columns—at Cahaba, site of Alabama's first permanent state capital, eleven miles southwest of Selma. The capital moved to Tuscaloosa where it remained for twenty years until Montgomery became Alabama's seat of government in 1846.

As you drive east on highway 80 from Selma to Montgomery you'll be following the route of the famous 1965 civil rights march, which passed along the way "solitary weathered pine shacks standing forlornly in the wide fields, wisps of smoke coming from their leaning brick chimneys, and people lined up on the broken porches, looking out at the passing spectacle on the highway with quiet, guarded astonishment," as Charles E. Fager described the scene in his book *Selma*. The marchers continued on past Lowndesboro, virtually unchanged from the time back in the mid-nineteenth century when the town was the Black Belt's cultural, educational and trade center. Settlers from South Carolina coveting the rich Alabama River Valley farmland moved to the area, bringing with them all their possessions—furniture, livestock, slaves—and founded the town in 1819. Atop the Methodist church perches the dome brought from Alabama's first capital at Cahaba. Lowndesboro's most famous resident was Dixon H. Lewis, U.S. senator from 1844 to 1848, believed to be the largest man ever to occupy a seat—or seats—in the Senate. Any voter wishing to complain about something to someone "big" in Washington could do no better than to contact Dixon Lewis, a six-foot tall, five-hundred-pound presence in the Senate. Old Homestead, his house in Lowndesboro, bears huge columns, as if to symbolize the owner's size.

Montgomery, Alabama's state capital, lies just to the east. Government buildings—both those of Alabama and relics of the Confederate States, whose capital Montgomery was for five months—abound in the town. Attractions include such official and once-official structures as the Capitol, where brass stars on the front portico mark the spot Jefferson Davis stood to take the oath as Confederate President; the First White House of the Confederacy (M.–F., 8–4:30; Sat. and Sun., 9–4:30, free), furnished as it was when President and Mrs. Davis lived there; and the Executive Mansion, official residence of the state's governors since the 1950s (for tour information: 205-834-3022). State-related museums include the Alabama Archives and History Museum (M.–F., 8–5; Sat. and Sun., 9–5, free), whose exhibits range from Confederate-era items to artifacts of Alabama's early days and such curiosities as the wooden leg of Charles Tait, a planter who owned more than a thousand slaves; the Alabama War Memorial (M.–F., 8–4:30, free); and the Lurleen Burns Wallace Museum (M.–F., 8–5; Sat. and Sun., 9–5, free), with displays devoted to Alabama's first woman governor, George Wallace's wife, installed in an antebellum mansion. Montgomery's newest sight, which opened in late 1989 on the grounds of the Southern Poverty Law Center, commemorates victims of the civil rights era. A tablet lists names of forty people killed during the movement, while down a wall slides a thin film of water over the words of Martin Luther King, Jr.: "Until justice rolls down like waters and righteousness like a mighty stream." Other historic corners of Montgomery include the Dexter Avenue King Memorial Baptist Church (for tour information: 205-263-3970), with a mural that recalls the life of King, whose first pulpit was at the church and who began his leadership of the civil rights movement in Montgomery after the famous incident in which police arrested Rosa Parks on December 1, 1955, when she refused to vacate her bus seat for a white man; the Drugstore Museum (open by appointment: 205-262-0027), housing a 1930s drugstore and displays on the history of pharmacy in Alabama; the Old North Hull Street Historic District (M.–Sat., 9:30–4:30; Sun., 1:30–4, adm.); and the Cradle of the Confederacy Railroad Museum (open by appointment: 205-265-8942), adjacent to Montgomery's imposing nineteenth-century Romanesque-style Union Station, near which stands a display of the Lightning Route traveled by the nation's first electric streetcar. The Montgomery State Farmers Market (open daily), installed in a building that suggests country fairs and old-time farmers' markets, offers not only produce but also a selection of Alabama handiwork, available as well at the Society of Arts and Crafts (called "Sac"), 1033 South Hull Street.

Some famous figures haunt Montgomery's past, among them country singer Hank Williams—his hit discs included such heartfelt laments as "Cold, Cold Heart" and "Your Cheatin' Heart"—who reposes at the Oakwood Cemetery Annex, in 1986 renamed the Hank Williams Memorial Gardens; Orville and Wilbur Wright, who in 1910 operated the world's first flight training school at what is today Maxwell Air Force Base (for tour information: 205-293-2017), which boasts the Defense Department's largest military library; and Montgomery native Zelda Sayre Fitzgerald, wife of F. Scott Fitzgerald (they met in 1918 when the author, stationed at nearby Camp Sheridan, espied Zelda, daughter of a local judge, at a country club dance in Montgomery) whose artwork hangs in the Montgomery Museum of Fine Arts. The museum (Tu.–Sat., 10–5; Sun., 1–6, free) occupies a new (1988) rather severely linear building next to the similarly boxy Alabama Shakespeare Festival Theater, which offers not only the Bard's works but a wide selection of other productions as well (for tour or performance information, the phone number—which has a pronounced Shakespearian ring to it—is 205-277-BARD).

Scattered around the northern fringes of Montgomery are additional attractions, including the Buena Vista Mansion (Tu., 10–2) near Prattville, an early nineteenth-century house prepared in Birmingham—England, not Alabama—and assembled on the site by English craftsmen; Fort Toulouse

(April 1–Oct. 31, 6–9; Nov. 1–May 31, 8–5, free), an eighteenth-century French fort tucked between the Coosa and Tallapoosa, which join there to form the Alabama River; Jasmine Hill Gardens (Tu.–Sat., 9–5, adm.), a flower-filled area with classical Greek statuary; and the Al Holmes Wildlife Museum (9–5; Sundays, 2–5, adm.), featuring more than five hundred animal species in areas resembling their natural habitats.

To the east of Montgomery lies the town of Tuskegee, home of the famous college founded in 1881 by Booker T. Washington and now a National Historic Site. As a child, the future famous black educator was listed on the property rolls of a Virginia tobacco farm as "1 negro boy," with a value of four hundred dollars. After working his way through college as a janitor, Washington became a teacher and eventually, on July 4, 1881, he established Tuskegee Institute with a two thousand dollar grant from the state of Alabama. Since those early days, when the first class of thirty students met in a dilapidated church and shanty, Tuskegee has grown to an academic community of some five thousand students, faculty and staff with more than one hundred and sixty buildings, among them The Oaks, the spacious house Washington built in 1899. In the second floor den of the residence (tours daily on the hour, 9–4, except 12 and 1, free), which remains much as it was when Washington lived there, stands furniture built by Institute students, while around the room are the educator's personal effects. The nearby Carver Museum (9–5, free) recalls the life and career of George Washington Carver, the famous scientist who developed various uses for peanuts and sweet potatoes. Carver arrived at Tuskegee in 1896 and taught, wrote and conducted research there for forty-seven years. Both of the famous black educators repose in the small burial area next to the campus's ultra-modern, angular brick chapel. Washington lies beneath a bulky rough-hewn grey stone, while on the grey stone slab that marks Carver's grave appears the inscription: "A life that stood out as a gospel of self-forgetting service. He could have added fortune to fame but caring for neither he found happiness and honor in being helpful to the world."

To the northeast of Tuskegee lie the university town of Auburn—whose campus includes a Historic District with buildings such as Samford Hall, a well-windowed red-brick pile embellished by striking Arab-like red and white arches— and Opelika, nine miles east of which, near Salem, stands one of Alabama's dozen surviving covered bridges, Salem-Shotwell, built with oak pegs that join the various components. Hidden away in the mean streets of nearby Phenix City, a grimy industrial town, is a touch of sentiment—the inscription on John Godwin's grave, in Godwin's Cemetery, composed by his former slave, Horace King, who erected the marker in "lasting remembrance of the love and gratitude he felt for his lost friend and former master." To the south, at the former Russell County seat of Seale, stands the 1868 courthouse, listed on the National Register, while farther west, at Union Springs, is the Register-listed Bullock County Courthouse Historic District, an attractive group of late nineteenth- and early twentieth-century commercial structures clustered around the handsome 1871 courthouse building. A similarly worthy group of century-old residential structures fills the College Street Historic District, also listed on the Register, at Troy, to the south, which also boasts the Pike Pioneer Museum (10–5; Sun., 1–5, adm.), with log houses, a country store and displays of antique agricultural and household objects.

On the way back out to Eufaula, one of Alabama's most picturesque towns, you'll come to Clayton, which claims two National Register houses, the 1850 Greek Revival cottage where Henry D. Clayton, author of the Clayton Anti-Trust Act, lived and Octagon House (1861), Alabama's only

surviving eight-sided antebellum residence. At the Clayton
Baptist Church Cemetery reposes W. T. Mullen, a heavy
drinker whose teetotaler wife erected a whiskey bottle tombstone as a lasting reminder of her husband's vice. Early
nineteenth-century architecture embellishes Eufaula, which
perches on a plateau two hundred feet above a bend in the
Chattahoochee River and spreads out onto low hills to the
west. Among the old buildings there, all listed on the National Register, are two Greek Revival-style residences, Hart
House and Welborn House; the 1836 Tavern, the town's first
permanent structure; and the neo-classic Shorter Mansion
(10–4; Sun., 1–4, adm.), a history museum that includes
one room devoted to former Joint Chiefs of Staff Admiral
Thomas H. Moorer, a native of Eufaula.

Six miles north of town is Tom Mann's Fish World (summer, 8–5; winter, 9–4; Sun., 12–4, adm.), supposedly the
world's largest freshwater aquarium, with ten 1,400-gallon
tanks and a path that takes you along an underwater walk.
On the grounds stands a monument to "Leroy Brown," a
large-mouth bass that for more than six years was a leading
attraction at Fish World. When Leroy expired, owner Tom
Mann erected a memorial that reads: "Most bass are just
fish, but—Leroy Brown was something special." More than
twenty parks and recreation areas—with facilities for boating, camping, fishing and other outdoor activities—line the
Alabama side of the Walter F. George and George W. Andrews lakes, which extend north and south of Eufaula
(for information on the recreation areas: 912-768-2516 or
768-3051). In the far southeastern corner of the state near
Columbia is the Farley Nuclear Visitors Center (M.–F., 9–4;
Sun., 2–5, free), a museum featuring displays on the history
of energy from prehistoric times to the nuclear age.

A series of attractions stretches across the southern edge
of Alabama that you can conveniently visit as you head back
west toward Mobile, covered in the next section. Dothan,

founded in 1885, is a relatively new city that lacks all traces
of antebellum atmosphere usually found in the Deep South.
Dothan's main claim to fame is its National Peanut Festival
held every year in October. At Ozark, to the west, stands
the 1852 Claybank Church (open daily, free), a well-
preserved log sanctuary, one of the state's few remaining
such buildings. Fort Rucker, south of Ozark, boasts the U.S.
Army Aviation Museum (M.–F., 10–5; Sat., Sun., and holidays, 1–5, free), where the ninety aircraft on display include
the world's largest collection of helicopters, among them
the "Army One" machine Dwight D. Eisenhower used when
he was President. At nearby Enterprise stands what is said
to be the world's only statue to a pest, the Boll Weevil Monument, erected to honor that cotton plant nemesis which for-
tunately forced farmers to diversify into other profitable
crops. The antique Depot at Enterprise houses a small history museum (Tu.–F., 11–4, free). Farther west lie two towns
with European names. Elba, whose turn-of-the-century
Romanesque-style Coffee County Courthouse is listed on
the National Register, took its name in 1851 when the town
of Bentonville was relocated a half-mile upriver on higher
ground following a yellow fever epidemic. Unable to agree
on a name for the new settlement, every adult male was
allowed to submit a suggestion, and one local, then reading
a book on Napoleon, offered the name "Elba," as the new
town's well-watered site reminded him of that island where
the French hero had been exiled. At Andalusia the oddly
named streets East Three-Notch and South Three-Notch,
along which stand a number of stately homes, originated
from the trail Andrew Jackson notched on his way to the
January 1815 encounter with the British in Louisiana, a clash
that became known as the Battle of New Orleans. If you're
heading north toward Montgomery, Greenville, which calls
itself "the camellia city," offers a scattering of old houses
and also the nearby Bates Turkey Farm (open to visitors:

205-227-4505) five miles east of Fort Deposit, two and a half miles east of I-65 exit 142 in Logan; while the obscure hamlet of Carlowville is a well-preserved early nineteenth-century rural village with some thirty buildings in its Historic District, listed on the National Register. The ambiance of Alabama small-town life in places such as Carlowville was captured in print by Harper Lee, whose Pulitzer Prize-winning novel *To Kill a Mockingbird* was set in a "tired old town" like Monroeville, the author's hometown to the southwest, where the Register-listed "courthouse sagged in the square," through which "People moved slowly. . . . They ambled across the square, shuffled in and out of the stores around it, took their time about everything. A day was twenty-four hours but seemed longer. There was no hurry, for there was nowhere to go, nothing to buy and no money to buy it with." Such is the sort of the sleepy, almost timeless type of town a traveler in Alabama—and, for that matter, throughout the South—finds while roaming the region's back roads and remote corners.

The Mobile Area

Mobile—Point Clear and the Gulf Coast

Just about every Southern state boasts its show city, a place like Charleston, South Carolina, or Savannah, Georgia, where the flavor of the Old South lingers. In Alabama Mobile is where you'll best get a sense of the antebellum way of life that typifies the Southern section of the U.S. French colonists, who settled in the area in 1702, built a fort at the site of what is now downtown Mobile in 1711. In 1763 England acquired the region, which it held until 1780 when a Spanish expedition sailed into Mobile Bay from New Orleans to take possession of the city. President James Madison ordered American troops to capture Mobile in 1813 to end Spanish aid to the British in the War of 1812. Mobile then became American but still today many reminders of the city's early development survive. For an overview of Mobile's past a good place to start your visit to the city is at the History Museum (Tu.–Sat., 10–5; Sun., 1–5, free) which occupies an 1872 Italianate-style townhouse. The Colonization Room, Civil War Room and other theme displays trace Mobile's evolution over the last nearly three centuries. Exhibits include gowns worn by Mobile's queens of the Mardi Gras, a celebration that predates the more famous festivities held in New Orleans, where former Mobilians established the tradition. Carl Carmer, in his somewhat outdated but still evocative *Stars Fell on Alabama,* published in 1934, maintains that "Mardi Gras in Mobile is the most formal and elaborate function in modern America," and even these days the celebration, whose origins can be traced back to 1704 and which later evolved with the nineteenth-century Cowbellion Society, is an elaborately choreographed minuet of balls and parades, the last of which every year includes a jester chasing a skeleton around a broken Doric column to symbolize the South's need to renew itself after its Civil War defeat. Other Mobile museums that offer a glimpse of the city's history include the Carlen House (Tu.–Sat., 10–5; Sun., 1–5, free), a French colonial-style Creole residence with period furnishings; the Phoenix Fire Museum (Tu.–Sat., 10–5; Sun., 1–5, free), installed in the attractive 1859 Steam Fire Company No. 6 building; the mid-1840s Condé-Charlotte Museum House (Tu.–Sat., 10–4, adm.), with displays on Mobile's existence under the flags of five powers; and the Heustis Medical Museum (daily, free).

Showplaces also abound in Mobile. Many such mansions are open only during the annual Historic Homes Tour held the second weekend of March, but three places can be visited year round: 1833 Oakleigh Mansion (M.–Sat., 10–3:30; Sun., 2–3:30, adm.), a pleasingly simple structure that now houses the Historic Mobile Preservation Society headquarters; the eighteen-room 1855 Bragg-Mitchell Mansion (M.–F., 10–4; Sun., 1–4, adm.), a truly lovely property, whose eighteen slender fluted columns lend the house a delicate and even fragile look; and the Richards-DAR House (Tu.–Sat., 10–4; Sun., 1–4, adm.), laden with equally delicate lace-like iron-work. Next to the Bragg-Mitchell Mansion stands the Exploreum Museum of Discovery (Tu.–Sat., 10–5; Sun., 1–5, adm.), featuring "hands-on" scientific exhibits, while other Mobile museums include the Fine Arts Museum of the South (Tu.–Sun., 10–5, free) and the "U.S.S. Alabama" (8-sunset, adm.) where you can tour that battleship, the adjacent submarine "U.S.S. Drum" and also see a display of military airplanes. Earlier martial memories linger at Fort Conde (9–5, free), reconstructed from drawings in French archives as a reproduction of the original 1735 brick fort at the site. After visiting the museums it's delightful to walk around town and enjoy the squares, historic districts and other antique areas that make Mobile such a pleasant place. Those lovely oaks and magnolias that embellish the city are controlled and protected by the Mobile Tree Commission, created in 1961 by the Alabama legislature.

Church Street Cemetery (1819) contains a number of impressive monuments, while at Magnolia Cemetery (1836) repose Chappo Geronimo, son of the Apache leader Geronimo, who for a time was imprisoned at Mount Vernon, Alabama, and Joe Cain, who revived Mobile's Mardi Gras after the Civil War. City Hall (1857), one of the nation's oldest municipal buildings still in use, occupies an Italianate structure where a market formerly functioned in the courtyard. The Cathedral of the Immaculate Conception (1849) stands on the site of the old Spanish burial ground, while another mid-nineteenth-century church, Christ Episcopal, contains Tiffany stained glass windows. Mobile's history-haunted squares include Spanish Plaza; Bienville Square, laid out in 1835; 1859 Washington Square, where children frolic on the famous cast-iron deer statue; and De Tonti Square, centerpiece of a nine-block Historic District filled with old houses. As for overnighting in Mobile, the Vincent-Doan Home, dating from about 1827, offers bed and breakfast accommodations (1684 Springhill Avenue, 205-433-7121), and you can book other bed and breakfast establishments in town and along the Gulf Shore through Bed and Breakfast Mobile, Inc., P.O. Box 66261, Mobile, AL 36606; 205-473-2939. For meals, the Pillars, 1757 Government Street, is perhaps the most elegant restaurant in town; Rousso's, a popular place across from Fort Conde downtown, specializes in seafood; and Wintzell's Oyster House, 605 Dauphin Street, established a half-century ago, is a local institution whose menu carries such witticisms as: "Good food takes time—yours will be ready in a second," "This will make you appreciate your wife's cooking," "If you have a gambler's instinct, try our gumbo, you may find some seafood," and "I am not stupid, I know the food is lousy, but everybody pays me for it."

Although the other main area attractions rim Mobile Bay, north of the city lie some historic sites with little remaining there to show for their previous importance—the Indian capital of Maubila, which gave its name to Mobile, located where the Tombigbee and the Alabama rivers flow together; Fort Mims, scene of the Indian massacre that precipitated the retaliation that led to Andrew Jackson's crushing of the Creeks at Horseshoe Bend; St. Stephens, once the colonial capital; and Citronville, in northern Mobile County, where the last Confederate forces east of the Mississippi surrendered on May 4, 1865. In the remote piney woods of that area reside three thousand or so so-called "Cajuns," a curious clan not connected with the more famous Louisiana Cajuns, who speak with a pronounced accent and in their everyday parlance use some French words. The Cajuns are believed to have traces of African ancestry, at least in an amount sufficient to have induced an Alabama judge to hold in the early 1940s that since the group's children were one sixty-fourth black they couldn't attend white schools.

To visit the various sights around Mobile Bay you can make a circle trip; a ferry (for information: 800-634-4027) connects the two nearly touching tips of land, Dauphine Island and Fort Morgan, out in the Gulf of Mexico. On the way out to Dauphine, along the west side of the bay, you'll pass the famous Bellingrath Gardens (7–sunset, adm.), with sixty-five acres of round-the-year flower displays and a collection of more than two hundred and twenty-five Boehm porcelain figures. The peaceful bird sanctuary, beaches and fishing pier equipped with lights for night anglers on Dauphine Island stand in contrast to the shell-shocked walls of Fort Gaines, an 1858 brick fortress built in a five-pointed design based on a plan by Michelangelo on the site where French, Spanish and English troops once stood watch to guard the entrance to Mobile Bay. It was during the Civil War Battle of Mobile Bay when Admiral Farragut uttered his famous cry, "Damn the torpedos. Full speed ahead!" Tunnels, bastions and cannons still survive at the well-preserved fort (9–5, free), used by the military as recently as 1946. Installed in Fort Morgan (8–sunset, adm.), just across the water, is a museum (8–5, adm.) that traces the history of the facility, one of the last Confederate strongholds to fall to Union forces, from the sixteenth century through World War II. From Fort Morgan out at the tip of the peninsula back to the mainland stretch thirty-two miles of sugar white sand beaches, a popular resort area that includes Gulf State Park (205-968-7544), offering an inn, a lodge, cottages and recreational facilities.

As you make your way around the eastern side of the bay you'll reach Point Clear, where the Punta Clara Kitchen (M.–Sat., 9–5; Sun., 12:30–5), a candy shop, occupies a delightful turn-of-the-century Victorian-style house listed on the National Register. Original furnishings fill the house where twelve children grew up. Over the parlor fireplace of the homey house, a mini-museum that recalls the century-old way of life once lived there, appears the heartwarming inscription: "For you this hearth fire glows." At the candy shop you'll get to sample the tasty treats, homemade and guaranteed to add pounds. A mile or so down the road stands the appropriately named Grand Hotel, one of the country's most attractive and tasteful hostelries. Inviting furniture fills the octagonal double-fireplace-equipped wood lobby, off of which nestles a small library, while to the rear stretches the glass-enclosed dining room that looks out onto the water of the bay. For more than a century and a half Point Clear has been a fashionable watering hole for Southern ladies and gentlemen from not only Alabama but also Mississippi, Louisiana and Georgia. "Dearest, I fear I shall not see you at Point Clear this summer," lamented a Southern lad to his lady in an 1860 letter. "I am leaving this evening for Vicksburg."

A bit farther on toward Mobile you'll pass through the unusual town of Fairhope, established in 1893 by Iowans aiming to prove the soundness of Henry George's single-tax theory. The Fairhope Single Tax Corporation, created in 1904, leases all the land in town for a single tax (rent) based on a valuation reassessed annually. This tax is used to pay for all community services, as well as all county, state and other taxes. In the early part of the century at Fairhope, whose library boasts the nation's highest per capita book circulation, a Minnesota schoolteacher founded the School of Organic Education, a kind of free-form, open-learning institution that still functions. Another rather unusual local educational institution is the United States Sports Academy, with a museum and archives (M.–F., 10–2, free) devoted to sports history, art and literature. The Academy is an independent graduate school that offers Master of Sport Science degrees in such fields as coaching, fitness and sports management. At nearby Malbis stands an odd sight for Alabama— the blue-domed Greek Orthodox Memorial Church (9–12, 2–5, free), spiritual center of a Greek community established in 1906 by Antonius Markopoulos, who prospered in the agricultural industry. It is perhaps passing strange to end a tour of Alabama with a Greek Orthodox church, but no more curious or unorthodox than visiting a coon dog cemetery, where our visit to Alabama began.

Alabama Practical Information

For Alabama travel information: 1-800-ALABAMA; within the state: 1-800-392-8096. The street address: Alabama Bureau of Tourism, 532 South Perry Street, Montgomery, AL 36104; 205-261-4169.

Alabama operates eight "Welcome Centers," tourist offices, on highways near state lines: in the northern part of the state at Ardmore on I-65; DeKalb at I-59 near the Georgia line; and the Hardy Center on I-20. In the central part of the state: Sumter County on I-59 near the Mississippi line; Lanett on I-85 near the Georgia line. In the south: Grand Bay on I-10 west of Mobile; Baldwin on I-10 east of Mobile; and Madrid on U.S. 231 near the Florida line.

Alabama operates twenty-one state parks, seven of them designated as resort areas. To reserve accommodations at Alabama's state parks: 1-800-ALA-Park (M.-F., 8–5); out of state: 205-261-3333. For fishing, hunting and camping information: Alabama Department of Conservation and Natural Resources, 64 North Union Street, Montgomery, AL 36130; 205-261-3467.

Information is available on areas in the northern part of the state from the Alabama Mountain Lakes Association, Box 1075, Decatur, AL 35602, 205-350-3500, and on the Gulf Coast from the Alabama Gulf Coast Area Chamber of Commerce, Drawer 457, Gulf Shores, AL 36542, 205-968-7511. For information on other popular tourist centers: Birmingham, 205-252-9825; Cullman, 205-734-0454; Decatur, 205-350-2028; Florence, 205-764-4661; Huntsville, 800-843-0468 outside Alabama, 800-225-6819 in-state; Mobile, 205-433-5100 and 800-662-1984; Montgomery, 205-834-5200; Selma, 205-875-7241; Tuscaloosa, 205-758-3072.

Bed and Breakfast Birmingham, Box 31328, Birmingham, AL 35222, 205-933-2487 can book accommodations for you in that city.

2. Mississippi

If Mississippi were any more Southern it would be like a foreign country. It's the quintessential "Deep South" state, complete with cotton plantations embellished by white columned mansions, magnolia trees (the official state tree), a laid-back and slow-paced way of life, a deep sense of history, and accents so drawling that a conversation with a Mississippian might take twice as long as with a Yankee.

The first Europeans arrived in the area in 1541 when Hernando de Soto marched through what is now Mississippi searching for gold. Instead he discovered the great river which gave its name to the state. In 1699 the Frenchman Iberville established on the Gulf Coast one of the first permanent European settlements in the lower Mississippi Valley, and in 1716 the French built a fort at Natchez as an outpost of their coastal colony. Lamothe Cadillac, who arrived in the area from France in 1713 to look for minerals, didn't think much of the territory: "This is a very wretched country, good for nothing. . . . [Nor] is it expected that for any commercial or profitable purposes, boats will ever be able to run up the Mississippi. . . . One might as well try to bite a slice off of the moon." When Cadillac's sponsor, Anthony Crozat, renounced his concession in the territory the Scotsman John Law stepped in to start up what became the famous "Mississippi Bubble" scheme. In 1717 the French king granted Law's Mississippi Company a twenty-five-year monopoly on all trade between France and a huge territory that included what's now Mississippi. Although the French public bid shares of the company to astronomical heights

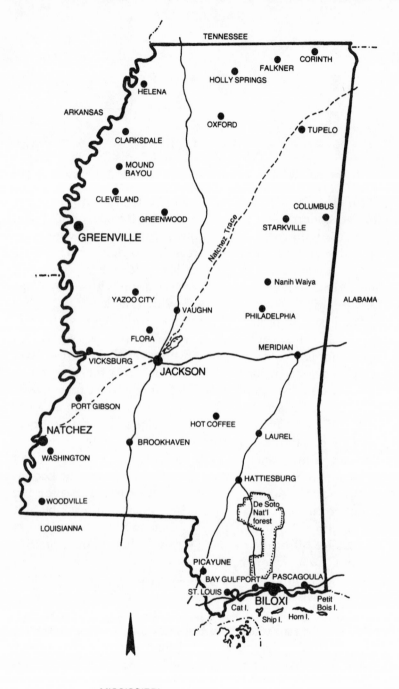

TENNESSEE

CORINTH

FALKNER

HOLLY SPRINGS

HELENA

ARKANSAS

OXFORD

TUPELO

CLARKSDALE

MOUND
BAYOU

COLUMBUS

CLEVELAND

GREENWOOD

STARKVILLE

GREENVILLE

Natchez Trace

Nanih Waiya

ALABAMA

YAZOO CITY

VAUGHN

PHILADELPHIA

FLORA

MERIDIAN

VICKSBURG

JACKSON

PORT GIBSON

HOT COFFEE

NATCHEZ

BROOKHAVEN

LAUREL

WASHINGTON

HATTIESBURG

WOODVILLE

De Soto
Nat'l
forest

LOUISIANNA

PICAYUNE

BAY GULFPORT

PASCAGOULA

ST. LOUIS

BILOXI

Petit
Bois I.

Cat I.

Ship I.

Horn I.

MISSISSIPPI

0   50   100m.

the investors failed to "bite a slice off of the moon" and the bubble burst.

From the very early days land, whether bubbled or earth-bound, played a major role in the state's history. Less known than the Mississippi Bubble but no less bubbly was the late eighteenth-century "Yazoo Act" manipulation, the largest land speculation in U.S. history, by which four companies acquired some thirty-five million acres in Mississippi (and Georgia) at less than two cents an acre and resold the land to the public. On the state's rich farmland eventually grew cotton, the white gold that created Mississippi's landed gentry, a class that so influenced the state's development or non-development, because the Delta's prosperity retarded much of the rest of the state. Cotton ruled supreme. Other governments favored a gold or silver standard but so dominant was cotton in Mississippi that during the Civil War the state issued a cotton currency, backed by bales of the valuable fiber. The pervasive influence of the cotton culture led to an almost feudal sense of structure, such as J. F. H. Claiborne described in *Mississippi as a Province, Territory and State*, the first volume of his history of the state (and the last, for the second volume's manuscript and all the author's archives burned in a fire at his plantation in 1884): "The relation between the owner and the slaves, particularly when they had been inherited, was strictly patriarchal. 'Old Massa' was not a tyrant, but the head of the family, of which they all considered themselves members. 'Old Missus' was the head nurse and waiting woman of the plantation, seeing to the sick and the children and distributing clothing and comforts all around."

Such were the roots of Mississippi's way of life. Traces of the old society remain, not "Massas," to be sure, but a certain agrarian and rural atmosphere and a settled, almost static feeling in many of the small towns that dot the state's hinterland. The past hangs heavy: Time, in Mississippi, seems somehow different as if, in an odd way, it "did not exist, the accumulating seconds and minutes and hours to which in its well state the body is slave both waking and sleeping, now reversed and time now the lip-server and mendicant to the body's pleasure instead of the body thrall to time's headlong course," so Mississippian William Faulkner described a character's convalescence. Similarly, in Mississippi, time—normally so destructive—hasn't enslaved yesteryear with oblivion for in Mississippi the past, with all its splendors and shadows, still lingers in an almost tangible way.

Northern Mississippi

Holly Springs—Corinth—Tupelo—Oxford

Northern Mississippi boasts the hometowns of the state's two most renowned figures—William Faulkner of Oxford and Elvis Presley from Tupelo. The two towns lie only fifty miles apart but a much wider gap separates the men, one a Nobel Prize-winning chronicler of the Old South, the other a modern-day pop culture phenomenon. Faulkner represents the old-fashioned, courtly plantation culture strain that runs through so much of Mississippi's history, while Presley seems to symbolize a down-home, hound dog and grits, rough-hewn way of life not uncommon in the Magnolia State.

Although Presley was a Mississippian born and bred, by now he's indelibly associated with Memphis and his Graceland mansion there. But after Elvis hit the big time he wanted a piece of his home state. If you're an incorrigible Presley fan you may, as you begin your driving tour of northern Mississippi, want to take a look at "the King's"

DeSoto County ranch. The property lies tucked away on a back road just below Memphis, about three miles south of the Tennessee-Mississippi state line, just west of Horn Lake on highway 301 about a half-mile south of Goodman Road. There isn't really much to see there, so your imagination will have to supply you with visions of Presley's previous presence on the property, which may soon be turned into a recreation park by the family that acquired the place in the early 1980s.

As you continue south on highway 51 you'll come to Hernando, where the DeSoto County Courthouse contains some 1903 murals from the old Gayoso Hotel in Memphis depicting the exploits of Spanish explorer Hernando de Soto, who in 1541 discovered the Mississippi River instead of the gold deposits he was seeking. Hernando also boasts the McIngvale Clock Museum (9–3, adm.) with a collection of more than seven hundred timepieces, the earliest dating from 1750. Just south of Hernando lies Arkabutla Lake, a dragon-shaped body of water said to be one of the South's windiest lakes and thus favored for sailing. At Como, farther south, stands Four Oaks (open by appointment, 601-526-5354), a late neoclassic revival-style mansion that recalls the days a century ago when Panola County was said to be the country's richest county, thanks to the cotton crop. Other mansions from those days stand on a street across the railroad tracks from Main Street, while a few blocks north of Main is the boyhood home of Stark Young, novelist and, from 1922 to 1947, drama critic for *Theatre Arts* magazine, *The New Republic* and *The New York Times*. Young, who died in 1947, is buried in Friendship Cemetery near Como. Other nineteenth-century Panola County houses grace Sardis, five miles south of Como, including the 1848 Heflin House, now a museum of area Indian history, Fairhill (1870) and the Johnson Tate Cottage (1873). For information on these houses: 601-487-3451.

To the east of Como and Sardis lies the village of Abbeville, where home-cooking-style Ruth & Jimmie's Cafe, installed in an old-time country store building, serves "grandma's Sunday dinner every day." Holly Springs, north of Abbeville, is a delightful "Old South" type of town with an attractive collection of antebellum buildings and a slow-paced, laid-back atmosphere. Much history haunts the town's houses, virtually each of which has some sort of tale or legend connected with it. Melrose (1858) was built as a wedding present, the front door at The Magnolias (c. 1850) still bears the scar left by a Federal soldier's bayonet, while Wakefield (1858)—whose one-time owner shocked the populace in the late 1860s by marrying a Union officer—once changed hands as the prize in a poker game. In Cuffawa (1832) lived a direct descendant of Virginia's first governor; in Hamilton Place (1838) resided the treasurer of the Illinois Central Railroad; at Crump Place (c. 1830) E. H. "Boss" Crump was born, the legendary mayor of Memphis; and writer Sherwood Bonner occupied Cedarhurst (1857). The daughter of a doctor, Bonner is considered by some to be Mississippi's leading pre-Faulkner fiction writer. In the early 1870s she moved to Boston to further her literary career and there became Henry Wadsworth Longfellow's secretary, collaborating with him in his *Poems of Places, Southern States.* Bonner, whose well-received 1878 novel *Like Unto Like* is set in the South during Reconstruction times, died at Holly Springs in 1883 at age thirty-four. Another local woman who enjoyed success in the arts was painter Kate Freeman Clark, a pupil of well-known artist William Merrit Chase. The Clark Art Gallery (open by appointment, 601-252-2511) contains more than a thousand of her paintings, supposedly the world's largest single collection by one artist. The Holly Springs Chamber of Commerce, Randall and College Streets, sells a booklet of the so-called Green Line Tour that guides you to the town's old houses, many of which are open the third weekend of April during the annual spring pilgrimage, the state's second oldest (1936) after the one in Natchez. For home and pilgrimage information: 601-252-2943.

Ripley

From Holly Springs it's convenient to head east for your first encounter with the history of the famous Faulkner family. The hamlet of Falkner, north of Ripley, was named after Colonel William C. Falkner (spelled then without the "u"), the famous novelist's great-grandfather. Old Colonel Falkner, who inspired some of the characters in William Faulkner's novels, was himself an author and well-respected citizen of Ripley. A contemporary account by Reuben Davis, a doctor, lawyer and Congressman from Mississippi, in *Recollections of Mississippi and Mississippians* published in 1889, recalls the Colonel as "firm and courageous" and the author of "several works of fiction which have given him prominence as a writer. He also conceived and carried out the idea of building a railroad from Ripley to Middleton, Tennessee . . . all by means of his personal influence, and skills as a financier. Beginning life without pecuniary resources, he has accomplished more than almost any man I have ever known." Such was the reputation of the family's founding father, who reposes in the Falkner family plot at the Ripley Cemetery. Rather more lively than the graveyard in Ripley is the bustling "Trading Day," a venerable event, held for more than a century, which takes place the first Monday of every month beginning at 8 a.m. at the Fairgrounds. Town and country folk from the region gather there to sell or swap a wide variety of goods. As for Colonel Falkner's more renowned great-grandson, William Faulkner was born in New Albany to the south, on the way to which you might want to stop at Blue Mountain to see the antique doll collection at the 1873 Blue Mountain College, listed on the National Historic Register (open by appointment, 601-685-4771). New Albany, apart from the old boxy brick bank building with gold lettering over the door down on Bankhead Street, offers little to see except for the plaque at the corner of Cleveland and Jefferson Streets which reads: "WILLIAM FAULKNER Here, September 25, 1897, was born the distinguished author, member of the American Academy of Arts and Letters, winner of the Pulitzer Prize and recipient of the 1949 Nobel Prize in Literature." On the west side of town William Faulkner Park honors the illustrious native son.

Before proceeding on to Tupelo, about twenty-five miles southeast of New Albany, the birthplace of that other world-famous Mississippian, Elvis Presley, you may want to see a few sights in the northeastern corner of the state. At Corinth, a few miles from the Tennessee state line, survive not only Civil War-era sights but also a certain nineteenth-century ambiance. An 1873 Corinth visitor named L. J. Dupree described the place in terms that are almost a caricature of sleepy Southern towns of today as well as of yesteryear: People were "sauntering in the hot sunbeams and loitering about the dramshops . . . as the locals move about lazily. They drag their feet and drawl out their words and stare listlessly at a stranger. . . . Laziness is in the very air one breathes. . . . The town grows, but lazily. There are houses begun and never finished. The owners are too lazy." Such lazy ways and slow days still typify many a town in the Deep South, perhaps not all bad in a sometimes too-busy era.

The Civil War time in Corinth is recalled at Battery Robinette, which commemorates the Confederate Army's (unsuccessful) assault on the Union artillery emplacement during the 1862 Battle of Corinth, fought in part on the twenty-acre site that now comprises the Corinth National Cemetery, where more than five thousand Union soldiers repose. Both Battery Robinette and the cemetery are listed on the National Register, as is the 1857 Curlee House (1–4, except Th., adm.) built by one of the founders of Corinth, which was established in 1854. During the Civil War the elegant white house with small graceful columns around it served as headquarters for, in turn, Confederate and Union generals. Before leaving town you may want to stop in at Borroum's, a picture-out-of-the-past establishment—with old wood fixtures, a cigar store Indian, antler-crowned stuffed animal heads on the wall—which is believed to be Mississippi's oldest drug store (1865). Heading south out of Corinth and then a few miles to the east you'll come to Jacinto, nearly a ghost town now but worth a visit for the handsome 1854 Federal-style two-story brick courthouse, which contains a historical museum (April to Dec., Tu.–Sun., other times by appointment, 601-287-7679, free), and for the village's other nineteenth-century structures. At Baldwyn, about halfway between Jacinto and Tupelo, is the Brice's Crossroads Museum (M.–F., 9–5, free) with Indian artifacts and Civil War relics from the nearby Brice's Crossroads Battlefield housed in a replica of an early nineteenth-century log cabin.

Tupelo, to the south, vies with Oxford as Mississippi's Mecca: readers and word people gravitate to Faulkner's town; while listeners and music folk make the pilgrimage to Tupelo, there to see the two-room frame house Vernon Presley built in 1934 with one hundred and eighty borrowed dollars. Here Elvis was born on January 8, 1935, and here the Presley family remained until the house was repossessed a few years later, after which the Presleys lived in several other Tupelo houses before moving on to Memphis in 1948. Although the birth house (9–5; Sun.,1–5, adm.) is the centerpiece of Tupelo's Presley memorials, serious fans can also visit such other Elvis sights as a Memorial Chapel (truly engaged fans can get married there), the Assembly of God church where the family assembled for services, Lawhon School where the boy attended grades one to five (in the fifth grade young Elvis won second place singing in a local talent contest), Milam Junior High where Presley went to grades six and seven, and Tupelo Hardware where the future star bought his first guitar. More Presley memories survive at the Tupelo Museum (Tu.–F., 10–4; Sat. and Sun., 1–5, adm.) in Ballard Park on highway 6 just west of the famous Natchez Trace Parkway. The museum also includes an old country store display, a turn-of-the-century Western Union office and other historical exhibits.

About five miles north of Tupelo lies the Natchez Trace Parkway visitor center and headquarters (8–5, free). If you plan to drive any part of the Trace—which cuts diagonally across the middle of Mississippi to Jackson, the state capital, and on to Natchez in the far southwestern corner of the state—it's well worth stopping in at the visitor center, where a museum and short film trace the history of the Trace. The historic roadway evolved from an Indian path to a rough wilderness trail which, in the late eighteenth century, pioneers followed to travel between Natchez and Nashville, Tennessee, four hundred and fifty miles to the northeast. Two years after the United States created the Mississippi Territory, with Natchez as its capital, mail service along the road began, and in 1801 President Jefferson ordered the army to clear the route. By 1820 more than twenty inns (or "stands" as they were then called) stood along the Trace, but soon after steamboats on the Mississippi, Ohio and other rivers began to draw traffic away from the overland route and the Trace fell into disuse. In the early twentieth century the Mississippi Daughters of the American Revolution began a movement to commemorate the Trace, and in 1938 Congress created the Natchez Trace Parkway as a unit of the National Park System. The Trace today is one of America's most attractive and delightful historical areas, and no doubt its longest and narrowest. Along the Parkway, a truly splendid road, unmarred by advertising signs and unspoiled by commercial establishments, are dozens of exhibit areas, Indian sites, nature trails, picnic alcoves and scenic vistas. Maps and pamphlets with information on these attractions are available from: Superintendent, Natchez Trace Parkway, R.R. 1, NT-143, Tupelo, MS 38801, 601-842-1572. If you happen to be heading south from Tupelo (perhaps via Houston where you'll find an old-fashoned country store tucked away in the basement area of Horn's Big Star grocery), you can stay in the only inn on the Trace, a delightful two-bedroom bed and breakfast establishment installed in century-old log cabins at French Camp (601-547-6835), eighty miles from Tupelo. A group of well-preserved nineteenth-century buildings at French Camp—the Huffman Log Cabin, the James Drane House, the still functioning 1885 Academy school—will serve to give you the flavor of old days on the historic Natchez Trace.   *Oxford*

Before continuing on to the central part of the state it's worth a detour, even a long one, to visit Oxford (fifty miles west of Tupelo), one of Mississippi's and the South's most alluring towns. Apart from Hannibal, Missouri, where Mark Twain and his characters are almost tangible presences, probably no other town in America is so haunted by the spirit of the author who captured the place in his works as William Faulkner's Oxford. Faulkner lived and wrote in and about Oxford, which he made famous in his books under the name "Jefferson" in the mythical Yoknapatawpha County. Fifteen of his nineteen novels were set in the "little postage stamp of native soil," as the author referred to the area. Oxford's centerpiece, and the best place to start absorbing the Faulkner atmosphere that pervades the town, is courthouse square, a typical, even archetypical, Southern county seat. In front of the 1870 "cotehouse," as the locals pronounce it, stands a Confederate soldier statue ("They gave their lives in a just and holy cause," reads the monument's inscription) and along the square's four sides run arcades and rows of shops where Oxonians meet to exchange large quantities of small-town gossip and maybe even to make an occasional purchase

or two. A stroll around the square will take you past such
establishments as Neilson's department store, a fixture in
Oxford since 1839; the First National Bank, founded in 1910
by the novelist's grandfather; and Gathright-Reed drugstore,
which Faulkner frequented to buy tobacco and to read magazines, occasionally becoming so engrossed in an article that
he'd sit on the floor while finishing the story.

A mile or so south of the square stands Rowan Oak, a
stately mansion set in a grove of oak and cedar trees. Faulkner
purchased the mid-nineteenth-century house in 1930 and
lived there until his death in 1962. Designated a National
Historic Landmark in 1977, Rowan Oak is now owned by
the University of Mississippi and maintained as a memorial
to the famous novelist (open during term time, M.–F.,
10–12, 2–4; Sat., 10–12; Sun., 2–4, free; for information:
601-234-3284 or 601-232-7318). Inside the handsome mansion, complete with Southern-style white columns, is Faulkner's library of twelve hundred books, as well as the author's
study where he wrote on an old-fashioned Underwood port-
able, still sitting on the same scratched wooden table by
the same window as the machine did when Faulkner used
the typewriter. Inscribed on two walls there in the writer's
cramped handwriting is the outline for his novel *A Fable*.
Faulkner's bedroom upstairs remains as it was the last time
he used it before his death on July 6, 1962. A pair of old
shoes reposes on the floor, and by the bed stands a bookcase
with paperback mysteries (*The Comfortable Coffin, Trent's Last
Case* and others) which furnished Faulkner's bedtime reading. While at Rowan Oak, it's pleasant to explore the spacious grounds where the outbuildings include the original
kitchen, used by Faulkner as a smokehouse, and the log stable, the oldest structure on the property.

West of courthouse square stretches the well-wooded
nearly twelve hundred-acre campus of the University of Mis-

sissippi, fondly known as "Ole Miss." When the legislature met in joint session in early 1841 to choose a site for the state university Oxford was chosen by one vote (fifty-eight to fifty-seven) over Mississippi City down on the Gulf Coast. In the fall of 1962 Ole Miss was the scene of what James W. Silver, in *Mississippi: The Closed Society,* called "the most explosive federal-state clash since the Civil War" when James Meredith arrived to register as the first black since Reconstruction to be admitted to the school. It took two deaths, dozens of injured and more than 23,000 U.S. and National Guard troops to get Meredith enrolled. The only original building remaining on the campus is the Lyceum (late 1840s), which was used as a hospital for Confederate troops after the 1862 Battle of Shiloh in Tennessee. Behind the Lyceum stands the university library where items from the Faulkner collection—manuscripts, books, the novelist's 1950 Nobel Prize diploma—are on display.* Among the most interesting exhibits are two oversized scrapbooks, crammed with Faulkner clippings assembled and donated to the library by J. R. Cofield, an Oxford photographer who took dozens of pictures of the town's most famous son.

Between the university and the square stands the Buie Museum (Tu., W., Sat., 10–12 and 1:30–4:30; Th., 9–12; F., 1:30–4:30; Sun., 2–5, free) with collections of Greek and Roman antiquities, early scientific instruments and primitive paintings by Oxford artist Theora Hamblett, as well as a

---

*The plaque at the site of Faulkner's birth house in New Albany mentioned above refers to his 1949 Nobel Prize, whereas the diploma bears the date 1950. By a vote of fifteen out of eighteen members the Swedish Academy selected Faulkner for the award in 1949 but the decision had to be unanimous. By the time the three dissenters joined the majority it was too late to award the prize in 1949 so Faulkner received the Nobel for 1949 in 1950.

flea wedding scene seen through a magnifying glass. If you
are overnight in Oxford two pleasant places to stay are the
Alumni House (601-234-2331) situated in a quiet corner of
the campus and the Oliver-Britt Inn, 512 Van Buren
(601-234-8043). For meals the locals gather at Smitty's Cafe
(as did Faulkner in his time) just off the square. Smitty's
menu lists such down-home dishes as catfish, country ham
steak, sausage "'n biskits" with grits and "other stuff when
you can git it or when the cook ain't sik." If your driving
tour through the South has sparked a more than passing
interest in the region, you might want to stop in at the Center
for the Study of Southern Culture installed in the old Barnard Observatory building on the university campus. The
Center houses a wide variety of resources and undertakes
a number of projects covering all phases of the South's culture, history and folklore.

To complete your visit to Oxford, stroll over to St. Peter's
Cemetery a few blocks east of the square. St. Peter's has
served as Oxford's burial ground since the town began in
1835. Buried there in a simply marked grave next to his
wife and near his forebears is the town's most famous figure.
His work done, Faulkner reposes in his beloved "little postage stamp of native soil," which nurtured and inspired him
and which now embraces him forever.

West-Central Mississippi

The Delta: Clarksdale, Greenwood, Greenville, Yazoo City—Jackson

L. P. Hartley's novel *The Go-Between* begins: "The past
is a foreign country; they do things differently there." So,
too, does the Mississippi Delta region seem a foreign coun-

try, for things are done differently there. The slow sleepy region—which has its own pace and rituals—is a throwback to the old days when cotton was king and the plantation culture represented an entire way of life. In Mississippi once upon a time—and, to a certain extent, in the Delta still today—the plantation was the goal and glory of every red-blooded, and blue-blooded, Mississippian. As the *Vicksburg Sun* put it in an article published April 9, 1860, (quoted in *Mississippi: Storm Center of Secession* by Percy Lee Rainwater): "A large plantation . . . [is] the Ultima Thule of every Southern gentleman's ambition. For this the lawyer pores over his dusty tomes, the merchant measures his tape, the doctor rolls his pills, the editor drives his quill, and the mechanic his plane—all, all who dare aspire at all, look to this as the goal of their ambition."

The rather distinct and self-contained region known as the Delta occupies an elliptical area about two hundred miles long extending some sixty miles east of the Mississippi at its widest point. In the famous phrase of David Cohn, from the Delta town of Greenville, "The Mississippi Delta begins in the lobby of the Peabody Hotel in Memphis and ends on Catfish Row in Vicksburg." From the names of some of the towns scattered about the Delta you could write a short story or, better yet, a blues song: Lula, Sledge, Darling, Rena Lara, Tippo, Alligator, Renova, Itta Bena and Nitta Yuma, Midnight, Bourbon, Money, Panther Burn and others.

Although the Delta may begin in the Peabody lobby you can conveniently start your visit to the area somewhat south of the hotel. Highway 61, the Delta's "Main Street," will take you south from Memphis down through Tunica County, one of the nation's poorest, and on into the heart of the Delta. At Friar's Point, a Mississippi River village a few miles west of 61, you'll find a museum (Tu., Th., Sat., and Sun., 2–6 and by appointment, 601-383-5514, adm.) with a small but widely diversified collection of Indian artifacts, Civil War relics and historical objects from the Delta area. Friar's Point was the town where the first Italian immigrants imported in the 1880s to work on Delta plantations settled. The first main Delta town you'll come to is Clarksdale, at a site on the Sunflower River where an Indian city named Quizquiz was located at the time Spanish explorer Hernando de Soto discovered the Mississippi in May 1541 not far from Sunflower Landing at nearby De Soto Lake. The main attraction in Clarksdale is the Delta Blues Museum (M.–F., 9–5, free), a collection of photographs, artifacts and archives relating to the blues-rich culture in the Delta where that music still blares forth in many a so-called juke joint, or dive, found in a number of the area's small towns. Coahoma County was home to such legendary bluesmen as W. C. Handy, Muddy Waters, Charlie Patton, Ike Turner, Son House and others, so the area is perhaps the epicenter of blues history and traditions. Since 1947 Early Wright, the South's longest-running black disc jockey, has spun blues and gospel music records starting at 7 p.m. on local station WROX.

Another famous one-time resident of Clarksdale was playwright Tennessee Williams, born in Columbus, Mississippi in 1911 and brought as a boy to Clarksdale where he lived with his grandfather, the Reverend Walter Dakin, in the rectory of St. George's Church. Williams drew an evocative word portrait of his early days in Mississippi towns such as Clarksdale and Columbus (as recounted in *Remember Me to Tom* by Edwina Dakin Williams, his mother):

My sister and I were gloriously happy. We sailed paper boats in wash-tubs of water, cut lovely colored paper-dolls out of huge mail-order catalogs, kept two white rabbits under the back porch, baked mud pies in the sun upon the front walk, climbed up and slid down the big wood pile, collected from neighboring alleys and trash-piles bits of colored glass that were diamonds and rubies and sapphires and emeralds. And in the evenings, when the white moonlight streamed over our bed, before we were asleep, our Negro nurse Ozzie, as warm and black as a moonless Mississippi night, would lean above our bed, telling in a low, rich voice her amazing tales about foxes and bears and rabbits and wolves that behaved like human beings.

Such were the days and nights and delights of at least one Mississippi lad long ago.

On highway 61 south of Clarksdale you'll pass through the somewhat forlorn town of Mound Bayou, a remnant of the all-black settlement founded in 1887 by Vicksburg resident Isaiah Montgomery. Montgomery acquired some seven hundred acres of land for seven dollars an acre, and by 1907 the settlement comprised 30,000 acres with 4,000 residents. A drop in the cotton price in 1920 from a dollar to under twenty cents a pound, migration to Northern cities during World War I and Montgomery's death in 1924 led to the town's decline. Merigold, just south of Mound Bayou, boasts Mississippi's first winery since Prohibition (Tu.–Sat., 10–5, free) and McCarty's Barn, a studio where Lee and Pup McCarty create pottery and jewelry items; while at Cleveland, five miles farther south, Delta State University offers art and natural history museums (M.–F., 8–5; Tu. to 7:30, free). Cleveland is also the center of the Delta's Chinese community. Chinese in Mississippi? It's true, for in the post-Civil War Reconstruction period planters initiated a plan to bring Chinese workers to the area to replace the freed blacks. Some of the Chinese families accumulated sufficient savings to open grocery shacks that catered to blacks. The Orientals thus "took up a strategic if unwanted position between the white and black population, providing goods and services to the latter, while preserving and protecting the caste superiority of the former," notes Stanford M. Lyman in the introduction to Robert Seto Quan's *Lotus Among the Magnolias*. On highway 8 in Cleveland stands the Chinese Baptist Church (the name appears over the door in both Chinese and English), behind which runs East Main Street where some of the local Chinese families reside.

Some fifty miles due east of Cleveland lies Grenada, site of the building that housed the now defunct 1840s-vintage Yalobusha Female Institute and of the restored 1890 Grenada Bank building, listed on the National Historic Register. Southeast of Cleveland is Greenwood, which bills itself as "cotton capital of the world." Cotton is intricately woven into the fabric and pattern of Mississippi history. The first mention of the cotton plant in the state was by the Frenchman Charlevoix, who saw some plants in a Natchez garden in 1722. Mississippi's first seeds, from Jamaica and Georgia, tended to rot, so the planters sought other seeds elsewhere. In 1806, the story goes, a man named Walter Burling of Natchez asked permission to take some cotton seeds with him out of Mexico. Although permission was refused, Burling took "home with him as many Mexican dolls as he might fancy. . . . The stuffing of these dolls was understood to have been cotton seed," noted an 1854 state report quoted in *A History of Mississippi* by Robert Lowry and William H. McCardle. Thus originated Mississippi's present-day cotton empire, for seeds from Mexico were the basis of the state's crop.

On the eve of the Civil War in 1860, America's cotton production reached almost a billion pounds, some two-thirds of the world's total supply, and the cotton kingdom of Mississippi included subjects ranging from "the Creoles and hillfolk, who raised cotton merely to cover their nakedness, to the so-called slavocrats who raised cotton largely to cover their indebtedness," as John K. Bettersworth put it in *Confederate Mississippi*. Greenwood's Cottonlandia Museum (Tu.– Sat., 9–5; Sun., 1–5, adm.) contains exhibits on the state's principal crop, while the Florewood River Plantation west of town (Tu.–Sat., 9–5; Sun., 1–5, adm.) presents a re-creation of an 1850s cotton plantation, complete with a planter's mansion, twenty-six outbuildings and cultivated cotton fields, as well as a cotton museum. Down in town by the Yazoo River stretches nineteenth-century Cotton Row, listed on the National Historic Register, with the nation's second-largest cotton exchange and Ram Cat Alley, once the town's nightlife center. Greenville's Leflore County Courthouse, a big boxy building that resembles a state capitol, occupies the site where Choctaw Indians once carried out executions. Now only contracts and writs are executed there. Stately old Southern mansions line lovely Grand Boulevard garnished with "Miss Sally's" oak trees, planted by North Greenwood founder Sally Gwin. In the rural areas of Leflore County people still today practice the old custom of dirt eating, known as geophagy. Connoisseurs of the clay-rich earth snack on baked dirt often seasoned with vinegar and salt. Dirt from hills is favored over the lowland variety, popularly referred to as "gumbo dirt." The locals occasionally mail shoeboxes full of the delicacy to relatives living elsewhere who crave the flavor of Delta dirt.

Driving from Greenwood to Greenville, a Mississippi River town to the west, you'll pass through Indianola where you can wash the locally grown nuts from the Pecan House (for phone orders: 800-541-6345 out of state; 800-541-6252 in Mississippi) down with wine from the Claiborne Vineyards (open by appointment, 601-887-2327), operated by the nephew of *New York Times* food writer Craig Claiborne. Also at Indianola is Delta Catfish processors, where you can tour the world's largest catfish-processing operation. Just before Greenville you'll pass through the typical small Delta town of Leland where the Little Bales of Cotton store sells a wide range of cottonland souvenirs—cotton-bale clocks, bale bookends, bale footstools and the like. In early December Leland hosts a floating Christmas parade on Deer Creek, which flows through downtown.

Something in the air or in the mint juleps—or maybe in the school system—at Greenville has activated the creative muse in an unusual number of the town's residents. Civil War historian Shelby Foote, Pulitzer Prize-winning editor Hodding Carter, novelist Walker Percy and his second cousin author William Alexander Percy, after whom the town library is named, all lived in Greenville. W. A. Percy's *Lanterns on the Levee* is a delightful memoir that evokes Greenville and the surrounding cotton country in the first part of this century. After graduating from Harvard Law School Percy returned in 1909 to his hometown, not "a thing of beauty in those days. The residences looked like illegitimate children of a French wedding cake. . . . Sidewalks were often the two-board sort that grow splinters for barefoot boys, and the roads, summer or winter, were hazards. There were lovely trees and crepe myrtles but where they grew was their business. There were flowers but no gardens. Just a usual southern town of that period, and its name was Greenville." Another local writer, David Cohn, found a similar profusion of foliage (described in his *Where I Was Born and Raised*) when he returned home in 1947: "Growing Greenville has been wise enough to preserve its superb trees. Birds still sing from its magnolias. . . . Weeping willows are cascades of tender green in springtime. Crepe myrtles in full bloom run through the streets with cloudy fire in their branches. The fruit of cottonwoods drift white in summer. There is an instinctive love of beauty here and of trees which inform it." Thus does the name "Greenville" well describe the well-garnished, shady and pleasant Delta town that you can most fruitfully visit by using the driving and walking tour brochure published by the Chamber of Commerce, 915 Washington (601-378-3141). Among the more interesting places are the Mississippi River Levee area and the displays at the Levee Board, located in 1883 buildings—the city's oldest commercial structures still used for their original purpose—at the corner of Walnut and Main Streets. Also at that corner stands the old (c. 1881) *Delta Democrat-Times* building. It was editorials Hodding Carter published in the "D D-T," as the paper is called, which won him the 1946 Pulitzer Prize. Farther along Main stand (at number 412) Gothic-style St. Joseph's Catholic Church, replica of a Dutch church; the Percy Library (number 341), installed in the former Elysian Club building; the First National Bank (number 302), a 1903 classic-style structure listed on the National Historic Register; and buildings on both sides of the 200 block of Main, so-called Cotton Row where cotton trading companies once operated. Greenville is home to Doe's, one of the Delta's best-known restaurants, which specializes in steaks cut to your specifications and cooked before your eyes and tastebuds in the kitchen visible from the eating area. At Greenville's Living Water Garden you can do more than watch your meal being cooked; you can catch it. Sportsmen can troll for their own catfish, while just plain hungry folk can order an already landed and prepared catfish, served with hush puppies—a kind of cat and dog meal. Plans are now under way in Greenville, home of the Delta's largest blues festival, to establish a concert facility dedicated to preserving that indigenous black music.

Near the hamlet of Scott, north of Greenville, spreads the 38,000-acre English-owned Delta and Pine Land Company, said to be the world's largest cotton plantation (no organized tours but visitors are welcome); while to the south, perched between Lake Washington and the Mississippi, lies the hamlet of Chatham, where the nearly century-and-a-half-old Italianate-style Mount Holly Plantation House, listed on the National Historic Register, offers overnight accommodations (601-827-2652). Near the house and also by the lake stand the ruins of St. John's Church, which fell into decay after the windows were removed during the Civil War to obtain the lead pane frames, melted down to make bullets. Farther south is Vicksburg and, to the southeast of Greenville, lie Belzoni—with the Ethel Mohamed Stitchery Museum (open by appointment, 601-247-1433) and the Antique Barn restaurant, which serves catfish dips, pâte and other such fishy concoctions—and Yazoo City. "Yazoo": a strange name. Yazoo City native Willie Morris—novelist, essayist, editor of *Harper's* magazine—says in his autobiography *North Toward Home* that "Yazoo" is an old Indian word meaning "death" or "waters of the dead." Morris recalls that overwhelming sense of place so common with Mississippi writers: "I knew Mississippi and I loved what I saw. . . . In Yazoo I knew every house and every tree in the white section of town. Each street and hill was like a map of my consciousness; I loved the contours of its land, and the slow changing of its seasons. . . . [and eventually I realized] how this land had shaped me, how its isolation and its guilt-ridden past had already settled so deeply into my bones." Morris's home town indeed has a certain comfortable, down-home feel to it.

Although a 1904 fire destroyed the downtown and many houses in the Mound Street residential area, some old structures remain in and around Yazoo City, whose center section, comprising one hundred and seventy-five buildings and residences, is listed on the National Register. Outside town is Bell Road, an unusual sunken roadway once used by oxcarts; in the old days a bell at each end served to signal that someone had entered the road, wide enough for only one vehicle at a time. South of Yazoo City near Satartia, where the Delta flatland meets the hill country, is the No Mistake Plantation, named after the prospective buyer's brother advised him in 1833 that he'd "make no mistake in buying that land." At Flora, to the southeast, you'll find the Petrified Forest (Memorial Day to Labor Day, 9–6; other months, 9–5, adm.), a stand of prehistoric trees turned to stone. The area, which offers a nature trail and a museum, is a National Natural Landmark site, but privately owned.

Before proceeding to nearby Jackson, the state capital, you might want to detour north to Pickens, near which stands the Rob Morris Little Red Schoolhouse (highway 17, west of Interstate 55, M.–F., 9:30–3:30, free), formerly the Eureka Masonic College building (1847), listed on the National Historic Register, where Morris founded the Masonic Order of the Eastern Star. Installed in an old train depot at Vaughan, not far to the south, is the Casey Jones Museum (Tu.–Sat., 9–5, adm.), which commemorates the famous railroad engineer killed in a train wreck a mile north of the museum in 1900. The third Saturday in October every year a Hobo Day celebration, featuring music, hobo stew and a hobo king and queen contest, enlivens the museum. Also at Vaughan, out on Possum Bend Road, is the workshop where furniture craftsman Greg Harkins fashions old-style chairs for "presidents, congressmen, celebrities, and other big dogs, but mostly just common folk," as the establishment's card says.

JACKSON

Like many state capitals Jackson, south of Vaughan, has amassed a goodly number of museums, cultural offerings and historical attractions. Seats of government somehow seem to end up with a disproportionate share of their land's resources. In addition to the usual array of official buildings—the state capitol; the Old Capitol, which houses the state historical museum; the attractive governor's mansion (tours available)—Jackson boasts a wide range of museums. There you will find the Mississippi Agricultural and Forestry Museum and the National Agricultural Aviation Museum (with exhibits on crop-dusting); the Mississippi Museum of Art; the Mississippi Museum of Natural Science; the Smith-Robertson Museum and Cultural Center, devoted to the state's black culture and history; the Mississippi Military

Museum; and, last but perhaps most unusual, the Dizzy Dean Museum, with memorabilia pertaining to the famous St. Louis Cardinal pitcher and, later, sportscaster. Every fourth year Jackson hosts an International Ballet competition (the most recent: 1990; for information, 601-960-1560) and the town boasts such pre-Civil War show houses as the Oaks (Tu.–Sat., 10–4; Sun., 1:30–4, adm.), occupied by General William Tecumseh Sherman during his 1863 siege of the capital, and Manship House (Tu.–F., 9–4; Sat. and Sun., 1–4, free), a Gothic-style small villa laden with frilly trim. Information on all these sites is available at the Jackson Visitor Center, 1510 North State Street (800-354-7695; in Mississippi, 601-960-1891).

Around Jackson are a scattering of attractions, some little known, worth a stop if you're headed in their direction. Out at Ridgeland on the Natchez Trace, to the north, is the Mississippi Crafts Center (9–5), where a log cabin houses a shop that sells a wide range of handicrafts. Also on the north side, at Tougaloo College in Tougaloo, is an art collection featuring African and Afro-American works (open by appointment, 601-956-4941, ext. 327, free). At Mississippi College in Clinton, to the west, is a museum and archive (M. and F. mornings; Sat. and Sun. afternoons, free) tracing the history of Baptists in the state. Founded in 1826, Mississippi College was the first coeducational college in the U.S. to grant degrees to women. At Raymond, just to the south, yet a third educational institution, Hinds Junior College, houses the Marie Hull Art Gallery (Sept.–April, M.–Th., 8–3; F., 8–12), with a permanent exhibit of works by Mississippi artists. The almost severely classical but beautifully proportioned Raymond Courthouse, built in the 1850s by slave labor, is listed in the National Archives as one of the nation's best built buildings. Farther from Jackson, to the southeast, are the towns of Piney Woods, home of the pioneering Country Life School, founded in 1909 to teach black children practical skills, and D'Lo, with the Ida Thompson Museum (open by appointment, 601-847-2754, free), housed in an old post office, exhibiting farming and domestic artifacts as well as photos on the history of Mississippi's tuberculosis sanatorium. With that rather diverse group of attractions you can end your tour of West-Central Mississippi.

East-Central Mississippi

Columbus—Starkville—Kosciusko— Philadelphia—Meridian— Laurel

The east-central section of Mississippi, which occupies the so-called plains area on the opposite side of the state from the Delta, contains a wide variety of attractions, including country-music shrines, antebellum plantations and Mississippi's only surviving Indian settlement. One of the region's most handsome towns is Columbus, where more than a hundred splendid nineteenth-century homes grace the city's tree-shaded streets. Almost every house has a story or a special feature connected with it. The Love Cottage (1109 Main Street), for example, contains thirteen doors, windows, squares in the walk and panes of glass around the front door, for the Love family considered the number "13" lucky; the carpetbagger who occupied the Frank Home (406 North 3d Avenue) during Reconstruction days hid his horde of gold in a well on the property; The Fourth Estate house (624 North 2d Avenue) sports fully sixty-eight outside windows; and at Twelve Gables (220 South 3d Street) a group of Columbus matrons originated the idea of putting flowers on graves of Civil War dead, which the ladies did in April 1865 at Friendship Cemetery, thus supposedly establishing what became the nation's Memorial Day observance. Many of the old houses are open during Columbus's annual Pilgrimage (for information: 601-329-3533), held the last weekend of March and the first week of April. One old residence, the 1847 Blewett-Harrison-Lee House (316 7th Street), is a museum with nineteenth-century objects on exhibit (Tu. and Th., 1–4, free).

On College Street between South 3d and 4th Streets stands the magnolia tree-garnished house where Thomas Lanier Williams first saw the light of day, an event memorialized by the plaque there: "One of America's leading playwrights, Tennessee Williams, was born here March 26, 1911. He received the Pulitzer Prize for *Streetcar Named Desire* and *Cat on a Hot Tin Roof.* Both stories set in the South." Later in life Williams, who also spent part of his boyhood in Clarksdale, Mississippi, reminisced: "I was born in the Episcopal Rectory in Columbus, Mississippi, an old town on the Tombigbee River, which was so dignified and reserved that there was a saying, only slightly exaggerated, that you have to live there a whole year before a neighbor would smile at you on the street." The river Williams referred to forms part of the two hundred and thirty-four-mile Tennessee-Tombigbee Waterway completed in 1985, which, via those two rivers, links the Gulf of Mexico with sixteen thousand miles of inland waters. For information on the waterway and tours of its locks and dams: 601-326-3286. The hundred and forty-five-passenger sidewheel paddleboat "Bigbee Belle" in Columbus offers excursions and dinner cruises on the Tombigbee. Columbus, originally named Possum Town, is also home to Mississippi Industrial Institute and College, the nation's first public college for women. The school occupies a rather old-fashioned-looking campus on the southeast side of town.

Perched by the Tombigbee River off highway 50 five miles north of Columbus is Waverly Plantation (open dawn to dusk, adm.), a National Historic Landmark-listed house which is one of Mississippi's most attractive antebellum buildings. Built in 1852, the house contains splendid twin circular stairwells that climb to the octagonal observatory atop the roof. The interior of the mansion—which stood empty for fifty years until Mr. and Mrs. Robert Snow, Jr. bought the place in 1962 and began to restore it—is a treasure trove of local lore and antiques, while outside in the garden stands what's said to be Mississippi's largest magnolia tree. About twenty-five miles west of Waverly lies the town of Starkville, where Mississippi State University dominates the town and its attractions. At the University you can tour the veterinary college as well as the food and dairy research and processing areas, and you can visit the Briscoe Art Gallery, and museums devoted to forest products, to insects, to mineralogy and to archeology. The local history museum occupies an old Gulf, Mobile and Ohio depot (Tu. and Th., 2–5, free), while the Northeast Mississippi Coca-Cola bottling plant on highway 12 west (W., 9–11, 2–4 or by appointment, 601-323-4150, free) houses a museum displaying more than 2,300 items of Coca-Cola memorabilia. If you overnight in Starkville the most atmospheric place to stay is the National Historic Register-listed Ivy Guest House, Main and Jackson (601-323-2000), built in 1925 as the Hotel Chester and restored in 1985.

From Starkville you can swing west out to Kosciusko where there's a museum and information center (9–5, free) on the Natchez Trace, with a slide presentation on the Parkway and a display on Taduesz Kosciuszko (the town's name omits the "z"), the Polish engineer who served as a general in the American army during the Revolutionary War. Around town stand some old houses of various styles, among them the D. L. Brown Victorian residence and the colonial-style Bluff Springs Manor, both listed on the National Register. Or you can head south from Starkville to

the Philadelphia area, one of the state's most interesting corners. Although the 1988 movie *Mississippi Burning* recalled
the murders near Philadelphia in June 1964 of three young
civil rights workers, another image of the area comes across
with a visit to the Choctaw Indian settlements in Neshoba
County. By the 1830 Treaty of Dancing Rabbit Creek the
Choctaws—whose language named the nation's greatest
river and the state: "mish sha sippukrie," or "father of
waters"—ceded more than ten million acres of land to the
U.S. Most left the area, but some elected to remain in the
original homeland and their descendants now live in seven
self-governing Choctaw communities that have established
factories and other enterprises that make the tribe Neshoba
County's largest employer. Tribal headquarters are located
in Pearl River on highway 16 eight miles west of Philadephia,
where the Choctaw museum (M.–F., 8–4:30, free) and an
arts and crafts shop give you an insight into the tribe's history and culture. The annual four-day Choctaw Indian Fair,
featuring dances, crafts, traditional ceremonies and the stick-
ball world series begins on the first Wednesday after the
Fourth of July. On highway 21 about twenty-five miles
northeast of Philadelphia rises the Nanih Waiya Mound,
which legend holds is the birthplace of the Choctaws; while
at Tucker on highway 19 seven miles southeast of town is
the Holy Rosary Catholic Indian Mission, founded in 1884
by a Dutch priest.

   On highway 21 seven miles from Philadelphia to the southwest is the Neshoba County Fairgrounds, listed on the National Historic Register, where what's said to be the nation's
only remaining campground fair takes place every year in
late July and early August. The event began a century ago
(in 1889) when a small group of farm families gathered to
compare produce and livestock. These days more than 12,000
people, joined by an additional 70,000 visitors, stay at the
fair's five hundred cabins and amuse themselves with cake-

walks, beauty contests, a rodeo, square dancing, singfests, horse racing and political oratory. As for Philadelphia itself, on Holland and Poplar Avenues between Rose and Main Streets stand four blocks of early twentieth-century houses that comprise the town's Historic District, listed on the National Historic Register. Another relic of the old days in Philadelphia is the 1907 Williams Brothers General Store, an establishment *National Geographic* magazine once described as a "needles to horse-collars" emporium.

With nearly 50,000 inhabitants Meridian, southeast of Philadelphia, is Mississippi's third-largest city, after Jackson and Biloxi. Gypsies and country music fans gravitate to Meridian, the former to visit the graves of the Mitchells, King and Queen of the Gypsies, in Rose Hill Cemetery, the latter to pay homage at the Jimmie Rodgers Museum (M.–Sat., 10–4; Sun., 1–5, adm.) where exhibits trace the career of the founder of country music. The first person to be inducted into Nashville's Country Music Hall of Fame, Rodgers became known as the "blue yodeler," the name that appears on the lid of a trunk on display at the museum. The last week in May Meridian hosts the Jimmie Rodgers Memorial Festival, featuring country music. Also in Highland Park, site of the Rodgers Museum, is the century-old Dentzel Antique Carousel, a National Historic Landmark, one of three such antiques still in operation. (Burlington, North Carolina, also boasts a similar such merry-go-round.)

Another local rarity is Merrehope, one of fewer than half a dozen buildings left standing in Meridian after General William Tecumseh Sherman's raid in February, 1864. A rather ponderous, many-columned pile, Merrehope was given that coined name—"Mer" for Meridian, "re" for restoration, and "hope" for hope—after the local restoration organization acquired the house in 1968. Another throwback to the past is the Temple Theatre, a 1928 movie house, listed on the National Register, which in its day was believed to

be one of the country's largest stages. Out at the airport
the Key Brothers Aviation Museum (open all day, free) contains displays relating to the brothers' world endurance flight
record set in 1935, and exhibits on the history of aviation.
Before leaving town you may want to stop by the Lincoln
Bed and Breakfast office, 2302 23rd Avenue (601-482-5483),
not an inn where you can stay but a firm that makes reservations at Mississippi bed and breakfast establishments. Lincoln
sells a list of such hostelries for three dollars. Meridian also
boasts Weidmann's, said to be the state's oldest (1870) restaurant, housed in a medieval-looking building at 203 22nd
Avenue.

At Causeyville, twelve miles southeast of Meridian on
highway 19, you'll find the 1895 General Store (M.–Sat.,
6:30–7; Sun., 1–5, free), listed on the National Register,
where stone- ground cornmeal, hoop cheese, homemade jel-
lies and other local specialities are on sale. To the south,
at Enterprise, lies rustic Dunn's Falls, a sixty-five-foot cascade once used to power a grist mill and machines to make
Stetson hats. A new working grist mill there by the Chunky
River now goes through its daily grind. Farther south, between Vossburg and Heidelberg, is another such antique,
Bound's Water Grist Mill, one of the state's most colorful
remaining mills. The mill occupies a log cabin by an em-
bankment and is powered by the spill of water from an adjacent lake. If you're traveling in this area in July you might
want to check the day of the World Championship Tobacco
Spitting contest, held the last twenty years or so at Billy
John Crumpton's pond on Cohay Road five miles west of
Raleigh.

To complete your tour of east-central Mississippi continue
on to Laurel, about fifty miles south of Meridian, where
the Lauren Rogers Museum of Art (Tu.–Sat., 10–5; Sun.,
1–5, free) owns an especially good collection, with works
by such well-known American artists as Homer, Whistler,

Sloan, Inness and painters of the Hudson River School, and canvases by European masters, including Daumier, Millet and Constable. Laurel, hometown of renowned opera singer Leontyne Price, is the seat of Jones County, a hotbed of Union sentiment in Civil War times. The citizens of Jones County, which had the smallest slave population in the state at 12 percent (the largest was 93 percent in Issaquena County in the Delta, an area that had the highest concentration of blacks in the country), burned in effigy their delegate to the 1861 Secession Convention. So "king cotton" and its agriculture and culture, much as they are identified with the state, didn't reign supreme in all of Mississippi.

Southern Mississippi

Vicksburg to Natchez—Hattiesburg—The Gulf Coast

Of all the cities in the South it's perhaps Vicksburg that is most haunted by memories of the Civil War. Strategically perched on bluffs overlooking the Mississippi, Vicksburg was a prize both sides coveted. At the beginning of the conflict President Lincoln noted: "The Mississippi is the backbone of the Rebellion; it is the key to the whole situation." The President went on: "We must be able to proceed at once toward Vicksburg, which is the key to all that country watered by the Mississippi and its tributaries." After a forty-seven-day siege by Union troops, the city finally succumbed to General Ulysses S. Grant on July 4, 1863. For more than a century after that dark day Vicksburg refused to celebrate the nation's Independence Day. The surrender took place at the Old Court House (8:30–4:30, Sundays from 1:30, adm.), built in 1858 on the city's highest hill by slave labor. Listed on the National Register, the building now houses a nine-room museum crammed with Civil War-era displays. Civil War memories also haunt the huge Vicksburg National Military Park (8–7 summer; 8–5 winter, adm.), where a sixteen-mile driving tour takes you through the battlefield. A visitor center at the park offers a good introduction to the history of the siege of Vicksburg, a city-shattering, era-ending event. The arrival of Union troops interrupted a Christmas ball at the 1836 Balfour House (9–5, adm.), used as headquarters by the Federals after the city fell, while the McRaven Home (9–5, to 6 summers, Sundays from 10, adm.) still bears scars, inside and out, from cannonballs. The Waterfront Theater, down on the levee, presents a show on the siege entitled "The Vanishing Glory" (every hour 10–8; to 5 winter, adm.), while on the nearby riverboat "Mamie S. Barrett" are staged dinner theater performances of "Gold in the Hills," the world's longest-running melodrama (more than half a century), so states the *Guinness Book of World Records*.

Museums in Vicksburg include the Biedenharn Candy Company (9–5; Sundays 1:30–4:30, adm.), where Coca-Cola was first bottled, in 1894; Yesterday's Children (Tu.–Sat., 10–4:30, adm.), a collection of antique dolls; Toys and Soldiers (9–4:30, Sundays from 1:30, adm.), with more than 25,000 toy soldiers. On the south edge of town spreads the seven-hundred-acre Waterways Experiment Station, a federal facility which conducts research on hydraulic and other environmental problems. Models of waterways, and other research facilities, can be visited on a self-guided tour (7:45–4:15 weekdays, free). Bed and breakfast establishments in antebellum mansions abound in Vicksburg. They include: Anchuca (601-636-4931, 800-262-4822), an 1830 Greek-revival-style house, from the balcony of which Jefferson Davis once spoke; the mid-1850s Duff Green Mansion (601-636-6968, collect calls accepted), used as a hospital during the war; Cedar Grove (601-636-1605, out of state 800-862-1300), listed on the National Register, which has a cannonball in the parlor wall; and Grey Oaks (601-638-4424), its front facade designed as a replica of *Gone with the Wind*'s Tara.

Between Vicksburg and Natchez to the south meanders a network of back roads that take you to areas evoking images of the long-vanished era of the Old South. Twenty-six miles south of Vicksburg on highway 61 is Port Gibson, whose nineteenth-century architecture recalls the comment made by Union General Ulysses Grant, during his march north in May 1863, that the town was "too pretty to burn." Port Gibson's most unusual building is the 1859 First Presbyterian Church, its steeple topped not by a cross but by a giant (twelve-foot high) cast metal hand, its index finger pointing skyward. A series of back roads leads from Port Gibson to the Mississippi, eight miles west. Tucked into a hill near the river is Grand Gulf Military Monument, a four hundred-acre park, listed on the National Register, which partly occupies the site of a nineteenth-century boom town that literally disappeared from the face of the earth when the Mississippi eroded the settlement's fifty-five- block business district. Displays at the museum (8–12, 1–5, Sundays, 10–6, adm.) recount the story of General Grant's attempt in April 1863 to cross the Mississippi and land his troops at Grand Gulf. Repulsed by the Confederates, Grant moved south and crossed at Bruinsburg, which you can reach on another back road out of Port Gibson. In a desolate area near Bruinsburg rise the haunting remains of the Windsor plantation house—twenty-two charred columns, forlorn remnants of the elegant mansion that once stood there. Completed in 1861, the stately home survived the Civil War only to burn down in 1890 when a careless house guest dropped his cigarette in some debris.

Back roads take you to Rodney, a nearly deserted river town too small and forgotten to appear on Mississippi's official highway map. The hamlet of forty-five or so souls boasts a delightful old Baptist church, still used, as well as an abandoned Presbyterian church where Confederate cavalrymen captured Union soldiers attending services in the sanctuary on September 15, 1863. Rodney is where the opening scene of *The Robber Bridegroom,* by Mississippi writer Eudora Welty, a lifelong resident of Jackson, takes place: "It was the close of day when a boat touched Rodney's Landing on the Mississippi River and Clement Musgrove, an innocent planter, with a bag of gold and many presents, disembarked." But no such dramas unfold at the forlorn hamlet of Rodney these days.

At Lorman, back out on the main road, highway 61, nine miles south of Port Gibson, stands a country store (8–6, Sundays from 12) established in 1875 and seemingly little changed since then. The present building, constructed in 1890, contains original fixtures and furnishings and an eccentric assortment of merchandise, while a museum, of sorts—a motley accumulation of miscellany—occupies the loft area where the emporium once stored barrels of meat, flour and molasses hauled by ox teams from steamboats that docked at Rodney. Nine miles south of Lorman at Fayette, where in 1969 Charles Evers became the state's first black mayor since reconstruction of a mixed-race town, you can head west on another back road, highway 553, to the Old Maryland Settlement, established in the eighteenth century by pioneers from Maryland. A dozen or so old plantation houses and other antique buildings dot the landscape of the Settlement, which affords a vivid impression of how the landed gentry lived in the old days. Among the stately structures open for tours are Cedars Plantation (1814), once owned by actor George Hamilton; Lagonia, the Settlement's oldest house, built in part from the timbers of a dismantled barge two hundred years ago; and Springfield, where Andrew Jackson married Rachel Robards in 1791. This marriage proved to be a bit of an embarassment, as Mrs. Robards, it turned out, hadn't been officially divorced from her husband, Lewis Robards. After the divorce finally went through, Andrew and Rachel married, or remarried, in January 1794.

Perched atop a knoll at a crossroads in the Settlement is Christ Church, an enchanting mid-nineteenth-century small stone sanctuary where Union troops once paused to play bawdy songs on the organ. Just across the road stands Wagner's, a rickety old country store established a century and a half ago. Although the store at Lorman seems a bit of a tourist come-on, Wagner's is a genuine, functioning old country store with an ambiance straight out of the last century. Around an old-fashioned stove might sit overall-clad locals swapping gossip—a scene like a Norman Rockwell painting come alive. On the way to Natchez, ten miles or so to the southwest, you'll pass through Washington, site of the history-rich (1802) Jefferson College, listed on the National Register, where artist John James Audubon taught, Confederate President Jefferson Davis studied, and where Aaron Burr was arrested for treason.

Natchez is a gem of a town. Although many European cities offer a coherent whole in style and tone, few such places exist in the United States. Charleston, South Carolina, is perhaps the nation's best example of an architecturally integrated city, but Natchez—with its more than five hundred well-preserved and maintained antebellum buildings— also offers that pleasing sense of regularity and wholeness so common in Europe and so rare in this country. Most show towns like Natchez, which live off tourism, seem eventually to take on a certain artificial, contrived air, but that old Mississippi settlement there on the Mississippi River appears to have escaped such a fate. Natchez boasts more buildings per square mile listed on the National Historic Register than anywhere else in the country. Many of the old houses remain open to visitors all year, while additional showplaces can be seen during the two pilgrimages: the fall event held for three weeks mid to late October, and the spring pilgrimage for a month during the last three weeks in March and the first week of April. For specific dates and other Natchez information: 800-647-6742; in Natchez, 446-6631. Some of the old houses offer bed and breakfast accommodations, among them Linden, once the residence of Mississippi's first U.S. senator and the place where part of *Gone with the Wind* was filmed; Dunleith, a striking white Greek-revival house surrounded by graceful columns, where scenes in *Huckleberry Finn* and *Showboat* were shot; and Monmouth, a magnificent mansion set on twenty-six flower-filled acres once owned by an early governor of Mississippi. All these palatial houses in upper Natchez—the area on the bluffs high above the Mississippi—recall the gilded age when the town supposedly boasted about half the millionaires in the United States.

Natchez, back in those days, however, had another side to it, the underside at Natchez-Under-the-Hill, a rough and raucous street beneath the bluffs frequented by hard-drinking riverboatmen. Mark Twain called Natchez-Under-the-Hill a "moral sty," and an 1818 visitor, Estwick Evans, described the place in *A Pedestrious Tour of Four Thousand Miles, Through the Western States and Territories,* as "perhaps one of the most wretched places in the world." In *Random Recollections of Early Days in Mississippi,* published in 1885, H. S. Fulkerson tells the story of an innocent Methodist preacher who, debarking from his riverboat moored at Natchez-Under-the-Hill, was lured into a gambling den where he promptly lost all his money. Learning of the fleecing, the ship's captain, John W. Russell, proceeded to the establishment and threatened to pull the house into the Mississippi if the money wasn't refunded. When no cash materialized, Russell returned to his boat and then "hitched on the undergearing of the house, and commenced backing his boat. As soon as the cracking of the timber was heard the gamblers called to him, shaking the money in their hands. He eased up, and they went aboard and delivered up all of the money!" Such was Natchez-Under-the-Hill in the bad old days. Nowadays you can get the flavor—if not the fighting and the fleecings—by walking along Silver Street there by the river and visiting the pubs, cafes and restaurants that still retain a nineteenth-century ambiance. If you'd find it fun to overnight down there where the river roustabouts once played and stayed, rather than remaining in the millionaire's area up on the hill, you can put in at the Silver Street Inn (601-442-4221), installed in a one-time bawdy house but now a perfectly tame restored, antique-filled bed and breakfast establishment, rather than simply a bed establishment.

More Southern history and ambiance linger at Woodville, thirty-four miles south of Natchez, where 1810 Rosemont House, listed on the National Register, was Jefferson Davis's boyhood home (M.–F., 10–4 from March 1 to Dec. 15, adm.). The Davis family moved to the property from Kentucky when Jeff, youngest of ten children, was two years old. In the center hall of the home, outfitted with many Davis family furnishings, hangs a whale oil chandelier, while near the house five generations repose in the family cemetery. Also at Woodville is the Pond Store (7–7), an old country store established in 1881. At Liberty, east of Woodville, stands the house of Gail Borden, who produced in the town the first can of condensed milk, and farther east at Columbia is the John Ford Home (Sat. and Sun., 1–5 or by appointment, 601-736-8429, adm.), the oldest residence (1792) and only original pioneer dwelling remaining in the region. To the northwest is Monticello, where in 1884 Andrew Longino, later governor, built his cottage-like home (open by appointment, 601-587-7732, adm.); while at Hattiesburg, to the east of Columbia, dozens of late nineteenth- and early twentieth-century homes (on Southern, Walnut and the adjacent streets in the east-central part of town) comprise the Hattiesburg Historic Neighborhood, listed on the National Register of Historic Districts.

The University of Southern Mississippi houses the Sam Woods collection of paintings, Flemish tapestries and antique furniture and the Lena de Grummond collection of children's literature, including illustrations, photos and manuscripts of more than seven hundred writers and artists. Hattiesburg boasts one of Mississippi's largest daily flea markets, forty shops at the Calico Mall, 309 East Pine (Tu.–F., 10–5; Sat. from 9; Sun., 1–5). At Petal, just outside Hattiesburg, is the International Checker Hall of Fame (M.–F., 9–3, adm.), with exhibits on that game and perhaps the world's largest checkerboard, which occupies a tile floor at the museum.

From Hattiesburg it's less than a hundred miles down to the Gulf Coast. If you take the eastern route you'll pass through Lucedale where there's a scale model, one yard to a mile, on twenty acres—representing four hundred miles—of biblical scenes in the Holy Land during the time of Christ (8–4 March–Nov., adm.). On a Saturday in early July Lucedale hosts its annual watermelon festival, with melon eating, seed-spitting and other such juicy competitions. The Mississippi coast stretches for eighty-five miles along the Gulf of Mexico. It should be stated at the outset that although the area offers some attractions of cultural and historical interest, much of the Coast is marred by rather touristy shops, fast food chains, neon bedecked motels and other such commercial establishments lining highway 90, the road that borders the Gulf. On the eastern edge of the Coast, south of Lucedale, is Pascagoula where exhibits at the Old Spanish Fort and Museum (10–4 except Th., adm.), said to be the oldest building (1718) in the Mississippi Valley, will take you back to the earliest days of the region, first settled by Europeans in 1699 when the Frenchman Iberville established a settlement a few miles to the west. Exhibits at Pascagoula's Scranton Floating Museum, installed in a seventy-foot shrimp boat (Tu.–Sat., 10–5; Sun., 1–5, free), will introduce you to the Gulf Coast's fishing and seashore activities. Poet Henry Wadsworth Longfellow versified that nautical way of life in "The Building of the Ship," supposedly written at the Longfellow House on the east side of town (3401 Beach Boulevard). The poem refers to "Pascagoula's sunny bay," into which flows Singing River, so-called for the humming sound the stream makes as it enters the sea there.

At Ocean Springs, just east of Biloxi, the metropolis of the Gulf Coast and Mississippi's second-largest city, you'll find the visitor center for the Gulf Islands National Seashore, which includes widely scattered National Park Service areas off the coasts of both Florida and Mississippi. The Park Service runs tours of the marshes and Davis Bayou near the visitor center, while Ship Island, part of the national preserve that lies twelve miles off shore, can be reached by boats from both Biloxi and Gulfport (summer schedule: daily at 9 and 12; spring and fall: weekends at 9 and 12). Just past the bridge from Ocean Springs to Biloxi is the relatively new (1986) Seafood Industry Museum (Tu.–Sat., 9–5; Sun., 12–5, adm.), which occupies the old Coast Guard barracks. Nets, photos, trawling equipment and other sea items shown in a series of well-mounted exhibits trace the history and operations of the area's fishing industry. As you continue west along highway 90 you'll pass the landmark Biloxi Lighthouse, a sixty-five-foot high cast-iron tower built in 1848. In the base of the lighthouse, painted black when Lincoln was assassinated and draped in black crepe when Kennedy was shot, is an exhibit of its history (May to Labor Day, Tu.–Sat., 10–5; Sun., 1–5, adm.). The 1847 Magnolia Hotel in downtown Biloxi, the Gulf Coast's oldest remaining hotel building, now houses an art gallery and a Mardi Gras exhibit

(M., Tu., Th., 9–12; W. and F., 2–5, adm.). The most
delightful place to eat in Biloxi is the Old French House
Restaurant (601-374-0163), 138 Magnolia, a two-hundred-and-
fifty-year-old residence that fairly reeks with atmosphere.

As you continue west you'll catch views of the world's
longest manmade beach, which stretches along the Coast
for twenty-six miles and was completed in 1951. Between
Gulfport and Biloxi stands Beauvoir, the small many-
columned house where Jefferson Davis spent the last years
of his life (9–5, adm.). For ten years after he was released
from the federal prison in Virginia, Davis sought a permanent residence. In 1877, when he was sixty-nine, he settled
at Beauvoir where he remained until his death twelve years
later. While at the house the former Confederate States President wrote his two-volume *The Rise and Fall of the Confederate
Government*. Next to the house in the former hospital building, constructed in 1924 for indigent Southern veterans, is
a Confederate museum. As recently as 1978 Jefferson Davis's
political career was a federal matter, for in that year Congress
passed without a dissenting vote a bill to restore U.S. citizen-
ship to the Confederate leader, eighty-nine years after his
death. On the western edge of the coast is a modern-day
high-tech government facility light-years away from Old
Mississippi and the days of the Civil War. At the National
Space Technology Laboratories, highway 607 just off I-10—
on terrain where pirate Pierre Ramaux once hid his
loot—technicians test the engines that comprise the main
propulsion system of the space shuttle. The visitor center
(9–5, free) contains exhibits on the history of rocketry, while
tours (10:30, 12:30, 2:30) take you past the three huge concrete and steel test-towers and other facilities at the installation. Just north of the complex lies the town of Picayune,
named for the New Orleans *Times-Picayune* in honor of Eliza
Jane Poitevent, a local woman who rejuvenated the then-
bankrupt newspaper. The Margaret Reed Crosby Library

in Picayune contains a collection of antiques and contemporary art (M., 9–8; Tu. to Th., 9–6; F., 9–5; Sat., 9–1, free).
If you overnight in Picayune, Candlelight Cottage bed and
breakfast, 1903 highway 11 north (601-798-2626) is a pleasant
place to stay. Temptingly close, to the south, lies New Orleans, forty-five miles away. But that's another state, another
trip.

Mississippi Practical Information

You can contact the Mississippi Division of Tourism at:
P.O. Box 849, Jackson, MS 39205; 800-647-2290. The
"Events Hotline" number (in Mississippi and from adjoining
states, plus Georgia and Texas) is 800-822-6477.

The state of Mississippi operates nine highway tourist offices, called Welcome Centers, which are open 8–5; Sundays,
1–5; U.S. 61 at Natchez; I-55, Hernando; I-10 and state highway 607 near Waveland; I-10 near Pascagoula; I-20 and I-59
near Meridian; I-59 near Picayune; I-55 near McComb; I-20
at Vicksburg; U.S. 82 and Reed Road, Greenville.

Mississippi operates twenty-seven state parks, many with
overnight facilities. For information: 601-961-5014. The six
National Forests in Mississippi occupy more than a million
acres. Many of the forests have trails, lakes and camping
facilities. For information: 601-965-4391.

Phone numbers for tourist offices in some of the main
cities are: Columbus, 800-327-2686; Corinth, 601-462-5637;
Jackson, 800-354-7695; Meridian, 601-483-0083; the Gulf
Coast, 800-237-9493; Natchez, 800-647-6724; Oxford, 601-
234-4651; Starkville, 601-323-3322; Tupelo, 601-841-6521;
Vicksburg, 800-221-3536.

You can book bed and breakfast accommodations in Mississippi through Lincoln, Ltd., P.O. Box 3479, Meridian,

MS 39303, 601-482-5483. The firm publishes a list of Mississippi bed and breakfast establishments ($3).

Pilgrimages—which usually include visits to antebellum houses, garden tours, historical pageants and other such special events—are held at approximately the following times: Aberdeen, the second week of April; Columbus, end of March and first week of April; Holly Springs, third weekend of April; Natchez, four weeks in March and early April and three weeks in October; Oxford, second weekend of April; Port Gibson, beginning of April; Vicksburg, last week of March and first week of April.

3. Louisiana

It is a slight exaggeration to say—as did Pierre Clément de Laussat, the French government representative in New Orleans at the time of the Louisiana Purchase—that "All Louisianians are Frenchmen at heart!" After all, the northern part of the state, quite distinct in culture and atmosphere from the Gallic south, is populated by plain old Anglo-Southerners, like much of the rest of Dixie. To be sure, northern Louisiana offers a number of tourist attractions, including museums, historic villages, local color, and the hometown of Huey Long, the state's second-most famous head of government, the most famous being Louis XIV, memorialized by the state's name. But it is the south, with that uniquely French flavor found in New Orleans and the Cajun country areas—places where the locals are indeed "Frenchmen at heart"—that attracts most visitors to Louisiana.

Louisiana became French in the late 1690s when secret agents of Louis XIV learned that the English planned to establish a colony in the region. The French took immediate steps to move into the country, in October 1698 sending an expedition led by Pierre le Moyne, Sieur d'Iberville, to the Gulf Coast. In the summer of 1699, a few months after the French established a small fort on the Coast, Bienville, d'Iberville's brother, sailed up the Mississippi where, near the site of New Orleans, he encountered a twelve-gun English ship reconnoitering the river for a place to gain a foothold. Bienville warned the English captain, Lewis Banks, that he was encroaching on French territory and that a nearby French fleet was prepared to enforce France's territorial claims. No such convoy existed, but Banks turned around and departed from that point in the Mississippi River, still today known as "English Turn."

In the eighteenth century European power politics kept changing the map of the New World. After the English defeated the French in Canada in 1763 the Acadians fled, many migrating to Louisiana where they founded the colorful Franco-Southern culture now known as Cajun. About the same time France ceded the Louisiana Territory to Spain, which retained the domain until the turn of the century. Only a few traces of the Spanish period remain, one of them, curiously enough, being some of the architecture in the New Orleans French Quarter, for fires in 1788 and 1794 destroyed most of the French city. Other such holdovers from the days Spain ruled the area include a Spanish mission near Natchitoches in west-central Louisiana, the Cajun town of New Iberia, Spanish by name though French in ambiance, and in St. Bernard Parish just south of New Orleans a colony of Spanish-speaking descendants of the Canary Islanders who settled there in the late eighteenth century. In the early nineteenth century the Europeans again reshuffled the map when France sold the Louisiana Territory to the Yankees in April 1803, a transaction that set Napoleon to gloating, "I have just given England a maritime rival that sooner or later will lay low her pride"—a prophecy that came true less than a decade later in the War of 1812. It was that year when Louisiana was admitted to the Union, so over only a dozen years the area changed from a French-speaking Spanish colony to a French dependency to a territory of the United States and, finally, to a state, the first west of the Mississippi.

After Louisiana became American the state added to its underlying Old World Frenchness an Old South antebellum way of life, thus creating the cultural mix which present-day visitors find so alluring. These were the years when, as Joe

Gray Taylor described the ambiance in *Louisiana: A Bicentennial History,* the state was "suffused in a soft golden glow made up of equal parts of nostalgia and moonlight. Tall, handsome gentlemen bow to beautiful ladies in crinoline; the sweet odor of magnolia blossoms fills the air; and the sound of a banjo is heard, far enough removed in time and space to make soft music for the singing of contented slaves." But this sort of dreamy life came to an end when the sound of guns rather than banjos filled the air. "The density of the smoke from guns and fire-rafts, and the scenes passing on board our own ship and around us," wrote Captain David Farragut in his May 1862 report to the Secretary of the Navy on the capture of New Orleans, was "as if the artillery of heaven were playing upon the earth."

Later, after the smoke cleared and heaven's artillery stilled, Louisiana reverted to its rather languid, laid-back ways, and still today a certain devil-may-care atmosphere prevails there, typified by the Cajun *laissez les bons temps rouler* ("let the good times roll") attitude and by the famous Mardi Gras celebrations. Perhaps Mardi Gras, called by New Orleanians simply Carnival, best symbolizes the state's rather romantic past—filled with pirates like Jean Lafitte, with a mixed Franco-Hispanic-American heritage, with an antebellum culture and with a kind of post-bellum decadence—and its easygoing present-day way of life. Carnival dates back to the mid-eighteenth century when the "Cowbellions," a group of free-spirited souls and perhaps spirit-drenched bodies, raided a hardware store and stole cowbells that the revelers rang as they roamed the streets of New Orleans. In 1857 the first of the famous "krewes" appeared—more than sixty such organizations now mount Mardi Gras parades and host its balls—and in 1872 many of the current rituals began when Alexis Alexandrovich Romanov, brother of the Russian Czar's heir apparent, showed up in New Orleans in pursuit of an opera singer. It was then when the first parades took

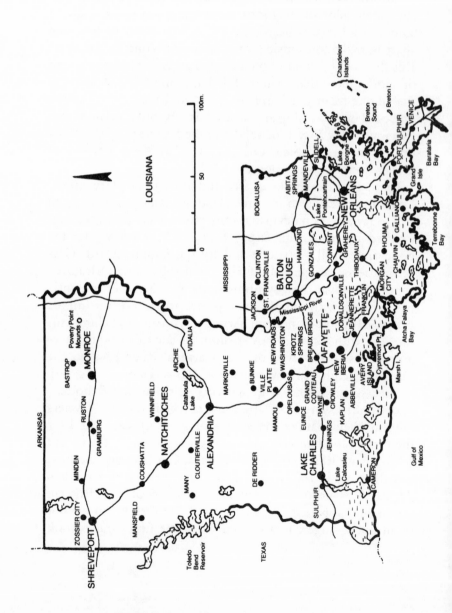

place and when the Mardi Gras theme song "If Ever I Cease
To Love" was first played, and it is for such history and
pageantry, revelry and romance that travelers from near and
far come to Louisiana, there to see the plantations and Cajun
regions and the Old World-New World city tucked like a
treasure into a pocket of the curving Mississippi River.

The River Road to New Orleans

St. Francisville—Baton Rouge—Plantation Country

In the early nineteenth century a young American lawyer
named Alexander Porter told Andrew Jackson he was moving to Louisiana. Jackson, who knew the area from his military campaign in the state during the War of 1812, advised
the young man: "And remember, Alick, you are going to
a new country. . . . You will find a different people from
those you have grown among, and you must study their
natures, and accommodate yourself to them." Still today,
Louisiana is different. The admixture of French and American culture, the many plantation houses that still survive
as relics of an old and to an extent still continuing way of
life, the laid-back "let the good times roll" attitude all con-
tribute to Louisiana's unique flavor and culture, an ambiance
unlike that found in any other Southern state.

Although just about all roads and itineraries in Louisiana
lead to New Orleans, that oddly shaped and sited city
crammed between two lakes and the Mississippi River and
artfully poised between past traditions and modern-day conditions, other parts of the state offer sights that recall the
territory's heritage and culture. The plantations, old houses
and historic attractions along and near the Mississippi River
north of New Orleans provide a good introduction to

Louisiana's charms. Two of the most beguiling parishes—
Louisiana's designation for "county," a carry-over from the
early days when the Catholic Church delineated not only
moral but also geographical boundaries—are West and East
Feliciana, the first areas of the state you'll come to if you
enter from Mississippi south of Natchez. Back in the 1850s
more than half of America's millionaires lived in the rich
Mississippi Valley region between Natchez and New Orleans. The plantations lining the river grew not only cotton
but also sugar cane, indigo and tobacco. One of the properties most evocative of that lush, plush yesteryear way of
life is Rosedown (March–Oct., 9–5; Nov.–Feb., 10–4, adm.),
an antique-crammed mansion at St. Francisville. Built in
1835, the house contains elegant furniture and fixtures imported from Europe by Daniel and Martha Turnbull, whose
1828 "Grand Tour" to England, France and Italy inspired
them to lay out at Rosedown a splendid garden in the European style. Beside the striking avenue of oak trees wind paths
leading to exquisitely maintained stands of flowers, arbore-
tums and even a medicinal herb garden. As recently as 1956
the now well-kept property lay in a decayed state, but in
the spring of that year Catherine Underwood of Houston
acquired the estate, which she restored into the showplace
it is today.

Other similarly attractive show houses embellish the area
around St. Francisville, among them Afton Villa Gardens
(W.–Sun., 9–4:30, March–June and Oct.–Nov., adm.), with
the ruins of an antebellum mansion and Louisiana's longest
oak alley; Catalpa Plantation (9–5, closed Dec. and Jan.,
adm.), owned by the same family since the eighteenth century, with an unusual elliptical oak alley; the 1795 Cottage
Plantation (9–5, adm.), with many original furnishings and
outbuildings still surviving; many-columned Greenwood
(twenty-eight of them), a rebuilt 1830-era house (M.–Sat.,
9–4; Sun., 1–5, adm.) that survived the Civil War only to

burn in 1960; and Myrtles Plantation (9–5, adm.), a 1796 structure that claims to be "the most haunted house in America." The Myrtles (504-635-6277), Barrow House (504-635-4791), an 1809 residence listed on the National Register, and the century-old St. Francisville Inn (504-635-6502) offer bed and breakfast accommodations. Exhibits in two area museums span the centuries: the West Feliciana Historical Society in St. Francisville offers displays on the parish's history, while the River Bend Energy Center on U.S. 61 south contains exhibits on atomic and other types of energy.

Between St. Francisville and Jackson to the east lies Locust Grove State Commemorative Area (9–5, free), a cemetery where Sarah Knox Taylor, Confederate President Jefferson Davis's wife, and Civil War general Eleanor Ripley repose. Southern soldiers also lie in the Confederate Commemorative Area in Jackson, a one-acre site adjacent to the Centenary Commemorative Area (9–5, adm.), where two old Centenary College buildings, an 1837 dormitory and a professor's house, contain exhibits on the history of the school and on education in the South. Jefferson Davis graduated from Centenary, which in 1908 moved to Shreveport, Louisiana. Nearby stands the Republic of West Florida Historical Association museum (Tu.–Sat., 10–5; Sun., 12–5, adm.), installed in a wing of the old Jackson High School buildings. Seven rooms contain a diversified group of exhibits, including Civil War relics, wildlife dioramas, World War II souvenirs and a propeller from a plane supposedly flown by Charles Lindbergh. Two establishments in Jackson, much of which comprises a National Register-listed Historic District, offer bed and breakfast rooms: Asphodel (504-654-6868), located among a group of nineteenth-century houses, in one of which *The Long Hot Summer* was filmed, and Milbank (504-634-5901), a spacious 1830s mansion, listed on the National Register. Bear Corners restaurant in Jackson is a popular local eatery with a country ambiance. With its turrets, spandrels and gingerbread decor Glencoe, on highway 68 near Jackson, is the state's finest example of Queen Anne-style architecture (to reserve rooms at Glencoe, a bed and breakfast house: 504-629-5387), while the Audubon Commemorative Area south of Jackson includes 1799 Oakley Plantation House (9–5, adm.) where artist-naturalist John James Audubon created eighty or so of his famous bird paintings. The mansion now houses a museum featuring memorabilia of Audubon, who lived in the area from 1821 to 1825. At the St. Francis Hotel in St. Francisville hangs a complete collection of Audubon's four hundred and thirty-five life-sized bird portraits. To the east of Jackson lies the attractive town of Clinton, established in 1824 to serve as the seat of East Feliciana parish. Old buildings, many listed on the National Register, fill the settlement, among them the 1840 Greek-Revival courthouse, the 1871 Victorian Gothic-style St. Andrew's Church, and nineteenth-century houses offering bed and breakfast, including Plovanich Place (504-683-8927), Brame-Bennett House (504-683-5241), Mt. DeLee Plantation House (504-683-8324) and Martin Hill (504-683-5594). Before leaving East Feliciana you may want to visit three other parish towns offering nineteenth-century architecture: Norwood, with a group of Victorian houses; Wilson, an old railroad town; and Slaughter, with some turn-of-the-century rowhouses and cottages.

Back to the west, near Zachary, where the McHugh House Museum (1–5, free) traces the history of the town, the six hundred and fifty-acre Port Hudson State Commemorative Area (April–Sept., 9–7; Oct.–March, 9–5, free) encompasses a huge battlefield where the longest siege in American history took place. Civil War gun trenches, evocatively named Fort Desperate, three viewing towers and seven miles of hiking trails recall the period between May 23 and June 9, 1865, when 6,800 Confederates held off nearly 40,000 Union troops. Before proceeding south to nearby Baton Rouge it is worth taking the ferry across the Mississippi from St. Francisville to New Roads to visit Parlange (9–5, adm.), one of Louisiana's most renowned plantation houses, built in 1750 on a land grant from the French crown. Still a working property after nearly two and a half centuries, Parlange— which stands near the odd little arc of water called False River, formed when the Mississippi changed course— belongs to descendants (the eighth generation) of the original owner, and may thus be the nation's oldest business still operated by the same family. Near Parlange on the "river," truly false as it is now a lake, stands Le Pointe Coupee Parish museum, installed in the area's oldest cottage. At the town of New Roads, Samson Galleries, housed in a turn-of-the-century building, sells antiques and Audubon prints, while Pointe Coupee Bed and Breakfast (504-638-6254) offers accommodations in three old houses. In Pointe Coupee Parish—where Ernest J. Gaines, author of *The Autobiography of Miss Jane Pittman,* set many of his books—lived pioneer Julien Poydras, who founded there three of Louisiana's earliest public schools and who introduced the bill that admitted the state into the Union in 1812.

Baton Rouge—a curious combination of port, oil town, seat of government and education center—is one of those rare cities, like Madison, Wisconsin, Austin, Texas, and Columbia, South Carolina, which boast both the state capital, established there in 1849, and the state university (1860), originally located in Alexandria, whose first president was none other than Yankee General William Tecumseh Sherman. Official buildings and attractions thus abound in Baton Rouge. The university, where in 1935 writer Robert Penn Warren and critic Cleanth Brooks, Jr., began publication of the once renowned *Southern Review,* offers the Museum of Geoscience (M.–F., 8:30–4:30, free); the Museum of Natural Science (M.–F., 8–4; Sat., 9:30–1, free); the Union Art Gallery (M.–F., 8–6; Sat. and Sun., 11–5, free); the Anglo-

American Art Museum (M.–F., 9–4; Sat., 10–12, 1–4; Sun., 1–4, free), with period rooms and decorative arts; and two Indian mounds; while L.S.U. also operates the off-campus Rural Life Museum (M.–F., 8:30–4), featuring nineteenth-century buildings with artifacts and objects that recall the early days in the state's rural regions.

At Baton Rouge's lesser-known Southern University, parent campus for what is supposedly the nation's largest predominantly black university system, are a Black Heritage exhibit, a Red Stick "Baton Rouge" monument recalling the marker that indicated the boundary between two Indian tribes, and the lair of LaCumba, the school's jaguar mascot. Government buildings in Baton Rouge include the new (1960) governor's mansion and the old chief executive's house (Sat., 10–4; Sun., 1–4, adm.), a small-scale replica of the White House built by Huey Long, with artifacts of the nine governors who occupied the residence; the Arts and Science Center Riverside Museum (Tu.–F., 10–3; Sat., 10–4; Sun., 1–4, adm.); the Arts and Science Center Planetarium (shows, Sat. and Sun., 2 and 3; summer, Tu.–F., 2, adm.); the Old Bogan Fire Museum (M.–F., 9–5, free), featuring fire trucks and fire-fighting equipment from the early part of the century; the Pentagon Barracks (Tu.–Sat., 10–4; Sun., 1–4, free), an early nineteenth-century structure built to house army personnel stationed at Baton Rouge and now an information center for the state capitol; the Capitol (8–4:30, free), at thirty-four stories the nation's tallest, with an observation tower, a craft display and a small plaque marking the spot where Huey Long was assassinated (he's buried in the Capitol gardens); and the 1849 Gothic-style Old State Capitol (Tu.–Sat., 9–4:30, free), adjudged the world's ugliest building (a "monstrosity") by Mark Twain who, after a blaze almost destroyed the eyesore, commented, "Dynamite should finish what a charitable fire began."

The "U.S.S. Kidd," a three hundred and sixty-nine-foot

long World War II destroyer berthed in an enclave on the Mississippi, offers tours (9–5, adm.), as do two plantation houses, Magnolia Mound (Tu.–Sat., 10–4; Sun., 1–4) and 1817-vintage Mount Hope Plantation (M.–Sat., 9–4, adm.), built by German planter Joseph Sharp on a four hundred-acre 1786 Spanish land grant. Mount Hope provides bed and breakfast (504-766-8600), while Southern Comfort Bed and Breakfast, 2856 Hundred Oaks, Baton Rouge, LA 70808 (504-346-1928 or 928-9815; for reservations, 800-523-1181, then 722), a reservation service for nearly forty Louisiana bed and breakfast houses, publishes a list of such establishments (three dollars). Catfish Town Marketplace, near the Mississippi just south of the "U.S.S. Kidd," includes a Food Court with nine restaurants featuring crawfish, catfish, gumbo and other regional specialties, while for music of the area Tabby's Blues Box Heritage Hall, 1314 North Boulevard, offers local blues performers.

Industrial and commercial Baton Rouge presents a different sort of picture than does the government-museum-university town most tourists know. Along the Mississippi River to the north stretches the city's huge refinery and tank-farm complexes. That industry arrived in Baton Rouge in 1909, eight years after oil was discovered in the state, and within ten years Louisiana boasted fifteen refineries. In 1924 Standard Oil of New Jersey (now Exxon) established at its Baton Rouge operation the nation's first health maintenance organization. With a daily production capacity of 455,000 barrels of crude, almost two million gallons, Exxon Baton Rouge refinery is second in size in the U.S. only to the company's Baytown, Texas, facility. Some two hundred miles upriver from the Gulf of Mexico, Baton Rouge is the country's fifth-largest port, handling more than seventy million tons of cargo annually, and the most inland deep-water port in the nation. The installation occupies the west bank of the Mississippi at Port Allen just across from Baton

Rouge. From the levee at the base of Court Street in Port Allen you can view the port and the river traffic, both barges and ocean-going craft, while the nearby Port Allen Locks facility, completed in 1961, is the world's largest free-floating structure of its kind. The West Baton Rouge Museum (Tu.–Sat., 10–4:30; Sun., 2–5), installed in the former parish courthouse, built in 1882, contains regional history exhibits, and at the 1878 Cinclare Plantation, just south of Port Allen, the old days survive at one of the region's few remaining sugar cane mills. Although the mill—which operates around the clock seven days a week in October, November and December, processing five thousand tons of cane a day—isn't open to visitors because of safety regulations, you can visit the plantation's office and see a restored "dummy," a small steam engine once used to transport cane from fields to the mill. By the levee at Brusly, farther south, stands the simple but attractive 1907 wood St. John the Baptist Church; while nearby, between Back Brusly and Back Back Brusly, rises a three-and-a-half-century-old landmark oak tree. At the Plaquemine Locks State Commemorative Area (9–5, free) a few miles south are the original locks, constructed in 1900, a viewing tower, a stair-step roofed pavilion, and a museum that interprets the Mississippi's history and its boat traffic. Next to the locks stands the 1848 Greek Revival Iberville Parish Courthouse, now a tourist information office.

All along the Mississippi south to near New Orleans stand stately plantation houses, relics of a bygone way of life. As Louisiana author Harnett T. Kane put it in *Plantation Parade,* published in 1945: "A century ago, along the Mississippi and its adjacent waters, the sugar and cotton plantations rose in a double file of splendor. For more than two hundred miles, beginning below New Orleans, hardly a foot of ground remained free from the hand of the cultivator; for most of this distance it was not possible to travel the river and be out of the range of a great house, serene and proud

and pillared." Although no longer so thick on the ground
as in the days of yesteryear, those columned mansions still
embellish the Louisiana countryside along the twisty Mississippi. The first major house you'll come to as you head
southeast toward New Orleans is Nottaway (9–5, adm.),
supposedly the South's largest plantation home, with three
floors occupying more than 50,000 square feet comprising
sixty-four rooms, twelve of them offering overnight accommodations (504-545-2730 or 545-2409). In 1849 sugar planter
John Hampden Randolph commissioned the vast pile, which
boasts lacy plaster work, hand-painted Dresden porcelain
doorknobs and a sixty-five foot Grand Ballroom where six
of Randolph's eight daughters (he had eleven children in all)
were married. During the Civil War a Union gunboat officer
who'd once been a guest of the Randolphs at Nottaway saved
the mansion, now owned by a man from Sydney, Australia,
from destruction.

On the south edge of the nearby town of White Castle
lies the Cora Texas sugar mill, while to the south at Donaldsonville, the state capital in 1830–31, you'll find a number
of century-old structures that comprise a National Register-
listed Historic District. Among the venerable buildings are
those occupied by Oschwald's Pharmacy, with a pressed tin
cornice; Lemann Brothers, Louisiana's oldest individually
owned department store (1877); Ace Hardware, installed in
the 1850 former Jewish synagogue; and the popular local
eatery, First and Last Chance Cafe, a Railroad Avenue fixture
since 1927. Displays at the Ascension Heritage Museum in
the 1867 parish courthouse building trace the history of the
area. Another well-known area restaurant is Lafitte's Landing, just by the Sunshine Bridge near Donaldsonville.
Named after the renowned early nineteenth-century pirate
Jean Lafitte—he preferred to call himself a privateer, not
an outlaw but a within-the-law businessman whose raids
were licensed by the authorities—the establishment occupies

a building moved from the old Viala Plantation in Ascension Parish. It is thought by some that the pirate-privateer's son, Jean Pierre Lafitte, married Marie Emma Viala in the house.

Although car ferries supposedly cross the Mississippi at points along the waterway those boats—unlike the river—run erratically, if at all, so it's best to take the Sunshine Bridge to reach the sights on the east side. Not far beyond the bridge—called when it was built the span that "goes from nowhere to nowhere"—rises Tezcuco, "resting place," named by its builder, Benjamin Tureaud, after the lake near Mexico City where Montezuma fled to escape the Spanish conquistador Cortez. Completed in 1855, Tezcuco (March–Oct., 10–5; Nov.–Feb., 10–4, adm.) bears wrought-iron decor and ornate detailing. If you want to overnight there, cottages on the attractive grounds of the well-named property offer a pleasant "resting place" (504-562-3929). Just down the road you'll find The Cabin, a restaurant featuring cajun food and a collection of antique farm implements installed in century-and-a-half-old slave quarters of the Monroe plantation, and Houmas House (Feb.–Oct., 10–5; Nov.–Jan., 10–4, adm.), another plantation property completed in 1840 as centerpiece of a sugar cane estate that occupied 20,000 acres. When Union general Benjamin Butler tried to occupy the property during the Civil War, owner John Burnside, an Irishman, claimed immunity as a British subject and Houmas was spared the indignity of being taken over by the Yankees.

If time permits you may want to continue on to see a few attractions back toward Baton Rouge. On highway 431 near Brittany is Rosewood Manor (9–5, adm.), a latter-day antebellum-style mansion incorporating architectural elements from nearly forty demolished old plantation houses. Nine rooms at Rosewood, crammed with displays of porcelain, crystal, antiques and objets d'art, take overnight guests (504-675-5781). Nearby Gonzales, named after Joseph "Tee

Joe" Gonzales, who operated a general store in the area in the 1880s, boasts that it's the "Jambalaya Capital of the World" and hosts an annual Jambalaya Festival the second weekend of June. A small local museum at Gonzales (W.–F., 1–5, free) contains historical exhibits and a collection of handmade lace. Nearby Carville, on the Mississippi, is the site of the nation's only leprosarium, an institution established by Louisiana in 1894 and taken over by the federal government in 1921, which houses about a hundred and thirty of the country's six thousand lepers.

The unusual Tree House in the Park (504-622-2850) at Prairieville takes overnight guests in a glass cabin perched on stilts above a swamp. Off to the east Livingston Parish is a jambalaya-like mixture of cultures and nationalities. At the descriptively named French Settlement the Creole House Museum contains antiques, archives and photos relating to the early inhabitants of "La Côte Française," the French Coast, where not only French but also German and Italian immigrants who reached the area via the Amite River settled starting in 1800. Port Vincent on the Amite, originally called Scivicque's Ferry after Italian settler Vincent Scivicque— presumably the locals switched from his last to his first name to make the town's name more pronounceable—served as parish seat from 1872 to 1881. Albany off to the east is the site of the nation's largest rural Hungarian settlement, known as Arpadhon. Originally attracted to the area in 1896 by the Brackenridge lumber mill, the Hungarians acquired cut timberland which they used to raise strawberries. The first weekend in October Albany celebrates the annual Hungarian Harvest Festival. Returning now to the Sunshine Bridge area, at the town of Convent on highway 44 to the south stands the plantation house of Judge Felix Pierre Poche, founder of the American Bar Association.

It's well to cross over the Sunshine Bridge back to the area west of the Mississippi, there to continue on toward

New Orleans. On the way to famous Oak Alley at Vacherie you'll pass through St. James, site of some of the first Acadian (Cajun) settlers in Louisiana who arrived there from Canada in 1756, and also where one of the state's oldest cemeteries, at St. James Church, is located. Although Oak Alley's interior (March–Oct., 9–5:30; Nov.–Feb., 9–5, adm.) is among the least interesting of the Mississippi River plantation houses, the estate's grounds present perhaps the most striking vistas of any property in the state and, for that matter, in the entire South. Back in the early eighteenth century an unknown French settler planted twenty-eight oak trees in two evenly spaced rows running between his modest house and the Mississippi. For two and a half centuries these trees, one of the nation's largest groves of mature oaks, have witnessed many and varied activities: the construction (1837–9) of the present plantation house by French sugar-planter Jacques Telesphore Roman, brother of two-time Louisiana governor Andre Roman; the Civil War; the gradual decay of the residence; and then its restoration, starting in 1925, by Scottish cotton broker Andrew Stewart and his wife Josephine, who first saw the mansion and trees from the deck of a riverboat cruising on the Mississippi. In 1972 Mrs. Stewart left the property to a nonprofit foundation administered by her great-nephew. The true treasures of the estate are the oaks, which form a magnificent quarter of a mile-long alleyway at the end of which rises the house, one of the State's hundred remaining ante-bellum plantation homes of the four hundred which survived the Civil War. Every year the trees, each of which bears a lightning rod, get fed with liquid fertilizer, while every third year they're pruned. The largest trunk among the trees—twice as wide as they are tall—measures nearly thirty feet around. In an outbuilding behind the "big house," as main plantation residences are often called, luncheon is served (11–3), while re-

cently restored cottages on the property offer bed and
breakfast accommodations (504-265-2151).

Although the Oak Alley trees are no doubt St. James'
Parish most famous vegetation, the parish also produces the
world's only "perique"-type tobacco, so called, some believe, from the vulgar slang expression for the phallus, whose
shape the dried compacted plug resembles. The best crops
of perique, a strong, distinctly flavored leaf, grow on the
vachery, or cattle land, an elevated area away from the river.
In the old days the curing of perique was so complicated—
with months of fermentation under pressure, a process that
extracted the tobacco's rich, winey juices—that the government required its growers to obtain manufacturer's licenses.
This strong black tobacco unique to Louisiana is used in
blends.

Adjacent St. Charles Parish, which formed part of the
so called "German Coast," contains reminders of the area's
early German settlers. In 1719 a group of some two hundred
German immigrants settled near Lake Des Allemands (Lake
"of the Germans") thirty miles from New Orleans. In 1721
more settlers from Germany arrived under the leadership
of Karl Friedrich D'Arensburg, who in 1768 led an uprising
against the repressive Spanish governor Ulloa, the very first
North American revolution against a foreign power. Although the Germans forced Ulloa out of Louisiana, the Spanish returned the following year and executed most of the
rebel leaders. A more recent German presence occurred when
Hahnville hosted German captives at a World War II prison
camp. Hahnville was named after Union agent Michael
Hahn, who served as Louisiana governor concurrently with
a Confederate who held the same office after part of the
state fell to the North in 1864. Every October Hahnville
cooks up a "German Coast" Food Festival. These days St.
Charles Parish is an industrial area with a few remnants of

yesteryear tucked among the Union Carbide, Monsanto, Shell, Occidental and other oil and chemical facilities.

Beyond Taft, where the 1985 Waterford III Nuclear Power Plant rises, stretches the Hale Boggs Bridge, the lower Mississippi's newest span (1983). The bridge will take you across to the road leading to 1787 Destrehan (10–4, adm.), said to be the oldest and best-documented plantation home in the lower Mississippi Valley. On highway 48 near Destrehan is St. Charles Borromeo Cemetery, with graves dating from the 1700s and the latest in a series of churches that have stood on the site for more than two centuries. Destrehan lies only twenty-three miles from New Orleans, and a mere eight miles from the airport, so it's necessary to head back up-country to escape the magnetic pull of the metropolis and to complete your tour of the river road region. Beyond Norco, named for the New Orleans Refining Company, sold to Shell Oil in 1920, you'll pass the Bonnet Carré Spillway, an aqueduct-like construction built by the U.S. Army Corps of Engineers at the site of an 1871 "crevasse," or levee break, to direct overflow from the Mississippi to Lake Pontchartrain, a function the spillway has served only three times since it opened in 1935.

Farther upriver you'll reach San Francisco Plantation House (10–4, adm.) rather incongruously stuck by a Marathon Oil installation. Built in 1856 by Edmond Bozonier Marmillion, the house boasts one of the state's fanciest interiors, with elaborate architectural details, antiques and five arresting ceiling frescoes. Valsin, the builder's son, originally named the pile "Sans Frusquin"—"broke"—because of the fortune spent to build the mansion. Only a dining room and various service quarters occupy the ground floor level, above which rise a gallery and the family's living area. San Francisco, the first and no doubt most elaborate residence built in "Steamboat Gothic" style, inspired the Frances Parkinson Keyes famous novel of that name. The house, along with all the others up and down the Mississippi between Baton Rouge and New Orleans, stands as silent witness to a long-gone era. In *Plantation Life on the Mississippi,* William Edwards Clement writes of the old days when a plantation servant "would be stationed on the levee-front landing to listen for the boat whistle" and, after the signal, he'd "start waving a large cloth or flag to get the pilot's attention, thus bringing the boat in for a landing. It was always an exciting moment as the big boat dropped its stage plank and the 'rousters' came ashore to tie up the boat." The planters would board, then the ship would steam on, its wake foaming and churning, its shrill whistle now and again sounding until, finally, all traces of the steamer vanished, as have those long ago days of paddle-wheelers and plantations.

Northern and Western Louisiana

Shreveport—Monroe—Natchitoches—Alexandria—Toledo Bend—Cajun Country: Lafayette, St. Martinsville, New Iberia—Morgan City—Houma

The contrast between soggy southern Louisiana, watered by bayous and swamps and oozing with Old South and French culture, and the north, a region of wooded scrubland populated by Anglo-Saxons almost Yankee in their laid-back nature, couldn't be greater. As Harnett T. Kane, resident expert on the state, noted in *Louisiana Hayride:* "Modern Louisiana is divided, as was the mother country, into three parts: the South, the North, and The City—New Orleans." Kane continues: "The South is tolerant, easy-going, Catholic. The North is tight-lipped, grim-eyed, Puritan, Protestant. Between the 'hard-shelled Baptist country' and the 'soft-shelled crab land' are barriers of economics, of race, of creed."

The population centers in the sparsely settled north are Shreveport and Bossier City, twin towns that flank the banks of the Red River. Shortly after Captain Henry Shreve managed to break up a hundred and sixty-five-mile long logjam on the river, he established in 1836 a village along the waterway called Shreve Town. Bossier City dates back to 1843 when General Pierre Evariste Jean Baptiste Bossier founded the town, later terminus of the unusual 1870s shed road, a nine-mile long covered turnpike which sheltered convoys that carried cotton out and brought supplies in to the settlement. Among the museums and old buildings scattered around the area recalling those early days are the Pioneer Heritage Center (Sun., 1:30–4:30, adm.), a collection of nineteenth-century structures installed on the Louisiana State University at Shreveport campus; Shreve Square, a renovated 1890s-era area of cobblestone streets and warehouses tucked under the Texas Street Bridge downtown; Spring Street Museum (weekends, 1:30–4:30, free), with dioramas, murals, archeological relics and other displays relating to the state exhibited in a doughnut-shaped structure on the State Fairgrounds (the Louisiana State Fair takes place in late October).

Art museums in town include the Norton Art Gallery (Tu.–Sun., 1–5, free), featuring works on the American West by Frederick Remington and Charles M. Russell; the Meadows Museum of Art (Tu.–F., 1–5; Sat. and Sun., 2–5, free), with three hundred and sixty 1930s drawings and paintings by French artist Jean Despujol on Vietnam, Cambodia and Laos; and the Barnwell Memorial Gardens and Art Center (M.–F., 9–4:30; Sat. and Sun., 1–5, free), a combination planting and painting place, with a rear gallery affording a panoramic view onto the Red River. Another horticulture display brightens the American Rose Center (hours vary according to the growing season; for information: 318-938-

5402; adm.), home of the American Rose Society, a one hundred and eighteen-acre park with more than 15,000 rosebushes in some forty different gardens; the roses bloom from April to December, while other flowers and plants show their colors in the winter months.

The Emile Weil-designed Strand, a renovated 1925 movie and vaudeville theater, occasionally presents entertainments (for information: 318-226-1481), while at the famous Louisiana Hayride (318-222-9391), the nation's second-oldest live-broadcast country music show, performances take place Saturday nights beginning at eight. Wildlife displays in the area include a collection of stuffed animals in the trophy room at the Coca-Cola bottling plant (for information: 318-222-8661) and two miles east of Louisiana Downs racetrack (the season is April–Oct., W.–Sun.) in Bossier City, more than four hundred mounted birds and animals at the Educational Museum of Natural History (Tu.–Sat., 9–5; Sun., 1–5, adm.). Nearby is Barksdale Air Force Base where the Eighth Air Force Museum (318-456-3065) contains dioramas, old barracks, antique planes and other aviation displays.

If you have time to linger in Shreveport you'll find some additional sights of historic interest, among them the Caddo Parish Courthouse, so admired by Harry Truman he both suggested the building as a model for the Kansas City Courthouse and later hired its architect Edward Nield to assist in restoration of the White House; the turn-of-the-century Romanesque-style Justin Gras Building (on Louisiana Street) whose old "Casino/Saloon" sign at the rear recalls the days when the hotel there served as a gambling house and brothel; the Slattery Building (corner of Marshall and Texas), said to be the finest and tallest office structure between St. Louis and New Orleans when built in 1924 by eighty-year-old John B. Slattery as a show of his faith in Shreveport's future; Austin Place, a Civil War-era choice residential district just south of historic Oakland Cemetery, where many early settlers repose and which includes Louisiana's second-oldest Jewish burial ground; the century-old McNeil Pumping Station, a National Historic Landmark, one of the nation's few remaining public steam-powered water pumps; a nineteenth-century-style post office tucked away in the east end of Shreveport's main post office at 2400 Texas Avenue; and the site of old Fort Humbug (on the grounds of the Veteran's Hospital a mile from downtown), so called as Confederate troops, lacking cannons, set up logs as dummy guns along the fortifications. If you overnight in Shreveport, two places offer bed and breakfast rooms: The Columns, 615 Jordan (318-222-5912) and Fairfield Place, 2221 Fairfield Avenue (318-222-0048), the latter in the Fairfield Historic District, an area of stately old homes.

From Shreveport you can proceed in various directions to the attractions in surrounding parishes. At descriptively named Oil City to the north is the Caddo-Pine Island Oil and Historical Society Museum (M.–F., 9–11, 12–5; Sat., 1–5, free), where displays recall the boom-town fever in the early part of the century when oil was discovered in the area. Early oil field artifacts, old photos, exhibits relating to the world's first offshore well at nearby Caddo Lake, as well as displays on the Caddo Indian culture, fill the former Kansas City Southern Railway depot building.

In DeSoto Parish to the south of Shreveport you'll find the grave of Moses Rose, only survivor of the Alamo, interred at the old Ferguson Cemetery in Logansport where he died in 1850, and the Mansfield State Commemorative Area (9–5, adm.), site of one of the most important Civil War encounters west of the Mississippi. Monuments and a museum recall the famous battle, the last major Confederate victory in the War Between the States. At Coushatta, east of Mansfield, you'll find two shopping areas with an old-time flavor: the former train depot now houses a quilt outlet, and Planters Emporium comprises a group of craft

and antique shops installed in a late nineteenth-century building listed on the National Register. East of Shreveport-
Bossier City lies the Germantown Colony and Museum
(W.–Sat., 9–5; Sun., 1–6, adm.), seven miles northeast of
Minden. Countess von Leon, widow of the Count who
founded the socialist-utopian settlement in 1835 and who
died before it could take hold, ran the colony, where two
reproductions and three original buildings, including the
Countess's cabin and the kitchen-dining hall, recall the frontier community.

The nearby town of Athens is flat Louisiana's highest settlement, all of four hundred and sixty-nine feet above sea
level, while Driskill Mountain, off highway 147 south of
Arcadia and to the southeast of Minden, is the state's highest
point, hardly a "mountain" at five hundred and thirty-five
feet. Homer, northeast of Minden, boasts the 1860 Greek-
Revival Claiborne Parish Courthouse, one of Louisiana's
four such pre-Civil War structures, and the Herbert S. Ford
Memorial Museum (M.–F., 8:30–4; Sun., 2–5, free), which
contains displays on area history, as does the Lincoln Parish
Museum (Tu.–F., 9–4:30; Sat. and Sun., 2–5, free) at Ruston
to the southeast. Ruston also boasts the century-old First
Presbyterian Church, a Gothic-style sanctuary with stained
glass windows depicting biblical stories; while out at Louisiana Tech University you'll find a museum with area artifacts,
a fifty-acre arboretum featuring the "Avenue of State Trees,"
and an Equine Center (M.–F., 8–5, free), a horse farm established to teach students all phases of breeding, training and
racing horses. Twin Gables, 711 North Vienna (318-255-
4452) in Ruston offers bed and breakfast in a century-old
Victorian-style house. Another area university, Grambling
State at Grambling, just west of Ruston, is a well-known
black college with a renowned marching band. Five miles
south of Gibsland to the west is the Stage Coach Trail Museum (Tu.–Sun., 2–5, free), while due north of Ruston—

which celebrates a Peach Festival the third week in June (an even more juicy event takes place the last week in July in adjacent Union Parish at Farmerville, which hosts a Watermelon Festival)—lies Dubach, near which the Unionville General Store (open by chance or appointment: 318-777-3601), Lincoln Parish's oldest business establishment, owned by the same family since 1888, provides a glimpse at an old-fashioned emporium.

Jonesboro, a town of five thousand souls twenty-five miles south of Ruston, is an unusual place, for it presents a well laid-back image, boasting that it offers "no museums, no week-long festivals, no historic points of interest, no tour of homes and no souvenir shops with junk made in Hong Kong." Then why go there, except to see what might be the nation's most nonpromotional town, "where there is nothing to do but relax"? Well, Jonesboro is proud of its sidewalks, finished with a shiny gravel pebble surface, and the place claims the world's longest uninterrupted sidewalk, stretching three miles to Hodge, where you can visit supposedly the world's largest kraft paper machine at the Stone Container factory (M.–F., tours at 10, 11, 12, free). So even self-effacing Jonesboro offers a few sights, in spite of the town's disclaimers. A rather more passion-possessed place is Calhoun, fifteen miles east of Ruston, where the Louisiana Passion Play, recounting the life and death of Jesus, is performed in an outdoor theater during the summer (June–Aug., Th.–Sat., at 8:30, adm.). On Brownlee Road near Calhoun is the 1843 Red Rock General Store, featuring antique wares, handicrafts and a front porch where you can laze the day away in rockers.

At West Monroe, ten miles east, Ole Susannah's Country Square offers more than twenty old-fashioned craft and specialty shops in renovated antique houses (for bed and breakfast there: 318-396-2960), while local arts and crafts are also sold at the Roundtree Gallery, 812 North 2nd Street, in Monroe. Downtown Monroe includes the nearby one square-mile Don Juan Filhiol Historic District, an area of old buildings, including the parish courthouse overlooking the Ouachita River, named after the town's Spanish founder, who in 1790 built Fort Miro on the site where trappers and Indians traded. Two other venerable Monroe buildings, both listed on the National Register, take visitors by appointment: Boscobel Cottage (318-325-1550), an 1820s West Indies-type (and later, Greek Revival) house, and the residence built in 1906 by Louisiana governor Luther E. Hall (318-323-1505). Another local show house is the ELsong property which, along with ELsong Gardens and a Bible Museum (Tu.–F., 10–4; Sat. and Sun., 2–5, free), were left to a foundation by Emy-Lou Biedenharn, daughter of Joseph A. Biedenharn, who in 1894 in Vicksburg, Mississippi, first bottled the then little-known fountain beverage called Coca-Cola. (The establishment where that momentous event took place is a museum store in Vicksburg.) The house and garden acquired the name ELsong when Biedenharn commented that the flower beds his daughter, a one-time singer, created were "Emy-Lou's song." Apart from the Bible Museum, Monroe also offers the Masur Museum of Art, installed in an English Tudor-style house (Tu.–Th., 10–6; F., Sat., Sun., 2–5, free); Rebecca's Doll Museum, 4500 Bon Aire Drive (open by appointment: 318-343-3361), with 2,000 antique dolls on display; the Northeast Louisiana University Museum of Natural History, in Hanna Hall on the campus, with archeological and wildlife displays; and the Louisiana Purchase Gardens, Zoo and Amusement Park (10–5, adm.), with floral displays, rides, a miniature railroad and animal exhibits, including an area with nocturnal species viewed by day under muted lights so the beasts can sleep undisturbed. For meals in the area, Warehouse No. 1 restaurant (5–10 p.m., except Sun.), installed in a former corrugated-tin food storage building on the Ouachita River, and the "Angel Patience," the world's

largest towboat restaurant—and, who knows, perhaps the
only one as well—moored in downtown West Monroe, offer
unusual places to eat. Greening the landscape around Monroe
are some 50,000 acres of protected natural enclaves, including
the Cities Service, Ouachita and Russell Sage Wildlife Management Areas, all open to the public, and the D'Arbonne
National Wildlife Refuge.

At Bastrop, north of Monroe, the Snyder Memorial Museum (M.–F., 9–4:30; Sat., 9–1) contains regional historical
items, while off to the east in East Carroll Parish lies Poverty
Point State Commemorative Area (9–5, adm.), where
mounds and a museum recall the Indian culture that flour-
ished there some three thousand years ago. The Mississippi
River, which marks the east edge of the parish, here reaches
its widest point in Louisiana, seventy-six hundred feet. Although it seems a paradox, the river tends to narrow rather
than gain volume as it proceeds south, mainly because toward its outlet at the Gulf of Mexico the waterway lacks
tributaries to augment it. Apart from the Red River, no
streams enter the Mississippi in Louisiana from the west,
while south of Baton Rouge none join it from the east.

Winnsboro, south of Poverty Point and southeast of Monroe, boasts the Jackson Street Historic District, the nation's
second-smallest, with just three houses, as well as the Commercial Historic District, featuring turn-of-the-century commercial buildings, and the diminutive Queen Anne-style
farmhouse where World War II Flying Tiger leader General
Claire Chennault lived as a boy. Back near the Mississippi
to the east is the Winter Quarters State Commemorative
Area (9–5, adm.), a plantation house built in three stages
using three styles over three generations, where Union General Ulysses S. Grant headquartered for a time during his
siege of Vicksburg, Mississippi. This part of Louisiana—
namely, Tensas Parish—was the very heart of the slave-
sustained pre-Civil War way of life, for the parish claimed

a hundred and eighteen of the state's sixteen hundred plantations, with at least fifty slaves each, that existed in 1860 on the eve of the great conflict. At Columbia, west of Winnsboro, the Louisiana Art and Folk Center Museum (Tu.–Sat., 9–5, free) houses antiques and artifacts recalling rural life a century and more ago.

Farther south, along and near U.S. highway 84, lie a number of historic attractions you can visit if you're heading east toward Natchez, Mississippi, reached by 84. The route west on 84 is covered in the next paragraph. In LaSalle Parish, south of Columbia, is the two-century-old Eden Methodist Church, said to be the oldest Methodist sanctuary west of the Mississippi and south of the Mason-Dixon Line. Just outside Jena, east of Eden, the parish museum occupies a building constructed in 1906 as headquarters for the Good Pine Lumber Company. Harrisonburg, farther east, is a picturesque little town with another old Methodist church, this one still riddled with Civil War bullet holes, as well as 1862 Fort Beauregard and the restored National Register-listed Sargeant House, once a hotel for steamboat pasengers and now a tourist office. Just north of Jonesville is the King Turtle Farm that produces for export more than half a million pet turtles a year. Near Jonesville is "Where Four Corners Meet," a junction virtually unique in the world—the only other such confluence lies, or flows, in Africa—where a quartet of streams merge: the Little, Tensas, Ouachita and Black rivers. The 1840s-vintage National Register-listed Frogmore Plantation House on U.S. 84 west of Ferriday is one of the parish's oldest residences and a good example of a Louisiana frame-raised home. Farther along on 84 near Vidalia and beyond Ferriday, boyhood home of country and western singers Mickey Gilley and Jerry Lee Lewis and evangelist Jimmy Swaggart, stands Taconey Plantation, also listed on the National Register, one of the state's top ten cotton-producing plantations before the Civil War, and thus a true remnant of the antebellum culture and agriculture. Long-time (1908–1940) Vidalia Sheriff Eugene Campbell's 1915 house, listed on the National Register, survives as the only residence left on the original site of the town, where famous frontiersman Jim Bowie killed Norris Wright in a renowned duel on a Mississippi sandbar in 1827.

If you head west in LaSalle Parish instead of east on highway 84 you'll pass near Rochelle, between Georgetown and Urania on U.S. 165, an abandoned settlement where remains of the early twentieth-century lumber town survive. Winnfield, to the west, is the town which gave to Louisiana the famous Long political clan. At the Earl K. Long Park in town stands an eight-foot bronze statue of the three-time Louisiana governor who liked to claim he was "the last of the red hot papas in politics." On the site of the park once stood the family home where Huey Long, Sr., and his wife Caledonia raised nine children (one daughter died at a young age). A statue of the most famous member of the clan, Huey Long, Jr., governor and U.S. senator, stands in front of the Winn Parish Courthouse. Although six of the Long children attended college, the money ran out by the time young Huey came of age so he worked a time as a traveling salesman, later passing the bar exam after studying only one year at Tulane University Law School. After election to the Public Service Commission in 1918 (then called the Railroad Commission), Long ran unsuccessfully for governor in 1924, an office he later won based on his populist share-the-wealth "every man a king" program. Elected to the U.S. Senate in 1930, "the Kingfish" was at the peak of his power when Dr. Carl D. Weiss, son-in-law of Judge Benjamin Pary, a long-time Long opponent, assassinated the politician in the Louisiana state capitol in September 1935. (A plaque at the capitol in Baton Rouge marks the site of the shooting.)

Tucked away in a heavily forested area at Goldonna, west of Winnfield, is the aptly named Backwoods Village Inn, where country and western and bluegrass bands perform Friday and Saturday nights and where Pioneer Day festivities take place the second and fourth Saturday of each month; for information: 318-727-9227. Nearby lies Natchitoches (pronounced by the locals NAK-uh-tush), said to be the oldest town in the Louisiana Purchase Territory. Natchitoches dates its beginnings from the construction of a fort built by the French in 1714 to block Spanish expansion in the area. At the Fort St. Jean Baptiste State Commemorative Area (9–5, free) stands a full-scale replica of the wooden fort and trading post established by the French. As for Natchitoches, old houses well garnished with stately trees, much history, a lingering air of yesteryear and a peaceful laid-back atmosphere make the town one of Louisiana's most attractive and interesting settlements. Among the beguiling nineteenth-century structures are Ducournau Square, fronted by lacy cast-iron balconies and in the rear a courtyard sporting a gracefully contorted iron spiral stairway; the Roque House, an eighteenth-century cottage, perched by the Cane River, with an oversized overhanging roof; and a series of attractive residences along Jefferson, the street that fronts the river, including the 1830 Lemee House (310 Jefferson); the 1821 Ackel House (number 146), the town's oldest brick residence; and the 1830s Levy House (number 328), where a French doctor practiced for twenty years until locals discovered his medical credentials were forged, whereupon the townsfolk rode him out of Natchitoches on a rail. Some of the city's showplaces are open during the annual pilgrimage held in early October (318-352-8072). On Sirod Street stands the wood-frame dwelling which houses Liz's Beauty Shop, featured in the movie *Steel Magnolias,* filmed in Natchitoches. For meals in Natchitoches, Lasyone's, a restaurant renowned for meat pies, a local specialty, is a popular eatery, while for overnighters the town offers Ducournau Square (318-352-5242), Jefferson House (318-352-5756) and Fleur-de-Lis (318-352-6621) bed and breakfast accommodations.

Some appealing attractions lie south of Natchitoches, but if you want to continue the itinerary across the state, head west to a cluster of commemorative areas: Los Adaes (9–5, adm.), listed on the National Register, capital of Spanish Texas for fifty years until abandoned in 1773 and site of a Spanish mission, the only one established in Louisiana, and of a fort built in 1721 by the Spaniards as a counterweight to the French Fort St. Jean Baptiste in Natchitoches; Rebel State, where country and blue grass performances are held during the spring and summer (for information: 318-472-6255) and the State Fiddling Contest takes places in June; and National Register-listed Fort Jessup (9–5, adm.) featuring replicas of a military installation established by Zachary Taylor in 1822 and later used as a departure point for troops sent to fight in the Mexican War. South of Fort Jessup lies the delightful village of Fisher, a turn-of-the-century sawmill hamlet, listed on the National Register, preserved in an unchanged picture-perfect state, with an opera house, church, post office, train depot and houses surrounded by white picket fences. The Spanish-style St. John the Baptist Church, also Register-listed, in Many recalls the eighty-three years Spain ruled the area, as does the historical marker that commemorates the disputed territory claimed by the United States and by Spain after the Louisiana Purchase, that monument standing at the Louisiana Tourist Information Center west of Many. It is a historical curiosity that the famous 1803 Purchase didn't include all of Louisiana. Since "Louisiana" had originally been defined as the drainage basin of the Mississippi River, a large triangular-shaped area in the southwestern part of the state not drained by the river was excluded. Although French Louisiana and Spanish Texas had recognized this prior to the Purchase, when the U.S. acquired the Territory the official papers left the boundary vague. Even Talleyrand, the French Foreign Minister, admitted he was unsure of the exact limits of the domain conveyed to the Americans, remarking to Robert Livingstone, who'd negotiated the purchase: "You have made a noble bargain for yourselves and I suppose you will make the most of it." And, indeed, the expansionist Yankees did so, in 1819 finally convincing Spain that the Sabine River marked America's western border. Toledo Bend Reservoir, formed in 1966 by a dam across the Sabine, is the South's largest man-made body of water and the nation's only public hydroelectric and water conservation project undertaken without permanent federal financing.

The twelve hundred miles of shoreline offer dozens of recreational facilities, while the lake brims with bream, bass, crappie and other fish. Highway 6 which crosses the reservoir follows the route of El Camino Real, the King's Highway, part of the San Antonio Trace from Natchitoches to Mexico City. The area's Hispanic heritage survives at Zwolle, whose annual Tamale Festival belies the town's Dutch name. Twelve miles south of Many lies Hodges Gardens, an enclave with greenhouses, floral displays, hiking trails and nature areas (8–sunset, adm.). Accommodations are available at the Gardens' lodge (318-586-3523) and at Toro Hills Resort Hotel just across highway 171 (800-451-3415 in Louisiana, 800-533-5031 out-of-state). At Leesville to the south the Museum of West Louisiana (Tu.–Sun., 1–5, free), located in a renovated depot, contains displays on regional history, including photos from early days of the lumber industry. Huckleberry Inn, 702 Alexandria Highway (318-238-4000), provides bed and breakfast rooms in a Victorian-era house surrounded by venerable oak trees. At New Llamo near Leesville remain some of the original buildings of a communal colony that functioned there without churches, police or a judicial system from 1917 to 1935, while at Burr Ferry, west of Leesville, survive earthen breastworks thrown up by Confederate troops to block an anticipated Union advance up the Sabine

River. Exhibits at the nearby Fort Polk military museum
(M.–F., 8–4; Sat. and Sun., 8–4:30, free) cover army history
from the American Revolution to the present. Down at
DeRidder stands a spooky old Gothic-style parish jail, now
unused, while the Beauregard Museum (Tu.–F., 1–4,
free), housed in an old train depot, contains displays of antiques and old china. Outside of town, Bundick's Creek
Country Store (open by appointment: 318-463-3338) houses
an old blacksmith shop, nineteenth-century artifacts and old-
fashioned wares.

Returning now to Natchitoches, the route south to Alexandria takes you through the delightful plantation-filled
Cane River country. Along the river lie such showplaces
as Starlight, Cherokee, Oakland and Roubieu plantations..
Open to visitors are Oaklawn (March–Oct., 10–5; Nov.–
Feb., 10–4, adm.), with the state's third-longest avenue of
oaks, and three National Register-listed properties: Beau
Fort (1–4, adm.); Melrose (12–4, adm.), with nine early
nineteenth-century buildings, including African House, decorated with scenes by primitive-style artist Clementine
Hunter (who lived on the plantation) and believed to be
the only Congo-type structure in North America; and Magnolia (1–4:30, adm.), still in the same family since the original French land grant to the LeComte clan in 1753. The
Bayou Folk Museum at nearby Cloutierville (mid-June to
mid-Aug., Tu.–F., 10–5; Sat. and Sun., 1–5; fall and spring,
Sat. and Sun., 1–5, adm.), installed in a house where author
Kate Chopin lived in the early 1880s, contains exhibits relating to the writer, whose short stories in *Bayou Folk* (1896)
and *A Night in Acadie* (1897) were set in the Cane River
country. The museum also houses antiques and household
objects from yesteryear which convey an image of the way
of life when Kate lived there with her husband, Oscar, whose
family owned a plantation in the area. Around the nearby
hamlet of Chopin, named after the family, spreads the Little

Eva Plantation, thought to be the setting of Harriet Beecher Stowe's famous novel *Uncle Tom's Cabin*. Local legend has it that plantation owner Robert B. McAlpin, portrayed in the book as Simon Legree, bought "Uncle Tom" at a sale in New Orleans and brought him back to the property. New Orleans back then, in the mid-nineteenth century, was the nation's greatest slave market, with "merchandise" on offer that had been sent down the Mississippi where the workers could fetch higher prices than up north. This arbitrage in slaves led to families being uprooted and "sold down the river," a term that still today connotes betrayal. About a quarter of a mile from the Little Eva Country Store (by highway 490, just off Interstate 49) stands a ramshackle shack of weathered wood, replica of the original Uncle Tom's Cabin removed from the property for display at the 1893 Chicago Exposition. In a small burial ground a half-mile or so beyond the cabin metal markers indicate the graves of the famous figures: Robert McAlpin, who "according to legend was the character portrayed as Simon Legree in . . . 'Uncle Tom's Cabin'" and "Here lies the body of the person said to be the character portrayed as Uncle Tom."

On the way to Alexandria to the southeast you'll pass through Boyce, home of Hot Wells Bath House (W.–Sun., 8:30–3, adm.), Louisiana's only mineral water spa. At Alexandria the Historical and Genealogical Library and Museum contains exhibits and archives on the area, and the Kent Plantation House (Oct.–April, M.–Sat., 10–4; Sun., 1–4, adm.), built in 1796, is believed to be the oldest structure in central Louisiana. Nearby 1840s-vintage Tyrone Plantation House also offers tours (9–5) as well as bed and breakfast (318-442-8528). Another historic place to stay in Alexandria is Hotel Bentley (800-624-2778 in Louisiana, 800-356-6835 out of state), a 1908 National Register-listed hostelry, just by the Red River, with a spacious and gracious lobby embellished by large square columns. A block away stands the

Visual Arts Museum (Tu.–F., 9–5; Sat., 10–4, free) and a few blocks away is River Oaks Square Arts and Crafts (M.–F., 10–4, free), an 1899 Queen Anne-style residence that houses studios and workshops for local artisans. On the grounds of the Veterans Hospital three miles out of town stood the first home of Louisiana State University, founded in 1860 and later moved to Baton Rouge.

At Pineville, adjacent to Alexandria, repose war dead at the Alexandria National Cemetery, while early settlers are interred at Rapides Cemetery, one of the state's oldest burial grounds. Mount Olivet Church (M.–F., free), built in 1857, served as a barracks for Union troops during the Civil War. Near Marksville to the south, where the National Register-listed early nineteenth-century Hypolite Bordelon residence houses a museum and tourist center, is the Marksville State Commemorative Area (9–5, adm.), which includes remnants of a two-thousand-year-old Indian culture, while at nearby Cheneyville the Loyd Hall Plantation (Tu.–Sat., 10–4; Sun., 1–4, adm.) and the Walnut Grove Plantation (Tu.–Sat., 10–4; Sun., 1–4, adm.), owned by the same family since it was built in the 1830s, recall the antebellum era. Trinity Episcopal Church in Cheneyville (open by appointment: 318-346-4217), built in the 1850s, contains the original furnishings and a slave gallery above the vestibule. Along highway 71 between Cheneyville and Bunkie stand several roadside antique shops. The town was named after a pet monkey owned by the daughter of local landowner R. B. Marshall who granted a railroad right-of-way provided the line called its station "Bunkie," the way the little girl pronounced "monkey."

To the south of Bunkie, toward the center of the Cajun Country, is the Louisiana State Arboretum (M.–Sat., 9–5; Sun., 1–5, free), the nation's first such state-supported facility, with labelled plants, stands of beech trees and a botanical library that preserves specimens of native flora. Farther south lies the pleasant little town of Washington, an old steamboat settlement so filled with historic houses that nearly 80 percent of the community is listed on the National Register. Among the showplaces are the Acadian Connection (Th.–Sun., 10–5, free) where area craftsmen sell their wares, and two bed and breakfast places: Carré Desantels (318-826-7330) and Camellia Cove (318-826-7362 or 826-7749). For meals the Steamboat Warehouse Restaurant, installed in an 1830 building on the banks of Bayou Courtableau, affords an unusual ambiance. Nearby Opelousas, Louisiana's third-oldest city, founded about 1720, offers more historic houses, including the 1850 residence occupied by Governor Henry Allen when the town served as state capital during the Civil War, and 1827 Estorge House (318-948-4592), which takes bed and breakfast guests. A small museum in Opelousas contains a miscellany of artifacts, including exhibits on Jim Bowie of bowie knife fame, a one-time local resident. Off to the west lie Mamou, where at Fred's Bar and Lounge Cajun music and dancing enliven things every Saturday from 9 p.m. to 2 a.m., and Eunice where more local music sounds forth at the Savoy Music Center Accordion Factory (Tu.–F., 9–5; Sat., 9–12, free), scene of Saturday morning Cajun jam sessions. The Eunice Museum (Tu.–Sat., 8–12, 1–5, free), housed in an old train depot listed on the National Register, presents exhibits on Cajun culture, including music and local Mardi Gras customs. Four plants that process crawfish, that Cajun country delicacy, operate at Eunice, which the last Sunday of March presents the World Championship Crawfish Etouffee Cook-off, claimed to be the nation's largest culinary contest. South of Opelousas lies Sunset, where Chretien Point Plantation, once a meeting place for pirate Jean Lafitte, boasts a staircase used as the model for the one at Tara in the movie *Gone with the Wind*. Sunset's major revenue source is cockfighting, legal in only four states. (The others are Arizona, Missouri, New Mexico and Oklahoma.)

Nearby Grand Coteau claims one of the country's few primarily rural National Historic Districts, with more than seventy structures in and around the town included. The 1821 Academy of the Sacred Heart, second-oldest women's institution of higher learning west of the Mississippi and the world's oldest Sacred Heart school, St. Charles Borromeo Church and cemetery, and century-and-a-half-old St. Charles College, a Jesuit school now occupying a 1909 building, recall the town's early days. Bed and breakfast is available in Grand Coteau at the 1850 Cobbler's House (318-662-5264).

Before proceeding on to Lafayette, capital of the Cajun country, covered in the second paragraph below, you might want to detour west to visit a few attractions in that direction. Near Interstate 10 west of Lafayette lies the frog-raising town of Rayne where not rain but twenty-four inches of snow, the heaviest on record in the state, fell in 1895. In Crowley are the Cajun Music Hall of Fame (M.–Sun., 10–6; Sat. from 3, free) and The Gallery (Tu.–F., 10–4; Sat., 10–1, free) with local handicrafts on sale, while outside of town a Rice Museum (admission by appointment: 318-783-3096) offers displays on that important local crop. On a farm near Jennings oil was found for the first time in Louisiana in 1901, a discovery recalled at the Oil and Gas Park in town, where a replica of the state's first well stands. At the Zigler Museum (Tu.–Sat., 9–5; Sun., 1–5, adm.) hang paintings by European and American artists, along with natural history exhibits. At Jennings you'll also find the Boudin King, a restaurant featuring the spicy sausage ("boudin") owner Ellis Cormier originally cooked up in his grocery store, converted in 1975 by the "King" into his not palatial but quite comfortable eatery. For more regional treats Taste of Louisiana—restaurants and food stalls installed in a restored old warehouse at Lake Charles to the west—offers some typical Louisiana dishes, while that city's Scarlett O's restaurant occupies former governor Sam Houston Jones's residence, located in the twenty-square-block Charpentier Historic District, embellished by Victorian-era homes. The Imperial Calcasieu Museum (Tu.–F., 10–5; Sat. and Sun., 1–5, free) houses regional and fine arts exhibits in the shadow of giant Sallier Oak, believed to be more than three centuries old. Lake Charles also boasts what's said to be the world's largest bird house, a feather-filled mansion that can hold more than five thousand purple martins.

To the west of Lake Charles lies Sulphur, where the Brimstone Museum (M.–F., 9:30–5, free) contains exhibits on the Frasch sulphur mining process, developed in 1894, a half-century after the nation's first deposits of the mineral were discovered in the area; Vinton, through which passes the West Calcasieu Old Spanish Trail, a history-rich route, and where the National Register-listed Old Lyons House (318-389-2903), a restored Queen Anne-style home, offers bed and breakfast; and, to the north, De Quincy, home of a railroad museum (1–4, free) housed in a former Kansas City Southern depot, and of the Dogtrot Museum, featuring a National Register-listed "dogtrot"-type house, along with a general store, blacksmith shop and other old buildings. (A "dogtrot" house, common in the South, contains an open center section where animals can trot, romp or otherwise occupy.) If you want to take the long way around back to the center of the Cajun country, the Creole Nature Trail beginning in Sulphur heads south on highway 27, passes through the Sabine Wildlife Refuge, continues on to the seashore, and goes on along the coastal highway, route 82, by windswept marshes and moss-draped oaks, to the Rockefeller Wildlife Refuge. To the east this road will bring you back north to the Lafayette-New Iberia area, via Kaplan, the nation's only town that celebrates Bastille Day; Abbeville, with the nineteenth-century Greek Revival Vermilion Parish Courthouse, Magdalen Square and nearby oyster bars;

A La Bonne Veillee Guest House (318-937-5495), offering bed and breakfast in a mid-nineteenth-century plantation house (on highway 339 north of Erath) listed on the National Register; and Delcambre, a colorful shrimping village with a fisherman's wharf, net repairs shops and trawlers, all at their busiest in April, May and August.

The Lafayette-New Iberia area is the core of the Cajun country and culture. The Cajuns of today descend from the Canadian Acadians who, fleeing the British, arrived in the area in 1765. Some 800,000 Cajuns, about half of whom still speak a French dialect, now live in Louisiana. Cajun culture and history from "A" (art) to "Z" (zydeco, the region's music) is covered in displays at Lafayette's Acadian Village (10–5, adm.), a reconstructed settlement; the Cajun Country Store (10–6, free), with handicrafts on sale; the Lafayette Museum (Tu.–Sat., 9–5; Sun., 3–5, adm.) installed in a two-century-old house listed on the National Register; and at the gallery of artist George Rodrigue, 1206 Jefferson, whose delightful paintings of regional scenes seem to capture the area's essence. Also Register-listed is the little gem of a building (note the odd canopy-covered balcony) on the main square that once served as the city hall and now houses CODOFIL, the Council for the Development of French in Louisiana. Lafayette's one-way streets may baffle you and you might have to revolve around town as often as the revolving Evangeline Maid loaf of bread sign turns, but you'll manage to find your way to such other old buildings in Lafayette as St. John's Cathedral and the adjacent St. John's Oàk, whose huge pole-supported branches stretch out over the churchyard. On the campus of the University of Southwestern Louisiana, whose Dupre Library contains archives from the French and Spanish colonial periods, is a man-made swamp and cypress-tree lake where you can see alligators, trees, birds and other regional natural features in a civilized setting. Lafayette bed and breakfast places include Bois des

Chenes Inn, 338 North Sterling (318-233-7816), installed in
an 1820s National Register-listed carriage house; Shag-
wood Manor, 1414 East Bayou Parkway (318-984-1674 or
233-4570); and Ti Frere's House, 1905 Verot School Road
(318-984-9347).

At Scott, just west of Lafayette, Floyd Sonnier's Beau
Cajun Art Gallery (M.–F., 10–5; Sat., 10–4, free), installed
in a 1902 saloon, houses the artist's pen and ink drawings
of early Cajun life, while at Breaux Bridge, to the east, Mu-
late's, one of the best-known regional restaurants, features
Cajun food and music, and Ransonet House, 128 Oak Drive,
offers bed and breakfast. From Henderson, farther east, de-
part excursion boats to the Atchafalaya Basin, a swampy,
soggy wilderness area. On the way south to St. Martinville
you'll pass the Longfellow-Evangeline State Commemorative Area (9–5, adm.), with a two-century-old Acadian home
and a craft shop, while down in the town itself stands the
Evangeline Oak and a statue of the famous heroine of Henry
Wadsworth Longfellow's poem about two lovers separated
when the Acadians were exiled from Canada. By the lovely
little bayou-side park, where a gazebo rises near the old oak,
stands the venerable Castillo Hotel building, listed on the
National Register, formerly Mercy High School and then
an inn for steamboat passengers and which now houses a
restaurant. On the main square a block away rise the Petit
Paris Museum (9:30–4:30, adm.), St. Martin de Tours
Church and a statue of Evangeline. Across Bayou Teche
you'll find the Olivier Store, with old documents on display,
and Oak and Pine Alley, a century-old tree-lined way along
which, local legend has it, a wedding party once rode beneath glittering webs dusted with gold and silver.

St. Martinville's 1876 Durande residence, now the post
office, is believed to be the nation's only private building
taken over by the federal government for preservation and
use as an official facility. Evangeline Oak Corner bed and

breakfast, 215 Evangeline Boulevard (318-394-7675), offers accommodations in St. Martinville. The nearby Loreauville Heritage Museum (9–5, adm.) includes an extensive collection of historic artifacts and such structures as a voodoo shack, while New Iberia down the road boasts such showplaces as Shadows-on-the-Teche (9–4:30, adm.), a striking manor house, built in 1834 and now owned by the National Trust for Historic Preservation, along with the Mintmere Plantation and Armand Broussard residences (10–4, adm.), adjacent houses both listed on the National Register. Mintmere offers bed and breakfast (318-364-6210), as does "Interlude," 2305 Loreauville Road (318-367-6704). Two interesting local commercial establishments are the Konrico Rice Mill (tours, M.–F., 10, 11, 1, adm.), supposedly the nation's oldest (1912), and the adjacent company store (M.–Sat., 9–5), and B. F. Trappey's Sons (M.–F., 8–3; Sat., 9–4:30), a shop and a factory that pickles peppers and bottles hot sauce. To see how the more famous Tabasco, the nation's second-oldest food trademark, is bottled, you can tour the factory (M.–F., 9–11:45; 1–3:45; Sat., 9–11:45, free) at nearby Avery Island, which also boasts a garden and bird sanctuary (9–5, adm.); while at Jefferson Island—like Avery, not an island but a huge salt dome—are the attractive steamboat-style house and the surrounding Live Oak Gardens (9–5, adm.) of nineteenth-century actor Joseph Jefferson.

As you head away from the Cajun country toward New Orleans you'll find a number of old houses and out-of-the-way places worth visiting. The Jeanerette Bicentennial Museum (M.–F., 10–4, adm.) contains displays on the history of the sugar cane industry, while Bed and Breakfast on the Bayou, 2148 West Main in Jeanerette (318-276-5061) puts up guests in a cottage on Bayou Teche. In nearby Charenton is a museum and craft shop devoted to wares of the Chitimacha Indians (M.–F., 7:30–4; Sat., 7:30–12, free), and in and near the photogenic town of Franklin stand a group of show homes, among them Arlington (c. 1830), Oak Lawn Manor (c. 1837), Bocage (1846) and Grevemberg (1850), all open to visitors, and Laurel Ridge Country Inn (318-7732 or 828-7669), offering bed and breakfast.

National Register-listed Calumet Plantation, near Morgan City to the east, houses an antique shop where high tea is served on Tuesdays (for reservations: 504-395-5882), and near town is the Wedell-Williams Memorial Aviation Museum of Louisiana (M.–F., 11:30–4:15, free), with a collection of antique planes and displays on crop dusting and oil-related aviation history. Morgan City is a one-time oil boom-town where rusty hulks of petroleum equipment now serve as mute witnesses to the industry's bust. A well monument to the currently unwell off-shore drilling industry recalls the world's first producing such installation, completed November 14, 1947, when the Kerr-McGee Company struck oil in the Gulf of Mexico forty-three miles south of Morgan City. The town boasts another "first"—the first *Tarzan of the Apes* movie was shot in the vine-thick swamps there in 1917, a distinction recalled at the town museum (M.–F., 9–5; Sat. and Sun., 1–5, adm.), installed in Turn-of-the-Century House once owned by the local mortician, where the old Tarzan silent classic is shown regularly. At Thibodaux rise the handsome 1856 Lafourche Parish Courthouse, listed on the National Register; Rienzi Plantation, built in 1796 by Queen Maria Louisa of Spain as a possible retreat in case of her defeat by Napoleon; 1844 St. John's, said to be the oldest Episcopal church west of the Mississippi; and Arcadia Plantation, whose original cottages were built in the 1820s by Jim Bowie, just north of which is Nicholls University, its library housing a museum to former U.S. Senator Allen Ellender.

Two miles south of Thibodaux lies the splendid old Laurel

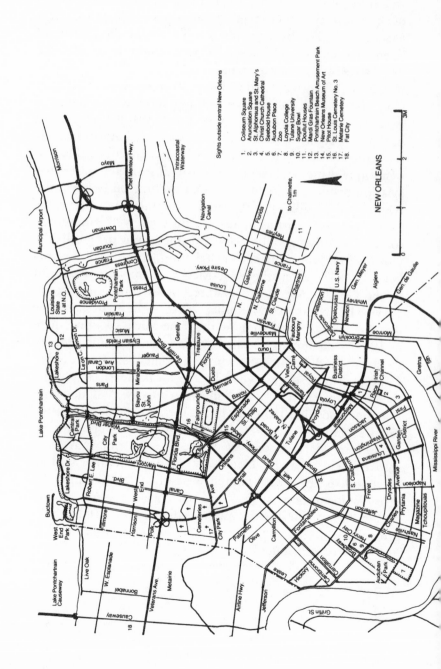

Sights outside central New Orleans

1. Coliseum Square
2. Anunciation Square
3. St. Alphonsus and St. Mary's
4. Christ Church Cathedral
5. Seebold House
6. Audubon Place
7. Zoo
8. Loyola College
9. Tulane University
10. Sugar Bowl
11. Doullut Houses
12. Mardi Gras Fountain
13. Pontchartrain Beach Amusement Park
14. New Orleans Museum of Art
15. Pitot House
16. St. Louis Cemetery No. 3
17. Metairie Cemetery
18. Fat City

NEW ORLEANS

Valley Plantation (10–4, free), listed on the National Register, whose seventy-six buildings make it the nation's largest surviving nineteenth-century sugar farm, while north of town are the 1790 White family house (9–5, adm.), homestead of Edward White, Sr., Louisiana governor and U.S. senator, and his son Edward, Jr., senator and for eleven years U.S. Supreme Court Chief Justice, and Madewood (10–5, adm.), an imposing old (1846) plantation house that takes bed and breakfast guests (504-369-7151). Another spacious antebellum house, listed on the National Register, contains the Terrebonne Museum (10–4, adm.), featuring history exhibits and a collection of Boehm and Doughty porcelain birds. The Wildlife Museum in Houma (Tu.–Sat., 10–6; Sun., 1–6, adm.) contains some seven hundred specimens, one of the world's largest private animal collections. Local shops specializing in Cajun or Louisiana items include Cajun Country General Store (M.–F. 8–5; Sat., 10–3), the Cajun at Heart arts and crafts bazaar (Sat., 10–5; Sun., 12–5) and A La Main Craft Co-op Shop (M.–Sat., 10–5; to 9 Th.). For tours of the area's wetlands, swamp veteran Annie Miller (504-879-3934), who lures alligators to her boat with meat treats (not her passengers), conducts boat excursions through the marshes, while tours of the U.S. Sugar Cane Experimental Station are available by appointment (M.–F., 8:30–4, 504-872-6326). For meals, Parrot's restaurant in Houma occupies the building that housed the town's first post office, and for accommodations the Cajun Connection, 311 Pecan Street (504-868-9519) offers bed and breakfast.

From Houma, roads south take you to seafood-processing villages where you can tour the packing plants: Indian Ridge Shrimp (504-594-3361) and ACLI Seafood (504-594-5869) in Chauvin and D'Luke's (504-563-2328) and Sea Tang (504-563-4586) in Dulac. In Chauvin you'll also find La Trouvaille, an eatery installed in a Cajun cabin specializing in regional dishes (W., Th., F., closed June through Aug.) and the

Boudreaux Canal Store, a general store established in 1865 (the present building is half a century old) with antique fixtures and an old-time atmosphere (M.–F., 7:30–4; Sat., 7:30–12). At the southern tip of the parish lies Cocodrie, a fishing village where the Louisiana Universities Marine Center (M.–F., 8–4, free) contains aquariums and an observation area affording a panoramic view of the bays, bayous and marshes. The other road south, U.S. highway 1, takes you to Golden Meadow, so named for the surrounding fields of goldenrod, where the "Petit Caporal" ("the little corporal" as Napoleon was called—but not to his face) shrimp boat, the oldest in the state (c. 1854), stands as a monument to the seafood industry. To the far south lies Port Fourchon, near which—out in the Gulf—is the nation's only offshore deep-water oil docking facility, which serves the supertankers. Off to the east stretches the eight-mile long, mile or so wide sliver of land named Grand Isle, a resort area where fish and bird life abound. Grand Isle State Park affords an unspoiled beach and a four hundred-foot long fishing pier. Here at this remote spot you are off the mainland, surrounded by coastal waters, and here Louisiana, and your tour, come to an end.

New Orleans and Surroundings

New Orleans—Kenner—Covington—Gretna—Venice

Apart from that other Old World named "New"—York—perhaps no city so symbolizes or dominates a state as does New Orleans. It must be a rare traveler to Louisiana who fails to visit "the big easy," "the Crescent City," "the city that care forgot," as New Orleans is variously known. The town exerts on visitors a strong and lasting impression. Lafcadio Hearn, the famous writer who lived in the city from 1877 to 1887, noted in *Creole Sketches:* "There are few who can visit her for the first time without delight; and few who can ever leave her without regret; and none who can forget her strange charm when they have once felt its influence."

Much of the city's "strange charm" emanates from the seven by fourteen square-block area known as the "Vieux Carre" or Old Quarter. Each part of the tightly packed Quarter seems to exude its own ambiance: Royal Street, with fancy shops; Bourbon Street, lined with honky-tonk nightspots; history-haunted Jackson Square. But the Vieux Carre is more than just a tourist quarter, commercial area and historical curiosity; the Quarter also serves as a residential part of town, home to some seven thousand people. So as you wander the narrow streets of the section you'll be visiting not only a famous tourist mecca but also New Orleans's most colorful neighborhood. In that way, the Quarter is both touristy and typical, a combination of characteristics that lends the Vieux Carre its unique flavor. In the Quarter—preserved so artfully thanks to the vigilant eye of the Vieux Caree Commission, established in 1936 to set strict architectural standards for the area—you'll find street after street of attractive old buildings, tempting eateries, browser-beckoning shops, ordinary and odd museums and people-watching opportunities.

A good place to start your visit is at the New Orleans City Tourist Center, also a state tourist office, at 529 Ann Street on Jackson Square. The Square recalls Paris street scenes: on one side of the artist-filled area rises St. Louis Cathedral, the third and most recent version (1794, with renovations) of churches on the site since the 1720s, flanked by the Cabildo and the Presbytere (both now units of the Louisiana State Museum). The elegant Pontalba Apartment Buildings, known as the country's first apartment houses (1850 and 1851), once novelist William Faulkner's residence,

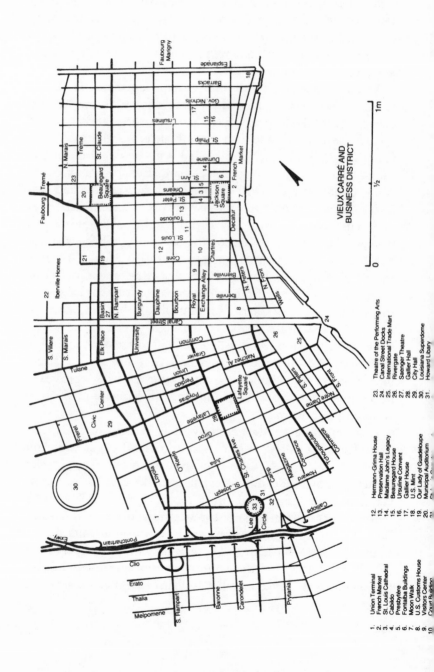

VIEUX CARRÉ AND
BUSINESS DISTRICT

0   ½   1m

1. Union Terminal
2. French Market
3. St. Louis Cathedral
4. Cabildo
5. Presbytère
6. Fontalba Buildings
7. Moon Walk
8. U.S. Customs House
9. Visitors Center
10. Court Building

12. Hermann-Grima House
13. Preservation Hall
14. Madame John's Legacy
15. Beauregard House
16. Ursuline Convent
17. Galier House
18. U.S. Mint
19. Our Lady of Guadeloupe
20. Municipal Auditorium

23. Theatre of the Performing Arts
24. Canal Street Docks
25. International Trade Mart
26. Rivergate
27. Saenger Theatre
28. Galier Hall
29. City Hall
30. Louisiana Superdome
31. Howard Library

stand alongside the Square. Scattered around the Quarter are such museums as the Old Pharmacy Museum, a Mardi Gras display at Arnaud's Restaurant, the Old U.S. Mint (in front stands "a Streetcar Named Desire," recalling the famous play Tennessee Williams wrote in his apartment at 632 St. Peter near Royal, along which the streetcar, since replaced by a bus, rumbled), the Historic New Orleans Collection, and the Voodoo Museum. (For clairvoyant consultations, tea leaf readings, or at least a spot of tea, visit Bottom of the Cup Tea Room, 732 Royal and 616 Conti.) Also in the Vieux Carre stand such historic houses (all open to visitors) as the 1850 House, Gallier, Hermann-Grima (with the Vieux Carre's last private stable), Fortier and Beauregard-Keyes, half named for Frances Parkinson Keyes who wrote there *Dinner at Antoine's* and other novels, and half for Confederate General P.G.T. Beauregard. When a young engineer Beauregard worked in the Egyptian-style Customs House on Canal Street, a splendid century-and-a-half-old granite building with a striking central marble hall, later used as headquarters by the intensely unpopular Union General Benjamin Butler during the occupation of the city by the Northerners. It was "Beast" Butler, as the locals dubbed him, who issued the famous "woman order," a decree stating that any female who cursed or abused Federal soldiers would be considered a prostitute under the law. The offended ladies of New Orleans supposedly obtained a measure of revenge against Butler by placing his portrait at the bottom of their chamber pots.

Other attractions in and around the French Quarter include the Mississippi levee Moon Walk, not a celestial reference but so called for a former mayor of New Orleans; Jackson Brewery, a recycled 1891 beer factory that now houses shops, bistros and the New Orleans School of Cooking; the French Market, which stretches down Decatur Street beyond the Cafe du Monde, a legendary establishment where you can get the delicious powdered sugar-covered "beignets" washed down by the famous chicory-coffee blend. Locals favor lesser known Morning Call out in Metarie for beignets. Free guided walking tours of the French Quarter, and other parts of town, start from the Jean Lafitte National Historical Park Visitor and Folklife Center at 916-18 North St. Peter Street. In October 1989 the Woldenberg Riverfront Park opened, giving pedestrians direct access to the Mississippi for the first time in a century. In 1990 a 110,000 square-foot aquarium with more than a million gallons of water opened nearby.

It would be a mistake to restrict your stay in New Orleans to the Vieux Carre, for scattered around town outside the Quarter are a number of other worthwhile attractions. In the mysteriously named "C.B.D."—not a secret code but the initials locals use to designate the "Central Business District," an area strangers, Yankees and other foreigners would call "downtown"—are Riverwalk, a rather too commercial and charmless stretch of shops in an indoor mall along the Mississippi; the Superdome (tours available); and the Top of the Mart, a lounge atop the World Trade Center where you'll revolve even if you don't imbibe as the room turns to afford varying views of the city thirty-three floors below. Other museums around town include Jefferson Barracks (admission by appointment: 504-271-6262), with military history displays installed in an 1830s powder magazine; the Confederate Museum; the Pitot House Museum, built in the early nineteenth century by New Orleans's first mayor; the Ursuline Museum, with historic documents and displays at the nation's oldest girls' school (1727); Longue Vue House and Gardens; New Orleans Museum of Art; and the Louisiana Nature and Science Center. One of the city's more unusual attractions is Mardi Gras World, 233 Newton Street in Algiers across the river (call to see if you can join a group tour: 504-362-8211), huge warehouses where workmen build Mardi Gras parade floats. Those parades start two weeks before Mardi Gras Day, which falls on February 15 in 1994 and on February 28, 20, 11, 24 and 16 from 1995 to 1999.

Two little-known local collections are housed at Tulane University out in the Garden District: pre-Columbian art from Mexico and Central America (for information: 504-865-5110) and an archive pertaining to jazz and New Orleans music (504-865-6634). Although fans of local music can find any number of jazz joints in the Quarter, less obvious places for music include gospel or jazz masses Sunday mornings at St. Francis de Sales, 2203 Second Street; St. Philip's, 1301 Metropolitan Avenue; and St. Monica's, 2327 South Galvez Street. Off-the-beaten-track nightspots include Jimmy's, 8200 Willow Street; Maple Leaf, 8316 Oak Street; and Tyler's, 5234 Magazine Street. For miles along Magazine, one of the country's most browse-worthy streets, stretch dozens of antique shops, bookstores, art galleries, pubs, cafes, eateries and other establishments where you can while the day away. Magazine borders the Garden District, an open tree-filled section of town originally populated by the first Americans who settled in New Orleans after the 1803 Louisiana Purchase, newcomers shunned by the Creoles who continued to live in the French Quarter. Along Coliseum, Prytania and other streets in the delightful neighborhood stand history-filled and architecturally rich nineteenth-century houses, among them the residence where Confederate President Jefferson Davis died in 1889, 1134 First Street, and the home occupied by renowned local author George Washington Cable, 1313 Eighth Street, hounded from town for his strong anti-slavery stand. In the Garden District you'll also find the century-and-a-half-old Lafayette Cemetery, one of those famous above-ground (because of the marshy soil) New Orleans graveyards, other examples of which include the three St. Louis Cemeteries northwest of the French Quarter, while at the history-haunted Metairie Cemetery every gravestone has a story behind, or under, it.

Along the edge of the Garden District runs St. Charles, down which rattle New Orleans's delightful old streetcars, the world's oldest (1837) continuously operating street railway. The twenty cars now in service date back to 1924. The route (exact fare required: sixty cents) takes you from the C.B.D. through the uptown section, past lovely old houses along St. Charles and to Tulane and the adjacent Audubon Place, an imposing private residential section, and Audubon Park, which boasts Monkey Hill, the below-sea-level city's only rise, built by the W.P.A. to show New Orleans children what an elevation looks like. St. Charles is where you'll find—as you might expect to find in a town as Gallic as New Orleans—a French Cultural Services Center, 3305 St. Charles (504-891-6901), with exhibits and French books, programs and classes. To see the river side of the city you can find ferries across the Mississippi—so contorted at New Orleans the sun rises over the river's west bank—at the foot of Jackson Avenue and at the Canal Street Wharf, where you can cross to Algiers Point, a picturesque quarter with Victorian architecture along tree-lined streets and from which also leaves the old time paddle-wheeler "Natchez" on cruises to Barataria, pirate Jean Lafitte's old haunt downriver; while the "Cajun Queen," which departs from Riverwalk, offers trips to plantation houses and a dinner cruise.

"Dinner": that word, or any other food expression, when spoken in connection with New Orleans, is freighted with folklore. English novelist William Makepeace Thackeray adjudged New Orleans "the city of the world where you can eat and drink the most and suffer the least." It's a great local sport for tourists and residents alike to discuss eating, an activity which in New Orleans has taken on many of the characteristics of a religion, without the disadvantages. As Mark Twain observed on sampling some pompano in New Orleans, the dish was "as delicious as the less criminal forms of sin." Virtually every book or article on New Orleans lists all the famous "brand name" restaurants such as Antoine's, Galatoire's, Arnaud's, Brennan's, Commander's Palace and others. But where do the residents eat? Here's a list of some lesser-known out-of-the-way places that knowledgable food lovers who live in New Orleans or frequently visit the city recommend: Chez Helene (soul food), Barron (catfish), Eddie's (Creole), La Riveria (Italian), Sidmars (a seafood place out in Bucktown in the West End by Lake Pontchartrain), Frankie and Johnny (seafood), Mais Oui (soul food and excellent gumbo), La Crepe Nanou (French), the Bean Pot (Mexican), Vera Cruz (Mexican), Kolb's (worthwhile as much for the old-time atmosphere as for the German cuisine, for the eatery houses a late nineteenth-century system of fans, that era's air conditioning), Gautreau's (Creole, specializing in fish; occupies a restored old pharmacy), Bayou Ridge (Italian), Clancy's (Creole), Little Greek, Mandinas (seafood), The Upper Line (Creole), Shogun, Bistro at Maison de Ville (French-Creole), Gambrill's (French-Creole), Cafe Savanna (seafood), Cafe Degas (French), Cafe Sbisa (bouillabaisse), Matassas, Christian's (Creole and seafood in a former church), Mid City (seafood), Liuzza's (Italian), Joey K's (seafood), Ruby Red's (hamburgers), Snug Harbor (burgers and seafood), Sitting Duck (lunch only), Domilises (a neighborhood bar with food) and Mystery Street Cafe.

As for places to stay in New Orleans, brand names also abound for hotels, as just about all the national chains have a presence in the city. But the many local inns and bed and breakfast establishments offer more pleasant and typical places to stay. In the downtown area such places include: Casa de Marigny Cottages, 818 and 822 Frenchmen Street (504-948-3875), A Hotel, The Frenchmen, 417 Frenchmen Street (504-948-2166), Lafitte Guest House, 1003 Bourbon (504-581-2678, 800-331-7971), Lamothe House, 621 Esplanade (504-947-1161), Maison de Ville Hotel and Audubon Cottages, 727 Toulouse (504-561-5858, 800-634-1600), New Orleans Guest House, 1118 Ursulines (504-566-1177, 800-654-4092), Quarter Esplanade Guest House, 719 Esplanade (504-948-9328), Soniat House, 1133 Chartres (504-522-0570, 800-544-8808), Villa Convento, 616 Ursulines (504-522-1793), St. Peter House, 1005 St. Peter (504-524-9232). Bed and breakfast places out in or near the Garden District include: Hedgewood Hotel, 2427 St. Charles (504-895-9708), Marquette House, 2253 Carondelet (504-523-3014), St. Charles Guest House, 1748 Prytania (504-523-6556), Terrell House, 1441 Magazine (504-524-9859), Park View, 7004 St. Charles (504-861-7564) and the splendid 1883 Columns, listed on the National Register, 3811 St. Charles (504-899-9308). Two reservation services in New Orleans are Bed and Breakfast (504-525-4640, 800-228-9711, then 184) and New Orleans Bed and Breakfast (504-822-5038 and 822-5046).

In the greater New Orleans area, as well as farther afield in southern Louisiana, lie other attractions. Out at Kenner, near the airport, is the Louisiana State Railroad Museum (Tu.–Sat., 9–5; Sun., 1–5, adm.), the Louisiana Wildlife and Fisheries Museum (Tu.–Sat., 9–5; Sun., 1–5, adm.) and Rivertown, USA, a combination of restored nineteenth-century buildings and commercial family attractions. Kenner has a bed and breakfast establishment, Seven Oaks, 2600 Gay Lynn Drive (504-888-8649), as does adjacent Metairie, La Chalet Guest House, 4201 Teuton Street (504-833-7982). Off to the east, six miles downriver from the French Quarter, lies Fort Chalmette National Historic Park (8:30–5, summer to 6, free), site of the Battle of New Orleans, the last major encounter in the War of 1812, where a museum and the battlefield recall Andrew Jackson's famous victory. Farther east at Fort Pike State Commemorative Area (9–5, adm.) stands another military installation, a fort built shortly after the War of 1812 to defend navigational channels leading to New Orleans. At St. Bernard, south of Chalmette, is a museum devoted to the Islenos, Canary Islanders who in the 1780s settled in the area where their Spanish-speaking descendants still reside.

To reach the region north of New Orleans it's an experience to cross the causeway over Estuary Pontchartrain, always called a lake but, due to its salt water and its connection with the sea, not really such. The twenty-four-mile roadways—one for each direction, opened in 1956 and 1969—comprise the world's longest over-water bridge. Back on Labor Day 1923 a man named Ernest C. Hunt swam twenty-two miles across Lake Pontchartrain in fifteen hours. North of the lake lie the picturesque towns of Covington and Madisonville, both with resident artists along with craft and antique shops, while nearby Hammond calls itself "the strawberry capital of the world." At Covington, where novelist Walker Percy lived, are such relics as 1846 Christ Episcopal Church, listed on the National Register, the 1876 H. J. Smith's Sons General Store and Museum and the 1907 Southern Hotel Building, which now houses offices of St. Tammany Parish, named after Delaware Indian chief Tammanend, adopted as a patron saint during the Revolutionary War, who also lent his name to the New York City Democratic political machine, known as Tammany Hall. The parish offers various bed and breakfast places: at Covington, Plantation Bell Guest House, 204 West 24th Avenue (504-892-1952), the Guest Cottage, 214 Lee (504-893-3767), and Riverside Hill Farms, 96 Gardenia Drive (800-375-1928 in Louisiana); at nearby Madisonville, River Run Guest House, 703 Main Street (504-845-4222); and at Amite to the north, Blythewood Plantation, 300 Elm Street (504-748-8183).

North of Amite lies the Camp Moore State Commemorative Area (9-5, adm.), with a Confederate Cemetery and a museum where displays recall the time when the facility served as one of the South's largest Civil War training camps. Nearby Washington Parish, a logging area, mounts what is supposedly the nation's third-largest county fair. At Abita Springs, a one-time popular health resort, the tiny Abita Brewing Company concocts Abita Gold and Abita Amber beers (tours by appointment: 504-893-3143). Near Mandeville to the south stands Louisiana's largest live oak, a nearly thirty-seven-foot in circumference specimen on the Seiler estate on Fountain Drive at Lewisburg. Like many of the state's stately oaks the tree, "Seven Sisters" by name, belongs to the Live Oak Society, organized in 1934. More than four hundred trees—each at least a century old with a girth of over seventeen and a half feet measured four feet from the ground—belong to the Society, whose members are the oaks themselves, represented by their owners or sponsors. This is perhaps the world's only organization with inanimate members. A member more conveniently located for viewing is "Martha Washington," at twenty-seven and a half feet the state's tenth-largest oak, which stands in New Orleans' Audubon Park.

Below New Orleans to the south, the state turns into a ragged-edged water-logged region. Just as the Pontchartrain causeway is the world's longest bridge, so the four and four-tenths-mile Huey P. Long span between Jefferson and Bridge City ranks as the longest railroad bridge in the world. You can get a good view of the well-named Long Bridge as you cross the Mississippi on the adjacent highway span, which takes you to Bridge City, "Gumbo Capital of the World." Off to the east is Westwego, so named for the expression "West we go," shouted by trainmen when railcars were rejoined after being ferried across the Mississippi before Long Bridge was completed in 1935. Farther east lies Gretna, whose National Historic District includes more listings—three hundred and fifty—than any other such area in the

U.S. Among the attractions so listed are the 1899 Infant Jesus College, originally a convent, with a splendid three-story cast-iron gallery; St. Joseph's, labeled an "outlandish" example of Spanish colonial architecture; the delightful little David Crockett Fire Hall, built in 1859, which houses the nation's oldest volunteer fire company (1841), and the antique Gould No. 31 Steam Fire Pumper, a still functioning piece of equipment said to be the only remaining such item in existence.

To the south the towns of Lafitte and Jean Lafitte recall the days nearly two centuries ago when the pirate of that name haunted the bayous around Barataria. The Lafitte National Historical Park, whose other units are the French Quarter in New Orleans and Chalmette, site of the Battle of New Orleans, includes some 8,600 square acres of coastal wetlands around Barataria. One way to see the area is from above: Southern Seaplane (504-394-5633 or 394-6959) offers flying tours over the bayous. You can also make your way by car through the oddly shaped delta region on roads that border the Mississippi, crossed by ferries at Belle Chasse and Pointe a la Hache. On the way to land's end you'll pass Woodland Plantation, immortalized on the label of the Southern Comfort whiskey bottle. Venice, probably your last stop, hardly lives up to its namesake, for the town is not much more than an unsightly assemblage of storage tanks, machinery and rusting equipment. This is the end of the road. Beyond lies watery Pilottown, an odd settlement with only a scattering of houses on stilts inhabited by riverboat pilots. Here the mighty Mississippi ends its long journey, finally disappearing into the sea, and here the land gives way to the Gulf. Down the waning river glide great ocean ships carrying coal, sulphur, grain and other commodities bound for far lands and distant ports of call—a long, long way from the plantations, Cajuns and culture of old Louisiana.

Louisiana Practical Information

Louisiana Office of Tourism, P.O. Box 94291, Baton Rouge, LA 70804, 504-925-3860, out-of-state 800-33-GUMBO. For information on the state's arts, archeology, culture, folklore and history: Office of Cultural Development, 504-925-3884. For information on Louisiana's forty state historic areas and parks: 504-925-3860.

Louisiana operates thirteen highway and city visitor centers. In the New Orleans area: I-10 near Slidell; I-55 near Kentwood; I-59 near Pearl River; at 529 Ann Street in New Orleans. In the Baton Rouge area: U.S. 61 north of St. Francisville; at 666 North Foster Drive and in the state capitol building in Baton Rouge. In the southwest (entering from Texas): I-10 near Vinton; I-10 and Lake Shore Drive. In the west: I-20 near Greenwood; highway 6 at Pendleton Bridge near Many. In the northeast: U.S 84 at Vidalia; I-20 at Mound.

For travel information in some of the state's main tourist areas: New Orleans, 504-568-5661; Baton Rouge, 504-383-1825; New Iberia, 318-365-6931; Lafayette, 318-232-3808; Natchitoches, 318-352-8072; Shreveport-Bossier, 318-222-9391, out-of-state 800-551-8682; Monroe-West Monroe, 318-387-5691.

For bed and breakfast accommodations in Louisiana: Southern Comfort, 504-346-1928 or 928-9815; for reservations, 800-523-1181, then 722. In New Orleans, Bed and Breakfast, Inc., 504-525-4640, 800-228-9711, then 184, and New Orleans Bed and Breakfast, 504-822-5038 or 822-5046.

II

The Mountain South

4. Kentucky

In Kentucky, called "the daughter of the East and the mother of the West," began the nation's expansion to the open areas beyond the Alleghenies. The first state to border on the Mississippi, Kentucky was an uninhabited garden spot settled by so disparate a mix of pioneers that Harry Toulmin, writing about 1800, noted in *A Description of Kentucky* how "These people, collected from different states, of different manners, customs, religions, and political sentiments, have not been long enough together to form a uniform and distinguishing character." This observation echoed the comment of John Filson, the state's very first historian, who wrote in his 1784 *The Discovery, Settlement and Present State of Kentucke* [sic] how the settlers, being "collected from different parts of the continent, they have a diversity of manners, customs and religions, which may in time perhaps be modified to one uniform." Filson, it's believed, also ghost-wrote the famous 1784 Daniel Boone autobiography, which starts with the stirring words: "It was on the first of May 1769 that I resigned my domestic happiness, and left my family and peaceable habitation on the Yadkin River, in North Carolina, to wander through the wilderness of America, in quest of the country of Kentucke," a region the frontiersman discovered to be a "paradise."

Through Kentucky's early history interweaves the story of Boone, a rather short and stocky fellow who favored a wide-brimmed hat rather than the coonskin cap he's usually depicted as wearing. Boone opened Kentucky in 1775 when he and his band of axmen passed through the Cumberland Gap and began cutting the Wilderness Road, and by April of that year they established at the trail's northern terminus Fort Boonesborough. Four years earlier Boone had spent three months alone in a remarkable solo feat "without a horse, dog, bread, salt, or sugar" exploring the forested Red River Gorge, and three years later, in 1778, the famous frontiersman had been captured near Blue Licks, a salt source, by Shawnee Chief Blackfish, so taken with Boone that the Indian adopted him. In 1776 the Commonwealth of Virginia designated Kentucky one of its counties, which by 1789 subdivided into the nine counties that constituted Kentucky in 1792 when it joined the Union, the first state on the western frontier and one of the very few carved out of another, most of them originating from territories. Kentucky called itself a commonwealth—a term used during Cromwell's time in mid-seventeenth-century England to designate an area free of royal domination—for the state had belonged to one of the nation's few commonwealths, Massachusetts and Pennsylvania being the only other such areas. As Kentucky developed, Boone grew restless for the "child of the wilderness," as Reuben Gold Thwaites described him in *Daniel Boone,* "was ill fitted to cope with the horde of speculators and other self-seekers who were now despoiling the old hunting grounds." Finally, in 1798, Boone departed from the state to head west to the less crowded wilds of Missouri, so ending an era in Kentucky's history.

It was about this time, quite early in the state's story, when three Kentucky traditions began to develop: colonels, thoroughbreds and bourbon. Isaac Shelby, the state's first governor, appointed his son-in-law Charles S. Todd as Kentucky's first honorary colonel. Nearly a century later in 1887 the legislature formalized the practice by authorizing the governor to choose "such aides or other officers" as the chief executive desired, and in 1932 the Honorable Order of Kentucky Colonels, whose members have included a wide range of luminaries, from Mae West and Al Jolson to "My

Old Kentucky Home" composer Stephen Foster, was established as a charitable organization, which every May gathers in Louisville for a gala Kentucky Derby eve banquet. The Derby, founded in 1875, symbolizes Kentucky's thoroughbred culture, which began a century earlier when the Boonesborough Assembly, the first legislative body west of the Alleghenies, passed a law relating to horse breeding. Four years later a group of horsemen met at Postlethwaite's Tavern in Lexington to form the Kentucky Jockey Club, and by 1780 that town boasted the first designated "race path" in the region. "Blaze," foaled in England, arrived in Kentucky in 1797 as the state's first full-grown thoroughbred, and soon the equine industry was off and running, with Kentucky replacing Virginia in the 1850s as the leading horse-breeding state. Inextricably connected with the Derby is the state drink, the mint julep, a potion of many recipies but none better than the one suggested by Louisville editor Henry Watterson: "Pour whiskey into a well-frosted cup, throw [all] the other ingredients away and drink the whiskey." In 1789, when a census counted more horses than people in Lexington, Elijah Craig, a Baptist preacher from Virginia, developed in nearby Georgetown a sour-mash whiskey dubbed in 1821 "bourbon," a name originating from Kentucky's Bourbon County. The state's fourteen operating distilleries now produce a million barrels of bourbon annually, more than 85 percent of the nation's supply.

Even more important to the state's economy is burley tobacco, a late-blooming crop that started only after the Civil War when the light-colored mild leaf first began to become popular. From November to February there operate in Kentucky thirty tobacco markets that generate cash sales of about a half-billion dollars, nearly a quarter of the state's farm income, well ahead of receipts from the sale of horses and mules, including stud fees, which amount to less than a fifth of the total. Before the Civil War Kentuckian Henry Clay,

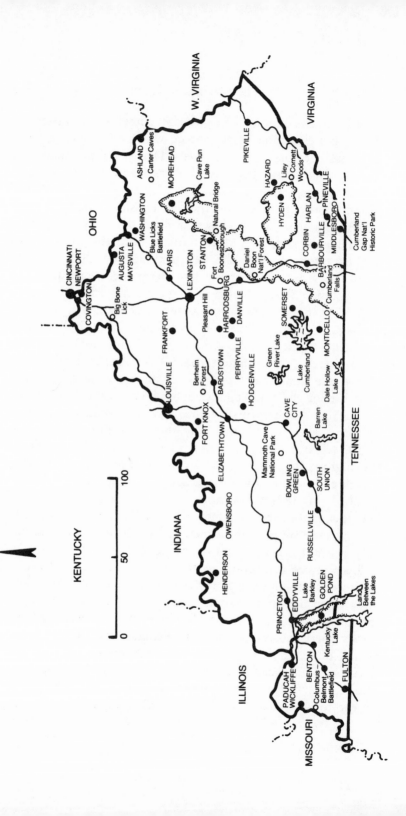

who died in 1852, acted as a conciliator between the North and the South. Clay's moderating influence is perhaps one reason why Kentucky, untypically for a Southern state, remained neutral during the war and never seceded, although a Confederate government existed briefly in Bowling Green. Mixed loyalties predominated, with the state supplying thirty-nine of its native sons as Union generals, along with 90,000 Yankee troops, as well as thirty-one generals and 45,000 soldiers to the Confederate side. Only one major encounter transpired on Kentucky soil, the October 1862 battle at Perryville, which ended Confederate attempts to dominate the state.

For some decades after the war Kentucky remained a rather rough-edged, isolated state influenced for years by the pre-industrial traditions established during the pioneer era. As Thomas D. Clark observed in *Agrarian Kentucky,* "Up to 1890, fully three-fifths of Kentucky's rural population lived in heavily wooded counties where conditions characteristic of the great American frontier had lingered through four generations." With its horse-based betting, bourbon and burley, its colonels and coal-country culture in the eastern mountain region, the Kentucky of today reflects its origins as a frontier state settled by a diverse populace that, in the words of Patricia Watlington in *The Partisan Spirit: Kentucky Politics 1779–1792,* made it "unique in that none of her adult citizens were natives of the area."

Still today Kentucky in a way recalls how the state seemed back in the late eighteenth century, as described by George Morgan Chinn in *Kentucky: Settlement and Statehood 1750–1800:* "It was a man's world of action more than thought, of physical more than intellectual strength and of bold assertion rather than meekness. It operated without the distinctions imposed by wealth or education, and frontier culture evolved from the day-to-day struggle to survive." It was perhaps this masculine tone typifying Kentucky that led suffrage leader Madeline McDowell Breckenridge—an avatar of the state, for she was Henry Clay's great-granddaughter, descendant of Kentucky senator and U.S. Vice-president John Breckenridge, relative of renowned early surgeon Dr. Ephraim McDowell of Danville, and wife of a *Lexington Herald* editor—to remark in 1915: "Kentucky women are not idiots—even though they are closely related to Kentucky men."

Eastern Kentucky

Ashland—Morehead—Prestonburg—Pikeville—Hindman—Harlan —Pineville—Middlesboro—Cumberland Gap—Big South Fork—Corbin—London

Mountains and coal mines, prosperity and depressions, friendly hospitality and family feuds have given the eastern Kentucky hill country its highs and lows, ups and downs. The term "mountain people," as the region's residents are described, refers not only to their Appalachian habitat but also to a rather basic and unadorned way of life that developed in isolation removed from the mainstream of American culture. Back at the turn of the century John Fox, Jr., whose books define and interpret his native state, noted in *Blue-grass and Rhododendron: Outdoors in Old Kentucky* that "the Kentucky mountaineer has been more isolated than the mountaineer of any other State. There are regions more remote and more sparsely settled, but nowhere in the Southern mountains has so large a body of mountaineers been shut off so completely from the outside world." And more recently historian Thomas D. Clark, in *Kentucky: Land of Contrast*, published in 1968, observed: "No part of the Kentucky story is more meaningful than the fact that its people have

been isolated by geography, provincial at all times." So remote did the mountain culture remain that just a generation
ago Fannie Casseday Duncan mentions in *When Kentucky
Was Young* how a little boy who first saw windows in a
cabin ran to tell his grandma about "a house with specs
on."

A good place to get an introduction to eastern Kentucky's
history and ways of life is at the Kentucky Highlands Museum (Tu.–Sat., 10–4; Sun., 1–4, donation) at Ashland, the
region's largest city, in the state's northeastern corner. Installed in a box-like three-story stone mansion built in 1917
by the widow of coal entrepreneur John C. C. Mayo, considered the region's richest man, the museum houses displays
that trace the area's past and culture, while west of town
you'll find more regional items at a replica of the "Wee House
in the Woods" occupied by Jean Thomas, known as "the
Traipsin' Woman" for her horseback excursions through the
eastern Kentucky mountains as a court stenographer in the
early twentieth century. The Jean Thomas Museum (M.–F.,
8:30–3:30, free), installed in the "Wee House"—wee but solidly and authoritatively built of brick—contains displays of
Appalachian folk arts, with many of the items collected by
Thomas, once a script assistant in Hollywood for Cecil B.
DeMille, during her treks through the countryside. Early
in Ashland's history, industrial activity started up with iron
smelting at the Argillite Furnace in 1818. The name of the
1881 Ashland Coal and Iron Railway summarizes the development and exploitation of the area's natural resources, as
do such companies as Ashland Oil and Armco Steel, both
founded in 1920. Among the city center's century-old structures, some on the National Register, is the 1892 Crump
and Field Building, now the Ashland Area Art Gallery (Tu.–
Sat., 10–4; Sun., 1–4, free), which retains its old cast-iron
front and original interior. The 1931 Paramount Theater
(M.–F., 8:30–4:30, free), restored as a performing arts center,

survives as one of the few such movie houses built as model film palaces around the country by Paramount Pictures. At Ashland, hometown of country singers Naomi and Wynonna Judd, the Coalton County Jubilee offers country music and dancing every Saturday night (summer, 8–midnight; winter, 7–11; for information: 606-928-3110) while the Chimney Grove is a popular local eatery.

Many of the mountain country's lore, legends and dramas local author Jesse Stuart captured in his fifty-seven books, most of them set in the region, called "Greenwood" in the stories. Perhaps the best known is *Taps for Private Tussie,* the tale of an irrepressible back-country family who didn't cotton much to work but at the drop of a hat, or a fiddle bow, would throw a lively Saturday night hoe-down, even if it wasn't Saturday. Stuart was born, grew up and lived in an isolated corner of the countryside twenty miles north of Ashland, beyond Russell, site of one of the world's largest freight rail-switching yards. In April and September the Jesse Stuart Foundation operates half-day tours (by reservation only: 606-329-5233) conducted by members of the Stuart family, which take you to tiny Plum Grove and the adjacent W-Hollow, named for its distinctive shape, where you'll see the house the author occupied for more than forty years until his death in 1984. After Stuart married, his father told him, "Jesse, you have the bird but you don't have the cage," prompting the young author to renovate and enlarge the then-primitive log cabin where he settled with his bride. You'll also visit the so-called "Bunkhouse" where he wrote many of his books and the cemetery where Stuart's grave, marked by a five-foot tall granite tombstone inscribed with his writings, nestles on a knoll overlooking the Kentucky hills he loved. Nearby reposes his lifelong chum, happy-go-lucky Charles Cottle, whose Stuart-composed inscription, its cadence and simplicity typical of the novelist's writings, reads: "'One life to live' was my philosophy. The good earth was and is a friend to me. And as good as the earth are the Plum Grove friends I have, the last to bear me to this Plum Grove grave." If you're unable to take the tour, you can hike through parts of W-Hollow on trails through the Jesse Stuart State Nature Preserve, an area the writer gave to Kentucky to keep as he knew it over the long years he lived there.

Six miles west of the Stuart enclave lies Greenboro Lake State Resort Park (800-325-0083), whose Jesse Stuart Lodge commemorates the famous author. This is one of the fifteen state-operated resort parks, all with attractive, reasonably priced lodges and extensive recreational facilities, that provide pleasant places to stay around Kentucky. On highway 7 north of the park nearly two-hundred-foot long Bennett's Mill Bridge—built in 1855 and, never painted, naturally weathered—survives as one of only fourteen remaining Kentucky covered bridges (twelve publicly-owned and two private), remnants of the more than four hundred such spans that originally stood around the state. Nine miles south of the park off highway 1 remains another such relic, the 1880 Oldtown Covered Bridge, listed on the National Register, which crosses Little Sandy River. Carter Caves State Resort Park (800-325-0059)—where the Strange Music Weekend takes place in early February, with melodies played on vacuum cleaners, antique instruments and other noteworthy oddities—is another of those attractive Kentucky resort facilities, this one featuring tours of some of the area's more than twenty caverns, including Bat Cave (shown only during the summer) where thousands of bats spend the winter.

At Morehead, thirty miles west, Morehead State University houses three displays evoking the region's culture: the Appalachian Collection (M.–Th., 8–10; F., 8–6; Sat., 9–4:30; Sun., 2–10 during term time, off-term 8–4:30, free) with documents, Jesse Stuart-related items and other printed materials shown on the fifth floor of the Julian Carroll Library;

the Folk Art Collection (M.–F., 8:30–4; Sat. during term time, 8:30–4, free), with quilts, wood carvings and other hand-crafted objects; and the Stewart Moonlight School (M.–F. by appointment only: 606-783-2829), the one-room school where in 1895 Cora Wilson Stewart established a much-needed adult education program, a night school—"moonlight," not to be confused with the area's not uncommon "moonshine"—which the first year attracted twelve hundred education-hungry students, nearly ten times the number expected. The last week in June the university sponsors the annual Appalachian Celebration, featuring regional music, crafts and literature.

Mary Jane's Country Kitchen in Morehead serves down-home meals, while Appalachian House (606-784-5421) takes bed and breakfast guests. West of town the Minor E. Clark Fish Hatchery (M.–F., 7–3, free) contains more than a hundred ponds that yield up to two million fish a year, while the huge nearly seven-hundred-thousand-acre Daniel Boone National Forest—whose Cave Run Lake offers recreational facilities and excellent muskie fishing—includes the Shallow Flats Goose Viewing Area, where Canada geese dwell, and near Salt Lick the unusual, if not unique, Pioneer Weapons Area where hunters are restricted to such antiquated arms as the longbow, crossbow, flintlock rifle, percussion cap rifle and muzzle-loading shotgun (for information: 606-745-3100). Farther south in the Boone Forest lies Natural Bridge State Resort Park (800-325-1710), with such features as the sandstone arch bridge formation and the nearby Red River Gorge, a rugged area of streams, limestone cliffs and other natural elements, including scenic attractions like Gray's Arch, Sky Bridge and a thirty-mile Loop Drive that passes through an old logging-train tunnel and near a dozen or so sandstone arches.

Back to the east West Liberty hosts on the last weekend of September the annual Sorghum Festival, when little brown jugs of sorghum molasses sweeten the scene, and farther east at Louisa on the Big Sandy River U.S. Supreme Court Chief Justice Fred M. Vinson first saw the light of day—in a jail. The future jurist, congressman and Treasury secretary was born in 1890 behind bars in Louisa where his father ran the jail. Elected to Congress in 1923, Vinson served (except for two years) until 1938, then in 1946 Harry Truman appointed him Chief Justice, a position the Kentuckian held until his death in 1953. Another famous Washingtonian once frequented the region—George Washington himself, who in the eighteenth century surveyed some two thousand acres in and around the area Louisa now occupies. At Paintsville, south of Louisa, where Kathleen Distel (606-686-2291) takes bed and breakfast visitors, was born another famous Kentuckian, Brenda Gail Webb, better known as country singer Crystal Gayle; while at nearby Van Lear singer Loretta Lynn, a "coal miner's daughter," was born and reared in Butcher Hollow. At nearby Salyersville Bella Jo's restaurant serves what some say is the best pizza in Kentucky, while Sam an Tonio's at Prestonburg specializes in Tex-Mex fare popular with the locals.

Jenny Wiley State Resort Park commemorates the thirty-year-old pioneer woman held captive by Shawnee Indians for eleven months in 1789 and 1790. After killing two of her children, the Indians sold Jenny to a Cherokee chief who coveted her as a wife. The Indians tied the young woman to a tree with dried deer thongs but, Wiley indeed, she managed to work her way loose and rejoin her husband, a happy ending to the episode. The story is dramatized at the Jenny Wiley Theatre (mid-June–Aug., 606-886-9274), which also presents three other musicals over the summer at the amphitheater near the park's lodge. In early September the Wiley Park hosts the annual Kentucky Highlands Folk Festival, with singers, dancers, storytellers, poets, musicians and other Appalachian area performers.

At the eastern edge of adjacent Pike County, the nation's largest coal-producing area and Kentucky's biggest land mass (excluding water) county, Breaks Interstate Park spreads across the state line into Virginia. The visitor center includes exhibits on coal mining and natural history, while the sixteen-hundred-foot deep, five-mile long canyon, or "break," is the largest gorge east of the Mississippi. Rhododendron Lodge (lodge: 703-865-4414; cottages: 703-865-4413), nestled on the canyon rim, offers scenic views of the area, while at the amphitheater every Labor Day sounds forth the annual Autumn Gospel Song Festival, held for more than forty years. At Pikeville—where Country Kitchenette serves up tasty cornbread and other down-home eats—the Cut Thru facility, one of the largest earth-moving jobs ever attempted, involved the removal of 18,000,000 cubic yards of dirt to create a new route for the Livisa Fork River. Pikeville, along with nearby Hazard and Corbin, also in eastern Kentucky, for some reason rank first, second and third in the nation in per capita consumption of Pepsi Cola. It was in Pike County where the famous Hatfield and McCoy feud erupted, a legendary affair that is the most renowned of the many such family grudges. Similar clan clashes once typified the Kentucky Appalachian region. As John Fox, Jr., noted in *Blue-grass and Rhododendron: Out-doors in Old Kentucky,* "It is the feud that most sharply differentiates the Kentucky mountaineer from his fellows."

The Hatfield-McCoy conflict originated during the Civil War when the Hatfields of West Virginia sided with the Confederate cause and the Pike County McCoys supported the North. During the war family leader Anderson Hatfield, nicknamed "Devil Anse," was accused of killing Harmon McCoy, brother of family patriarch Randolph, in 1863. Fifteen years later Randolph McCoy accused Devil Anse's cousin of stealing a hog, a claim that led to a lawsuit to recover the porker. A jury comprised of six Hatfields and six McCoys decided seven to five in favor of "Hog Floyd," as Hatfield later became known, with Selkirk McCoy casting the deciding vote against his own kin. Without delay, the McCoys expelled Selkirk from the family, but the Hatfields immediately took him in. Two years later, in 1880, the feud heated up when Johnse, Devil Anse's oldest son, met and wooed Rose Anne McCoy, Randolph's daughter. Although Devil Anse refused to let the boy marry a member of the hated McCoys, later Johnse did wed a McCoy girl.

In 1882 flared up the most violent confrontation between the families when three McCoy boys, sons of Randolph, stabbed to death the brother of Devil Anse, who took revenge by executing the trio. Gunfire broke out across the Tug Fork branch of the Big Sandy River which demarks the Kentucky-West Virginia state line, a waterway that separated the territory each clan claimed. At least twenty people died before the shooting stopped when both sides ran out of ammunition. In the next decade revenge slayings frequently bloodied the landscape as each family retaliated, but the vendettas stopped about 1895. Finally, in 1914, Randolph McCoy died, followed to the grave seven years later by his mortal enemy, Devil Anse Hatfield. Up until as recently as 1984 a direct descendant of the original families survived— Jim McCoy, Randolph's oldest son, who died on February 11 that year at age ninety-nine. In 1976 McCoy, a coalminer, met with a member of the Hatfield family to officially end the feud, erecting a peace monument in the old McCoy cemetery at Blackberry Fork, near Hardy, Kentucky. As a final gesture of goodwill Jim McCoy requested that the Hatfield Funeral Home in Toler, Kentucky, handle the arrangements for his funeral and burial at the McCoy graveyard in Burnwell, a former coal camp six miles from Toler.

As you head west from Pike County the sinuous back roads on the way to Hindman pass through Pippa Passes, so named not for mountain passes but after Robert

Browning's poem about a simple mill girl who innocently affects the lives of people listening to her songs of joy as Pippa passes through a town one New Year's Day. It is passing strange that "Pippa Passes," as the English poet entitled his verse, came to designate a remote Kentucky settlement, but the name originated when Alice Lloyd of Boston solicited funds for a college in the village from New England Robert Browning Societies, which requested her to name the settlement after the poem. In 1922 Mrs. Lloyd established Caney Creek Junior College, renamed Alice Lloyd College in 1962 after her death and in 1980 expanded from a two-year to a four-year school. The campus also includes the June Buchanan School, a college preparatory school that offers accelerated classes. Hindman, just to the west, boasts another famous educational institution, the 1902 Settlement School, the nation's first such rural organization. In 1899 "Uncle" Solomon Everidge, a mountain country patriarch, asked for outside help to bring to the area educational opportunities. Some years after the Settlement began there on the forks of Troublesome Creek the public school system developed, and now the facility provides such supplementary services as music and art training, remedial tutorials, adult education and workshops on Appalachian life. The second weekend in September Hindman hosts the annual Gingerbread Festival, featuring the world's largest gingerbread man, based on the old-time practice of politicians who handed out the treats to influence voters. At Vest, a secluded hamlet on highway 1087 off 80, Quicksand Crafts (M.–F., 8–5, free), which serves as a training center to promote hand weaving, offers for sale placemats, bedspreads, tablecloths and other such items woven there.

A winding road west of Hindman takes you via Dwarf—named for a diminutive local, Jeremiah "Short Jerry" Combs—over to Hazard, from which in April 1915 departed the region's first complete coal train, thirty-three cars, an event that stimulated the development of the area's mines, whose output could henceforth be conveniently transported to markets far afield. A film and an underground tour of a simulated mine (M.–F., 8–3, free, by appointment only: 606-436-3101) at the Vocational Technical School will introduce you to the coal industry, honored the third weekend in September with the Black Gold Festival in Hazard, while the Hazard-Perry County Museum (M., Tu., Th., 10–12, 1–4; W. and Sat., 1–4, free) contains artifacts and photos that trace the area's history, which began in 1751 when land scout Christopher Guest discovered coal deposits in the region. Hazard's first non-coal-related firm, the Chazco Fixture Company, which produces retail display fixtures, parts bins and shelving, offers factory tours (606-439-1000), while Bailey's Restaurant is a popular local eatery.

Off to the west of Hazard lies Buckhorn Lake State Resort Park (800-325-0058), and in the nearby town of Buckhorn stands the outstanding log church, listed on the National Register, built as part of a mission established there in 1927 for the "Society of Soul Winners." Apparently more souls were lost than won, as the mission eventually closed, but a log gym that belonged to the Buckhorn School and the splendid sanctuary survive. Built of native white oak by local residents and students at the school, the church presents a pleasingly angular appearance, the neatly emplaced logs separated by thick layers of white chinking. The spacious beamed-ceiling interior, medieval in mood, recalls Scandinavian wooden churches, while the renovated pipe organ lends a hymnal piety.

Farther north, beyond the hamlet of Shoulderblade, lies Jackson, which in early September celebrates the annual Breathitt County Honey Festival, while the Old Country Inn there offers old fashioned home-cooked meals. Off to the west of Jackson at Beattyville—which in late October hosts the Wooly Worm Festival, with worm races and the

official Lee County Wooly Worm Survey, whose results the
locals furnish to the National Weather Service as a predictor
of winter weather—another down-home restaurant, the Purple Cow, features chicken and dumplings and home-baked
cream pies. Fourteen miles south of Jackson on Highway
15 Grass Roots Quilters (M.–F., 8–6, free), a cooperative,
offers handmade quilts for sale. Down at Viper, south of
Hazard, three elderly but spry sisters confect corn-shuck
dolls, a typical regional craft item, in their Slab Town Holler
residence.

At Hyden, off to the west of Hazard, operates the Frontier
Nursing Service (visits by appointment: 606-672-2913), established in 1925 by Mary Breckinridge, recalled at the annual Breckinridge Festival the first week in October, who
brought medical care to the area with her "horseback angels"
traveling nurses. The Service, whose chapel sports fifteenth-
century stained glass (definitely not a typical Kentucky craft
item), operates a School of Midwifery, the nation's oldest
such facility. At Whitesburg off to the east the Appalshop
(M.–F., 9–6, tours at 2, free) functions as a media center
that produces work on Appalachian history, culture and folk
ways. Local creative types gather at the cozy Courtyard Cafe
in town. Residents also patronize Frazier's Farmer Supply
to buy such animal products as Mane 'n Trail, a potion made
for horses but used by locals for hair care, and Bug Balon,
a cow udder ointment townspeople favor for chapped skin.
South of the Lilley Cornett Woods—which preserves an
original stand of unlogged forests like those that once covered eastern Kentucky's mountains and now serves as an
ecological research area (tours May 15–Aug. 15, 8–4:30;
April–mid-May and mid-Aug.–Oct., Sat. and Sun. only)—
lies Kingdom Come State Park, named for John Fox, Jr.'s,
book *The Little Shepherd of Kingdom Come,* the first of a
series of works the author wrote about Appalachian life and
the first American novel to sell more than a million copies.

Near Harlan, farther west, rises 4,145-foot Black Mountain, Kentucky's highest peak. The last week in June Harlan hosts the annual Poke Sallet Festival, featuring one of those curious mountain country customs the outside world often finds quaint and sometimes even strange. Poke salad ingredients include poke plant leaves, which supposedly possess healing powers. Only the poke bush's young shoots and leaves can be eaten, for the mature leaves and berries are poisonous. Bert Combs, elected governor of Kentucky in 1959, cooked up for fellow politicos, cronies, journalists, government workers and "smoke-filled room" types another unusual dish, a Varmint ("varmit") Supper featuring a menu, as John Ed Pearce described it in *Divide and Dissent: Kentucky Politics 1930–1963,* that included "Possum, raccoon, squirrel, groundhog, and even—some say—snake." Even more poisonous than the mature ramp and more biting than the Varmint Supper's wild meats are the snakes that on occasion kill members of some Appalachian area religious sects. In 1909 a man named George Hensley founded a snake-handling sect based on the biblical admonition in Mark 16:18, "They shall take up serpents." In the Tennessee and Kentucky hill country deaths from snake bites during a church ceremony eventually prompted both states to pass laws to ban serpent handling during religious services. As recently as 1989 a Harlan man who used a rattlesnake in a service at Ages Pentecostal Church died from the rattler's bite. It was labor unrest, rather than snake bites, that gave the name "Bloody Harlan" to the area, for back during the Depression, when the United Mine Workers vied with the left-wing National Miners Union to organize the coal workers, much blood reddened the coal country. On May 5, 1931, occurred a clash called the "Battle of Evarts," named for the town east of Harlan, and in June more violence caused casualties in the area. Novelist Theodore Dreiser arrived on the scene to publicize the miners' plight but he soon departed after facing a charge of being an accessory to adultery by a resident of Pineville, seat of Bell County to the west.

High above Pineville perches a huge boulder known as Chained Rock. When curious tourists used to ask locals what kept the rock from tumbling down into town, the residents would explain that a chain held the formation in place. After one sharp-eyed couple correctly observed that no chain existed, the townspeople formed the Chained Rock Club, whose members proceeded to obtain a one hundred-foot long chain they lugged up the mountain aided by mules and, toward the top, by Boy Scouts and Civilian Conservation Corps workers. Finally, on June 3, 1933, the workers attached the chain to the boulder, a device unnecessary to hold the rock but simply a cosmetic touch that now satisfies curious tourists. Nearby Pine Mountain State Resort Park (800-325-1712), one of those public areas offering attractive lodge and cottage accommodations, became Kentucky's first state park in 1924 when area citizens donated the land. Since the 1930s the Mountain Laurel Festival enlivens the park the last weekend in May when the laurel bursts into full bloom, while the third week in September the park hosts the Great American Dulcimer Convention, with concerts, crafts and folk dancing. South of Pineville, near the Tennessee state line, lies Middlesboro, where music also sounds forth at the mid-October Cumberland Mountain Fall Festival, which includes the Official State Banjo Playing Championship. Middlesboro, established in 1889 as a model English-type town and the nation's only city built within a meteor crater, boasts both the country's oldest golf course still in use, constructed in 1895 by English investors, and the Coal House, built in 1926 with forty tons of bituminous coal from the surrounding mines.

Just south of Middlesboro, where Kentucky, Tennessee and Virginia meet, gapes the Cumberland Gap, discovered in 1750 by Dr. Thomas Walker. In 1769 Daniel Boone passed through the Gap to enter Kentucky and later the opening served as the funnel through which poured thousands of settlers bound from the eastern states to the great open spaces of the West. At the Cumberland Gap National Historic Park survives part of the two hundred and eight-mile Wilderness Road, which ends at Fort Boonesborough to the north near Lexington, carved by Boone and his thirty axmen through the countryside in 1775. By 1783 some 12,000 settlers had reached Kentucky, most of them through the Cumberland Gap, whose history is recalled by exhibits at the visitor center (Memorial Day–Labor Day, 8–6; Sept.–May, 8–5). On Pinnacle Mountain an overlook affords views onto three states and the wooded hills that for a century and a half seemed to present an insurmountable barrier to westward expansion. Off the beaten track high in the hills nestles the unusual Hensley Settlement, a remote enclave in the park containing nearly thirty original log structures hand built around the turn of the century by the Hensley clan, who carved out their own little corner of the countryside far from electricity, horseless carriages and other such newfangled conveniences. A decade or so after Sherman Hensley, the last resident, left the isolated community, restoration began and now Hensley Settlement presents a frozen-in-time picture of an antiquated Appalachian back-country hamlet. To reach the enclave, which lies in Kentucky, requires a three and a half-mile hike up Cumberland Mountain on the Chadwell Gap Trail, which starts from Caylor, Virginia, or a five-mile trip by four-wheel-drive vehicle up Brownies Creek Road from Cubbage, Kentucky.

From Pineville back to the north you'll find handicraft co-ops at Red Bird Mission Crafts (M.–Sat., 9–4), specializing in rag rugs and corn-shuck flowers, seven miles north of Beverly to the northeast, and off to the west at Friendship Mountain Crafts (M.–Sat., 10–5; closed W. and July 15–Aug. 15), featuring willow furniture, located off highway

904 ten miles east of Williamsburg, named for Indian fighter William Whitley. Williamsburg serves as seat of McCreary County, the last Kentucky county organized and the only one formed in the twentieth century (1912), all of which lies within the Daniel Boone National Forest. Scenic and historic attractions abound in the vast forest. In the middle of the woodland Cumberland Falls State Resort Park (800-325-0063) perches just by the cascade that plunges sixty-eight feet into a boulder-filled gorge. Rafts (summer Tu.–Sun., hourly 12–4; weekends, Sept. and Oct.) carry you on a so-called Mist Ride out to the falls for a close-up look at the hundred and twenty-five-foot wide plunging waters, second in the East only to Niagara Falls. Under a full moon at Cumberland Falls glistens one of the world's only two moonbows (the other is in Africa), a phenomenon that recalls Kentucky writer James Lane Allen's comment that in the horse-happy state a nocturnal observer could "see in the halo around the moon a perfect celestial racetrack." Cumberland Outdoor Adventures (606-523-0629), on highway 90 just west of U.S. 25, runs float trips on the Cumberland River from May to October. A mile west of the park Tombstone Junction (Memorial Day–Labor Day, Tu.–Sun., 10–6, weekends May and Oct, adm.), a recreated Western frontier town, presents entertainment, mock Wild West gun fights, rides on a steam train and country music (Sun., 1 and 4:30).

Down in the southwestern corner of the Boone Forest stretches the Kentucky portion of Big South Fork National River and Recreation Area. Logging and coal mining once denuded and disfigured much of the Cumberland Plateau, but within the protected National Area—known because of its many gorges as "the Yellowstone of the East"—new vegetation blankets the countryside and covers many of the old logging camps, mining settlements and roads. At Stearns a reconstituted company store and a museum (mid-April–early Nov., W.–Sun., 10–6) portrays how a company-owned mining community functioned. The nearby abandoned town of Blue Heron, rebuilt and restored as the National Park Service's newest major attraction, presents a vivid picture of a company town where the firm owned all the structures, even the church, and paid miners in scrip spendable only at the company store.

Between Stearns and isolated Blue Heron, a coal town that operated for twenty-five years until 1963, runs the Big South Fork Scenic Railway (mid-April–early Nov., W.–Sun., from Stearns, 11 and 3; from Blue Heron, 1 and 5, 800-462-5664), a delightful open-sided excursion train that follows the scenic six-mile route once used to transport coal from the mines deep in the woodlands. Newly constructed trails and old logging roads—which take you to such areas as hundred and thirteen-foot Yahoo Falls, Kentucky's highest cascade, and abandoned settlements—criss-cross the Big South Fork Area, which offers four campgrounds, while rapids, falls and swift currents on the Big South Fork and its two main tributaries, the Clear Fork and the New River, present white-water challenges to rafters and kayakers. The more tranquil waters of Lake Cumberland encircle the General Burnside State Park, an island at the western edge of Boone National Forest near Burnside, where Kentucky's last stagecoach route, which operated until 1915, connected the town with Monticello to the south.

Back on the eastern edge of the forest lies Corbin, spreading across three counties. Near Corbin, where the family-owned Ramsey's Country Kitchen serves tasty meals, snakes Laurel River Lake, while in the city originated another "Lake"–Arthur Silverlake, who as Arthur Lake portrayed comic-strip character Dagwood Bumstead in more than two dozen movies. Although Louisville claims the home office of Kentucky Fried Chicken, Corbin boasts the Colonel Sanders Original Kentucky Fried Chicken Restaurant (7 a.m.–11 p.m., exhibits free), a still-functioning eatery with a museum and original furnishings, where the colonel cooked up his famous recipe in the 1940s.

In early October nearby Barbourville, where the first Civil War shot in Kentucky exploded, celebrates the annual Daniel Boone Festival, with Cherokee Indians from North Carolina, an arts and crafts fair and locals clad in pioneer attire. A few miles southwest of Barbourville is Himyar, briefly the state's fastest-growing town after its founding and thus named for Kentucky's then-fastest race horse. The nearby Thomas Walker State Historic Site (9 a.m.–9:30 p.m., free), which contains a replica of the state's first dwelling, recalls that in this area arrived the earliest explorers of the Kentucky territory. In 1750 Walker led a team into Kentucky to survey 800,000 acres for the Loyal Land Company of Charlottesville. On the way to the area the party reached a seemingly impassable wall of mountains, but off to the east the men glimpsed an opening noted by Walker in his journal entry for April 13, 1750, the first written description of the Cumberland Gap, so named by him for a military hero of the time, the English Duke of Cumberland: "The Mountain on the North Side of the Gap is very steep and rocky, but on the South side it is not so." After passing through the Gap Walker built in Kentucky a cabin to serve as a base camp while he explored the area. Over the next four months he covered two hundred miles in the rugged, hilly forests, a difficult terrain that disappointed Walker, who failed by only a short distance to discover the nearby lush bluegrass country. On Stinking Creek, in the northeastern part of Knox County off road 718, hides the Lend-A-Hand Center, a social services organization established in 1958, where rather quaint hand-built structures, including houses, barns and a barn-like red wooden church, dot the Center's secluded property.

More early Kentucky history lingers at London, to the north. At Levi Jackson State Park the Mountain Life Museum (May–mid-Sept., 9–5, adm.) includes pioneer-era artifacts exhibited in old log buildings reassembled on the site, while at the park's McHargue's Mill, an antique grist grinder on tree-lined Little Laurel River, you'll find what is perhaps the nation's largest collection of millstones. An old burial ground survives as the only remaining known graveyard along the Wilderness Road, the wagon route blazed in 1775 by Daniel Boone and his men. At the park you can hike portions of both Boone's Trace, which the frontiersman cut from Cumberland Gap to the Kentucky River, and the Wilderness Road, along which more than 200,000 pioneers entered Kentucky in the last quarter of the eighteenth century. Nearly century-old Sue Bennett College in London hosts an Appalachian Festival in early April, while Bernstadt, five miles west, offers homemade cheeses that recall the heritage of the village, founded in the early 1880s by Swiss settlers.

Farther west, on highway 1956, Rockcastle Adventures (606-864-9407) and Renegade Rick's Rockcastle River Runners (800-541-RAFT) outfit canoe, raft and kayak trips on the pristine Rockcastle, which flows through the heart of Daniel Boone National Forest. The waterway is one of nine rivers—all except the Green, in Mammoth Cave National Park, located in the state's eastern region—selected by Kentucky under 1972 legislation as a "wild river" (for a complete list and other information: 502-564-3410). The portions of the nine waterways so designated—among them the Cumberland, the Red, the Big and the Little South Fork and nearby Rock Creek—comprise a total of one hundred and fourteen miles of unspoiled streams, a tiny fraction of the 54,000 miles of rivers that flow through the state. Along these scenic "wild rivers," where Mother Nature survives untouched except by the whims of Father Time, you can see Kentucky as it appeared centuries ago before Thomas Walker discovered the Cumberland Gap, before Daniel Boone cut the Wilderness Road and before the pioneers began to arrive.

Central Kentucky

The center of central Kentucky, the Inner Bluegrass area
around Lexington, contrasts greatly with the mountainous,
wooded eastern part of the state. Here stretches rolling
meadowland partitioned by neat stone walls or elegant white
or black wooden fences. Perhaps it could be said that the
Bluegrass country was America's first national park, for so
lush and game-rich was the region that apparently the Indians
agreed to preserve it as "the Happy Hunting Ground... An
unwritten agreement seems to have existed among the various tribes that this land would never be settled," suggests
George Morgan Chinn in *Kentucky: Settlement and Statehood
1750–1800.* So enticing was the land, as fetchingly described
by James Lane Allen in *The Blue-Grass Region of Kentucky*—in
early spring "spreads a verdure so soft in fold and fine in
texture, so entrancing by its freshness and fertility, that it
looks like a deep lying, thick-matted emerald moss"—that
the white men couldn't resist rushing in where the Indians
had feared to tread. Thanks to the rich mineral content of
the limestone-based soil, the land's bluegrass—so called because of the blue hue that colors the fields when the plant's
bluish-purple buds bloom in the spring—proved the ideal
food to create strong, ivory-smooth bones and sinewy mus-
cles in thoroughbreds. In 1806, when politician and states-

man Henry Clay of Lexington bought "Buzzard," foaled in England, for $5,500, the sport and business of horses began to develop in the Bluegrass country. Up until the 1870s breeding and racing remained for the most part a sideline enjoyed by politicians and Kentucky colonels, but then newly rich Easterners, barons of industry, began to take a fancy to the "sport of kings" and the thoroughbred industry took off like—well, like "Aristides," who on May 17, 1875, won the first Kentucky Derby.

On a passing visit to the Bluegrass country it's impossible to gain more than a superficial "once-around-the-track" impression of the horse culture, for the thoroughbred community remains in many ways a world apart and a closed society, one with its own customs and traditions and a language almost like a foreign tongue: A "horse" denotes not simply a horse but a male over four years old, with those under four called colts; all thoroughbreds celebrate the same birthday, January 1, regardless of when they were born; names of thoroughbreds can't exceed a total of eighteen letters and spaces, and names can be reused only after sixteen years; "bug boy" doesn't describe an employee of an exterminator but an apprentice jockey, so called because an asterisk ("bug") stands by the rider's name in a race program. As Thomas D. Clark observed in *Kentucky: Land of Contrast:* "The horse world of the Bluegrass lives apart. The course of its life is guided by its own folk mores, an unorthodox kind of economics, and its peculiar needs are served as they arise."

The justifiably renowned Kentucky Horse Park (9–5, adm.) offers an introduction to this exotic world. You'll find there not only exhibits—such as the International Museum of the Horse, the American Saddle Horse Museum, antique horse-drawn vehicles and the Calumet Farms trophy collection—but also live horseflesh on a working farm. Because of a series of horse-barn fires in 1968, most of the farms around Lexington closed their gates to outsiders, but the tourist office in town (606-233-1221) can advise you which estates still receive visitors. In any event, you can see the famous horse farms from afar by driving out such roads as Paris Pike, Frankfort Pike and other routes that fan out north of Lexington. At the Red Mill Harness Track free morning workouts take place in June, September and November through March while horse sales are conducted year-round at Fasig-Tipton and Keeneland, the latter a nonprofit organization established in 1936 on part of a 1783 land grant from Virginia governor Patrick Henry. At Keeneland—which boasts a splendid stone wall that bankrupted John Oliver Keene several times during its construction, which lasted some twenty years—morning workouts take place from 6 to 10 a.m. April through October. The Keeneland Library (M.–F., 8:30–4:30, during meets 9–11 a.m.) offers a treasure trove of equine printed material, and The Track Kitchen, a cafeteria-style eatery, provides a good place to rub shoulders with owners, trainers, track officials and other members of the thoroughbred community.

Other attractions in Lexington, one of America's few major cities not on a waterway, include such show houses as Ashland (May 1–Oct. 31, M.–Sat., 9:30–4:30; Sun., 1–4:30; Nov. 1–April 30, M.–Sat., 10–4; Sun., 1–4, adm.), home for nearly fifty years of U.S. senator, Secretary of State and three-time Presidential candidate Henry Clay; the Mary Todd Lincoln House (April–Dec. 15, T.–Sat., 10–4, adm.), where Abraham Lincoln's future wife lived from ages six to twenty-one when, in 1839, she moved to her sister's home in Springfield, Illinois, there to meet and marry Lincoln; Waveland State Historic Site (March–Dec., Tu.–Sat., 10–4; Sun., 2–5, adm.), an 1847 mansion built by Daniel Boone's grandnephew, typical of dwellings occupied by Kentucky's gentry before the Civil War; Loudoun House (Tu.–F., 12–4; Sat. and Sun., 1–4, free), listed on the National

Register; and the Hunt-Morgan House (Tu.–Sat., 10–4; Sun., 2–5, adm.), ancestral home of John Hunt Morgan, leader of the Civil War "Morgan's Raiders" and called by Southerners "Thunderbolt of the Confederacy"—Northerners dubbed him "King of the Horse Thieves"—and of his nephew, Thomas Hunt Morgan, 1933 winner of the Nobel Prize for medicine for his findings on the role of chromosomes in heredity. The Hunt-Morgan House stands in Gratz Park, a delightful leafy enclave surrounded by late eighteenth-century and nineteenth-century houses, churches and other historic structures. Rebecca Gratz, sister of hemp magnate Benjamin Gratz, once a resident of the park named for him, was a friend of author Washington Irving, whose description of her to Sir Walter Scott inspired the character Rebecca York in Scott's novel *Ivanhoe*. At one end of the park rises the law office of Henry Clay, who reposes in the spacious park-like 1848 Lexington Cemetery on West Main Street, along with such other notables as John Hunt Morgan, U.S. Vice-president John Breckinridge and University of Kentucky basketball coach Adolph Rupp, who over forty-two years gained eight hundred and seventy-nine wins against only one hundred and ninety losses. The university campus includes an art museum (Tu.–Sun., 12–5, free) and the Museum of Anthropology (M.–F., 8–4:30, free), with exhibits on the culture and history of Kentucky, while adjacent to Gratz Park lies venerable Transylvania University, established in 1780 and home of the first medical and law schools west of the Alleghenies. "Transy's" 1833 Old Morrison Hall houses not only the school's administrative offices but also the remains of the brilliant but eccentric Rafinesque, linguist, botanist, explorer and sometime professor at the school. On the third floor of Old Morrison, once described as "the purest, simplest piece of architecture in the state of Kentucky," is a collection of antique scientific instruments. Another local museum, the Headley-Whitney (April–Oct., Tu.–F., 10–5;

Sat. and Sun., 12–5, Nov.–March, closed M. and Tu., adm.) out on the edge of town houses a widely diversified collection of curious objects, among them ostrich-egg candlesticks, miniature jewel-encrusted figures, Chinese robes with "forbidden stitches" (tiny stitches outlawed because seamstresses went blind sewing them) and a shell grotto. For less artifice and more natural scenes the Raven Run Sanctuary (W.–Sun., free) six miles from town encompasses a lovely corner of the countryside along the Kentucky River. Rokeby Hall (606-252-2368) and Joe and Ruth Fitzpatrick (606-255-4152) offer bed and breakfast accommodations in Lexington.

The Lexington-Frankfort area, with its universities, state capital, cultural attractions and attractive outlying towns, recalls the Raleigh-Durham region in North Carolina. Halfway between Frankfort, seat of government, and Lexington lies descriptively named Midway, listed on the National Register, the first town in Kentucky established by a railroad (1832). Still today, a century and a half later, train tracks run through the middle of Midway along Railroad Street, lined with antique shops, restaurants and other retail establishments installed in late nineteenth-century buildings, among them the distinctive c. 1882 Iron Horse Gallery sporting a cast-iron facade, a conical turret and an oddly angular clock tower. Elsewhere around town D. Lehman and Sons, established in 1854, survives as the settlement's oldest business still in operation; the mid-nineteenth century Porter House recalls the turn-of-the-century hotel of that name where the "Porterhouse" cut of steak originated; and Midway College, successor to the c. 1846 Kentucky Female Orphan School, still functions as Kentucky's only women's college, one of the degrees it offers being in equine management. Holly Hill Inn (606-846-4732) serves meals and takes overnight bed and breakfast guests. Not far away, where South Elkhorn Creek crosses U.S. highway 421, stands Weisenberger Mill, operated by the same family since 1862 and believed to be the state's oldest commercial water-powered mill.

At nearby Georgetown rises a new (1988) Toyota factory, a sign of the times, and the old (1853) Ward Hall mansion (May–Oct., M.–Sat., 9:30–5; Sun., 1–5, adm.), a relic of former times. The spacious antique-filled red brick and white-columned pile stands on land once owned by Colonel Robert Johnson, whose three sons served in the U.S. Congress at the same time in the 1820s. At Georgetown College, the oldest Baptist school west of the Alleghenies (1829), stands the 1840 Greek Revival-style Giddings Hall, built of handmade bricks by students and faculty, while another venerable structure, the restored late eighteenth-century home of pioneer Elijah Craig, now a restaurant called Elijah's, recalls the early-day hero who in 1789 made the first bourbon whiskey (an honor also claimed by Virginia's Berkeley Plantation on the James River), a potion so named as the area then formed part of Bourbon County, Virginia. It is thought that Craig created the liquor in the corner of town where Royal Springs still gushes forth seven and a half million gallons of water a day when he stored white grain liquor in white oak kegs burned within to cleanse the wood and eliminate splinters. The oak gave the whiskey its characteristic color and bouquet, and before long demand for the mellow liquor created along the region's creeks a series of stills, increasing from five hundred in 1792, the year Kentucky became a state, to two thousand twenty years later. In *Bluegrass Craftsman,* the delightful reminiscences of paper maker Ebenzer Stedman, the Georgetown area resident observes, "In the Citty & County of Fayette thare ware in 1811 one Hundred & thirty nine Distilleries. Think of that!" Georgetown, which the last weekend of September hosts the Festival of the Horse, boasts the state's largest antique mall, with nearly a hundred dealers installed in four buildings on West Main Street. You'll also find antiques for sale at the 1820

Breckinridge House (502-863-3163), which takes bed and breakfast guests, as does the Log Cabin (502-863-3514).

Other area towns, such as Nonesuch and Versailles, also abound with antique shops. Near Versailles, on one of the many rustic roads that criss-cross the Bluegrass countryside, spreads Woodburn Farm, established in 1790 as the nation's first horsebreeding farm. Not far from town you'll find the Bluegrass Railroad Museum (Sat., 9–6; Sun., 12–6, adm.), with displays and an eleven-mile long train excursion past horse and tobacco farms (Sat., 10, 1, 4; Sun., 1, 4, adm.). In Versailles the 1911 Louisville and Nashville depot now houses Nostalgia Station Toy and Train Museum (June–Dec., W.–Sat., 10–5; Sun., 1–5; Jan–May, weekends only, adm.), and the former 1819 Big Spring Church now serves as the Woodford County Historical Society Museum (M.–F., 9–4), with displays on the area's equine culture. The 1812 Pisgah Church off to the east, established in 1784, was the first Presbyterian sanctuary west of the Alleghenies, while south of town stands the c. 1797 Jack Jouett House (April–Oct., Tu. and Sat., 10–4; Sun., 2–4:30, donation), home of "the Paul Revere of the South," who in 1781, when a Virginia resident, rode forty miles to Monticello to warn Thomas Jefferson and then to the Swan Tavern in Charlottesville to warn Patrick Henry and other leaders that the redcoats, British troops, were coming. Jouett moved the following year to Kentucky, where he became one of the state's first importers of thoroughbreds. In Versailles, where Queen Elizabeth II of England attended Sunday services at St. John's Episcopal Church during one of her private horse-connected visits to the area, Sills Inn (606-873-4478) provides bed and breakfast accommodations. Over at Lawrenceburg the Wild Turkey Distillery offers unusually complete tours (M.–F., 8:30–2:30, free) of the bourbon-producing operation, including visits to the laboratory, the fermenting rooms, the warehouses and other areas.

Frankfort is one of the nation's smallest state capitals (population: 27,000) and one of the most attractive. The town
nestles by the Kentucky River, spanned by the 1890 metal
"Singing Bridge" that hums beneath automobile tires, below
green hills that surround the quiet, laid-back settlement.
Apart from the rather overbearing twenty-four-story Capital
Plaza, a boxy office building in a complex designed by
Edward Durrell Stone that towers above the low-rise low-
key city, most of the town's structures remain close to the
ground, lending Frankfort a pleasant, intimate feeling. As
usual with seats of government—and Frankfort boasts the
city and county governments as well as that for Kentucky—
the town contains a number of state-sponsored museums
and official buildings, among them the Capitol (M.–F.,
8–4:30; Sat., 9–4; Sun., 1–5, free), with statues of such notables as Kentuckians Abe Lincoln, Jefferson Davis and Henry
Clay, murals depicting Daniel Boone's adventures in Kentucky, and a collection of dolls representing the state's First
Ladies. Also, the adjacent Floral Clock, perched in a tilted
position, embellished with 20,000 blooms; the ponderous
native limestone National Register-listed Governor's Mansion (Tu. and Th., 9–11, free), modeled rather undemocrat-
ically after Marie Antoinette's Petit Trianon in Versailles
(France, not Kentucky); the Old Governor's Mansion (Tu.
and Th., 1:30–3:30 free), occupied by the chief executive
from 1798 to 1914 and now the lieutenant governor's residence; the Kentucky Military History Museum (M.–Sat.,
8–5, free); the 1830 Old State Capitol (M.–Sat., 9–4; Sun.,
1–5, free), set in an attractive park-like area—with a statue
of William Goebel, one of the few American governors ever
assassinated (1900), inscribed with his last words "Tell my
friends to be brave and fearless and loyal to the great common
people"—and containing within one of the nation's two self-
supporting circular stone stairways (City Hall in New York
houses the other one); and the Kentucky History Museum

(same hours as the Old Capitol, free), its central corridor lined with oil paintings of the state's governors, featuring such displays as "Old Yellow," a moonshine still confiscated in 1950, and a room devoted to "Bluegrass, belles and bourbon: Kentucky in the nation's mythology." Along one side of Broadway opposite the Old State Capitol stand century-old buildings housing antique dealers, craft shops and Poor Richard's Books, whose second floor contains shelves crammed with dust-covered tomes, but you can't tell a book by its cover so bookworms will enjoy burrowing, browsing and, inevitably, buying, thus making "poor Richard" richer.

Show houses in Frankfort include Liberty Hall (Tu.–Sat., 10–4; Sun., 2–4, closed Jan. and Feb., adm.), a handsome brick dwelling built in 1796 by John Brown, one of Kentucky's first two U.S. Senators; Orlando Brown House (same hours as Liberty Hall, adm.), constructed by Senator Brown in 1836 for his son Orlando, owner and editor of *The Frankfort Commonwealth;* the National Register-listed Zeigler House (private), Kentucky's only Frank Lloyd Wright-designed structure; and the c. 1820 Federal-style Vest-Lindsay House (M.–F., 9–4, free), boyhood home of George Graham Vest, U.S. senator from Missouri for twenty-five years but best remembered for the few-minute oration, "Tribute to a Dog," he delivered to a jury hearing a dog-shooting case in Warrensburg, Missouri. In the area, known as "Corner of Celebrities," stand nineteenth-century dwellings where nine U.S. senators, six congressmen, two U.S. supreme court justices, two cabinet officers, nine governors and three admirals once lived, as well as the house of John Bibb, who developed Bibb lettuce in his garden.

In a wooded setting overlooking Frankfort lies the supposed grave of Daniel Boone, who died and was buried in Missouri in 1820 and later perhaps removed to Kentucky, although some say the remains of another person, rather than Boone's, were in fact transferred, so both states now claim his grave. Nearby century-old Kentucky State University, which displays the slogan "Onward and Upward" to inspire the campus community, houses archives on the state's black heritage as well as the butterfly and moth collection assembled by Egypt's King Farouk; while Luscher's Farm Relics (Memorial Day–Labor Day, M.–Sat., 10–4:30; Sun., 1–4:30, adm.) outside town contains a display of early agricultural equipment and implements, including a goat- or dog-powered churn. The nearby Ancient Age Distillery (M.–F., 8:30–3, free) offers tours, including a stop at the tiny One-Barrel Warehouse which holds the two-millionth barrel—and only the two-millionth barrel—of bourbon produced by the firm, in 1953, since the repeal of Prohibition twenty years earlier. An easy way to sample Kentucky bourbon is with the tangy, tasty Whiskey Cremes confectioned by Rebecca-Ruth, the Frankfort candy company installed in a cozy white frame house in town decorated with a red and white striped awning. Ten years after two schoolteachers named Rebecca Gooch and Ruth Hanly founded the firm in 1919 a woman with the improbably redundant name of Fanny Rump lent money to enable the business to survive. In 1936 Ruth devised the idea of adding bourbon to her candy, thus creating those sweetly sinister confections that so tempt those cursed with a sweet tooth. Until 1986 government regulations prohibited the shipment of liquor-laced sweets across state lines, but now Rebecca-Ruth, which offers tours of its kitchen, sends its products to customers around the country. Bed and breakfast choices in Frankfort include the 1832 Taylor-Compton House (open, March–Dec. 15, 502-227-4368), Bixler's (502-223-7008) and Olde Kantucke (502-227-7389).

Across the North Fork of Elkhorn Creek on highway 1262 near Switzer, northeast of Frankfort, stretches the c. 1855 Switzer Covered Bridge, listed on the National Register, while Shelbyville, west of the capital, is a pleasant old town filled with antique shops, including the museum-like Wakefield-Scearce Galleries (M.–Sat., 9–5) specializing in silver and English furniture, installed in the former Science Hill School, a private girls' academy from 1825 to 1939, listed on the National Register. The school library now houses a bookstore while the cafeteria serves as the Georgian Room Restaurant. The downtown area and much of residential Main Street in Shelbyville, home of Martha Layne Collins, Kentucky's first woman governor, are also listed on the Register. On highway 60 west of town the Claudia Sanders Dinner House, until recently run by Colonel Sanders's widow, who lives in Shelbyville, occupies the former Kentucky Fried Chicken headquarters, filled with Colonel-related memorabilia, and at nearby Simpsonville the Register-listed nearly two-century-old Old Stone Inn, a former stagecoach stop, serves Southern-style meals. Simpsonville's Whitney M. Young, Jr., Job Corps Center, formerly Lincoln Institute, a boarding school for blacks run by the elder Young, recalls the one-time head of the National Urban League who grew up in the area. You'll find another pleasant eatery not far away at Jeffersontown, near Louisville, where the Unicorn Tea Room serves lunch as well as afternoon tea (M.–F., 3–4).

Louisville, a pleasant Ohio River city, presents an open, spacious appearance, thanks in part to the town's more than 9,000 acres of parkland, a system designed a century ago by Frederick Law Olmstead, father of landscape architecture and of New York City's Central Park. At Louisville originated cheeseburgers, first served at Kaelin's Restaurant in 1934; flavored chewing gum, invented about 1880; the first coin boxes for streetcars; the first public display of electricity, by Thomas Alva Edison in 1883; and the song "Happy Birthday to You," written in 1893 as "Good Morning to You" by two sisters, Patty and Mildred Hill. Lying closer to such cities as Toronto, Philadelphia and Buffalo than to New Orleans, Louisville is not an especially Southern town, although it does host that quintessential event of Dixie—the mint julep-irrigated Kentucky Derby. At Churchill Downs the Kentucky Derby Museum, open (9–5, adm.) to display the history of "every Derby every day but Derby day," recalls "the most exciting two minutes in sports" with artifacts, memorabilia and a film presentation (every hour on the half hour, 9:30–4:30) on an encircling screen that forms a complete oval as if mimicking a racetrack. Once asked what the Derby meant to Churchill Downs, Kentucky humorist Irvin Cobb, a native of Paducah, replied, "If I could explan that I'd have a larnyx of spun silver and the tongue of an anointed angel."

Louisville also boasts a selection of unusual and even unique museums, among them the John Conti Coffee Museum (M.–F., 9–5, free); the Colonel Harland Sanders Museum (M.–Th., 8–4:45; F., 8–3, free) at the home office of Kentucky Fried Chicken, a latter-day antebellum-style mansion; the World Boxing Hall of Fame (M.–Th., 5–9; Sat., 12–3, adm.); the Sons of the American Revolution Historical Museum (M.–F., 9–4, free), installed in the organization's national headquarters; the Eisenberg Museum of Egyptian and Near Eastern Antiquities and the Nicol Museum of Biblical Archeology (M.–F., 8–11; Sat., 8–5, free) at the Southern Baptist Seminary, where you'll also find the archives of evangelist Billy Graham and whose School of Church Music presents recitals (student performers, M. and F. afternoons; faculty and guest artists, Tu., 8 p.m., free; for information: 502-897-4115); and at Bellarmine College the manuscripts, notebooks, letters and other materials relating to Thomas Merton, the famous monk who lived at Gethsemane Monastery south of Bardstown (for access to the Merton archives: 502-452-8187).

Other museums in town include the Water Tower Art Association (M.–F., 9–5; Sun 12–4, free), installed in the

splendid 1861 Grecian temple-like building over which towers the standpipe in the style of a Roman triumphal column;
the Kentucky Railway Museum (June–Aug., Tu.–Sat., 10–5;
Sun., 12:30–5:30; May, Sept., Oct., weekends only, adm.),
featuring old equipment and a train excursion; Park Place
Museum (M.–Sat., 12–6), a large collection of antique clothing and artifacts; the J. B. Speed Art Museum (Tu.–Sat.,
10–4; Sun., 1–5, adm.), the state's largest and oldest (1927)
such gallery, with Old Masters and contemporary works;
the Museum of Science and Industry (M.–Th., 9–5; F. and
Sat., 9–9; Sun., 12–5, adm.); and the Portland Museum
(M.–F., 10–4:30, adm.), with a terrain model of the Falls
of Ohio, the rapids that led to the city's founding in 1778
by George Rogers Clark. When Clark descended the Ohio
to launch his Revolutionary War campaign in the British-
held western (now Middle West) territory he, like his predecessors on the river, avoided the rapids, formed by an
outcropping of limestone rocks, by a portage around the
falls. The soldiers' families who remained in the area proceeded to establish the settlement that became Louisville.
A public platform near 26th Street and Northwestern Parkway affords a view of the McAlpine Locks and Dam that
now permits navigation of the once intimidating Falls.
Moored in the Ohio, closer to downtown, floats the new
(summer 1988) Louisville Falls Fountain, a computer-
controlled installation with forty-one jets, colored lights and
other enhancements that combine to create a series of water
displays (May–Dec., 8 a.m.–midnight) culminating in a
fleur-de-lis formation to honor Louis XVI, whose name
Louisville commemorates. Facing the Ohio on the Indiana
side of the river looms the forty-foot Colgate Palmolive
clock, second in size in the U.S. only to the timepiece at
the Colgate factory in New Jersey across from Manhattan.

One of Louisville's most attractive features is its architecture. This ranges from the trendy, glossy twenty-seven-story

Humana Building (1985), occupied by the health care company—embellished with granite of five colors, marble, a waterfall, a pair of two-millennium-old Roman statues, a bronze sculpture by Giacometti, and other enhancements— to old houses and nineteenth-century commercial structures sporting more cast-iron facades than anywhere outside New York City. Many of those buildings lie between Sixth and Tenth Streets on West Main, along which stand renovated antique structures that house the Kentucky Art and Craft Gallery (M.–Sat., 10–4, free) with a tastefully chosen selection of the state's handmade artifacts on display and on sale, and the Actors Theater of Louisville (performances, Sept.– June, 502-584-1205), in an 1837 National Register-listed bank building, which hosts every March the well-known Humana Festival of New American Plays. Some fifty nineteenth-century houses fill the Old Louisville neighborhood in and around the area between Third and Sixth Streets clustered near Central Park and James Court less than a mile south of Broadway. Nearby stands the Filson Club, organized in 1884 as a historical society, which houses paintings, archives, books and a museum (club, M.–F., 9–5; museum, M.–F., 9–4; Sat., 9–12, free).

Other historic areas and houses include Bakery Square, a restored bakery now a shopping center located in the old Butchertown area east of downtown; the nearby Thomas Edison House (Sat., 10–2, or Tu.–Th. by appointment: 502-585-5247, free), listed on the National Register, where the nineteen-year-old Edison lived in a rented room while working as a telegrapher at Western Union, which fired him for conducting experiments while on the job; Register-listed Farmington (M.–Sat., 10–4:30; Sun., 1:30–4:30, free), built in 1810 after a plan by Thomas Jefferson, with a hidden stairway, a posted thank-you note from 1841 guest Abraham Lincoln and other such touches; Register-listed Locust Grove (same hours as Farmington), a late eighteenth-century plantation house where George Rogers Clark lived and where he received Meriwether Lewis and his brother William Clark after their famous early nineteenth-century Lewis and Clark Expedition up the Missouri River. For natural history the Kentucky Botanical Garden (M., W., Th., 11–3; Sat. and Sun., 12:30–4:30, adm.) and the Louisville Zoo (May–Aug., 10–5; Sept.–April, Tu.–Sun., 10–4, adm.) offer plants and animals, and the Cave Hill Cemetery (8–4:45, free), last resting place of George Rogers Clark, Colonel Harland Sanders and other notables, also includes an arboretum, while at the Zachary Taylor National Cemetery (8–5, free) reposes the nation's twelfth President.

Factory tours in Louisville include the American Printing House for the Blind (M.–F., 10 a.m. and 2 p.m., free), the world's largest producer of Braille and talking books; the Bourbon stockyards (by reservation: 502-584-7211), with livestock auctions and a museum; Hadley Pottery (M.–F., 2 p.m., free) and Louisville Stoneware (M.–F., 10:30 a.m. and 2:30 p.m., free), two producers of well-known dinner and ornamental ware; the Philip Morris cigarette manufacturing center (M.–F. on the hour, 8–4, except 2, free), one of the company's three such plants in the South open for tours (the others are at Richmond, Virginia and at Concord in Cabarrus County, North Carolina); and, to see the famous Louisville Slugger baseball bats crafted, the Hillerich & Bradsby Company's Slugger Park factory, no longer in Louisville but just across the river at Jeffersonville, Indiana (summer, M.–F., 10 a.m. and 2 p.m., closed late June–mid-July; for tour schedules in spring, fall and winter: 812-288-6611). For more relaxed views of downtown Louisville you can take evening tours in a horse-drawn carriage (502-581-0100) or ride on the Toonerville Trolley (also claimed by St. Mary's, Georgia), a bus reproduction of an old-time streetcar named for the nationally syndicated cartoon strip by Louisville native Fontaine Fox. The old fashioned 1914 stern-

wheeler "Belle of Louisville" (502-625-BELL), listed on the
National Register, and the sleekly modern "Star of Louisville" (502-589-7827) offer sightseeing tours and dinner
cruises on the Ohio. Two restored turn-of-the-century hostelries in Louisville are the Brown Hotel (502-583-1234), now
a Hilton, home of the Hot Brown turkey and cheese sand-
wich, the place Herbert Hoover was staying when the stock
market crashed in October 1929, and the splendid 1905
Seelbach (800-626-2032), a showplace embellished with an
ornate mural-decorated lobby and other enhancements sufficiently plush for Tom Buchanan to marry Daisy there "with
more pomp and circumstance than Louisville ever knew before," so F. Scott Fitzgerald described the event in *The Great
Gatsby*.

The area north of Lexington and northeast of Louisville
contains some scattered attractions worth seeing if you're
heading to or from Cincinnati. Just across the river from
that Ohio city lies Covington, whose German heritage appears at the Main Strasse Village, with antique shops and
restaurants in an old-country enclave that stretches across
thirty blocks in West Covington. Two blocks west of the
Goose Girl statue that serves as the neighborhood's symbol
rises the hundred-foot high Bell Tower (spring–Dec., caril-
lon concerts on the hour, 9–dusk) that contains a "glocken-
spiel," an animated clock with twenty-one figures that
portray the Pied Piper of Hamelin tale. Although Covington
once enjoyed, or suffered from, a reputation as a sin city
for Cincinnati, the party town also has a religious side, with
churches such as the Gothic-style Basilica of the Assumption
(M.–F., 8–4:30; Sat. and Sun., 8–6:30, free), brightened by
murals and more than eighty richly hued windows, including
the world's largest stained glass window; Mother of God,
topped by two-hundred-foot high towers and also boasting
murals and stained glass; the American Gothic-style 1865
First United Methodist; the six-by-nine-foot native field-

stone Monte Casino Chapel, at Thomas More College, built in 1910 by Benedictine monks and believed to be the world's smallest house of worship; and also the Garden of Hope (daylight hours, Easter–Nov., free), a replica of Jesus' tomb set in a garden with biblical plants.

The 1867 John Roebling-designed suspension bridge, a prototype of his Brooklyn Bridge, connects Cincinnati with Kentucky which, oddly enough, begins not at mid-river but on the north bank. When Ohio became a state in 1803 it sued Kentucky to get the boundary moved south to the middle of the Ohio rather than the low-water mark at the north bank as claimed by Kentucky when it entered the Union in 1792. Only in the 1980s was the case, perhaps the longest in the nation's history, decided in favor of Kentucky. In the spring of 1990 River Center, the first phase of a ten-year commercial development along two miles of the Covington waterfront, opened just west of the Roebling bridge. The Landing, the retail and entertainment complex there, occupies a football field-sized barge. In the Riverside National Historic District stands the c. 1815 home of Daniel C. Beard, 322 East 3rd Street, founder of the Boy Scouts of America; while Mansion Hill in neighboring Newport, where an unusual all stone steeple tops 1871 St. Paul's Episcopal, encompasses a Victorian-era neighborhood with century-old houses.

Back in Covington, in spacious and hilly Devou Park stands a mansion that houses the Behringer-Crawford Museum (Feb.–Nov., Tu.–Sat., 10–5; Sun., 1–5, adm.), with cultural and natural history exhibits, while the Railway Museum (May–Oct., Sat. and Sun., 1–4, adm.) includes more than fifty examples of rolling stock, among them a 1906 business car, a 1920s sleeper and a post office car. Out in the suburb of Fort Mitchell the Oldenberg Brewery and Entertainment Complex (11–10 for brewery tours, entertainment Tu.–Sun. evenings) churns out Premium Verum

(German-style pilsner) and other brews and presents in the Great Hall musical entertainments and food. Festivities in the outdoor Bier Garten (seasonal) and an English-type pub also enliven things in the huge brick building, which houses what's supposedly the world's largest collection of brewing memorabilia. The nearby Vent Haven Museum (May–Sept., M.–F., 9–6 by appointment only: 606-341-0461, adm.) houses the world's only collection of ventriloquist dummies and related items, many assembled by a fellow with the rather dramatic name William Shakespeare Berger. Among the five hundred or so figures from twenty countries on display are those once used by Edgar Bergen, mouthpiece for Charley McCarthy and Mortimer Snerd. For four days at the end of June every year a gathering of dummies takes place at the International Ventriloquist Convention—featuring a dealers' room with figures and memorabilia for sale, workshops and performances—held in the Drawbridge Inn next to the Oldenberg Complex. BB Riverboats (606-261-8500) and Barleycorn's Riverboats (606-581-0300) at Ludlow just west of Covington offer cruises on the Ohio, while the 1850s Amos Shinkle Townhouse (606-431-2118), owned by a former mayor of Covington, takes bed and breakfast guests.

East and west of Covington the erratic Ohio pushes Kentucky's boundary to the south. Off to the east, five miles southeast of Falmouth, the town of Bachelor's Rest takes its name from the single men who used to sun themselves in front of the local store. Up on the river perches the town of Augusta, which survives as a delightful nineteenth-century village, much of it listed on the National Register. Along Riverside Drive stands a row of old houses—the Piedmont Art Gallery (Th.–Sun., 12–5) occupies one of them—fronted by neat lawns that stretch down to the Ohio, crossed here by the Augusta Ferry (7 a.m.–dusk), a two-century-old (c. 1798) operation and one of only two ferries still operating on the river. So picturesque is Augusta that the village played the role of St. Louis in the 1880s in the TV mini-series *Centennial,* and it also served as the setting for a film of *Huckleberry Finn,* of an even earlier era. In town lived Senator Thornton F. Marshall, who cast the deciding vote to keep Kentucky in the Union—one of the four slave states, along with Delaware, Maryland and Missouri, that didn't join the Confederacy—as well as Dr. Joseph S. Tomlinson, first president of Augusta College, the world's first Methodist college (1822) and uncle of Stephen Foster, who some believe was inspired by Augusta's down-home atmosphere to write "My Old Kentucky Home." White Hall, built in the early 1800s, is the ancestral home of World War II chief of staff, and later Secretary of State, George C. Marshall. The c. 1796 Beehive Tavern serves meals, and Lamplighter Inn (606-756-2603) and Schweier's Inn (606-756-2135) offer bed and breakfast in the village. At Brooksville stands the handsome 1915 Bracken County Courthouse, and near Wellsburg on highway 1159 survives 1824 Walcott Bridge, the state's oldest covered span.

Farther east on the river lies Maysville, a late eighteenth-century river port town where some fifty buildings downtown, an area listed on the National Register, recall the days when the settlement served as a trade, cultural and educational center. The historic structures include Register-listed "Phillips' Folly," started in 1825 by William B. Phillips, who ran out of money but eventually completed the job in 1828 with funds he supposedly won at gambling; c. 1850 Mechanics Row, whose frilly iron grill work reflects the New Orleans influence brought about by river trade; the red brick house on Rosemary Clooney Street where the singer grew up; and Rand-Richeson Academy, an old boys' school whose graduates included Ulysses S. Grant, who lived in town with his uncle Peter Grant, interred in the old graveyard behind the nearby library. Dioramas and other displays at the Mason

County Museum (Tu.–Sat., 10–4, free) recount the area's history. With eighteen auction warehouses, Maysville functions as the world's second-largest burley tobacco market (after Lexington, with twenty-eight warehouses), which operates from late November to February (visitors welcome; for information: 606-564-5534). In 1864 a farmer in Brown County, Ohio discovered the mild type of burley, an odd-hued white or lemon yellow leaf, and within a few years the new tobacco replaced older, harsher varieties. About one third of an American-made cigarette consists of burley, now grown on 200,000 acres throughout Kentucky, which produces about a fifth of the nation's tobacco, a crop accounting for a quarter of the state's cash farm receipts.

In 1848 Mason County moved its seat of government to Maysville from Washington, which stopped growing and remained the tiny frontier-type town it is today, little changed from a century and a half ago. Back then travelers heading south from the Ohio River would pause there after their day-long struggle up the steep hill on the Buffalo Trace, the oldest trail in the North American interior, formed by buffalo heading to area salt licks. The town began in 1785 on land owned by the colorful Simon Kenton, a well-known Indian fighter, explorer, frontier adventurer and scout for Daniel Boone and George Rogers Clark. Through the years much history unfolded in the settlement, which boasted the first public waterworks (twenty-two wells) and the first post office west of the Alleghenies, along with three hemp walks used to weave ropes. For about a century, beginning in 1775, hemp featured as one of Kentucky's leading crops, with seventy tons produced in 1840, the peak year. The Bluegrass area supplied most of the nation's hemp, used to make twine, rope, gunny sacks, bags and rigging for American merchant ships. Foreign competition, especially jute from the Philippines, eliminated the industry, but when World War II interrupted overseas supplies production in Kentucky resumed for a time. Perhaps the plant still grows there, less openly now, for hemp is none other than marijuana. At stately Federal Hill (1800), perched on a rise just by the village, John Marshall was born, one of fifteen children, U.S. Supreme Court Chief Justice from 1801 to 1835. In 1833 Harriet Beecher (Stowe) visited Washington where she witnessed a slave auction that supposedly helped inspire her famous antislavery novel, *Uncle Tom's Cabin*. Brodrick's Tavern, established in 1794, still caters to travelers, serving lunch and dinner to visitors to Washington, listed on the National Register, a splendid relic that provides a picturesque picture out of the past.

In this part of Kentucky covered bridges abound. Near Dover stands the 1835 Lee's Creek Bridge; over by Tollesboro to the east survives the 1870 National Register-listed Cabin Creek Bridge; and down in Fleming County you'll find three covered bridges, all Register-listed: Hillsboro (c. 1870), on highway 111, tucked into the countryside by the verdant Appalachian foothills; 1867 Ringos Mill, on highway 158, built to serve a grist mill; and Goddard, on highway 32, with a delightful view of a country church through the c. 1820 (reconstructed in 1968) span, while down at Alhambra off highway 165 in Robertson County remains the Register-listed 1874 Johnson Creek Bridge. At nearby Blue Licks Battlefield State Park (9–5, free) a museum contains bones of the prehistoric animals that trekked to the area for the salt springs. In 1778 Indians captured Daniel Boone at the salt deposits, whose son died in an August 19, 1782, encounter with Indians and British renegades at Blue Licks, an engagement known as the last battle of the Revolutionary War since it took place nearly a year after Cornwallis's surrender at Yorktown. At Mt. Olivet stands the 1872 Register-listed courthouse, the only original such building still in use in Kentucky, which serves Robertson County, the state's least populous and second smallest in size, with one hundred and one square miles.

At Flemingsburg, where The Depot and Sorrell's both serve up tasty country cooking, Civil War soldier of fortune James J. Andrews plotted the "Great Train Robbery" exploit in the Fleming Hotel. At the nearby Elizaville Cemetery stands a monument to Marine Corps Private First Class Franklin Sousley, who helped raise the flag at Iwo Jima, a famous feat frozen on film in a renowned World War II photo. South of the lovely little village of Sherburne, Boyd's Family Restaurant offers home-style meals at Owingsville, as does Garrett's over at Carlisle, from where Daniel Boone, seeking "more elbow room," left his last Kentucky home in 1798 to move on west to Missouri. You'll find other typical small-town eateries in North Middletown, at Skillman House, and at Family Restaurant in Camargo near Mt. Sterling, where Maplewood (606-498-4025 or 498-5383) offers bed and breakfast and which in mid-October hosts Court Days, with trading and swapping in the nineteenth-century tradition.

On the way to Paris, back to the west, you'll find on highway 537 eight miles east of town the 1791 Cane Ridge Meeting House (March–Dec., 9–5:30; Sun., from 1:30, free), supposedly the nation's largest one-room log structure, birthplace in 1804 of the Disciples of Christ Church, founded during the great religious revival period of that era. A museum on the grounds recalls the early history of Cane Ridge, so named by Daniel Boone for the extensive area cane brakes. In Paris, whose native son Garrett Morgan invented the tricolor traffic light system, the 1788 Duncan Tavern and the adjacent c. 1801 Anne Duncan House (Tu.–Sat., 10–12, 1–4; Sun., 1:30–4, adm.) contain twenty rooms that hold a rich collection of pre-1820 antiques and a historical library with such treasures as the original manuscript of Kentucky author

John Fox, Jr.'s 1903 novel *The Little Shepherd of Kingdom Come*. The Tavern serves meals to groups by advance reservation (606-987-1788). Murals in the dome of the Bourbon County Courthouse depict the region through the seasons, while the town's Paris Winery, the first such establishment licensed in the state in the twentieth century, features Kentucky wine. It must be a brave vintner to produce wine in Bourbon County, but there it is. Around the county spread Bluegrass horse farms, some open to visitors by previous arrangement (606-987-3205), and up near Colville you'll find a National Register-listed covered bridge built in 1877. At nearby Cynthiana, where the 3M plant turns out the nation's entire supply of "post-it" pads, Blanke's is a popular local restaurant, and National Register-listed Broadwell Acres (606-234-4255) puts up bed and breakfast guests in restored slave quarters. At Cynthiana, established in 1793 and named for two daughters of early settler Robert Harrison, stand the original c. 1790 log courthouse and its stately white brick 1853 successor, with archives that include papers of Henry Clay, who practiced law in the town at the turn of the century.

Returning now to the Covington area, you'll find a few attractions off to the west toward Louisville. On the Ohio River perches the hamlet of Rabbit Hash, one of the dozens of quaintly or graphically named settlements that dot the Kentucky map—among them Dot as well as Black Gnat and Bugtussle, Chevrolet, Co-operative, Summer Shade, Subtle, Mummie, Oddville, Pride and Humble, Tobacco, Love and Never Divide, Million, Goodluck, Awe, Meeting and Place, Full, Felt, Farmers, Quality, Paradise and Hell-for-Certain, Open Fire, Add, Dimple and Butt, Bow and Arrow, Dreaming, OK, I've Said and many others in case you "Needmore." With all of forty inhabitants, Rabbit Hash serves as the metropolis of this stretch of the Ohio—mainly, however, by default, as no other settlements exist in the area. Settled in 1789, the village changed its name from Carlton, often confused with Carrollton downriver, to the definitely more distinctive Rabbit Hash, which commemorates the popular local dish served when flooding forced bunnies from their warrens along the Ohio up into the hills where residents could easily catch the animals. After the flood of 1978 nearly washed the hamlet away, local Lowell Scott bought the settlement, comprised of a few log cabins, the Iron Works gift shop that sells quilts and carvings made in the area, a blacksmith shop and such supplementary structures as a woodshed, chicken coop and two outhouses. At the 1831 general store, where the hoi-polloi of Rabbit Hash gather to swap yarns, if not to buy yarn and other staples, boxes filled with such necessities as pork chitterlings, Penetro Nose Drops and Putnam Fadeless Dyes litter the shelves. The most recent excitement to enliven old Rabbit Hash, once described as "just around the bend and back a few years," is the "Buckeye" ferryboat that started in 1983 (Memorial Day–Labor Day, weekends, and holidays, 10–6, cars not carried) to connect the village with Rising Sun, Indiana, across the Ohio.

Off to the east of Rabbit Hash lies Big Bone Lick State Park where indoor and outdoor displays at the Museum (April–Oct., 8–8; for off-season schedule: 800-255-PARK, adm.) recall the prehistoric animals who died mired in the swampland where they came to get salt. In 1807 President Jefferson sent an expedition to collect a sample of the huge bones at Big Bone Lick, discovered in 1729 and still the world's most extensive ice-age animal graveyard. Farther downriver at the confluence of the Ohio and the Kentucky lies Carrollton. Some three hundred and fifty nineteenth-century commercial and residential structures that form the town's National Historic District recall the days in the 1830s when Carrollton rivaled Fort Washington (Cincinnati) and Corn Island (Louisville) as a river port and tobacco-

producing center. In Carrollton, where eight tobacco warehouses still operate to store and auction burley, stand the
solidly built century-old brick county courthouse, through
which sailed boats during the 1937 flood, and the boxy 1880
stone jail, used until the late 1960s and now a museum.
The 1790 Masterson House (Memorial Day–Labor Day,
Sun., 2–5, free) east of town and the 1825 General William
Butler Home, residence of the commander of U.S. forces
in Mexico in 1848 and nominee for U.S. Vice-president,
survive from the area's early days. The newly renovated
(1989) Butler Home stands in the hilly General Butler State
Resort Park (800-325-0078), which offers an attractive lodge
and splendid views of the river-veined lowlands and, from
mid-December to mid-March, skiing. The Carrollton Inn
provides a pleasant place to eat and the P. T. Baker House
(606-525-7088 weekdays, 502-732-4210 weekends) offers bed
and breakfast, while over at Owenton Fannie's Country
Kitchen serves home-cooked-style meals. Owen County
gained the name "Sweet Owen" back in 1851 when the area
gave to John C. Breckinridge enough votes to win an upset
victory for Congress. In 1857 he became the youngest Vice-
president (thirty-six) in the nation's history, under James
Buchanan. Later Confederate Secretary of War, Breckinridge
served his full term as Vice-president even though he was
elected to the U.S. Senate in 1859. At Lockport to the south,
Kathleen Hayes (502-947-5435) takes bed and breakfast
guests.

On a small farm near Port Royal in Henry County resides
farmer, environmentalist and writer Wendell Berry, whose
essays, novels and poems argue for a more natural way of
life, rooted in the land and devoted to the essentials of existence rather than to consumer values. Preaching what he
practices, Berry farms his hillside land without chemical fer-
tilizers and uses draft horses instead of modern-day machinery. La Grange, where the Robin's Nest is a popular local

eatery, was the hometown of famous early film director D. W. Griffith. In rural Trimble County you'll find an 1837 stone jail at Bedford, the county seat, and at Milton, one of Kentucky's oldest towns, established in 1789, a bridge takes you across the Ohio to Madison, Indiana, a truly delightful town filled with antique architecture and well worth a detour.

Returning now to Lexington, the hub of the Bluegrass country, the itinerary south takes you first to Winchester, whose National Register-listed Main Street survives as one of the state's few intact nineteenth-century commercial districts. The oldest of the buildings, many sporting elaborate trim and other architectural details, is the former clothing store (1830s) on the corner of South Main across from the courthouse. Residential relics fill Thomson Subdivision, established along Boone Avenue in 1888, while at the 1813 Clark Mansion (May–Sept., Sun., 2–4, free), known as "Holly Road," lived Kentucky Governor James Clark. The new (late 1988) Pioneer Telephone Museum (M., 1–4, or by appointment: 606-745-5400, free) in the phone company building at 203 Forest Avenue contains antique equipment dating from as early as the 1870s, including a turn-of-the-century directory promoting the newfangled convenience with the slogan: "The mail is quick, the telegraph is quicker, but the telephone is instantaneous." Back in the 1920s G. L. Wainscott held one of the nation's first contests to name a product, with the winning entry "Ale-8-One" ("a late one") chosen to designate the locally produced soft drink which has dominated the market since the product's debut in 1926. Winchester's High Court Inn serves tasty meals, as does Mildred's Diner over at Stanton to the east not far from Pilot Knob State Nature Preserve, which includes a seven hundred and thirty-foot high rise, the Cumberland Plateau's tallest point. This is believed to be the spot from where in 1775 Daniel Boone first gazed upon the lush Bluegrass country, an area one of his companions, Felix Walker, described in idyllic terms: "A new sky and strange earth seemed to be presented to our view. So rich a soil we had never seen before. . . . It appeared that nature, in the profusion of her bounty, had spread a feast for all that lives, both for the animal and rational world."

At a restored grist mill eight miles west of Winchester the well-known Iroquois Hunt Club meets, whose hunters, attired in traditional black hats and red coats, ride to hounds across the countryside between October and March, while six miles south of Winchester stands the late eighteenth-century Old Stone Church, the oldest active sanctuary west of the Alleghenies, where Daniel Boone and his family worshiped. At nearby Fort Boonesborough State Park (April–Oct., 9–5:30; closed M. and Tu. after Labor Day, adm.) stands a reproduction of the log stockade built by Boone's band in mid-1775 there on the Kentucky River, which the "Shawnee Chief" plies in the summer (May–Sept., 1:30, 3 and 4:30). Not far away rises the red brick white-frilled 1799 White Hall mansion, a state historic site (April–Oct., 9–5:30; closed M. and Tu. after Labor Day, adm.), home of Cassius Clay, not the contemporary boxer but a famous fiery and fierce opponent of slavery. No timid soul or false hero with feet of clay, Clay dueled with a political opponent, took a bowie knife to a man who tried to shoot him and whacked his hickory cane over the head of a rival for the hand of his beloved, Mary Jane Warfield, whom Clay married and brought to White Hall. Lincoln appointed Clay minister to Russia, where the Kentuckian became involved with Anna Petroff, a member of the Imperial Ballet, and a decade later a mysterious veiled woman deposited on the doorstep of White Hall a ten-year-old boy, claiming the child was Clay's Russian-born son. This ended his marriage to Mary Jane, but later, at age eighty-four, Clay married a sharecropper's fifteen-year-old daughter, who after three years left the old man. The firebrand died in 1903 at age ninety-three, going out with a bang by shooting while reclining in his deathbed a fly that annoyed him by buzzing around the ceiling. The room still bears the bullet hole blasted by Clay's shot. From early June to mid-August *The Lion of White Hall* (Th., F., Sat., 8:15 p.m., 606-623-0759), based on Clay's *Memoirs*, dramatizes the "Lion's" life. By Valley View on the Kentucky River near White Hall operates a toll car-ferry, established in the 1780s and believed to be the state's oldest continuous business. The James B. Beam Distilling Company (described below) near Bardstown is supposedly Kentucky's oldest still-existing manufacturing business (1795).

At Richmond stands a group of historic old houses, many of them along West Main Street, including the residence of two-time governor James B. McCreary, who reposes in the Richmond Cemetery next to the grave of his pet parrot, memorialized with a small tombstone. Around the cemetery runs an ornamental iron fence that once enclosed the many-columned Greek Revival-style 1850 courthouse, listed on the National Register, where Union prisoners were confined during the Civil War. On Lancaster Street stand other old houses as well as Eastern Kentucky University, whose Hummel Planetarium, the nation's tenth-largest, hosts stargazing sessions and space shows (for information: 606-622-1547). Ma Kelly's, a homey cafe in Richmond, cooks tasty food, including homemade fruit cobblers and corn muffins you can take hot from the stove. Nine miles east of Richmond, hometown of Western scout Kit Carson, lies Waco, the hamlet where Bybee Pottery (M.–F., 8–12, 12:30–4:30; Sat., 9–12, free) has operated since about 1809. The fifth generation of the Cornelison family now runs the firm, which every spring digs more than a hundred tons of clay, considered among the purest in the world, to use in crafting some 125,000 pieces of pottery annually.

Kentucky's most craft-rich town, however, is Berea to

the south, where more than thirty craft workshops, galleries and stores display the attractive wares turned out by residents of the lovely mountaintop enclave, home of Berea College. In addition to the school's Log House Sales Room (M.–Sat., 8–5), the showplace for furniture and site of the Wallace Nutting furniture collection, and the gift shop at student-staffed Boone Tavern Hotel (606-986-9358), a tastefully understated place with a pleasant and peaceful ambiance, you'll find in the village such other craft establishments as Churchill Weavers, with tours of the loom house (M.–F., 9–12, 1–4, free), the Appalachian Quilt Shop, woodworker Warren A. May who carves furniture and dulcimers, the Upstairs Gallery, with the work of more than a hundred area artists and craftsmen, and many others. (There's also a branch of the Berea College crafts shop at the Galt House Hotel in Louisville.) None of the fifteen-hundred Berea College students, 80 percent of them from Appalachia, pays tuition but each works at least ten hours a week to earn his or her way. Tours of the college—established in 1855 by, among others, the redoubtable Cassius Clay—leave from the Boone Tavern lobby (summer, M.–Sat., 9, 10:30, 1:30, 3; during the school year, M.–F., 9 and 2; Sat., 9, free) and proceed to the craft workshops and other areas on the attractive tree-shaded campus, where the Appalachia Museum (M.–Sat., 9–6; Sun., 1–6, adm.) contains exhibits on the region's culture, including an offbeat display on the impact of the advent of mail-order houses on the previously self-sufficient mountain country settlements, which in the old days improvised to make such items as door hinges from worn horseshoes, a banjo from a fruitcake tin and a bird cage from a gourd. Although Berea College seems to emphasize arts and crafts, in the 1920s William J. Hutchins, brother of University of Chicago president Robert Hutchins, developed the school's liberal arts curriculum. A festive community, Berea hosts craft festivals in May, July and October, a Mountain Folk

Festival in April, the McLain Family Band Festival in August, the Celebration of Traditional Music Festival in October, and in November and December a month-long Christmas celebration (for specific dates: 606-986-2540). Holly Tree (606-986-2804) in Berea offers bed and breakfast accommodations.

Off to the west of Berea on Fisherford Road near Lancaster, where the Academy Inn restaurant occupies historic old quarters, stands the birth house of Carrie Nation, the hatchet-wielding temperance crusader. Born to a plantation-owning family there in 1846, she moved to Missouri after the Civil War and in 1900, unleashing her hatchet attack for the first time, Carrie demolished the saloon in the Carey Hotel in Wichita, Kansas, a feat that earned her seven weeks in jail, one of the thirty times she spent during her smashingly successful career behind bars—or perhaps better expressed, because of her anti-alcohol crusade, in the hoosegow. Almost six feet tall and weighing in at a hundred and seventy-five pounds, Carrie carried out a lesser-known anti-tobacco campaign—a bold endeavor for someone from Kentucky—that led her to snatch cigarettes from people's mouths. Nation died in 1911 and she reposes at Belton, Missouri, near Kansas City, beneath a monument that reads: "She hath done what she could."

To the south stands the c. 1780s William Whitley House (June–Aug., 9–5; Sept.–May, Tu.–Sun., 9–5, adm.), built as a residence and a fortress against Indians by Kentucky pioneer Whitley, who received there such notables as Daniel Boone and George Rogers Clark. Rifle ports, a hidden stairway, two-foot thick walls and other defensive features recall the dwelling's use as a haven against the Indians. In 1785 Whitley laid out on the property the nation's first circular racetrack, directing that the horses run counter-clockwise in defiance of the British practice, thus establishing the tradition still used at all American tracks. Farther south, near

Mt. Vernon—Jean's Restaurant there (motto: "Nothing instant but the service") serves up memorable fresh blackberry and peach cobbler and other delicious dishes—lies Renfro Valley, where the Seafood House also offers homestyle meals. In November 1939 local John Lair started off the new Renfro Valley music radio show with the announcement that the performance was "the first and only barn dance on the air presented by the actual residents of an actual community." Now, more than half a century later, music still sounds forth from the village, with the Barn Dance (March–Nov., Sat., 7:30 and 9:30, adm.), the Jamboree (March–Nov., Sat 7:30 and 9:30, adm.), the Gatherin' (Sun., 8:30 a.m., free) and the Friday Night Barn Dance (April–Nov., F., 8, adm.). In town you'll also find an old-time country store, craft and antique shops, a c. 1860 one-room school and a small museum. In early August the All-Night Gospel Sing and in early November the annual Fiddlers' Convention enliven Renfro Valley. For information and tickets to the shows in the village: 606-256-2664. More festivities unfold the last full week in September at Liberty off to the west—the Village Restaurant there features country cooking—with the annual Casey County Apple Festival, which boasts the world's largest apple pie, filled with eighty bushels of the fruit and weighing 3,000 pounds, served starting at noon on Saturday.

To the south Lake Cumberland, with more than 63,000 acres and nearly 1,300 miles of shoreline, snakes over the Kentucky landscape. One of the world's largest man-made bodies of water, the lake was formed in 1950 by Wolf Creek Dam across the Cumberland River, Kentucky's only major stream that flows in a southerly direction rather than north. Recreational opportunities abound at such facilities as the Jamestown Resort and Marina (502-343-LAKE, outside Kentucky 800-922-7008), the southeast's largest floating marina, with some six hundred boat slips as well as excursions on "The Jamestown Queen" paddlewheeler, and the Lake Cum-

Russell Cave, Bridgeport, Alabama

*Lake Guntersville,
Alabama*

Boll Weevil Monument,
Enterprize, Alabama

U.S.S. Alabama, Mobile, Alabama

Moundville Archaeological Park, Alabama

Pope's Tavern, Florence, Alabama

Sturdivant Hall,
Selma, Alabama

State Capitol, Jackson,
Mississippi

Cypress Swamp, Mississippi

B.B. King, blues singer, Mississippi

Ruins of Windsor, Port Gibson, Mississippi

Mississippi River

D'Evereux, Natchez, Mississippi

Chalmette, New Orleans, Louisiana

The Myrtles, St. Francisville, Louisiana

The Myrtles, St. Francisville, Louisiana

Lincoln Family Farm, Knob Creek, Kentucky

Shaker Village of Pleasant Hill, Harrodsburg, Kentucky

Ashland, Henry Clay's Estate, Lexington, Kentucky

Tennessee Valley Railroad Museum, Chattanooga, Tennessee

Carnton, Franklin, Tennessee

Old State House, Little Rock, Arkansas

Eureka Springs, Arkansas

Edwardian Inn, Helena, Arkansas

Cossatot River, Arkansas

Ozark Folk Center, Mountain View, Arkansas

Boyhood Home of Bill Clinton, Arkansas

Governor's Mansion, Little Rock, Arkansas

berland State Resort Park, offering two lodges and cottages (800-325-1709) and the new (1989) indoor swimming pool, with a view onto the lake. At the lake's northeastern branch, or tentacle, near descriptively named Touristville, Mill Springs boasts a mill with the world's largest overshot water-wheel as well as a splendid view of Lake Cumberland.

Southwest of the lake near Burkesville, where Thomas Lincoln, father of the President, served as constable in 1802 and 1804, Martin Beatty accidentally discovered oil in 1829 when drilling for salt water, thus creating the nation's first oil well. The petroleum, which a Burkesville physician bot-tled and sold for medicinal purposes, spilled out onto the Cumberland River and burned for some days. Farther west, near Tompkinsville, which hosts the annual Watermelon Fes-tival in early September featuring "Rolley-Hole" marble con-tests, a game unique to the area, runs Kentucky's only state-owned ferry, established about 1948 (the state bought it twenty years later) to connect two sections of highway 214. The nearby Old Mulkey Meetinghouse (9–5, free), a state historic site, includes the 1804 sanctuary, the state's oldest log religious building, whose twelve corners suppos-edly represent the Apostles and three doors, the Trinity. Rev-olutionary War soldiers and Daniel Boone's sister, Hannah, repose in the graveyard.

The hamlet of Bugtussle on highway 87 down by the Ten-nessee line takes its name from the itinerant wheat threshers who slept in barns where the workers had to tussle with the insects that infested the hay beds. Subtle, Eighty Eight, Wisdom, Mud Lick, Marrowbone and Breeding designate some of the area's other hamlets, and at Summer Shade, almost a poem of a name, headquarters White's Lazy W Rodeo, which travels around the state putting on Wild West—or Wild South—rodeos. At Sulphur Well to the North, Porter's restaurant specializes in country ham, a Ken-tucky delicacy. The Country Inn at Columbia, which in early

September hosts the Adair County Bell Pepper Festival, features country cooking as well, while September also brings to Greensburg, to the north, the annual Cow Day Festival, complete with Annie, a life-sized fiberglass cow that visitors can milk to obtain flavored drinks. At Greensburg, established in 1794, stands the native limestone 1803 courthouse, used until 1932, believed to be the oldest west of the Alleghenies, built by Thomas "Old Stonehammer" Metcalfe, later Kentucky governor and U.S. senator. Not far away stretches Green River Lake, completed in June 1969 as southern Kentucky's newest major water recreation facility.

The route southwest out of Lexington takes you to a series of historic towns. In Nicholasville stands the rather funky but delightful courthouse, pocked with round and arched windows and topped by an elaborate tower. Other late nineteenth-century structures embellish the historic district that encompasses the downtown area. In the lobby of the Sargent & Greenleaf Company south of town you'll find the world's largest lock collection (M.–F., 8–5, free), with security devices dating back to 1303, including keys and locks from Buckingham Palace, Diamond Jim Brady's safe and a padlock used by the Crusaders. The last weekend of September Nicholasville, where the Country Kettle dishes out delicious meals in attractively decorated premises, hosts the Jessamine Jamboree, featuring the outdoor show *Jessamine,* which dramatizes the history of the area, named for its many jessamine flowers. A seventy-five-mile stretch of grey limestone cliffs, seen from viewing points along U.S. highways 68 and 27 and state road 29, form the attractive Kentucky River Palisades, while the 1877 High Bridge, the highest span over a navigable stream in the nation, began the era of modern bridge building in America.

Near High Bridge and beyond Wilmore, a town of craft and antiques shops and home of Asbury Theological Seminary, one of the nation's five largest such schools, lies well-named Pleasant Hill, the lovely Shaker village virtually unchanged from the days of its beginnings a century ago. Like the Moravian Old Salem enclave in Winston-Salem, North Carolina, Pleasant Hill presents a delightful picture out of the past that vividly recalls a vanished era. Twenty-seven restored original buildings of the communal religious settlement, antique Shaker furniture and artifacts designed with the group's characteristic restrained beauty, impeccably produced crafts and reproductions of early Shaker artifacts, beautiful grounds, complete tranquility, and delicious meals—featuring the famous rind-filled lemon pie and a menu that reads "We Make Thee Kindly Welcome"—at the handsome Trustees' Office Inn all combine to provide an outstanding experience to visitors. Pleasant Hill is the nation's only historic village offering overnight accommodations in original buildings, available in more than seventy guest rooms (for room and meal reservations: 606-734-5411) installed in the simply furnished but quite comfortable quarters colony members once occupied. At one time the settlement numbered among the largest of the eighteen communal villages established in the late eighteenth and nineteenth centuries by the United Society of Believers in Christ's Second Appearing, called Shakers for their practice of trembling with emotion during services. Although a few members of the once six thousand or so-strong sect survive at Canterbury, New Hampshire, and Sabbathday Lake, Maine, no Shakers live at Pleasant Hill, now run by a nonprofit educational corporation. Through the year the settlement hosts various special activities, including September Harvest Weekends, while the "Dixie Belle" excursion boat plies the waters of the Kentucky River and on summer weekends horse-drawn wagons roll through Pleasant Hill's pleasant land. Two miles from Shakertown, Canaan Land Farm Bed and Breakfast (606-734-3984) offers accommodations in a National Register-listed 1795 country house where you can

participate hands-on in milking goats, birthing lambs (mid–
Nov. through Dec) and other such rural chores or delights.

More history haunts Harrodsburg, Kentucky's first permanent settlement (1774), where the Old Fort Harrod Park
(9–5:30, winter closed M., adm.) contains a full-scale reproduction of the outpost built by James Harrod. A pioneer
cemetery, the cabin where Abraham Lincoln's parents married, the Mansion Museum, and the McIntosh Gun Collection recall the early days when Daniel Boone, George Rogers
Clark, who planned at the fort his famous Northwest Territory Revolutionary War campaign, and other frontiersmen
frequented the area, an era dramatized in *The Legend of Daniel
Boone* (mid-June–late Aug., M.–Sat., 8:30 p.m., 606-734-
3346) presented in the outdoor theater, while the mid-August
Pioneer Days Festival in town also evokes the old days. At
The Gathering Place Marti Williamson presents folk songs
and tales as she plays the dulcimer and Autoharp (mid-June–
Aug., Tu.–Sat., adm.), and at Old Harrodsburg Pottery
you'll find a tearoom and gift shop installed in a restored
original building. Morgan Row, built in 1807, includes four
brick structures that comprise the state's oldest rowhouses,
while the National Register-listed Beaumont Inn (606-734-
3381) serves meals and takes bed and breakfast guests in a
century-and-a-half-old mansion.

At Danville the Constitution Square State Historic Site
(9–5, free) reproduces a log courthouse, the state's first Presbyterian church, a meetinghouse and jail which, along with
the original post office, supposedly the first west of the
Alleghenies—although Washington, Kentucky, also claims
this honor—serve to commemorate the early importance
of the town where the state's founding fathers adopted
Kentucky's first constitution in 1792. Along the square
stands Fisher's Row, early nineteenth-century brick structures that house the Historical Society Museum, an art gallery and exhibits on the history of 1819 Centre College,

whose attractive small campus nestles in the center of Danville, home also to the 1823 Kentucky School for the Deaf, the nation's first such publicly funded institution. Grayson's Tavern in the square once hosted political meetings and now houses changing exhibits, while the McDowell House (M.–Sat., 10–12, 1–4; Sun., 2–4; closed M., Nov.–Feb., adm.) commemorates pioneer surgeon Ephraim McDowell, who on Christmas day 1809 performed the first successful removal of an ovarian tumor. The Pioneer Playhouse outside Danville, where the movie *Raintree County* was filmed, presents five shows a year at Kentucky's oldest outdoor theater (mid-June–late Aug., 606-236-2747), located in a reproduction of an eighteenth-century village. Back in that era Danville resident Thomas Johnson, Jr., issued *The Kentucky Miscellany,* the first book of poems published in the state (1796). Known as the "Drunken Poet of Danville," Johnson, who died of alcoholism, complained in his poem "Danville" about "Accursed Danville, vile, detested spot, / Where knaves inhabit, and where fools resort," an attack that recalls John M. Harney's bitter "Farewell to Savannah."

Five miles south of Danville the Isaac Shelby Cemetery State Historic Site (9–5, free) preserves the grave of Kentucky's first and fifth governor (died 1826) and chairman of the 1792 constitutional convention, while west of Danville the Perryville Battlefield State Historic Site (grounds, April–Oct., 8–9; Nov.–March, 8–5; museum, April–Oct., 9–5; Nov.–March, by appointment, 606-332-8631, adm.) recalls the fierce October 8, 1862, encounter called by one Union general "the bloodiest battle of modern times," when some 7,500 casualties resulted during a clash between nearly 40,000 troops as Northern forces blunted the Confederacy's attempt to control Kentucky. On the weekend closest to the battle date several hundred men uniformed and equipped with Civil War-era gear reenact the battle on the ground where it unfolded. The antebellum Elmwood Inn at Perryville, tucked in a grove of trees by the Chaplin River, once housed an academy and now contains an attractive restaurant whose specialities include desserts topped with bourbon-flavored sauce.

Off to the west at Lebanon, the exact geographic center of Kentucky, the 1867 National Cemetery is one of the country's oldest such burial grounds. Tobacco auctions take place from November to January at five warehouses in Lebanon, also known for its ham, celebrated with the annual late September Country Ham Days Festival. You'll find bed and breakfast in Lebanon at Mytledene (502-692-2223) and also in nearby Springfield at Maple Hill Manor (606-336-3075) and at Glenmar (606-284-7791). The 1855 Tudor Gothic-style St. Rose Church and St. Catherine Motherhouse, a Dominican institution established in 1822, recall the area's early Catholic heritage. The postmaster at St. Catherine's eighteen square-foot post office, perhaps Kentucky's smallest, is a nun. The 1816 Washington County Courthouse, the state's oldest in continuous use, contains the 1806 marriage documents of Nancy Hanks and Thomas Lincoln, Abe's parents. North of town, beyond the 1870s-vintage Beech Fork Covered Bridge, off highway 55, the Lincoln Homestead State Park (April–Oct., 9–5, weekends only, Oct., adm.) contains a replica of the 1782 cabin where Tom Lincoln lived as a boy, the original cabin of the Hanks family and pioneer era-type blacksmith and carpenter's shops. The Mordecai Lincoln House adjacent to the park, built by Abe's uncle, survives as the only remaining residence built and occupied by a member of the Lincoln family still on its original site.

Before continuing on to nearby Bardstown you may want to visit the area's other Lincoln attractions. At Knob Creek on U.S. highway 31 E stands a reproduction of the cabin (April 1–Nov., summer 9–7; spring and fall, 9–5, adm.) where the Lincoln family lived from 1811 to 1816 on a farm at the site; while at Hodgenville to the south the Abraham Lincoln Birthplace National Historic Site (April–Oct., 8–5:45, to 6:45 June–Aug.; Nov.–March, 8-4:45, free) preserves what is thought to be the cabin where, on the morning of February 12, 1809, "Tom Lincoln and the moaning Nancy Hanks welcomed into a world of battle and blood, of whispering dreams and wistful dust, a boy," as Carl Sandburg in *The Prairie Years* dramatically described baby Abe's appearance. Lingering at the rude cabin, a visitor can't help but evoke in his imagination the famous life that began there and hear in his mind's ear the echo from over the long years of Lincoln's stirring words that tried to preserve and then to heal a divided nation. The granite shrine that protects the cabin contains fifty-six steps, one for each year of the martyred President's life, recalled in twelve wax figure scenes at the new (1989) Lincoln Museum (M.–Sat., 9–6; Sun., 1–6, adm.) in town. Lakeside (502-358-3711) at Hodgenville offers bed and breakfast, as does Country Charm (502-324-3722) at Magnolia to the south, while over at Glendale the Whistle Stop, installed in an old train depot furnished with antique fixtures, offers such taste treats as asparagus ham rolls and "box car" fudge cake guaranteed to derail your diet.

At Loretto to the east—where you can tour the Sisters of Loretto Motherhouse (9–4:30, free), home of one of the nation's first female religious communities, founded in 1812—nestles the delightful National Register-listed century-old Maker's Mark Distillery (M.–Sat., tours every hour, 10:30–3:30, free), where rustic red-shuttered buildings turn out wax-topped bottles of premium Kentucky sour-mash whiskey. The hard-to-find enclave hides in a tiny valley on Hardin's Creek on a site where liquor has been distilled since 1805. A mock toll gate greets visitors at the entrance to the grounds, where the restored Quart House, believed to be the nation's oldest surviving retail liquor store, recalls the days when locals filled their quart jugs there. The tour takes you to the spotless still house where the potion is fermented and distilled, then to the bottling operation and on to a warehouse where the whiskey ages four to eight years in charred white-oak barrels.

On the way to Bardstown to the north it's convenient to stop in at the Abbey of Gethsemane Monastery, the nation's first Trappist monastery (1848), where the famous contemporary contemplative monk writer Thomas Merton lived. His simply marked grave (1968) stands outside the church, where you can attend one of the seven services held there every day—and night: vigils take place at 3:15 a.m. The rest of the monastery is off limits to visitors, unless you're on a retreat, but it is pleasant to linger a time in that tranquil and remote corner of the Kentucky countryside to get an idea of the other-worldly way of life lived by the monks, who no doubt enjoy there the "peace that passeth all understanding."

To switch from the sacred to the profane, Bardstown's Heaven Hill Distilleries operation (tours, M.–F., 10:30 and 2:30, free) is, like Maker's Mark, one of the very few, and the largest, of the nation's family-owned liquor manufacturing firms. At Bardstown's historic Spalding Hall (c. 1826)—which served as St. Joseph College and Seminary, and as a Civil War hospital and a preparatory school—the excellent Oscar Getz Museum of Whiskey History (May–Oct., M.–Sat., 9–5; Sun., 1–5; Nov.–April, Tu.–Sat., 10–4; Sun., 1–4, free) traces the drink's development over the last two centuries. Items in the collection, assembled over fifty years by the head of Barton Distilling Company, whose boxy metal warehouses stand at the south edge of town, include early documents, bottles to hold liquor for medicinal purposes, a bottle cap equipped with a combination lock to secure the contents, cabin-shaped containers sold by Philadelphia liquor dealer E. C. Booz, whose name in the 1840s came to designate "booze," and stuck in the top of a boot nestles a small bottle stagecoach travelers could refill at taverns along the route, a procedure that gave rise to the expression "bootlegger." The other section of Spalding Hall houses the Bardstown Historical Museum, with displays on the Lincoln family's land title problems, Jesse James' exploits in the area, and other local historic memorabilia and exhibits. Next door stands 1819 National Register-listed Saint Joseph Proto Cathedral (M.–F., 9–5; Sat., 9–3; Sun., 1–5, free), the first cathedral in the west, built to serve the Bardstown diocese, which extended north to Detroit and south to New Orleans, established in 1808 along with those in Boston, New York and Philadelphia.

Other historic places around town include 1818 Federal Hill Manor, better known as "My Old Kentucky Home" (May–Oct., 8–5; to 7:30 June–Sept.; Nov.–April, 9–5; closed M. Jan. and Feb., adm.), the estate that supposedly inspired Stephen Foster to compose his famous song, recalled by *The Stephen Foster Story* musical (mid-June–Labor Day, Tu.–Sun., 8:30 p.m.; Sat 3 p.m., 800-626-1563); 1817 Wickland (M.–Sat., 9–7; Sun., 1–7, adm.), the residence of two Kentucky governors and one Louisiana chief executive; the nearly two-century-old Register-listed Old County Jail (May–Labor Day, 10–8; Sept.–April, 10–6; closed Jan. and Feb., adm.), used until 1987; Old Bardstown Village (mid-May–Oct., Tu.–Sun., 10–6, adm.), an assemblage of nineteenth-century structures; the John Fitch Monument, which honors the inventor of the steamboat; and the 1851 National Register-listed Mansion (tours 5:30 and 6:30, adm.), where the Confederate flag first flew in Kentucky. The Miniature Soldier Museum (Tu.–Sat., 10–5, adm.) contains thousands of toy martial figures, while the Doll Cottage (April–Dec., M.–Sat., 11–5, adm.) also offers a display of toy figures. From May to October horse-drawn carriages leave from Court Square (6 p.m.–midnight), while the My Old Kentucky Dinner Train (May–Dec., varied departures, 502-348-7500) chugs into action for evening excursions with 1940s-vintage dining cars through nearby Bernheim Forest, which includes an arboretum and a nature museum (March 15–Nov. 15, 9–7, free).

For bed and breakfast in Bardstown you can spend the night in jail at the Jailer's Inn (502-348-5551 or 348-3703); The Mansion (502-348-2586); Bruntwood Inn (502-348-8218 or 348-6808); 1812 McLean House (502-348-3494); and at 1779 Old Talbott Tavern (also 502-348-3494), believed to be the nation's oldest stagecoach stop west of the Alleghenies, a veritable museum—with Audubon prints, old furniture and other antique touches—where you can eat as well as stay at the historic establishment patronized through the years by Audubon, the Lincoln family, Jesse James, George Rogers Clark, Daniel Boone and exiled French king Louis Philippe, who in 1797 painted in an upstairs room colorful murals James supposedly used for target practice, pocking the pictures with bullet holes. The venerable tavern also serves as the setting for Washington Irving's short story *Life of Ralph Ringwood* about a stolen kiss, purloined there at the Talbott in 1802. Other area bed and breakfast places include Glenmar (606-284-7791) off highway 150 east of town, and the Deatsville Inn (502-348-6382) up at Deatsville.

At Bloomfield, where the nineteenth-century D. B. Sutherland & Sons Mill still operates, repose Ann Cook and Jeroboam O. Beauchamp, figures in the 1825 intrigue involving Cook's seduction by prominent attorney Solomon P. Sharp, later stabbed in revenge by her husband Jeroboam, a celebrated affair dramatized by Kentucky native Robert Penn Warren in his 1950 novel *World Enough and Time.* At Clermont by Bernheim Forest operates the Jim Beam distillery, believed to be Kentucky's oldest continuing manufacturing business (1795). The distillery itself doesn't take visitors but at the American Outpost (M.–Sat., 9–4:30; Sun., 1–4, free) you can watch a film on the bourbon-making process, look at more than five hundred collectors' decanters, see a re-creation of a nineteenth-century cooperage shop and visit a whiskey warehouse. In late July and most of August Camp Crescendo (502-833-2827) at Lebanon Junction functions as a training center for high school bands, hosting some thirty-five ensembles from five states.

To the west spreads the extensive Fort Knox Military Reservation, named after Revolutionary War general and first Secretary of War Henry T. Knox. The grounds include what must be the most valuable terrain on earth—the U.S. Treasury Gold Depository, built in 1936 to house the nation's supply of the precious metal. Behind a twenty-ton vault door in the two-story steel, concrete and granite basement are stored twenty-seven and a-half-pound gold bars. Round-the-clock guards stand watch over the hoard, and no one staff member knows the entire combination necessary to unlock the vault. The Depository offers no free samples or tours. The Depository—bristling with floodlights, observation cameras, barbed wire and other such unfriendly security devices—doesn't even let you get close, and you're allowed to view the installation from afar from U.S. highway 31 W or Bullion Boulevard for no longer than five minutes. Even the tanks and other armored weapons down the road at the Patton Museum of Cavalry and Armor (M.–F., 9–4:30; Sat. and Sun., May–Sept., 10–6; Oct.–April, 10–4:30, free) seem friendly after you've seen the forbidding Gold Vault building. The museum highlights the history of the armor branch and development of the tank, and also includes a section devoted to George S. Patton, including the famous ivory-handled pistols the general sported. Another military figure, Confederate General John Hunt Morgan, leader of the famous Morgan's Raiders, once headquartered at Brandenburg up on the Ohio River thirty-five miles west of Louisville, but these days the quiet town of less than 2,000 people offers the tranquil Doe Run Inn (502-422-2982), a century-and-a-half-old stone structure, built in part by Abe Lincoln's father, nestled in a rustic setting next to the Doe Run, a stream discovered in 1778 by Squire Boone, Daniel's brother. Standing on land deeded in 1786 by Virginia governor Patrick Henry, the inn offers basic but pleasant rooms and tasty country cooking, all at rock-bottom prices.

To complete your tour of central Kentucky it's worth visiting in Elizabethtown the unusual Schmidt's Coca-Cola Museum (M.–F., 9–4, adm.), believed to be the world's largest collection of memorabilia pertaining to the beverage. Crammed with advertising novelties, antique bottles and equipment, signs, mementos, a complete 1890s soda fountain and other items bearing the characteristic white "Coca-Cola" script on a bright red background, the museum occupies the upper level at the local bottling plant, owned by the Schmidt family since 1901. In the lobby of the modern facility a dispenser offers free samples of the beverages you can see being produced, bottled and canned on the production lines viewed from an elevated walkway. Down in town a building on the main square still bears a cannonball imbedded when Morgan's Raiders attacked Elizabethtown. Nearby stands the c. 1825 Brown-Pusey House (M.–Sat., 10–4, free), originally a stagecoach inn, occupied for two years by General George Custer, of Little Big Horn fame, when he was stationed in the town, while out at Freeman Lake Park survives the Lincoln Heritage House (June–Sept., Tu.–Sat., 10–6; Sun., 1–6, adm.), built in part by Abe Lincoln's father, Thomas, who lived in the area for ten years. The brand new (June 1990) *The Lincoln Drama* (late June–Labor Day, Tu.–Sun., 8:30 p.m., 502-737-6881) tells the story of the sixteenth President's Kentucky origins and upbringing. Olde Bethlehem Academy Inn (502-862-9003) offers bed and

breakfast at Elizabethtown, which in June hosts the annual
Kentucky Renaissance Festival, featuring jugglers and jous-
ters, Henry VIII-era costumes, magicians and musicians,
Shakespearean actors, and other such Olde England activi-
ties—a true time and place warp there in the heart of central
Kentucky, U.S.A.

Western Kentucky

*Owensboro—Henderson—Mammoth Cave—Bowling
Green—Hopkinsville—Land Between the
Lakes—Murray—Paducah*

Although Owensboro is the state's third-largest city, it
claims less than 60,000 people, an indication that Kentucky
remains a land of small towns and large rural areas, many
of them scattered across the western territory. An Ohio River
settlement in the northern part of western Kentucky, Owensboro has redeveloped its downtown waterfront area,
which sports a metal-roofed gazebo and benches above the
steep levee overlooking the scene near the blue steel girder
bridge that crosses to Indiana. In an industrial area along
the river at the east edge of town stretches Glenmore Distilleries (tours, M.–F., 1:30, free), while out at 2100 Frederica
grows what is believed to be the world's largest sassafras
tree, first noticed for its size in 1883—more than a hundred
feet tall, sixteen feet in circumference and at least two hundred and fifty years old. In early May Owensboro, which
calls itself the "Bar-B-Q Capital of the World," a claim many
other places in the South would no doubt dispute, hosts
the annual International Bar-B-Q Festival, while for typical
local fare, along with country, gospel and Bluegrass music,
you might want to try Goldie's Best Little Opry House

(shows F. and Sat., 8 p.m.). At Owensboro, hometown of singer Florence Henderson and site of Kentucky's last legal public hanging (1936), Friendly Farm (502-771-5590 or 771-4723) offers bed and breakfast.

At Hawesville off to the east you'll find the Hancock County Museum (May–Sept., Sun., 2–4), with steamboat, courtroom and history displays in a 1903 train depot. In 1827 a young Abe Lincoln won his very first trial here, successfully defending himself against a charge of operating a ferry without a license. To the south lies Rough River Dam State Resort Park, scene in mid-July of the Old Time Fiddlers Contest, one of the fifteen attractive state-run lodges around Kentucky (800-325-1713). The Bel Cheese company in Leitchfield offers an assortment of cheeses made on the premises, and at Pine Knob just to the west local folklore dramas in a new amphitheater (June–Aug., F. and Sat., 8:30 p.m., 502-879-8190) enliven the rural community, which includes a 1938 country store and a century-old church. Nearby Rosine—birthplace of "father of Bluegrass music" Bill Monroe and the town where Uncle Penn, celebrated in song by Monroe, reposes—hosts over Labor Day weekend the annual Bluegrass Festival. Monroe's Blue Grass Boys band gave its name to the now-famous music, featuring the banjo and other string instruments playing songs that evolved from a mixture of mountain ballads, folk tunes, jazz, gospels and country and western.

Back along the Ohio, Henderson, west of Owensboro, boasts the excellent John James Audubon Memorial Museum (April–Oct., 9–5; Nov.–March, Sat. and Sun. only, 9–5, closed Jan., adm.), installed in an imposing WPA-built French Norman chateau-like structure. The museum houses a complete collection of Audubon's famous *The Birds of America,* published between 1826 and 1838, as well as memorabilia pertaining to the renowned artist-naturalist, including his painting chair, diaries, letters and records from the store he ran in Henderson, where the Audubons lived from 1810 to 1819, finally leaving after a mill he invested in went bankrupt. Among the other losers in this venture was George Keats, brother of English poet John Keats who had counted on money from the business in far-off Kentucky to help him marry Fanny Brawne. The museum at Henderson, which lies on the Mississippi Flyway migratory route that brings many birds to the area, nestles in the nearly seven hundred-acre Audubon State Park, the very woodland where the naturalist would "ramble" (his favorite word) looking for feathered specimens, a passion that prompted his wife to remark, "Every bird is my rival." Audubon painted not only dead birds he'd mounted but, on at least one occasion, a deceased human. The artist wrote in 1819 that a Louisville minister disinterred his child so Audubon could paint a portrait of the dead youngster. Other Audubon works and a large collection of books about the artist reside at the Henderson Public Library in town, not far from Wolf's Tavern, a longtime (since 1878) local hangout.

At Henderson, where McCullagh House (502-826-0943) takes bed and breakfast guests, Mother's Day originated, first celebrated in 1887 by schoolteacher Mary Wilson, who suggested the observance to her pupils. Near Corydon, south of Henderson, was born (1898) another famous Kentucky character, A. B. "Happy" Chandler, impoverished but always happy. When young Chandler arrived at Transylvania University in Lexington he brought with him, he said, "a red sweater, a five-dollar bill, and a smile." After working his way through school and then attending the University of Kentucky Law School Happy was elected governor in 1935 at age thirty-seven, later serving in the U.S. Senate and as Commissioner of Baseball before running for governor again in 1955 with the slogan, "Be like your pappy and

vote for Happy." An earlier politician, Abe Lincoln, delivered his only Kentucky political speech on the courthouse
lawn at nearby Morganfield, where the nation's largest Job
Corps project operates.

In the southern part of western Kentucky lies, or burrows,
Mammoth Cave, the world's largest known cave system—
two hundred and ninety miles of it mapped—chosen by the
United Nations cultural organization UNESCO as a World
Heritage Site. Back about 1798 a man chasing a bear discov-
ered Mammoth Cave, first opened to the public in 1816 and
now visited by more than a million and a half people annually. Various tours operate at Mammoth, among them Frozen
Niagara, which includes the gypsum-encrusted Snowball
Dining Room, Echo Lake, and a six-hour Wild Cave Tour
(by reservation only, for information: 502-758-2328). At the
Mammoth Cave National Park visitor center (summer
7:30–6:30; spring, fall, winter, 8–5, free) the *Voices in the
Cave* movie recalls some of the underworld's history and
lore. In the park operate two National Park Service-owned
ferries, one serving the hamlet of Forks, the other known
as Houchins' Ferry. At the Baptist graveyard, not far from
Mammoth Cave Hotel (502-758-2225), reposes Floyd Collins, a local spelunker who perished in 1925 while trapped
for sixteen days in an area cave, an incident that captured
national attention.

Stimulated by the mammoth tourist traffic to Mammoth
Cave, any number of other attractions operate in the area,
among them boat cruises on the Green River (April–late
Oct.), the nation's deepest waterway for its size; water recreation at Nolin River Lake and at Barren River Lake—the
name "barren" originating in the early days when Indians
periodically burned away trees to facilitate buffalo hunts in
the area—which features a state-operated lodge (800-325-
0057); four or so commercial caves, including Mammoth
Onyx Cave (summer, 8–6; winter, 8–5, adm.), above which

grazes a herd of buffalo (free observation areas); and Horse Cave Theatre (July–late Sept., 502-786-2177), which performs in an old opera house, one of the nation's eight rural professional theaters and Kentucky's only professional stage company outside the Louisville area.

Around the cave country region history lingers at such places as Park City, with the remains of 1830 Bell's Tavern, a renowned stage stop burned in 1860, famed for its peach and honey brandy and frequented by famous figures of the time, and at Munfordville, where in 1829 the c. 1810 log Old Munford Inn, also a popular way-station, hosted for the night Andrew Jackson, en route to Washington for his inauguration as the nation's seventh President. At Smith's Grove, Bruce's offers down-home meals and at Glasgow—which in early June celebrates the Glasgow Highland Games, featuring a parade of tartans, gathering of clans, Scottish dancing, kilt-clad runners and a *ceilidh* (a Scottish social gathering with traditional music, dancing and storytelling)—Four Seasons Country Inn (502-678-1000) and "307" (502-651-5672) take bed and breakfast guests. While in Glasgow you may want to take a look at the historic old burial ground, Munford-Crenshaw Cemetery, which contains a Revolutionary War section.

Off to the west of Mammoth Cave lies Morgantown, where the state's only Civil War memorial to honor both Yankee and Dixie soldiers stands on the Butler County courthouse lawn. The *Magic Belle* drama (last two weekends in Aug.) recalls the turn-of-the-century era as viewed by local photographer George Dabbs, while the new Green River Museum (mid-April–mid-Sept., M.–Th., 12–6; F.–Sun., 12–8, free) contains displays pertaining to the riverboat days. At nearby Rochester a ferry crosses the Green River just by Lock Number 3 dam, built in 1840 and operational to 1965 as one of the oldest navigation systems west of the Alleghenies, another remnant of which survives at Lock and

Dam Number 4 in Woodbury. Bowling Green, named according to local legend for a lawn bowling game town founders Robert and George Moore brought to the area from the east coast in 1798, served during the Civil War as the Confederate capital of the Southern-sympathizing section of divided Kentucky. During the war Southerners used as a munitions depot Riverview-The Hobson House, listed on the National Register, now a show mansion (Tu.–Sun., 2–5, adm.). Atwood Hobson's oldest son was the Union army's youngest colonel, with future President William McKinley serving as one of his officers. Bowling Green, home of the world's only Corvette factory (tours, M.–F., 9 and 1, free), boasts five National Register-listed Historic Districts: Downtown Commercial, the three residential areas of St. Joseph's, Upper East Main and College Hill, and part of Western Kentucky University where the Kentucky Library (M.–F., 8–4:30; Sat., 9–4:30, free) and Museum (Tu.–Sat., 9:30–4; Sun., 1–4:30, free) contain rich collections of materials relating to the state's history.

Duncan Hines grew up at Bowling Green, born there in 1880, and during the twenty-six years he spent as a traveling salesman collected the names of a hundred and sixty-seven choice restaurants he listed on his 1935 Christmas card. The following year Hines expanded his list into the book *Adventures in Good Eating,* the first edition of his soon-famous guide, produced at the new firm's national headquarters installed in what's now the Hardy and Sons Funeral Home on Louisville Road. Local restaurants Hines might have favored include the Sassafras Tea Room at The Glass Place; Mariah's, located in a National Register-listed brick house; the Parakeet Cafe; and Lone Oak, with home-style cooking. Bed and breakfast choices in Bowling Green include Alpine Lodge (502-843-4846), the Bowling Green (502-781-3861) and Walnut Lawn (502-781-7255).

West of Bowling Green lies the Shakertown at South

Union settlement, listed on the National Register, site of the last western Shaker community, which functioned between 1807 and 1922. The more famous Shaker village at Pleasant Hill southwest of Lexington tends to overshadow South Union, where you can also get the flavor of the Shaker heritage. Recalling the settlement's early days are a museum (May–Sept., M.–F., 9–5; Sun., 1–5, adm.), the annual tenday festival in July featuring the *Shakertown Revisited* drama (daily 8:15 p.m., 502-542-4167) and the Shaker Tavern (W–Sat 5:30, Sun 12–2:30), a restaurant housed in the original 1869 hotel.

Off to the west at Russellville the c. 1810 Old Southern Depot Bank suffered an 1868 robbery by members of the gang led by Jesse James, whose parents and brother Frank were born in Kentucky, while the c. 1822 Bibb House (Tu.–Th., 12–5, adm.) recalls Major Richard Bibb, whose son John developed Bibb lettuce in Frankfort in the 1850s. The old-style but modern (1976) Log House southeast of town offers bed and breakfast (502-726-8483) as well as attractive woven goods made and sold in the Fiber Studio on the grounds. Kentucky is the only state with two distinctly separate coal regions, one in the hill country off to the east and the western mining area centered in Muhlenberg County where TVA's Paradise Power Plant, one of the nation's largest, requires forty-two million pounds of coal a day. Country music personality John Prine's lyrics, "Down by the Green River Where Paradise Lay," recall the region that gave to the world such singers as Merle Travis, from Drakesboro, and the Everly Brothers, who in mid-August return to Central City for the recently inaugurated (1988) Music Festival. At Madisonville, which celebrates Mule Day in early May, stands the reconstructed log cabin (M.–F., 1–5, adm.) where Governor Ruby Laffoon was born in 1869. His parents, who omitted to name their son, called him "Bud" for the first ten years until the boy named himself for a friend, John

Ruby, owner of a general store. Dixie Bee in nearby Providence serves up delicious country biscuits, ham, sausage, cornbread, pies and other treats. From highway 91 operates across the Ohio the historic ferry, established in 1823, that takes you to Cave In Rock, Illinois, a one-time lair of pirates who preyed on river traffic.

In Todd County, back to the south and east of Hopkinsville, two of Kentucky's most notable native sons first saw the light of day. In Fairview Jefferson Davis was born (1808), commemorated by a three hundred and fifty-one-foot high monument, atop which you can enjoy a splendid view of the countryside (May–Oct., 9–5, adm.). It is a historical curiosity that both Civil War Presidents, Lincoln and Davis, were born in Kentucky less than a year and a hundred miles apart. A modest red brick dwelling (Tu.–F., 10–4; Sat. and Sun., 1–4, free) at Guthrie was the birthplace a century later (1905) of Robert Penn Warren, the only winner of Pulitzer Prizes for both fiction and poetry (twice). The year before Warren was born an angry group of tobacco farmers gathered in Guthrie to organize a Protective Association to combat the Tobacco Trust, which bought leaf at monopoly-controlled prices. To harass the 30 percent of the growers who refused to join the Association, bands of so-called Night Riders destroyed fields and intimidated the independents in the Black Patch, named for the dark tobacco common in the region. Warren's 1938 novel *Night Rider* tells the story of this war, eventually won by the growers. Warren died in September 1989. In Daysville every Friday, Saturday and Sunday folks gather for a fleamarket and country music, a kind of mini-Grand Ole Opry event.

Nearby Hopkinsville took its name from a Revolutionary War officer and its nickname, Hoptown, from the time in the 1890s L & N Railroad passengers traveling between Evansville and Nashville would hop off to buy liquor at the only place on the route alcohol was legally available.

The Pennyroyal Area Museum (M.–F., 8:30–4:30, adm.)—
the curious name refers to the pennyroyal (or pennyrile)
plant, an aromatic medicinal herb used by pioneers to brew
tea for colds—contains exhibits on the area's history, including renowned clairvoyant Edgar Cayce (in Virginia Beach,
Virginia, there is an association devoted to Cayce) and the
Cherokee Indian "Trail of Tears," also recalled at Commemorative Park where statues and gravesites memorialize Fly
Smith and White Path, two chiefs who died there during
the tribe's forced march twelve hundred miles from North
Carolina to Oklahoma in 1838. Hopkinsville native Cayce,
born there in 1877, first encountered "the Universal Consciousness" when, as a schoolboy, he claimed he learned his
spelling lessons by sleeping on his ABCs book. He later
used his skills to diagnose illnesses and predict events. Unless
Cayce has somehow reincarnated himself or otherwise mi-
grated body or soul elsewhere, the psychic reposes in Riverside Cemetery.

To the south at Fort Campbell the Don F. Pratt Museum
(M.–F., 12:30–4:30; Sat., 10–4:30; Sun., 12–4:30, free) houses
exhibits on the history of the 101st Airborne Division, while
at Dawson Springs to the north a museum (Tu.–Sat., 1–5,
free) features photos of the town in the early 1900s when
it served as a popular spa. Pennyrile Forest State Resort Park
includes a Kentucky-run lodge (800-325-1711), and you'll
find area bed and breakfast places at Oakland Manor in Hopkinsville (502-885-6400) and at Round Oak (502-924-5850)
in Cadiz, site of the mid-October Trigg County Ham Festival, featuring best-dressed porker and greased-pig contests,
as well as the world's largest country ham biscuit. The recently opened B & B County Gourmet Store near Cadiz
offers for sale Broadbent's champion country ham, so adjudged at the Kentucky State Fair.

Cadiz serves as the eastern gateway to Land Between the
Lakes, an extensive recreational area developed by the TVA

featuring the world's largest man-made body of water. The Golden Pond visitor center (9–5, to 6 June–Aug., free) will introduce you to the area, watered by Kentucky Lake and Lake Barkley, created by two dams only two miles apart across the Cumberland and the Tennessee rivers. Lodging facilities include three state-run lodges: Lake Barkley (800-325-1708), Kenlake (800-325-0143) and Kentucky Dam Village (800-325-0146). Among the between-the-lakes attractions are The Homeplace-1850 (March–Nov., 9–5, adm.), a living history farm portraying the area's way of life in the old days; the nearby Buffalo Range; Woodlands Nature Center (March–Nov., 9–5, free); the Empire Farm (March–Nov., 9–5), an agricultural demonstration area; and remains of furnaces that recall the time when a booming iron industry enriched the region.

Up at Princeton, whose downtown area—anchored by the Caldwell County Courthouse, designed to resemble Fort Knox's Gold Vault fortress—is listed on the National Register, stands Adsmore (Tu.–Sat., 11–4; Sun., 1:30–4, adm.), an impeccably restored 1857 house filled with original furnishings. At Grand Rivers, perched on the northern edge of Kentucky Lake, the Iron Kettle serves tasty meals, and at Smithland on the Ohio River was filmed *How the West Was Won*. (Another movie, 1978 *Harper Valley PTA*, also made use of Kentucky facilities, which it acknowledged by crediting the horse "Seattle Slew" for providing the manure that vexed the film's PTA secretary.) Benton to the south hosts two unusual festivals: the early April Tater Day, the nation's oldest continuous "Day," held since 1843; and in late May the Big Singing, established more than a century ago, featuring old-time harmony concerts. At Murray, the nation's used-car capital, with more than a hundred and fifty reconditioning shops that process some 40,000 autos a year, the new (1989) National Scouting Museum (June–Labor Day, 10–7, adm.), which boasts forty-five Boy Scout oils by Norman Rockwell, presents the lore, legends and history of the Scouting movement, founded in 1907. In 1892 local Nathan B. Stubblefield demonstrated the principles of radio three years before Marconi at Murray, where you'll find bed and breakfast at Diuguid House (502-753-5470).

To the west lies Mayfield, seat of Graves County, the only one of the state's hundred and twenty counties—third in number only to Georgia and Texas, and all but ten of them named for people—formed by four straight lines. Mayfield boasts the Wooldridge Monuments, eighteen sandstone and marble statues, known as "the procession which never moves," that H. G. Wooldridge erected in the 1890s at the grave he soon occupied, and also the Fancy Farm Picnic, dating from 1881, the world's largest such event, held the first Saturday in August. Traditionally a great political conclave, the event attracts politicians from near and far who orate to the crowds, especially in uneven years when Kentucky holds its state elections, one of the few jurisdictions to do so in odd-numbered years. In mid-September Fulton, farther west, hosts the International Banana Festival, which recalls the time when 70 percent of the nation's bananas passed through the area, while in the little town of Cayce grew up John Luther Jones, who took the nickname Cayce— later altered to Casey—to distinguish himself from other Joneses who worked for the railroad. It was on April 30, 1900, when Jones was thrown from the cab and killed as his "Cannonball Express" hit a freight train parked on the tracks at Vaughan, Mississippi. For many years whenever a train passed his grave in Jackson, Tennessee, the engineer would salute Casey by sounding his whistle. Beyond Hickman, where a ferry that affords an outstanding view of the Mississippi operates, curls the Madrid Bend, a corner of Kentucky separated from the "mainland" by the convulsions of the 1811–1812 New Madrid earthquakes and reached only through Tennessee. To the north at Columbus—during the War of 1812 considered as a possible new national capital—the Columbus-Belmont Battlefield State Park contains part of the mile-long chain Confederates stretched across the Mississippi to hinder Union river traffic, while the museum (May–Sept., 9–5, adm.) houses exhibits on the November 1861 Battle of Belmont, Ulysses S. Grant's first active Civil War engagement.

Paducah—which lies at the confluence of the Tennessee and Ohio rivers and boasts more miles of navigable waters than any other inland city in the nation—is the largest settlement in the Purchase, the name given to the far western Kentucky territory Andrew Jackson purchased for the United States from the Chickasaw Indians in 1818. When William Clark of Lewis and Clark fame founded the town in 1827 on land he bought from the estate of his brother, George Rogers Clark, for $5, he named the new settlement for Chickasaw chief Paduke, whose imposing statue by renowned sculptor Lorado Taft is at 19th and Jefferson Streets, while in Noble Park rises the craggy-faced image of a feather-capped Indian. The Market House Museum (Tu.–Sat., 12–4; Sun., 1–5, adm.), in the National Register-listed downtown district, contains historical exhibits, including the interior of the 1877 DuBois drugstore and displays on Alben W. Barkley, Truman's Vice-president, and humorist Irvin S. Cobb, both Paducahans. Displays at the Barkley Museum (Sat. and Sun., 1–4, adm.) and a few items at the Register-listed White Haven (April–Sept., 8–8; Oct.–March, 8–6, free), an 1860s showplace that serves as a state tourist office, also recall Barkley, the nation's oldest "Veep" (seventy-one), as he was called, when he took office in 1949, while the youngest was Kentuckian John Breckinridge, thirty-six when inaugurated in 1857. Another museum, the McKinley Antique Auto Collection (M.–Sat., 10–6; Sun., 1–5, adm.) offers not an antique Veep but old and classic cars.

One of the most attractive features of Paducah—a pleasantly laid-back, slow-paced Southern city that seems a long way from the state's Appalachian mountain country in the east—is its varied and appealing architecture. In the downtown area stands the angular, modernistic 1965 City Hall, designed by Edward Durrell Stone and modeled after the U.S. embassy in New Delhi, India. Many of the 2nd Street structures sport cast-iron facades. The Federal Building displays a mural depicting the city's history, while attractive old residences fill the nearby National Register-listed Lower Town neighborhood. Along the Ohio, where in 1884 Clara Barton led the first major flood-disaster relief operation of the Red Cross, still operates Paducah Marine Ways, a barge manufacturer founded in 1854, the oldest industry in Paducah, where Ehrhardts (502-554-0644) offers bed and breakfast. Alben Barkley (died 1956) reposes in Mt. Kenton Cemetery near Lone Oak south of town, while Irvin S. Cobb (1944) lies in Oak Grove Cemetery where his cremated remains were carried by pallbearers who earned the honor, as the humorist specified, in a card game won by players who could "cuddle to their bosoms three of a kind in a dollar limit game." This "corn on the Cobb" kind of humor recalls early nineteenth-century Kentuckian U.S. Chief Justice John Marshall's comment about Kentucky, its gentry and its bourbon, a remark that seems to summarize much about the place and with which we can end our tour of the state:

> In the Blue Grass region,
> A paradox was born,
> The corn was full of kernels,
> And the Colonels full of corn.

Kentucky Practical Information

The Kentucky Department of Travel Development is at Capital Plaza Tower, Frankfort, KY 40601, 800-225-TRIP and 502-564-4930. Kentucky operates lodges and cottages in fifteen state-resort parks; for information on these and the other twenty-nine state historic sites and recreational parks: 800-255-PARK. For information on the state's extensive water recreational facilities: Kentucky Marina Association, Box 266, Kuttawa, KY 42055, 502-388-7925; and for information on recreational facilities in the extensive Daniel Boone National Forest: 100 Vaught Road, Winchester KY 40391, 606-745-3100. For bicycle excursions in the Lexington area and other scenic corners of Kentucky: Bluegrass Bicycle Tours, Box 23212, Lexington, KY 40523, 606-278-2453.

Kentucky operates six highway tourist offices: in the north on I-75 near Covington, U.S. 68 in Maysville and I-64 in Ashland; in the west on I-24 at Paducah; in the South on I-65 near Franklin and I-75 south of Williamsburg.

For information on some of the more popular tourist areas: Bardstown, 502-348-4877; Berea, 606-986-2540; Covington, 606-261-8844, outside Kentucky 800-354-9718; Danville, 606-236-7794; Frankfort, 502-875-8687; Land Between the Lakes, 502-924-5602; Lexington, 606-233-1221; Louisville, 800-633-3384 in-state, outside Kentucky 800-626-5646; Paducah, 502-443-8783.

For reservations at many of Kentucky's more than one hundred bed and breakfast establishments: Bluegrass Bed & Breakfast, Route 1, Box 263, Versailles, KY 40383, 606-873-3208; Kentucky Homes Bed & Breakfast, 1431 St. James Court, Louisville, KY 40208, 502-635-7341; and Ohio Valley Bed & Breakfast, 6876 Taylor Mill Road, Independence, KY 41051, 606-356-7865.

5. Tennessee

The terrain that's now Tennessee was discovered in the west when Spanish explorer Hernando de Soto entered the Chickasaw Indian territory near present-day Memphis in 1541. But the state was settled in the east by rough-hewn Americans—once removed from the culture and ways of the Atlantic seaboard European population—who crossed the Alleghenies into East Tennessee in the late eighteenth century. In 1779 a group of those early pioneers pushed still farther west into Middle Tennessee where they founded Nashborough, now called Nashville, and later, after the Chickasaw ceded their lands to the United States in 1818, Memphis, now the state's largest city, was founded. Three areas, each with a different appearance and a distinctive culture, comprise the state, which stretches across some four hundred and fifty miles: the mountainous East, covering about a quarter of the area, contains two-century-old settlements in a rugged region inhabited by hill-folk who follow country ways; the farm-rich Middle, with its rolling terrain of bluegrass pastures, occupies about half the state and recalls the genteel countryside of Kentucky; and West Tennessee, a quarter of the total area, is a flat region, dotted with more recently established towns, that seems to belong to the Deep South.

Tennessee's multifaceted personality has given it two official state insects, the firefly and the ladybug, four capitals—Knoxville, Kingston, Murfreesboro and Nashville—and fully five state songs, among them the "Tennessee Waltz." The wide-ranging state—which borders on eight others, more than any except Missouri—has also enjoyed, or suffered

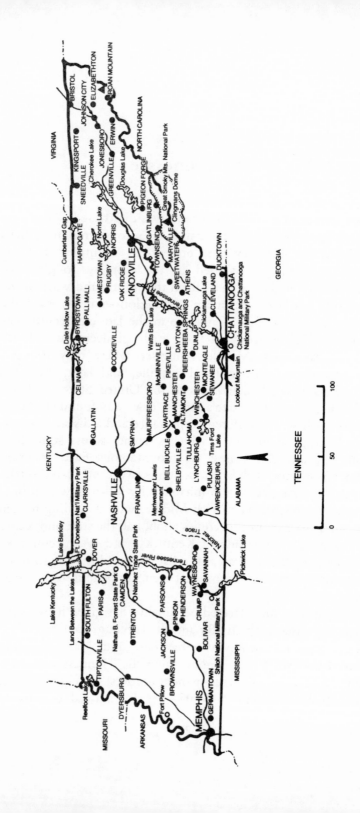

TENNESSEE

from, a split personality in politics, East Tennessee being rock-ribbed Republican and the rest by and large Democratic. Although the state endured more Civil War encounters than any other (apart from Virginia), Tennessee—the last to leave and the first to rejoin the Union—was one of the Confederacy's least radical members. East Tennessee, in fact, remained a hotbed of Union sympathizers: as early as 1819 *The Manumission Intelligencer,* an anti-slavery journal, began publication at Jonesborough, and shortly before the Civil War abolitionist "Parson" Brownlow wrote in his paper, the *Knoxville Whig:* "We have no interest in common with the Cotton States. We are a grain-growing and stock-raising people. . . . We can never live in a Southern Confederacy and be made hewers of wood and drawers of water for a set of aristocrats and overbearing tyrants."

One observer suggests that those varying cultures and regions that typify Tennessee have tended to soften the state's politics: "Tennessee's cultural multiplicity may well be the reason why the Volunteer State's responses to events, issues, trends, and reform movements were normally moderate," maintains William R. Majors in *Change and Continuity: Tennessee Politics Since the Civil War.* Perhaps only in such a pluralistic, temperate state could two brothers run against one another for high office. The 1886 "War of Roses," as the campaign was dubbed, became a kind of internal "civil war," pitting Democrat Robert Taylor against brother Alfred, a Republican, for the governorship. These "two roses from the same garden" functioned as a "Bob and Alf" show, with both playing the fiddle and telling corny jokes and country yarns during their series of forty-one joint debates. Brother Bob, the eventual winner, liked to note that both candidates "were born of the same mother and nursed at the same breast—but Alf's milk soured on him and he became a Republican." The sweetly-suckled Democrats have, indeed, dominated Tennessee politics, for the state has favored the

Grand Ole Opry over the Grand Old Party, but back in 1948 the two grand institutions met in the person of Opry singer Roy Acuff, who ran unsuccessfully for governor on the G.O.P. ticket.

The Opry seems in many ways to typify Tennessee's down-home country way of life, and it's certainly more attuned to the state's culture than Grand Opera. When an Italian company presented a performance of *Lucia di Lammermoor* in the mid-nineteenth century the *Nashville Gazette* felt it necessary to advise readers: "If a man in his death agony is heard to sing, the hearer must not become disgusted." Tennessee's popular version of Grand Opera started on Nashville's WSM when one Saturday night in 1925 the announcer introduced his Barn Dance show, which followed a classical music program, by saying: "Ladies and gentlemen, in the past hour we have been listening to music taken largely from Grand Opera, but from now on we will present 'The Grand Ole Opry.'" This kind of low-brow, country culture runs through the state's history, from the time of coon-cap clad Davy Crockett (the raccoon is the official state animal) to the latter-day U.S. Senator Estes Kefauver—head of the Democratic ticket that beat Roy Acuff in 1948—who, compared by Memphis Mayor E. H. "Boss" Crump to a domesticated raccoon, replied, "I may be a pet coon but I'm not Mr. Crump's pet coon." For good measure Kefauver adopted as his campaign symbol a coonskin hat.

The state's most famous politician, Andrew Jackson, one of the three U.S. Presidents from Tennessee—the others were Andrew Johnson and James K. Polk—was a rough-hewn, rugged frontier lawyer, land speculator and military leader in the best Tennessee tradition of the common man. He even gave his name to the political doctrine that glorified the country's common folk—Jacksonian Democracy. When the great man died on June 8, 1845, Jeremiah George Harris, editor of the *Nashville Banner,* praised the lost leader by comparing him to George Washington: "The mother shall teach her infant to lisp their names in unison." And—who knows? —perhaps to this day babies all around Tennessee so lisp.

Lisping is about the only sort of sound Tennesseans haven't set to song. Dulcimers and fiddles sound forth throughout the Smokies, while blues, rock 'n' roll and country—as personified by W. C. Handy, Elvis Presley and the Opry cast— have made Tennessee a music mecca. Jamborees, fiddlers' conclaves and "buck dancing"—a flat-footed rhythm-rich technique—echo around the state. Tennessee is also a nature lover's paradise, with more than fifty state parks, TVA recreation areas, the half-million-acre Smoky Mountains preserve, twenty major lakes and some 19,000 miles of streams, including more navigable waterways than any other state. As you travel through the oddly shaped four hundred and thirty by one hundred and ten-mile rough rectangle that encloses Tennessee you'll find a rich variety of old towns, country ways, traditional music, scenic panoramas, natural features and historic attractions, all of which form the pattern and the past of the "Volunteer State."

East Tennessee

Elizabethton—Johnson City—Jonesborough—
Bristol—Kingsport—Cumberland Gap—
Greeneville—Knoxville—Gatlinburg—Chattanooga—
Dayton— Rugby—Oak Ridge

In the early days of the dis-united states North Carolina extended from the Atlantic to the Mississippi River, and what is now Tennessee comprised the western half of North Carolina. Twenty years after a commission headed by Peter Jefferson, Thomas Jefferson's father, surveyed the northeastern boundaries of what was to become the state of Tennessee in 1749, the first American settlements outside the original thirteen colonies took hold near the Watauga River in East Tennessee. In 1772 those early pioneers formed the Watauga Association, a governing group that adopted the first written constitution in American history, and three years later the settlers acquired the land they occupied from the Transylvania Company, which had previously purchased twenty million acres from the Cherokee in the largest private land transaction ever known. When the Revolutionary War broke out, the settlers of Watauga—the so-called "Over Mountain" men—joined forces at Sycamore Shoals with John Sevier, an early political and military leader, from where they proceeded eastward to win a famous victory over the British emplacements at Kings Mountain, on the border between the Carolinas, on October 7, 1780.

In 1784 the Watauga Settlement, and the newer settlements in the Cumberland River region in Middle Tennessee, petitioned North Carolina for the "salutary benefits of government," whereupon Carolina immediately ceded the entire Over-Mountain territory to the federal government. Taking matters into their own hands, the East Tennessee settlers met in 1784 at Jonesborough to plan a new state, called Franklin, and in March 1785 another conclave gathered at Greeneville to choose officials to join Governor John Sevier in administering the proposed state of Franklin. Alarmed by the upstart start-up state to the west, North Carolina revoked the cession act and ordered the new government to disband. After Sevier refused, he was captured and taken to North Carolina and held at Morganton for trial but—in the best tradition of frontier escapades and derring-do—the governor's friends freed him from jail and carried him away on horseback. After four years of conflict between Franklin and North Carolina, Tennessee was again ceded to the federal government in 1789, this time definitively so, for the following year Congress organized the Southwest Territory, which included the previously orphaned area. Six years later, by which time the population exceeded the sixty thousand required to become a state, Tennessee was admitted to the Union, bringing with it a constitution adjudged by no less an authority than Thomas Jefferson to be "the least imperfect and most republican" of any state.

In the far eastern corner of East Tennessee lie a number of history-rich towns and areas that recall those early days in the state's formation. Just west of the Appalachian Mountains, which form the jagged eastern boundry of Tennessee, is Elizabethton where the state, in effect, began. At the Sycamore Shoals State Historic Area (8–4:30, free), site of the first permanent American settlement outside the colonies (1772), a replica of Fort Watauga, a museum and a movie entitled "The Overmountain-People" will introduce you to Tennessee's beginnings. It was at Sycamore Shoals where land speculator Richard Henderson met with the Cherokee Indians in 1775 to negotiate the purchase of twenty million acres, the largest private real estate transaction in history. A year later settlers built the fort to protect against attacks led by Chief Dragging Canoe, who tried to retake the land for the Cherokee. Near Sycamore Shoals stands the Carter Mansion (May 15–Sept. 15, 9–5, free), built about 1780 by John Carter, elected chairman of the Watauga Association in 1772. A bronze slab in front of the Elizabethton Courthouse marks the site of the Association's formation. Carter's son Landon served as secretary of state of the short-lived so-called "lost state of Franklin." The Elizabethton Historic District—most of which lies between Second, Fourth, East and Sycamore—includes a number of nineteenth-century structures. One unusual remnant from that era is the splendid century-old (1882) Doe River Covered Bridge, a lovely white wood single-span structure that stretches a hundred and thirty-four feet across a rustic stream. In mid-June

Elizabethton hosts its annual covered bridge and country music festival, while in December candlelight tours at the Carter mansion, decorated for the holidays in eighteenth-century style, celebrate the season.

Elizabethton serves as gateway to nearby Cherokee National Forest, a more than 600,000-acre spread of woodlands (the southern section of the forest lies beyond Great Smoky Mountain National Park) with campsites, hiking trails—more than a thousand of them, including the famous Appalachian Trail—scenic roads and five white-water rivers. For forest information: 615-476-9700. Tennessee's Roan Mountain State Park occupies part of the terrain within the forest. Atop the sixty-three-hundred foot high peak, one of the highest mountains in the eastern U.S., spreads a six hundred-acre rhododendron garden, the largest natural field of those flowers in the world. In the winter Roan Mountain—where cozy cabins offer simple but comfortable accommodations (for reservations: 800-421-6683)—serves as the South's only cross-country ski area, although other Southern states offer downhill skiing. Just the steps of the old Cloudland Resort Hotel, which once crowned the crest of the peak, remain, but the nearby Miller Homestead, with a log barn and nineteenth-century outbuildings, serves to recall the mountain people who settled in the area.

At the hamlet of Laurel Bloomery, in the far northeastern corner of the state, the Iron Mountain Stoneware company offers tours of the nation's only high-fired stoneware factory, where hand-painted dishes are produced; while on U.S. 321 west of Elizabethton on the way to Johnson City stands Sinking Creek Baptist Church, a hand-hewn log structure believed to be the state's oldest surviving religious building. The Carroll Reece Museum (M.–F., 9–4; Sat. and Sun., 1–5, free) on the East Tennessee State University campus in Johnson City contains displays relating to the region's history, which lingers more vividly at the Tipton-Haynes Historical

Farm (April 1–Oct. 31, M.–F., 10–6; Sat. and Sun., from 2, adm.), where a two-story restored house, barn, Greek Revival-style law office and other venerable structures present a picture out of the past. A similar remnant of the old days is Rocky Mount (M.–F., 10–5; Sun. 2–6; weekends only, Jan. and Feb., adm.), a two-story 1770 log home where William Blount, governor of the region south of the Ohio River, set up the seat of the new territorial government in 1790. Rocky Mount thus became the capital of the first official government west of the Alleghenies. A museum on the grounds houses exhibits on the pioneer period in East Tennessee, while at Erwin, south of Johnson City, is the Unicoi County Heritage Museum, with historical displays installed in a Victorian-era home formerly occupied by the superintendent of the nearly century-old (1897) National Fish Hatchery, which produces some eighteen million rainbow trout eggs annually. The rapids that churn through Nolichucky Canyon near Erwin offer one of the state's most challenging white-water rafting runs.

Just west of Johnson City lies Jonesborough, Tennessee's oldest town and one of its most delightful. Traces of Tennessee's earliest days fill old Jonesborough, established in 1779. Along a five-block stretch of Main Street stand any number of early structures built in a wide variety of styles, including Federal, Georgian, Greek Revival, Gothic Revival, Victorian and Italianate. In some cases two different—and even clashing—styles decorate, or confuse, a single structure, such as the Federal-type Robert May House that sports an Italianate porch. Sister's Row, built in the 1820s by a Philadelphian to provide each of his daughters with a separate but equal residence, is the town's oldest brick structure, while the 1797 Chester Inn—which hosted in its time many celebrities, including the three Tennessee U.S. Presidents, Andrew Jackson, Andrew Johnson and James K. Polk—is the oldest frame structure in Jonesborough. Old-fashioned lantern-like street-lamps stand by the Inn's delightful long front arcade and covered porch, fronted by posts holding graceful wooden arches. The local History Museum (M.–F., 8–5, April–Dec.; also Sat., 10–5, and Sun., 1–5, adm.) contains displays on Jonesborough, capital of the "lost state of Franklin," and on East Tennessee. Through the year the old town hosts various special events, including Historic Jonesborough Days in early July, the National Storytelling Festival, established in 1973 and held in early October, and a Christmas in Old Jonesborough holiday celebration in the month of December. Jonesborough restaurants featuring regional fare include Widow Brown's, the Dinner Bell and the Parson's Table, installed in a century-old church on Woodrow Avenue. Before heading north to some attractions near the Virginia border you may want to look in at the Grape Patch Winery (W.–Sat., 11–6; Sun., 1–5, free), one of Tennessee's dozen or so wine establishments, on route 75 near Telford, and the Davy Crockett Birthplace Park (April–Oct., 8–10; Nov.–March, 8–6, free) near Limestone, where a replica of the log cabin in which the famous frontiersman was born in 1786 stands in a rail fence-enclosed compound. The Snapp Inn at Limestone (615-257-2482) offers bed and breakfast accommodations in an 1815 antique-furnished house.

On U.S. highway 19 E south of Bluff City, near Bristol to the north, you'll find Ridgewood, a well-known barbecue restaurant, once adjudged the "best" such eatery in America, and a bit farther north lies the settlement of Blountville, which boasts more original log houses than any other Tennessee town. In the center of Blountville, founded in 1792, stand twenty eighteenth-century log and nineteenth-century frame and brick homes and public buildings, including the log, frame and stone Old Deery Inn (c. 1801) and its many outbuildings, and the John Anderson Townhouse (c. 1811), made of rough-hewn boards, where Blountville's officials assembled in the early days. Like Texarkana in Arkansas, Bristol, just to the north of Blountville, spreads across state lines, in this case Tennessee and Virginia. Brass markers in the middle of State Street indicate the boundary between the two states. A well-known downtown sign proclaims "Bristol a good place to live" with arrows pointing impartially to both "Va." and "Tenn." The old Bristol Train Depot recalls the time when the eastern seaboard rail lines were first linked up with a Mississippi Valley route when Norfolk and Western tracks joined the Southern Railway line in Bristol in 1856. Bristol also boasts the Grand Guitar, a music museum built in the shape of that instrument.

At Kingsport, due west of Bristol, remain other relics of early Tennessee history, including Exchange Place (Sat. afternoon, M. morning, free), a restored nineteenth-century farm that once served as a stagecoach stop where horses were exchanged and Virginia currency changed for Tennessee money or vice versa. A leaf-shaped cookie cutter found among some old family effects led to adoption of the sassafras leaf as symbol for Exchange Place. Promoted by the saying, "Drink sassafras in March and you won't need a doctor all year," the plant was exported to England as a health tonic ingredient. Another stagecoach stop was the Netherland Inn, a tavern and hostelry with a delightful three-tiered rear porch, that operated for more than a hundred years. Period furniture fills the beautifully restored old inn (May 1–Sept. 30, F., Sat., Sun., 2–4:30, adm.), located in the Boatyard Historic District by the Holston River where pioneer families fabricated their watercraft for the trip west. Near the Boatyard lies Long Island where the warring Cherokee signed a peace treaty in 1777 with the white encroachers, and where began the Wilderness Road, blazed in 1775 by Daniel Boone, Tennessee's first road platted by a white man. The 1915–1930 Church Circle District along Sullivan Street in the center of Kingsport recalls the town plan, much ignored, developed for the city in 1915. Kingsport's Bays Mountain Park furnishes an urban nature preserve of three thousand unspoiled acres which include hiking trails and a nature center. As you leave Kingsport and head for Rogersville to the west, you'll pass Allendale Mansion, an art- and antique-filled residence of a prominent businessman who bred Tennessee walking horses on the well-landscaped grounds (April–Oct., Tu.–Sat., Sun. afternoons, all year, adm.).

The Rogersville Historic District remains a relatively unchanged early nineteenth-century neighborhood of Federal and Greek Revival-style buildings nestled along tree-lined streets. The Hawkins County Courthouse at Rogersville, laid out in 1787, is one of Tennessee's few original such structures still in use, while the 1824 Hale Springs Hotel (615-272-5171), the oldest continuously operated (except for the Civil War period) inn in the state, offers delightful accommodations in antique-furnished rooms named after Jackson, Johnson and Polk, the trio of Tennessee Presidents who stayed there. In the backwoods areas of Hancock County, just to the west, reside the rather mysterious Melungeons, swarthy-looking people of undetermined ancestry. Some say the dark-complexioned clan is a mixed breed of blacks and Indians, others that they're of Portuguese descent, while legend has it that the Melungeons—a name derived from the French word "mélange," or mixture—descended from Sir Walter Raleigh's lost colony of Roanoke in Virginia. When the Tennessee state convention of 1834 disenfranchised all people of color, the Melungeons took to the hills and, resentful of the whites, stole their cattle and food and also set up moonshine and counterfeiting operations. Probably the best-known Melungeon was one Mahala Mullins, who lived with a brood of children in a log cabin on Newman's Ridge in Hancock County where she ran a bootlegging business. Revenue agents never arrested her, as they couldn't get the culprit through the cabin door: Mahala weighed some seven hundred pounds. A neighbor recounted that when Mahala died part of the cabin had to be dismantled to remove the body. A few Melungeons still lurk in the backwoods of the Cumberland Mountains but in recent years members of the one-time reclusive group have intermarried with outsiders and dispersed.

From Rogersville you can either head west to the Cumberland Gap area or proceed south to some historic places between the Alleghenies and the Appalachians. The famous Gap—a "V"-shaped indentation in the mountains where Tennessee, Virginia and Kentucky meet—now forms part of a National Historic Park near the town of Harrowgate. In 1775 Daniel Boone, an employee of the Transylvania Company, which had acquired from the Cherokee the twenty million acres of land (referred to at the beginning of this section) south of the Kentucky River, led thirty axmen in blazing a trail known as the Wilderness Road through the Gap. After the Revolutionary War pioneers swarmed west via the funnel through the mountains, a migration Frederick Jackson Turner described in his famous essay on the significance of the frontier in American history: "Stand at Cumberland Gap and watch the procession of civilization, marching single file—the buffalo following the trail to the salt springs, the Indian, the fur-trader and hunter, the cattle-raiser, the pioneer farmer—and the frontier has passed by." At the National Park (June–Aug., 8–7; Sept.–May, 8–5, free), dedicated in 1959, remain two miles of the Wilderness Road, the ruins of an early iron furnace, and Civil War fortifications. The Abraham Lincoln Museum (Feb. 1–Dec. 20, M.–F., 9–4; Sat. and Sun., 1–4, adm.), on the campus of Lincoln Memorial University in Harrowgate, also recalls the Civil War. Established in 1897 by Union General O.O. Howard as a memorial to his former commander-in-chief, the museum contains more than 225,000 items which form one of the country's most complete Lincoln and Civil War collections.

The road south out of Rogersville will take you to Greeneville, one of the state's most attractive and historic towns. The Greeneville Historic District includes a number of old commercial, residential and religious structures, among them Cumberland Presbyterian Church, its brick wall breached by a Civil War cannonball still embedded there, and the Federal-style Sevier House, occupied by Valentine Sevier, brother of John Sevier, organizer of the "lost state of Franklin" and later first governor of Tennessee. A log replica of Franklin's last capitol stands off route 70 northwest of town. On the courthouse lawn at Greeneville rises a monument to General John H. Morgan headed "Thunderbolt of the Confederacy" while a nearby marker bears the dedication, "To the memory of the Union Soldiers who enlisted in Union Army from Greene County, War 1861–1865." This is perhaps the only place in the U.S. where adjacent monuments honor both Yankee and Dixie combatants. Greeneville's most famous resident was Andrew Johnson, who became the nation's seventeenth President after Lincoln's assassination. The Andrew Johnson National Historic Site (9–5, adm.) includes a cemetery where the President reposes, his restored residence, a visitor center that contains a museum, and the tailor shop where Johnson worked in the 1830s. Lacking a formal education, young Andrew hired readers so he could keep up to date on current events by listening to government reports, newspapers, books and political speeches read to him as he toiled at his tailor's bench. Big Spring Inn, 315 North Main (615-638-2917), offers bed and breakfast accommodations in a three-story Victorian-style house.

In Tusculum, to the east, stands the two-story 1818 Samuel W. Doak home on the campus of Tusculum College, founded in 1794 as the first college west of the Alleghenies,

while west of Greeneville lies Morristown, with a reproduction of the tavern operated in the 1790s by John Crockett,
Davy's father (March 15–Nov. 15, M.–Sat., 10–5; Sun., 1–5;
June 1–Sept. 15, M.–Sat., 9–6, adm.). Built from materials
taken from nearby structures of the same vintage, the tavern
now houses a museum of items used in the time young
Davy Crockett—hunter, Indian-fighter, raconteur, state legislator and three-term U.S. congressman—grew up there.
At Jefferson City, to the west, stands the twenty-seven-room
five-story Glenmore Mansion, built in 1869. This huge, ir-
regularly shaped pile—so vast the family wintered in a
smaller adjoining replica that was easier to heat—is one of
Tennessee's most imposing mansions (Sat. and Sun., 1–5,
adm.). The Attic Restaurant at Talbott, three miles east of
Jefferson City, occupies a century-old farmhouse to which
the establishment moved from the attic of a shoestore in
Morristown. Waitresses clad in nineteenth-century garb
serve Tennessee country-style cooking. To the south lies
Dandridge, the state's second-oldest town, where the Jefferson County Museum houses historical displays, including
a marriage bond signed by "D. Crockett" in 1806. Dandridge also boasts thirty buildings listed on the National
Register, a Revolutionary War cemetery and the venerable
Shepherd's Inn. In 1988 police seized more marijuana in
Cocke County, off to the southeast, than in any other continental U.S. county, and more in Tennessee than in any other
state except Hawaii.

Dandridge brings you into the "magnetic field" of Knoxville, Gatlinburg and the Great Smoky Mountains National
Park. In 1786 James White, a captain in the Continental
Army, built a settlement on the banks of the Tennessee River
and before long other pioneers moved to the village, chosen
by Governor William Blount as capital of the territory south
of the River Ohio. After Tennessee entered the Union in
1796 Knoxville served as the first state capital until 1812

and then again in 1817–18. Much evidence of Knoxville's early history survives, including the James White Fort (April 15–Oct. 31, M.–Sat., 9:30–5; Sun., 1–5; Nov. 1–Dec. 15 and Feb. 1–April 14, open to 4, adm.), with the original cabin, the city's first residence, a reconstruction of the old fort and other buildings, and a museum. Another remnant of the early days is the 1792 Blount Mansion (April–Oct., Tu.–Sat., 9–5; Sun., 2–5; Nov.–March, Tu.–Sat., 9:30–4:30, adm.), listed on the National Register, where William Blount lived. Behind the house stands the governor's office, Capitol of the Southwest Territory from 1792 to 1796, where the Tennessee Constitution was drafted, while adjacent to the residence rises the 1818 two-story Federal-style Craighead-Jackson House, a visitor center for the Blount Mansion. Other antique houses in Knoxville, Tennessee's third-largest city, include 1834 "Crescent Bend" (March 1–Dec. 31, Tu.–Sat., 10–6; Sun., 1–4, adm.), with the Toms collection of furniture, old English silver and eighteenth-century decorative arts; the fifteen-room antebellum "Bleak House" (Nov.–March, Tu.–Sun., 1–4; April–Oct., 2–5, adm.), with Civil War era displays; the 1797 Ramsey House (April 1–Oct. 31, Tu.–Sat., 10–5; Sun., 1–5, adm.), an unadorned two-story stone structure, starkly lovely in its simplicity; and (near Knoxville) Marble Springs (April 1–Oct. 31, Tu.–Sat., 10–12, 2–5; Sun., 2–5, adm.), a two-story log house where John Sevier, the state's first governor, lived from 1790 to 1815. At the Knox County Courthouse are the graves of Sevier and his second wife, Catherine Sherrill, whom he affectionately called "Bonnie Kate." On the governor's marker appears his famous war cry, "Come on boys. Come on!"

Museums at Knoxville include the East Tennessee Historical Center (M. and Tu., 9–8:30; W.–F., 9–5:30; Sun., 1–5, free), installed in the 1874 U.S. Customs House, listed on the National Register, with displays on the state's history;

the Academy of Medicine Museum (by appointment only, 615-524-4676, free); the Museum of Art (Tu.–Sat., 10–5; Sun., 12:30–5, adm.), whose displays include the unusual Thorne Miniature Rooms, furnished with tiny antiques; and the Frank H. McClung Museum (M.–F., 9–5; Sun., 2–5, free), with a mixed bag of exhibits on such varied subjects as archeology, fine arts, science, history and natural history housed in a building on the campus of the University of Tennessee, established two centuries ago as Blount College, unusual for its time in that the school was coed. Five dorms at the university bear the names of the first coeds, while the university library contains displays on U.S. Senator Estes Kefauver's political career, now best remembered for his coonskin-cap campaign symbol. Along Laurel Avenue, adjacent to the grounds where the 1982 World's Fair took place, stretches the Eleventh Street Artists Colony, a neighborhood with galleries, craft shops and some Victorian-style houses. The renovated 1928 rococo-style Tennessee Theatre, at 605 Gay downtown, recalls the early days of movies, while the area's early history haunts the First Presbyterian Church burial ground, 620 State, where the town's and state's founding fathers, James White and William Blount, repose. If you overnight in Knoxville, Mountain Breeze Bed and Breakfast, 501 Mountain Breeze Lane (615-966-3917), provides comfortable accommodations in a noncommercial setting.

Near Sevierville, which lies between Knoxville and Pigeon Forge, you'll find another bed and breakfast establishment, Blue Mountain Mist Country Inn (615-428-2335), installed in a roomy old white wooden house with a spacious porch furnished with rocking chairs. Gladys Breeden's Restaurant at Sevierville is a local institution, a truly down-home eatery where you can serve yourself from pots atop the stove. If the nine-stool counter or three tables inside—where hundreds of business cards decorate, or at least paper, the walls— are filled, you can eat outside on the porch. The century-old

Sevier County Courthouse, listed on the National Register, somewhat resembles a Romanesque-style church, although high above the building rises an elaborate clock tower rather than a steeple. Pigeon Forge, just to the south, was once a sleepy village in the foothills of the Smokies, but nowadays about the only old-time rustic touch remaining in the town is the National Register-listed Old Mill, in continuous operation there on the bank of the Little Pigeon Forge River since the installation was built in 1830 by William Love, whose family owned the iron forge for which the town is (half) named. Apart from that rustic corner Pigeon Forge is an agglomeration of fast-food franchises, factory outlet stores, tourist shops, hillbilly music shows and other establishments featuring such fun and games as go-cart racing, miniature golf, bumper boats, "waltzing waters" and country singer Dolly Parton's "Dollywood" theme park.

Gatlinburg, just down the road to the south, gives Pigeon Forge a run for its money in the way of commercialism. Among the hundreds of come-ons—Gatlinburg claims some three hundred shops alone, plus all the other tourist-tempting places—two a cut above the others are the Smoky Mountain Winery, which occupies a pseudo chateau-like structure whose cellar houses oak barrels and casks that contain aging wine, and the Municipal Black Bear Habitat in Ober Gatlinburg, reached by the two and two-tenths-mile aerial tramway, said to be the world's longest, where the bears, most of them orphans, live in a natural-looking environment while waiting to be returned to the wild someday. Unless you're a connoisseur of fast food or "shop until you drop" activity, the main reason for going to Gatlinburg is to gain access to the Great Smoky Mountain National Park, the most visited of all the parks, with some ten million people a year enjoying the trails, pristine streams, campsites, rugged terrain and spectacular scenery. The Park's half million acres include the highest mountains in the eastern part of the country, with 6,643-foot Clingmans Dome towering above all the other peaks. At the slightly lower Mount Le Comte (6,593 feet) is a delightful lodge (615-436-4473) whose serenity is preserved by the half-day hike necessary to reach the facility. The Wonderland Hotel, which used to be a peaceful and secluded place to stay in the Great Smoky Mountain Park no longer shelters travelers, as the rustic relic, built in the early part of the century, was razed in 1992. Many guests who returned year after year will miss this delightful twenty-seven-room establishment with its old-fashioned ambiance and veranda affording splendid views. At Cades Cove in the western end of the Smokies the Park Service has recreated farmsteads much like those that operated in the area's back hills before Congress established the park in 1934. An eleven-mile loop road takes you past fields tended by descendants of the original settlers, log cabins, white frame churches, barns, mills and other structures, all preserved as they were a century ago. For information about the many natural attractions in the Great Smoky Mountains you can contact the Park Headquarters: 615-436-5615. Outside the park not far from the Cades Cove scenic drive entrance and near the village of Walland is Blackberry Farm Inn (615-984-8166), located in Miller's Cove, which boasts the region's oldest church as well as a venerable schoolhouse and mill. Six miles north of nearby Maryville stands another schoolhouse, the state's oldest (M.–Sat., 9–5; Sun., 1–5, free), a rebuilt log structure where Sam Houston taught in 1812, receiving eight dollars per term tuition in a combination of cash, corn and calico. Houston, one of the nineteenth century's most colorful characters, served as a lawyer, adopted Cherokee, governor of Tennessee, U.S. congressman, president of the Republic of Texas and U.S. senator from Texas.

Alcoa, just to the north of Maryville, claims to be the world's largest aluminum-producing area, while to the west at Vonore stands reconstructed Fort Loudoun (April–Oct.,

8–dusk; Nov.–March, 8–4:30, adm.), built by the English in 1756–7 in the heart of the Cherokee Nation to check French advances into the Mississippi Valley. After a Cherokee siege of the diamond-shaped fortress for five months in 1760 the English surrendered and withdrew under a safe-passage agreement with the Indians, who promptly proceeded to massacre twenty members of the evacuating party. Not far from Fort Loudoun is the Sequoyah Birthplace Museum (March–Dec., adm.), which memorializes the Indian who developed the Cherokee language alphabet. The museum houses displays on the tribe's culture and history. Nearby Sweetwater claims the world's largest underground lake, a four and a half-acre body of water in Craighead Caverns (9–dusk, adm.), which also boasts one of the world's few anthodite "gardens"—rare flower-like rock formations. In May 1989 at Sweetwater started up the Tennessee Meiji Gakuin, the nation's first fully accredited Japanese high school installed in the defunct Tennessee Military Institute boarding school.

At Tellico Plains, perched at the edge of Cherokee National Forest to the south, you'll find a bed and breakfast establishment, Creekside (615-253-3446), while Coker Creek, farther south, holds an annual Gold Festival in early October to celebrate America's first gold strike. Another unusual observance takes place in late April at Benton to the west, site of a festival for the ramp, a wild onion-like delicacy—sometimes described as "the sweetest tasting, vilest smelling plant that grows"—found only in the Appalachian Mountains. On the way to Cleveland you'll pass on U.S. 64 a valley known as Copper Basin, the so-called Tennessee Badlands, a fifty-six square-mile area denuded by copper mining in the late nineteenth century. Miners stripped ore and then timber to feed the copper roasters, a spoliation that along with erosion and sulphur dioxide from smelters destroyed the vegetation, turning the terrain into a barren

but many-hued landscape not unlike that found at the Grand
Canyon. Displays at the museum in Ducktown, named for
Cherokee Chief Duck, recall the early mining days in the
area. Also along highway 64 runs the five-mile long Ocoee
Flume, a wooden spillway built in 1912 by the East Tennessee
Power Company and later rebuilt by the TVA, while closer
to Cleveland lies the Primitive Settlement, a collection of
nineteenth-century restored log cabins furnished with household items used by pioneers. At the Red Clay State Historic
Area south of Cleveland—where a cluster of landmark buildings embellishes the downtown area—stands a replica of the
Cherokee Nation council house, as well as a museum
(8–4:30, free) and the spring-fed pool that originally attracted
Indians to the site. At Red Clay begins the famous "Trail
of Tears," the route the Cherokee traveled when the U.S.
uprooted 13,000 Indians in 1838, forcing them to emigrate
to the Oklahoma Territory.

Chattanooga nestles by a sweeping bend of the Tennessee
River above which towers Signal Mountain to the northwest,
Missionary Ridge to the east and, to the southwest, Lookout
Mountain. These strategic heights, along with the city's rail
lines that ran to such Southern centers as Memphis, Richmond, Atlanta and Charleston, made Chattanooga a much
fought-over Civil War prize. Union strategy sought to seize
the Confederate transportation nexus there, and in September 1863 the two sides clashed at Chickamauga Creek, south
of the city in Georgia, in one of the bloodiest encounters
in American military history, with more than a quarter of
the 124,000 combatants killed, wounded or missing. The
conflict moved on to Lookout Mountain where the "Battle
Above the Clouds" raged in a heavy mist until the morning
of November 25 when the Confederates retreated. Union
units then settled into Chattanooga where they gathered their
forces for General Sherman's famous "March to the Sea"
across Georgia. Chickamauga and Chattanooga National

Military Park, the nation's oldest (1890), largest and most-visited such park, occupies eight thousand acres scattered around the area. (The Georgia portion is covered in the chapter on that state.) The park includes Chickamauga Battlefield, where a seven-mile driving tour takes you to the main sights, and Point Park on Lookout Mountain. Cravens House (9–5, adm.), which served in turn as Confederate and as Union headquarters, contains a museum with antique-filled period rooms, while the Ochs Museum (named for the family of Adolph Ochs who owned the *Chattanooga Times* and who in 1896 purchased the then-bankrupt *New York Times*) houses photos, weapons, uniforms and equipment used by both armies. The Confederama at the foot of Lookout Mountain near the National Register-listed Incline Railway— said to be the world's steepest passenger train (near the top the grade reaches nearly seventy-three degrees)—uses five thousand miniature figures to present a history of the local battles (9–5; June to Labor Day 9–8, adm.). Two other commercial attractions on Lookout are Ruby Falls, a hundred and forty-five-foot underground waterfall, and the renowned Rock City, made famous not so much by its intrinsic merit as by the pervasive "See Rock City" signs painted on barns for miles around. Back in the 1950s more than eight hundred such advertisements brightened barns in eighteen states in the middle part of the country.

At the foot of Lookout Mountain runs Reflection Riding, a scenic drive through a garden and nature area. More Civil War history resides in the Confederate Cemetery and in the National Cemetery, the latter one of the South's largest and most attractive burial grounds, with graves of James J. Andrews and seven of his men, a band that seized the Confederate steam locomotive "The General" in April 1862 and drove it toward Chattanooga with the intention of destroying the line. Near their graves stands a replica of the engine, a curiosity but virtually unknown compared to that other local locomotive, the renowned "Chattanooga Choo-Choo," a name given in 1880 by a reporter covering the maiden run of the city's first post-Civil War train to connect North and South. During World War II, when Tex Beneke and the Glenn Miller band popularized the "Chattanooga Choo-Choo" tune, the train was on everybody's lips. The domed 1909 restored train station houses stores and restaurants as well as a Hilton Hotel featuring rooms in old-time sleeping cars connected to an 1880s wood-burning engine similar to the original Choo-Choo. No trains chug into the station these days, so for a choo-choo ride in Chattanooga proceed to the Tennessee Valley Railroad Museum (June to Labor Day, M.–Sat., 10–5; Sun., 12:30–5; Sept.–Nov., weekends only, adm.), which offers train displays and an old-fashioned steam train that takes you on a six-mile ride along a line listed on the National Register that passes over Chickamauga Creek and through a nearly thousand-foot long pre-Civil War tunnel. Other museums in Chattanooga include the Hunter Art Museum (Tu.–Sat., 10–4:30; Sun., 1–4:30, free), perched high on a hill overlooking the Tennessee River, and the nearby Houston Antique Museum (Tu.–Sat., 10–4:30; Sun., 2–4:30, adm.), with glassware, porcelain and a collection of 15,000 pitchers; the new TVA Energy Center (M.–Sat. 9–5, free); a gallery made to order for machairologists—the National Knife Museum, with more than 5,000 cutlery items displayed at what is supposedly the world's only museum devoted to knives (a "machairologist" is a knife collector); and—another weapons exhibit—the Fuller Gun Museum, said to be the world's most complete display of military shoulder arms (one gun sports a coffee grinder in the stock), installed at the headquarters building of the Chickamauga-Chattanooga National Military Park (summer, 8–5:45; winter, 8–4:45, free), located off U.S. 27 ten miles south of Chattanooga. A block from Rock City up on Lookout Mountain the Chanticleer Inn, 1300 Mockingbird Lane

(404-820-2015), offers bed and breakfast accommodations. Visitors to Chattanooga always wonder about the castle-like structure atop the Mountain: it's Covenant College, a private institution.

As you head north from Chattanooga back to the center of East Tennessee you'll reach Dayton, site of the famous 1925 "Monkey Trial," which pitted William Jennings Bryan against Clarence Darrow in the suit accusing local school-teacher John T. Scopes of violating a state law by using a book containing Charles Darwin's theory of evolution. The trial, which lasted for eleven days, is recalled in a well-mounted museum installed in the 1891 National Register-listed Rhea County Courthouse (M.–Sat., 8–4, closed W. afternoon, free), scene of the action. Nearly a thousand spectators jammed the courtroom—still used for Rhea County trials—which looks much the same now as it did during the proceedings more than a half-century ago. Overhead stretches an old-fashioned pressed-tin ceiling, while under-foot the venerable wooden floor bears the marks of time—tobacco stains, cracks, worn areas. Just after Bryan, who believed in literal interpretation of the Bible, won the case he died in Dayton. For some time following the famous event, visitors passing through town would often ask if there were any monkeys living in Dayton, to which the standard reply was, "No, but a lot of them pass through."

Near Crossville, farther north, is the unique settlement of Homestead, listed on the National Register, a planned community begun during the Depression when the federal government acquired 29,000 acres that were divided into small farms homesteaded by families chosen to develop the land. The settlers used traditional techniques and materials to construct the houses, built of stone, hand-split shingles, hand-hewn oak beams and hand-wrought ironware. The Homestead School and the Tower Museum, an attractive fieldstone building, stand across from the delightful Cum-

berland General Store—"Goods in endless variety for man
& beast," proclaims a sign on the outside—crammed with
old-fashioned and rural-type merchandise such as horse collars, cuspidor brushes, hand-tied tobacco and mule bits. At
nearby Cumberland Mountain State Rustic Park, created in
1938 as a recreational area for the homesteaders, stand sandstone buildings constructed by Civilian Conservation Corps
workers. The Cumberland County Playhouse in Crossville
offers professional theater, while the Talavera De La Reina
("Tavern of the Queen") restaurant, about twelve miles north
of town, furnishes not only meals but also extensive displays
of Hollywood memorabilia, including autographed photos
of stars, and garments worn by such luminaries as Betty
Grable, Mae West and Marilyn Monroe, all collected by
owner Amy Brissler, who for forty years worked as a TV
and movie costume designer. In Crossville itself the Bean
Pot Restaurant also offers food and atmosphere, with country cooking, a dummy figure that talks to customers, waitresses clad in bib overalls and red and white checkered shirts,
and a menu complete with a "mountain talk" dictionary.

Jamestown, farther north, was for several years the home
of John M. Clemens, father of Mark Twain. Clemens owned
large tracts of Fentress County land that outsiders tried to
buy up by paying the taxes or encroaching on the properties.
The efforts of Clemens's heirs to retain the land led to much
litigation with meager results but perhaps fortunate ones:
Samuel Clemens (Mark Twain) might otherwise have ended
up as a real estate developer rather than as an author. Squire
Si Hawkins in Twain's *The Gilded Age* was modeled after
John Clemens, while the novel's "Obedstown" is Jamestown.
Beggar's Castle, a German-style garden restaurant, and
Highland Manor Winery, the first licensed in Tennessee,
offer pleasant places in Jamestown to snack or sip. The first
land transaction in Fentress County was a deed conveying
property to Conrad Pile, a friend and hunting partner of

Davy Crockett and great-great-grandfather of another gun-bearing type, Alvin York, the famous World War I hero, memorialized at the rustic bright-red Alvin York Gristmill (summer, 8–8; spring and fall, 9–5, free) in Pall Mall to the north of Jamestown. York, a backwoods mountain-country marksman, captured the nation's imagination when he captured more than a hundred German prisoners, wiped out an enemy machine-gun nest and killed twenty-five German soldiers in France's Argonne Forest in October 1918.

Nearby, at Byrdstown, stands the small log cabin (Memorial Day to Labor Day, Th.–M., 10–6, free) where statesman Cordell Hull was born. A visitor center next to the cabin contains displays on the native son's diplomatic career. Although Hull is best remembered as Secretary of State, an office he occupied from 1933 to 1944, and as winner of the 1945 Nobel Peace Prize, perhaps his most lasting accomplishment—and certainly the most pervasive—was his authorship of the Federal Income Tax Law of 1913. Seventeen miles east of Jamestown lies the hamlet of Rugby, remnant of the English colony founded in 1880 by writer and social reformer Thomas Hughes, author of *Tom Brown's Schooldays* and other books. Hughes wanted to establish a place in the New World for the English gentry's younger sons who, denied by law the right to inherit, found it difficult to obtain positions in the overcrowded fields of medicine, law and the ministry, the only professions acceptable for young gentlemen. Hughes acquired some 75,000 acres in the Cumberland Mountains, and by 1884 the little English outpost in the American wilds boasted more than four hundred inhabitants and sixty-five major buildings. Gradually the colonists drifted away and today only seventeen of those structures remain, while Rugby's population has dwindled to forty or fifty residents. Some of the old buildings, listed on the National Register, can be visited on a forty-five-minute walking tour that leaves from the visitor center at Percy Cot-

tage (March 1–Dec. 15, M.–Sat., 1–5; Sun., noon–5, adm.).
The Harrow Road Cafe in Rugby offers homestyle meals,
and accommodations in the village are available at Pioneer
cottage and Newbury House Inn (615-628-2441).

To complete your tour of East Tennessee you can head
back east toward Knoxville, perhaps via Wartburg—
established as a German and Swiss colony in the mid-
nineteenth century—and Harriman, founded in 1890 as an
alcohol-free town, based on the idea that industrial progress
depended on a liquorless society. Each of the lots sold at
auction in February 1890 were transferred with deeds containing a "no saloon" clause, and the settlers built a Temperance Temple where anti-alcohol groups met. An economic
depression in 1893 contributed to the experiment's failure.
To the east of Harriman lie Lenoir City—near which the
Crosseyed Cricket restaurant, specializing in trout and catfish, occupies a mid-nineteenth-century-log cabin next to
a grist mill—and Oak Ridge, the atomic city built from
scratch in the countryside west of Knoxville. In 1940 the
entire population of Anderson County numbered 26,000 but
by war's end fully three times as many people lived at Oak
Ridge alone. After the government marked the enclave "Restricted Area" and posted guards all around the seventeen-by-
nine-mile site all sorts of rumors arose, among them that
the new city was producing Roosevelt campaign buttons and
that the mysterious plants churned out face powder for
WACs or dehydrated water for troops in the field. But Oak
Ridge's true function was to produce enriched uranium, used
in the atomic bombs dropped on Hiroshima and Nagasaki.
After the bomb blasted Hiroshima on August 6, 1945, the
local *Journal* newspaper ran a headline "Oak Ridge Attacks
Japan." On the morning of March 19, 1949, the installation's
gates were flung open and the atomic city was secret no
more. At the Oak Ridge National Laboratory you can see
the Graphite Reactor, listed on the National Register, used

to produce the first plutonium-239, and at the American Museum of Science and Industry (9–5, to 6, June through Aug. free) are displays on energy as well as exhibits on the development of the World War II "Manhattan Project" atomic program, while a self-guided thirty-eight-mile driving tour takes you to other sights around the atomic city.

North of Oak Ridge lies Norris Dam State Resort Park, with a lake formed by 1933 Norris Dam, often called TVA's first project, although TVA actually started not in Tennessee but in Alabama. The Lenoir Museum (April 15–Oct. 31, 9–5; otherwise, weekends only, free), located next to a still-functioning 1795 gristmill, contains a collection of early artifacts, and the Museum of Appalachia (8:30–twilight, adm.) in nearby Norris consists of a working Tennessee mountain farm with twenty-five or so original log structures—among them the National Register-listed Arnwine Cabin—and 200,000 pioneer items on display. These two museums serve to summarize the culture and past of East Tennessee, a historic area where "the Volunteer State" began two centuries ago.

Middle Tennessee

*Nashville—Clarksville—Columbia—Franklin—
Murfreesboro—Gallatin—McMinnville—Winchester—
Lynchburg—Shelbyville*

After the War of 1812 central Tennessee's development shifted the center of political gravity from the state's eastern section to the middle. Central Tennessee evolved in a way somewhat unlike the rough-hewn pioneer regions to the east. Middle Tennessee "developed along different lines from those prevailing in the eastern part of the state," observes Thomas

Perkins Abernethy in *From Frontier to Plantation in Tennessee.* "The great fertility of the Cumberland basin attracted wealthy investors and speculators. . . . The society which grew up under these conditions, though much affected by the circumstances of the frontier, tended gradually to model itself upon the pattern set in old Virginia and the Carolinas."

From the earliest days of Middle Tennessee, Nashville was the leading settlement, and so that city still remains. The town began back in the winter of 1779–80 when James Robertson, a leader of the Wautauga Settlement in East Tennessee, built Fort Nashborough on the Cumberland River in the central part of the state. A log replica of the original Fort Nashborough settlement (Tu.–Sat., 9–4, free) stands by the Cumberland, a rather incongruous enclave of old-style structures there in the midst of modern-day Nashville. Scattered around Nashville are other buildings that recall the city's early days, among them Travellers' Rest (M.–Sat., 9–4; Sun., 1–4, adm.), the restored 1779 home of John Overton, judge and political associate of Andrew Jackson, and site of the Battle of Peach Orchard Hill, a decisive engagement in the 1864 Battle of Nashville; Belle Meade Mansion (M.–Sat., 9–5; Sun., 1–5, adm.), an 1853 plantation house with a collection of carriages and oil paintings of the famous thoroughbreds raised on the farm there; 1836 Tulip Grove, residence of the nephew of Andrew Jackson's wife, and the nearby Hermitage (9–5, adm.), the most famous of all of Nashville's old houses, built in 1819 on a site selected by Rachel Jackson, who died there in January 1829 shortly before her husband became President. Behind the house, outfitted with the family's furniture and personal effects, repose Andrew and Rachel beneath hickory trees grown from nuts given to Jackson in 1830. Government attractions in Nashville include the National Register-listed state Capitol (9–5, free), designed by William Strickland, entombed in the building's northeast wall; the Tennessee State Museum (M.–

Sat., 10–5; Sun., 1–5, free), with historical exhibits and a separate section, housed in the nearby War Memorial Building, devoted to military history; and the Farris Agricultural Museum (8–4, free).

Other Nashville museums offer displays on various subjects: the Cheekwood Botanical Gardens and Fine Arts Center (Tu.–Sat., 9–5; Sun., 1–5, adm.) include beautifully kept grounds and a sixty-room Georgian mansion filled with paintings and art objects; the Museum of Beverage Containers and Advertising in Goodlettsville (M.–Sat., 9–5; Sun., 1–5, adm.), which houses more than twenty-five thousand old beer and soda cans, along with period promotional items; the Museum of Tobacco Art and History (Tu.–Sat., 10–4, free), with a large collection of antique pipes, snuff containers, cigar-store figures and posters; the Vanderbilt University Art Gallery, featuring a large display of prints, Oriental art and of Italian Renaissance paintings from the Kress Collection; and the Van Vechten Gallery (Tu.–F., 10–5; Sat. and Sun., 1–5, adm.), which offers contemporary art at Fisk University, where you'll also find Jubilee Hall, the oldest permanent higher education building for blacks in the country. Nashville's country music subculture is a world unto itself with its own museums, such as the Country Music Hall of Fame and Museum (June–Aug., 8–8; Sept.–May, 9–5, adm.), the Hank Williams, Jr., Museum, Minnie Pearl's Museum, Barbara Mandrell Country, and any number of other displays, shops and recording studios along "Music Row" on Division and Demonbreun Streets. The mecca for country-music lovers is the old Ryman Auditorium (8:30–4:30, adm.) which from 1943 until March 16, 1974, housed the Grand Ole Opry, now installed at the ultra-modern theater at Opryland theme park whose one hundred and twenty-acre grounds are crammed with rides, games, restaurants, shops and entertainment areas. Although the Grand Ole Opry is not all that "ole"—it began on radio station WSM

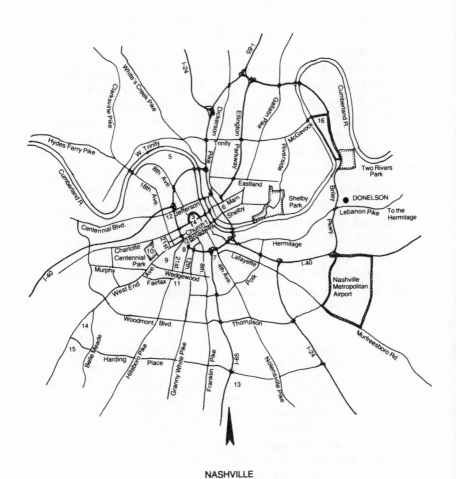

NASHVILLE

1   Fort   Nashborough   and
    Second Ave. historic district
2   Union Station
3   State Capitol
4   Tennessee State Museum
5   Metro Center
6   Edgefield
7   Cumberland Museum
8   Music Row
9   Vanderbilt University
10 Tennessee Parthenon
11 Belmont
12 Fisk University
13 Traveler's Rest
14 Belle Meade
15 Cheekwood
16 Opryland U.S.A.

in 1925—Nashville does boast some attractive older attractions, all listed on the National Register, including the 1847 St. Mary's Catholic Church, designed by William Strickland, architect for the state Capitol; the 1851 Egyptian Revival-style Downtown Presbyterian Church, also designed by Strickland; the 1903 Arcade, a two-tiered enclosed shopping mall modeled on Milan's famous Galleria; and the Historic Second Avenue District, a row of late nineteenth-century commercial buildings noted for their cast-iron and masonry facades and architectural detail.

Out in Centennial Park stands a "pseudo-old" exact-size replica of the Parthenon in Athens, a concrete building completed in 1930 to replace the original frame and stucco version erected in 1897 for the Tennessee Centennial Exposition (Tu.–Sat., 9–4; Sun., 1–4:30, free). At the Exposition's dedication ceremony on May 1 that year Governor Robert Taylor, victor over his brother Alf in the "War of the Roses" gubernatorial campaign, presented a lighthearted version of the world a century hence, namely now:

> I see the sun darkened by clouds of men and women flying in the air. I see throngs of passengers entering electric tubes in New York and emerging in San Francisco two hours before they started. . . . I see swarms of foreign pauper dukes and counts kissing American millionaire girls across the ocean through the kissophone. I see the women marching in bloomers to the ballot box and the men at home singing lullabies to the squalling babies. I see every Republican in America drawing a pension, every Democrat holding an office . . . and then I think the millenium will be near at hand.

Middle Tennessee attractions lie scattered in all directions from Nashville, which sits near the center of the area. Off to the northwest is Clarksville, a photogenic two-century-old town, with much of its Downtown Historical District listed on the National Register. Old-fashioned gas lanterns light Public Square, and on one antique building appears an old-time ad: "J. F. Couts Sons Furniture & Undertaking." Even back in those days firms diversified. The Clarksville/ Montgomery County Historical Museum occupies an odd looking many-gabled structure built in 1898 to serve as post office and customs house. Above the solid-looking brick county courthouse (1879) rises an equally solid clock tower, while the 1830s Emerald Hill Mansion, home of Confederate Senator Gustavus A. Henry, is also a sturdy brick pile fronted by tall elegant white columns. At Clarksville, which hosts the annual Tennessee Old-Time Fiddlers' Championship in April, lived poet Allen Tate who joined with John Crowe Ransom (born in Pulaski, Tennessee), Robert Penn Warren and other literary types to form the so-called "Fugitive" group of poets at Vanderbilt University in the 1920s. Tate's wife, Caroline Gordon, set several of her novels in the Cumberland River region. At Gate 4 of Fort Campbell on U.S. highway 41-A north of town near the Kentucky border you can find tours of the installation, home of the 101st Airborne Division, and access to the visitor center and museum (M.–F., 12:30–4:30; Sat. and Sun., 1–4:30, free). Off to the east at Port Royal State Historic Area near Adams, which every July hosts a threshers show, featuring antique steam-powered engines, are a 1904 covered bridge, an old Masonic Lodge and other relics of the days a century or so ago when the settlement served as a river port and logging center. Off to the west lies Fort Donelson National Military Park (8–4, free) with gun emplacements and other relics of the 1862 battle in which General U.S. ("unconditional surrender") Grant captured 13,000 Confederates and gained control of the strategic Cumberland River fortress. Just to the west of the park lies the TVA-managed Land Between the Lakes, a forty-mile wide peninsula filled with trails, wildlife, fishing and watersport areas nestled between Lake Barkley and Kentucky Lake. For information on the facilities: 502-924-5602. The Homeplace-1850, in the southern part of the Land Between the Lakes, is a living history farm with sixteen original log structures restored and assembled on a nineteenth-century farm site (March 1–Nov. 26, W.–M., 9–5, adm).

As you cut back toward the center of Middle Tennessee you'll pass by Erin, which during the week of St. Patrick's Day, celebrates its annual Irish festival, featuring a parade, leprechauns and Tennessee-type Irish blarney, or perhaps it's Irish-type Tennessee tall tales. Farther on, near Dickson, followers of English art critic and social theorist John Ruskin founded a communal colony not far from Ruskin Cave. The experiment disbanded in 1899 but ruins of the settlement remain, located about ten miles north of Dickson on Yellow Creek (also Erin) Road. Montgomery Bell State Park to the east boasts not only an attractive inn (for reservations: 800-421-6683) but also remnants of the iron ore and furnace operation that Bell, a Pennsylvania native, built up in the early nineteenth century. The entrepreneur engineered a nearly three-hundred-foot long tunnel cut through solid rock to supply waterpower for his iron forge on the Harpeth River, a project believed to be the nation's oldest man-made tunnel, commemorated at the nearby Narrows of the Harpeth State Historic Area.

Farther south, beyond Grinders Switch, hometown of the Grand Ole Opry's Minnie Pearl, who once published the *Grinder's Switch Gazette* newspaper, with all the news fit to print about the town, runs a stretch of the parkway that follows the Natchez Trace, the famous early nineteenth-century route from Nashville through southwestern Tennessee and across Mississippi to Natchez. On the Trace near Gordonsburg lies Meriwether Lewis Park where the famous explorer who co-led the 1804–1806 Lewis and Clark Expedition up the Missouri River met a mysterious death at Grinder's Inn the night of October 11, 1809. Displays at a log

house modeled on the original inn outline the history of
the Trace and of the expedition. Near the house runs a section of the long abandoned Trace, while in the Pioneer Cemetery, a grassy oval area not far away, rises a tall concrete
pillar that marks Lewis's grave. At the nearby town of
Hohenwald six or so stores specializing in used clothes
house stacks and racks of cast-off garments on offer for a
fraction of their original prices. The rummage shops buy
1,200-pound bales of old clothes from the Salvation Army
and other charitable organizations. Items unsold, the stores
vend to factories that recycle the garments into rags, thus
completing the riches to rags cycle suffered by orphaned
or outmoded designer clothes. Near Lawrenceburg to the
south the David Crockett State Park (7–9, free) honors the
famous frontiers- and backwoodsman who lived in the area
from 1817 to 1822 while serving in the Tennessee legislature.
Near the site of the grist mill, powder mill and distillery
Crockett operated on the banks of Shoal Creek around 1819
stands a latter-day grist mill.

Eighteen miles east of Lawrenceburg is Pulaski, where
six local citizens founded the Ku Klux Klan on December
24, 1865, an event memorialized by a plaque on the wall
of the one-time law office of Judge Thomas Jones a half-
block southwest of courthouse square. A few days later a
second session took place at a house where the group devised
the idea of wearing white robes.

Pulaski's newest attraction is Milky Way Farm, established
in 1932 by Mars Candy Company family member Frank C.
Mars and opened to the public in June 1992. The mansion
includes twenty-one bedrooms, twelve baths and the state's
largest (28 x 21 feet) private dining room table.

The road north from Pulaski back toward Nashville takes
you to two attractive old Tennessee towns with all-American
names: Columbia and Franklin. At Columbia stands the
house of Tennessee's third U.S. President (along with the

two Andys—Jackson and Johnson), James K. Polk. The simple yet attractive two-story Federal-style house (April–Oct., 9–5; Nov.–March, 9–4; Sun., year around, 1–5, adm.) was built in 1816 by Polk's father. Listed on the National Register, the residence contains many of the original furnishings President and Mrs. Polk used, including their White House china and such other items as an unusual fan Polk gave his wife for the inauguration bearing portraits of the first eleven chief executives and a picture of the signing of the Declaration of Independence. A daguerreotype of the President and his cabinet is possibly the earliest photograph of the interior of the White House. Down the street from the Polk House stands the Athenaeum, an exotic-looking Gothic Revival structure with Moorish arches, the last remaining building of a private girls' school that operated between 1852 and 1902. The nineteenth-century atmosphere in Columbia lingers at The Magnolia House, believed the oldest residence in town (c. 1812), a National Register-listed structure, also known as the "Doctor's House," where lunch is served (Tu.–Sat., 10–2). In early April every year Columbia celebrates its Mule Day, with mule sales and shows and other mulish activities.

A number of stately antebellum mansions scattered around Maury County present a picture of the genteel way of life that prevailed in Middle Tennessee a century and a half ago. Out U.S. highway 43 south you'll find such showplaces as Rattle and Snap and Clifton Place, as well as the lovely country churches, St. John's Episcopal and Zion Presbyterian; while U.S. 31 north, a scenic parkway, will take you past Haynes Haven Farms, Rippavilla and, in Spring Hill—site of the huge (more than four-million-square-feet) new General Motors factory built to produce the Saturn, GM's first new name-plate since 1918—Grace Episcopal Church, which boasts an unusual altar, its leaf and grape motif carved from walnut wood by a local teacher in the 1800s. Franklin, a two-century-old settlement to the north, is one of Tennessee's most delightful and evocative towns. The city's entire fifteen-block downtown section is listed on the National Register. Around the 1830 Carter House (May–Oct., 9–5; Nov.–April 9–4, adm.), a brick structure with stair-step lateral wall tops, swirled the November 1864 Battle of Franklin, which left more than 2,000 Northerners and over 6,000 Confederates wounded or dead, including five Southern generals, taken for interment at 1826 Carnton Mansion (Jan.— March, M.–F., 9–4; April–Dec., M.–F., 9–4; Sun., 1–4, adm.) where, in the nation's only privately owned Civil War cemetery, repose nearly 1,500 men who lost their lives in the battle (the generals are buried elsewhere). Dozens of other history-haunted houses line historic Franklin's shady streets. On Third Avenue stands the Eaton House (c. 1805), one of the town's oldest dwellings, occupied by the mother of John H. Eaton, Secretary of War for Andrew Jackson, who stood by him when Washington society snubbed Eaton's wife, an innkeeper's daughter.

St. Paul's Episcopal Church (1834) on Main is the state's oldest Episcopal church, and over on Fourth Avenue stands the Walker-Ridley House, home of Rogers Caldwell, a financial tycoon said to have been the South's richest man prior to the 1929 stock market crash. Two delightful restaurants in Franklin, both on Main, are Choices, installed in the century-old Bennett Hardware Building, and Dotson's, with one wall filled by autographed photos of country and western music stars who frequent the place. Windsong Farm out on Sweeney Hollow Road offers bed and breakfast accommodations (615-794-6162). Along highway 31 between Franklin and Brentwood, a southern suburb of Nashville, stand a series of antebellum stately homes, including Wyatt Hall, begun in the late 1700s; Creekside, whose floors became so blood-drenched when Confederates used the house as a hospital no one could ever remove the stains; and 1840 Green

Pastures, embellished with a wrought-iron entrance gate from Killarney Castle in Ireland and a sundial that supposedly once belonged to Anne Boleyn, wife of Henry VIII.

From Columbia you can cut across to Smyrna—now heading to the area east of Nashville—where the Sam Davis property, still a working farm (March–Oct., 9–5; Nov.–Feb., 10–4; Sun., 1–5, adm.), commemorates the young Confederate soldier tried and executed in Pulaski November 1863 as a spy. Before riding to the gallows perched on the coffin he was to occupy, the twenty-one year old wrote home: "Oh how painful it is to write to you. I have got to die tomorrow morning—to be hung by the Federals. Mother do not grieve for me. I must bid you good-bye forever more—Mother I do not hate to die. Give my love to all. Your Dear Son, Sam." More Civil War history lingers at nearby Murfreesboro where the Stones River National Battlefield and Cemetery (8–5, free) commemorates the bloodiest battle fought west of the Appalachians, with 10,000 Confederate and 13,000 Union casualties. Among the many markers and mementos of the encounter is the 1863 Hazen Brigade Monument, the nation's oldest Civil War memorial. Oaklands Mansion (Tu.–Sat., 10–4; Sun., 1–4, adm.) in Murfreesboro, embellished with a graceful arch-rich front porch, served as headquarters for both sides. In December 1862 Confederate President Jefferson Davis was entertained at the house, furnished as in the old days, where you'll also find a medical museum. Another holdover from the early days is Cannonsburgh (May 1–Nov. 1, Tu.–Sat., 10–5; Sun., 1–5, free), a reconstructed pioneer village, while the 1859 Rutherford County Courthouse—successor to the building that housed the Capitol of Tennessee from 1818 to 1826—is one of the state's six still-functioning pre-Civil War such structures. The east side of the courthouse faces Main Street—chosen to participate in the National Main Street historic preservation program—which is lined with Victorian, Georgian and Neo-Classical-style buildings, one of them, Clardy's Guest House, 435 East Main (615-893-6030), offering bed and breakfast accommodations. At Readyville just to the east stands a five-level wood water-powered mill, perhaps Tennessee's largest and best preserved such facility. The original mill, built in 1812 by Charles Ready, was burned during the Civil War and then rebuilt. Readyville became one of the nation's first electrified rural communities when the installation's owners linked a generator to the mill in 1902 and offered electric service to locals for about fifty cents a month.

Toward the north, and east of Nashville, the Cedars of Lebanon State Park preserves one of the nation's largest red cedar forests, while at the nearby town of Lebanon is 1842 Cumberland College, Cordell Hull's alma mater. Hendersonville boasts not only such alluring attractions as Music Village, U.S.A.—with museums and displays devoted to such country music luminaries as Willie Nelson, Ferlin Husky and Johnny Cash—and Twitty City, where Conway Twitty lives and offers "hello darlin' hospitality," but also historic Rock Castle (April 1–Oct 1., Tu.–Sat., 10–5; Sun., 1–5, adm.), a venerable Federal-style structure built before Tennessee was admitted to the Union two centuries ago. Other early houses stand at nearby Gallatin—Cragfont (Tu.–Sat., 10–5; Sun., 1–5, adm.), a handsome limestone residence built in 1798 by James Winchester, a founder of Memphis, and National Register-listed Trousdale Place (June–Oct., 8:30–4, free), which houses Sumner County historical displays—and at Castalian Springs, one of Middle Tennessee's oldest settlements, with the 1828 stagecoach inn and mineral springs resort Wynnewood (M.–Sat., 10–4; Sun., 1–5, closed winter Sundays, adm.). Built mainly of oak, Wynnewood is an imposing one hundred and forty-two-foot long building thought to be the largest such structure ever built in Tennessee. The Walton Hotel dining room at Carthage, to the east, is a period piece turn-of-the-century eatery, and at the nearby vividly named town of Red Boiling Springs—so called for a bubbling spring whose water contains a red sediment—the annual Folk Medicine Festival, with home remedy nostrums and practitioners, takes place in late June.

In the southeastern section of Middle Tennessee such unique attractions as walking-horse country and homey Lynchburg, with the Jack Daniel Distillery, typify the state's rather rustic way of life. At Fall Creek State Resort Park off to the east, the system's second-largest unit, the striking Fall Creek Falls plunges two hundred and fifty-six feet into a secluded pool. An attractive lakeside inn at the park, which boasts what *Golf Digest* magazine adjudged one of the nation's top twenty public courses, offers pleasant accommodations (for reservations: 800-421-6683). Cumberland Caverns near McMinnville—headquarters of the National Caves Association—includes a huge underground network of labyrinthine passageways first discovered in 1810 (June–Aug., 9–5; May, Sept., and Oct., weekends only, adm.). Few out-of-staters happen on the out-of-the-way old summer resort village of Beersheba Springs, secluded high on a hill above McMinnville, but it's well worth driving the winding way up the mountain to visit the delightful hamlet little disturbed by the twentieth century. The Methodist church now owns the century-and-a-half-old hotel, used these days for retreats and meetings. Just across from the venerable inn perches a splendid lookout point, next to which stands the hamlet's one-time general store, artfully converted into a house and used for years by the Burch clan (notice by the front door the marks drawn to indicate the height of the various children), one of the many prominent families that frequented the hilltop resort. On the way to Sewanee you'll pass through Tracy City, where the Dutch Maid Bakery sells its famous liquor-laced fruitcakes, and then through Monteagle, another resort, where the Smoke House restaurant offers typical hill country fare, featuring turnip greens, biscuits and other such country delicacies.

The Sunday School Assembly, founded in 1882 as a "Southern Chautauqua," is an attractive compound with summer cottages, a bandstand and pleasant pathways. The 1896 Adams Edgeworth Inn (615-924-2669), an antique filled National Register showplace on the Assembly grounds, offers bed and breakfast. At Sewanee is the University of the South, modeled after the architecture at Oxford in England. Chapel windows tell university history while a hillside marble cross memorializes Sewanee's World War I soldiers. At the foot of Monteagle Mountain lies Cowan, where the Railroad Museum (May 1–Oct. 31, Tu.–Sat., 10–4; Sun., 1–4, free) occupies the area in and around a century-old depot. The Old Jail Museum (mid-March to Sunday before Christmas, Tu.–Sat., 9–5; Sun., 1–5; to 4, Nov. and Dec., adm.) at nearby Winchester houses six rooms with displays on regional history; while the National Register-listed Hundred Oaks Castle (Tu.–Sun., 10–3; lunch served, 11–2., adm.) is a medieval-type chateau built in 1921 by a Tennessee governor's son, Arthur Marks, who died of typhoid fever at age twenty-eight before he could reign as lord of the manor. At 1873 Falls Mill, twelve miles west of Winchester, Dinah Shore's hometown, turns the huge (thirty-two-foot) overshot waterwheel, believed the largest in the U.S. still in regular use. The old mill nestles in a lovely wooded corner by pristine Factory Creek where The Country Store sells local handicrafts and mill-ground flour.

Although Lynchburg to the west is best known as home of the Jack Daniel Distillery, the village of four hundred or so merits a visit in its own right, for the hamlet preserves to perfection picturesque small-town scenes that recall Norman Rockwell paintings. Around the town square, dominated by the 1884 Moore County Courthouse, are the White

Rabbit Saloon, once owned by Jack Daniel himself, no longer a tavern but now an old-fashioned cafe; the Ladies Handiwork Shop, with handmade quilts, baby dresses and other such items on sale; and the Hardware & General Store—complete with a pot-bellied stove around which locals, some also pot-bellied, gather to gossip—that advertises "All goods worth price charged." A block off the square stands the Soda Shop, a venerable emporium sporting a turn-of-the-century soda fountain.

Tours of Jack Daniel Distillery (8–4, free), located at the edge of town, begin in a replica of one of the thirty-six or so seven-story high warehouses, each containing about a million gallons of whiskey, which loom above the distillery on the green hills around Lynchburg. The tour visits such places as a distilling area; the company's original office, filled with antique furnishings; and the nearby five-foot-two-inch Jack Daniel statue, life size except for the feet, enlarged by the sculptor so the figure would be solidly based on the pedestal. At tour's end visitors receive refreshments but no Jack Daniel, for Moore County has been dry since 1909. If possible, try to schedule "dinner" at Miss Mary Bobo's Boarding House (M.–Sat., 1, by reservation only: 615-759-7394), where family-style home cooking is served in a Civil War-era residence. Lynne Tolley, a great-grandniece of Jack Daniel, currently carries on the tradition started by Mary Bobo in 1908. There are accommodations at Lynchburg Bed and Breakfast (615-759-7158) in an 1877 residence, and also in nearby Fayetteville to the west at the Old Cowan Plantation (615-433-0225) and near Tullahoma to the east at 1884 Ledford Mill (615-455-1935 or 455-2546), where a cozy apartment occupies part of the National Register-listed nineteenth-century mill there by Shippmans Creek. A museum at the mill (Th.–Sat., 10–4, adm.) contains old tools, while a shop there sells handicrafts and mill-ground products. Tullahoma also offers tours of the George Dickel distillery (M.–F., 8–3, free) where Tennessee Sour Mash whiskey is brewed, and after the tour you can browse at the Dickel General Store, a mock old-time establishment filled with antiques, photos and souvenirs.

Not far from Tullahoma you'll find two more atmospheric places to stay, one at Normandy, which offers the Parish Patch Farm and Inn (615-857-3441) on seven hundred and fifty acres of rolling farmland along the Duck River once owned by Charles Parish, who headed the world's largest baseball manufacturer, and the other at Wartrace, the Tennessee Walking Horse Hotel (615-389-6407), virtually unchanged from when it was built in 1917. Behind the three-story brick verandah-fronted establishment stand stables and a marble monument to "Strolling Jim," the first Tennessee Walking Horse, a one-time plow nag trained to fancy-walk by hotel owner Floyd Carothers in 1939. Since that year nearby Shelbyville has hosted the annual Tennessee Walking Horse National Celebration, held for ten nights ending the Saturday night on the weekend before Labor Day. The horse set in Shelbyville gathers at folksy Pope's Cafe, a 1950s eatery. Photos and paintings of the champion steeds decorate the headquarters building of the Walking Horse Breeders' and Exhibitors' Association in Lewisburg. To complete your tour of Middle Tennessee, you might want to look in at Bell Buckle, just up the road from Wartrace. Local lore has it that the town received its name from an Indian or pioneer carving of a bell and a buckle on a large creekside beech tree. Once a railroad town—Railroad Square looks like a Western movie set—the village now contains a cluster of arts and crafts studios and shops and is also home of the Webb School, established there in 1886. At the Junior Classroom (8–5, free), an old-fashioned one-room schoolhouse used well into the twentieth century, once studied pupils who won ten Rhodes Scholarships and became the governors of three states, so this Middle Tennessee

"Buckle" has held together the reputation of the state's mid-section.

West Tennessee

Memphis—Bolivar—LaGrange—Shiloh—Jackson—Union City—Reelfoot Lake

Memphis, Tennessee's biggest city, is stuck in the state's far southwestern corner nearly five hundred miles from Bristol in the northeast. Bristol, in fact, lies closer to Philadelphia than to Memphis, which in ambiance as well as location seems detached from the rest of Tennessee. A Mississippi Delta sort of city and the urban center of a flat cotton-country hinterland, Memphis, along with its surrounding area, little resembles the hilly Appalachian towns and terrain of East Tennessee or the tidy settlements and rolling fields of the Cumberland Plateau in Middle Tennessee. Memphis is not a city of immediately apparent charm, but it does boast a few historic areas and colorful corners. Perhaps the best place to start a visit to the Mississippi River city is National Register-listed Beale Street, recently revitalized with new cafes, music joints and nightspots that recall the early days when Beale witnessed the birth of the blues. Today a stroll up fabled Beale Street is a walk down a musical memory lane. At Fourth and Beale stands the narrow "shotgun" house (moved from south Memphis) where blues composer W. C. Handy lived and wrote until he moved to New York in 1918. Just up the street is the funky, gaudy old Daisy Theater and nearby stands a plaque to PeeWee's Saloon, the tavern where "father of the blues" Handy parented many of his noteworthy songs. In Handy Park rises a statue of the famous composer, while up and down Beale are music

spots from which the blues blare. Along Beale also stands
A. Schwab, a nineteenth-century dry goods store where the
past is almost palpable. Piled high atop the antique wooden
fixtures are suspenders, shirt collars, men's garters, bib-sized
neckties and other seemingly outdated or outsized merchandise. The store's motto: "If you can't find it at Schwab's,
you're better off without it."

At the bottom end of Beale near South Main rises a nine-
foot statue of that other famous Memphis music maker, Elvis
Presley. All around town remain landmarks anointed with
Presley's presence in bygone years. On the south side down
toward the Mississippi border rises Graceland (June–Aug.
8–7; to 8 mid-June to mid-Aug., Sept.–May, 9–6; from 8
in May, adm.), the "King's" castle, now a mecca for some
600,000 of Elvis's fans who each year visit the mansion,
the singer's grave and a myriad of other Elvisian attractions
there on Elvis Presley Boulevard. Back toward the downtown area stands Sun Studio (10–6, adm.), where Elvis cut
his first disc and where such other stars as Johnny Cash,
Carl Perkins, Ringo Starr and Roy Orbison have also recorded. More highbrow, if less renowned, Memphis
attractions include the Victorian Village Historic District,
embellished with mid-nineteenth-century houses; the Brooks
Museum of Art (Tu.-Sat., 10-5; Sun., 1-5, adm.) and the
Dixon Gallery (Tu.–Sat., 10–5; Sun., 1–5, adm.); the Pink
Palace Museum (Tu.–Sat., 9:30–4; Sun., 1–5, adm.), housed
in part in a pink marble mansion built by Clarence Saunders,
who invented the supermarket concept; the National Ornamental Metal Museum (Tu.–Sat., 10–5; Sun., 12–5, adm.),
the nation's only museum devoted to metalworking; the
Chucalissa Indian Village (Tu.–Sat., 9–5; Sun., 1–5, adm.),
a reconstruction of a millennium-old Indian settlement, with
tribal art and artifacts displayed at the C. H. Nash Museum;
and the Mississippi River Museum on Mud Island (park and
museum hours vary seasonally; for information: 901-576-

7241), a park on a Mississippi River island, featuring a 2,600-foot long scale model of the great waterway, along which you can walk from Memphis to New Orleans in a few minutes.

Two old parts of town worth visiting are Front Street, lined with cotton companies and home of the 1912 Carter Seed Company, the last of the early cotton-row seed stores, and the South Main Historic District where early twentieth-century structures near the old train station remain as relics of the once bustling area. On Mulberry, a block east of Main, stands the rebuilt Lorraine hotel, site of the 1968 assassination of Martin Luther King, Jr., which now is the location of the new (1991) National Civil Rights Museum (10-5, Sun. from 1, adm.). The Arcade, at 540 South Main, is said to be Memphis's oldest cafe (1919), while two other off-beat old eateries are the Fourway Grill, Mississippi and Walker, a soul-food cafe founded more than forty years ago by the wife of long-time Memphis mayor E. H. "Boss" Crump's chauffeur, and the homey Buntyn, near Memphis State University at 3070 Southern, where plate lunches cost less than what the tip might be at fancier establishments. One unusual Memphis attraction is a tour through the "Hub," the sorting facility at the Federal Express home office near the airport. (For reservations for the tour, which starts at 11:30 p.m. when the packages are in full flow, call 901-395-3480 or, after 5 p.m., 901-797-7196.) Memphis was also the home city of Holiday Inns, now Promus Companies, whose world headquarters at 1023 Cherry Road near Audubon Park occupies a lovely old mansion on a twenty-six-acre wooded lot, an enclave worth a look. As might be expected, Holiday Inns abound in the area, but if you prefer bed and breakfast accommodations they're available through Bed and Breakfast in Memphis, 901-726-5920, or at the Lowenstein-Long House, 217 North Waldran (901-527-7174 or 274-0509).

Different routes fan out from Memphis in various directions. In the southern part of West Tennessee lie some attractions you'll pass if you're traveling to or from the Chattanooga area. At Somerville, scene of an early-October egg festival featuring a chicken beauty contest to determine the local pecking order, stands a National Register-listed old courthouse. Magnolia Place in Somerville, an antebellum home at 408 South Main, offers bed and breakfast accommodations (901-465-3906), while at the Silver Moon Cafe on the square you can get a glimpse of local characters and a taste of local chow. Another bed and breakfast place— Magnolia Manor, 418 North Main (901-658-6700)—operates at nearby Bolivar, where you'll find the Little Courthouse Museum, installed in the region's oldest-surviving courthouse building (1824), and The Pillars, a historic mansion where such personalities as Sam Houston and James K. Polk—whose grandfather reposes in the Polk Cemetery at the outskirts of Bolivar—were entertained. Out on U.S. highway 64 at Bolivar, from where Hernando de Soto headed west on the march that led to his discovery of the Mississippi River in 1541, is Backermann's, a Mennonite bakery with a variety of Pennsylvania Dutch-type baked goods. Farther west at Adamsville is a museum devoted to the exploits of a McNairy County law man with the redoubtable name of Buford Pusser. Hero of the three *Walking Tall* movies, Pusser suffered eight bullet wounds and seven knife slashes as he tried to bring law and order to the area during his time as sheriff from 1964 to 1970.

The route out of Memphis on highway 57, farther south, takes you to LaGrange, one of Tennessee's least spoiled and most attractive villages. At the entrance to the tiny town a sign (in poor French but with good accuracy) proclaims "La Belle Village," and a pretty-as-a-picture place it is, with beautiful mid-nineteenth-century houses and churches dotting the green fields. A small museum occupies the Walley Store building, across from which stands the still operating century-old Pankey General Store, a true period piece. Since 1896 the 18,500-acre Ames Plantation at nearby Grand Junction has hosted every February the National Field Trials, a bird dog competition documented in the unusual Field Trial Museum installed at Dunn's Supply Store, which offers a large selection of outdoor equipment. Farther west, near the Tennessee River, lies Shiloh National Military Park, scene of one of the Civil War's bloodiest battles, which resulted in 23,000 casualties after two days of fighting. At issue was control of the Mississippi and Tennessee River valleys and of the area's railroad corridors. William Tecumseh Sherman and future U.S. Presidents U.S. Grant and James Garfield participated in the 1862 battle, as did John Wesley Powell, who lost an arm in the fighting and who seven years later led the first expedition down the Colorado River through the Grand Canyon. A museum (9–5, to 6 Memorial Day to Labor Day, free), monuments, gun emplacements and a National Cemetery with rows of simple white grave markers parading in long files beneath stately trees, seen on the nine-and-a-half-mile self-guided driving tour, evoke the clash of arms that once bloodied the now tranquil terrain. At nearby Counce—a few miles south of Pickwick dam and recreational area, where an attractive state park inn (for reservations: 800-421-6683) stands by the levee—the Homestead House Inn offers bed and breakfast accommodations (901-689-5500, winter 667-3556).

Another itinerary out of Memphis, the route toward Nashville, takes you across the center of West Tennessee. At Mason you'll find Bozo's Pit Barbecue Restaurant (open, M.–Sat.), a nearly seventy-year-old eatery with a reputation for some of the best pork barbecue around. Covington boasts Tennessee Gins, supposedly the world's second-largest automated cotton gin (open for visits); and at the little town of Henning (less than seven hundred inhabitants) stand a number of historic old houses, among them Belle Grove,

whose marble and slate front walk came from the lobby
at Memphis's old Gayoso Hotel. It was across these stones
in that lobby that Confederate General Nathan Bedford Forrest's brother rode his horse in a famous incident. But
Henning is known as the hometown of author Alex Haley, who
on the porch of his grandparents' house from 1921 to 1929
heard the family stories that inspired his Pulitzer Prize-winning
novel *Roots* and more recent *Henning, Tennessee.* Haley, who died
in 1992, is buried in the front yard. A museum of Haley memorabilia and family furnishings now occupies the ten-room residence (Tu.–Sat., 10–5; Sun., 1–5, adm.), while in the Haley
lot at Bethlehem Cemetery a mile east of town reposes
"Chicken George," the *Roots* character who led the family
from North Carolina to Tennessee. To the west of Henning,
Fort Pillow State Historic Area (8–10, museum open to 4:30,
free)—near the hamlet of Golddust, so called when founder
John Duncan espied on the Mississippi the steamer "The
Gold Dust" just as he was about to name the settlement—
contains fortifications used in encounters between Yankees
and Confederates, who established the redoubt to block a
possible invasion from the north along the Mississippi. Since
the war era the river has moved a mile west, leaving the
cannon batteries high and dry.

On the way east toward Jackson you'll pass through
Brownsville, an attractive town with the College Hill Historic District and two National Register-listed religious
buildings: Zion Church and Temple Adas Israel, a century-
old Gothic-style synagogue with notable stained glass windows. Casey Jones Village (9–5; Jan.–March, 10–4, adm.)
at Jackson is a somewhat commercialized area that includes
the home, now a train museum, occupied by the legendary
railroad hero from Cayce, Kentucky; a replica of Steam Engine 383 the engineer piloted when it crashed into a stalled
train at Vaughan, Mississippi in April 1900; the Carl Perkins
Music Museum; and an old-style general store crammed with

antiques and turn-of-the-century fixtures. Near Jackson is Pinson Mounds State Archeological Area (M.–Sat., 8;30–5; Sun., 1–5, museum closed weekends, mid-Dec.–March 1, free) with ancient Indian burial and ceremonial mounds. Farther east lies another state property, Natchez Trace Resort Park, the system's largest, at 43,000 acres, with the attractive lakeside Pin Oak Lodge (800-421-6683) as well as the nation's third-largest pecan tree, supposedly grown from a nut a local settler received from one of Andrew Jackson's men as the general's troops returned from the Battle of New Orleans. In mid-April the nearby little town of Holladay hosts the annual Old Time Blue Grass and Fiddlers Jamboree.

Farther north is the Nathan Bedford Forrest State Historic Area, named for the famous Confederate general who won history's first victory by cavalry over a naval force by attacking and destroying a Union munitions depot and supply ships at nearby (old) Johnsonville in 1864. Up at Paris, to the northwest, a week-long catfish festival called the "world's biggest fish fry" takes place in late April and early May, while South Fulton at the Kentucky border hosts an International Banana Festival, featuring a one-ton banana pudding, the third week in September. Trenton to the south, home of the world's largest teapot collection, housed in City Hall, celebrates an annual Teapot Festival the second week in May. At the nearby hamlet of Skullbone, famous around the turn of the century for bare-knuckle boxing bouts, is an old general store; the village of Bradford claims to be the world center for a hot spicy dish called Doodle Soup, a claim apparently not yet challenged; Kenton boasts a flock of rare white squirrels; and near Rutherford stands a reproduction (using the original materials) of the cabin Davy Crockett built when he moved to the area in 1823 (late May– late Oct., 9–5, adm.).

To complete your tour of West Tennessee continue on north to Union City to see the Dixie Gun Works, one of

the world's best-known dealers in antique guns and a manufacturer of firearms replicas. The establishment displays hundreds of old powder horns, bullet molds and weapons, part
of a collection begun in 1894. An old car museum occupies
the same site. Nearby stretches Reelfoot Lake, Tennessee's
most recent natural feature not made by man: the violent
New Madrid earthquakes of 1811 and 1812 shook into existence a lake where a dense forest once stood. Bald cypress
trees with knobby "knees" bristle from the water, while between November and mid-March bald eagles winter around
the lake, so the bald truth is that the fearsome quakes left
Tennessee with an appealing nature preserve, one of the nation's most recently created such areas. Bus tours (for information: 901-253-7756) to observe the eagles leave in the
winter from the unusual Airpark Inn, a state facility (for
reservations: 800-421-6683) built out over the lake, part of
which comprises a National Wildlife Refuge. Here in its
upper corner Tennessee impinges on Missouri, part of the
Middle West, another region. We are now a long way in
place and time from the two-century-old Watauga Settlement, near the Atlantic states of North Carolina and Virginia, where the history of Tennessee and our tour of the
state began.

Tennessee Practical Information

The state tourist office is: Tennessee Tourist Development,
P.O. Box 23170, Nashville, TN 37202; 615-741-2158. Tennessee operates ten tourist offices, called Welcome Centers
(open twenty-four hours a day) on Interstate highways near
the entrance to the state: in the southwest, at Memphis;
northwest, Dyersburg; north central, Mitchellville and
Clarksville; south central, Ardmore; southeast, Nickajack,

Tiftonia and Chattanooga; northeast, Jellico and Bristol.

Phone numbers of tourist offices in some of the main tourist centers include: (1) *East Tennessee:* Elizabethton, 615-543-2122; Jonesborough, 615-753-5961; Gatlinburg, 800-822-1998; Knoxville, 615-523-7263; Smoky Mountains, 615-984-6200; Chattanooga, 800-338-3999 (in-state), 800-322-3344 (outside Tennessee). (2) *Middle Tennessee:* Nashville, 615-259-3900; Clarksville, 615-643-2331. (3) *West Tennessee:* Memphis, 901-576-8181 and 800-447-8278; Jackson, 901-423-2341.

Tennessee operates fifty-one state parks, many with lodges, inns, cabins and campsites. For reservations, 800-421-6683; for other state park information, 615-742-6667. For information on fishing in the state: Tennessee Wildlife Resources Agency, P.O. Box 40742, Nashville, TN 37204. For information on TVA recreation areas: 800-362-9250 (in-state), 800-251-9242 (from surrounding states). For bed and breakfast accommodations: Bed and Breakfast Host Homes of Tennessee, P.O. Box 110227, Nashville, TN 37222, 615-331-5244, and Bed and Breakfast of Middle Tennessee, P.O. Box 40804, Nashville, TN 37204, 615-297-0883.

6. Arkansas

Arkansas is among the least Southern of all the states covered in this book. Although cotton plantations and an antebellum ambiance survive in the southeast, near the Mississippi River city of Helena, other parts of Arkansas seem suffused with a Western and with an Ozarks hill-country atmosphere. The typical early settler in Arkansas was less a gentleman planter wearing satin than a buckskin-clad frontiersman. As John Gould Fletcher noted in *Arkansas,* "One may say that there are roughly two regions in Arkansas: the highlands, occupying the northwestern half, and the lowlands, occupying the southeastern half of the area. These two are distinct in types of population, in scenery, and in culture." The different ways of life in those two regions appear in both obvious and subtle ways. In *Life in the Leatherwoods,* a memoir of hill farmers in the Arkansas Ozarks in the 1870s and '80s, John Quincy Wolf observes, for example, that "Among the settlers in the Leatherwood Mountains in the 1870s hospitality was a very common virtue and a very genuine one, but it was very different from the hospitality of the Old South in that it was utterly unselfconscious and informal to the last degree. To the White River folks it was not an obligation or a matter of etiquette."

Arkansas, then, the smallest state west of the Mississippi, encompasses a diversity unknown in some of the bigger states. In addition to the Ozark highlands and the Southern farm areas, that diversity includes a Western tone around Fort Smith. The frontier survived in Arkansas, the most western of the Southern states, long after the first migration of pioneers had continued on to the Great Plains. One reason

277

for that lingering frontier atmosphere is that only Arkansas, of all the states west of the Mississippi, found the further westward advance of its citizens blocked by Indian Territory. Unlike Virginia, South Carolina and Georgia with their bluebloods, western Arkansas was a land of redskins and white hunters.

As for the highlands, the upper third of Arkansas—some part of which lies north of each of the surrounding states and thus merges with the Middle West—belongs to the Ozarks, a hilly rural region dotted with log cabins and re-mote villages and veined with rivers. Of the culture in those parts, some outsiders claim there is none and, moreover, some say the people of Arkansas, a state with large areas of remote back country, suffer from a sense of backwardness. But an exaggerated hill-billyism also prevails there in the Ozarks, as if the locals enjoy "putting outsiders on." As Ozark folklorist Vance Randolph entitled one of his collec-tions of back-country tales and legends: *We Always Lie to Strangers*.

Arkansas has suffered from the greatest out-migration and smallest immigration in the twentieth century of any one-time Confederate state, but this has left the area with a low population density and large swatches of unspoiled country-side—more than eighteen million acres of forest, covering nearly two-thirds of the state. Paradoxically, in recent years "Backwardness has become a sought-after attribute where retirees in particular, beset with the maladies of progress, come to seek a more tranquil conclusion to their lives. Thus through an irony of fate, Arkansas has become a sanctuary for many of its long-time detractors," writes Charles E. Thomas in *Jelly Roll* (the title refers to the nickname of a section of a town near El Dorado).

Predecessors of those recent arrivals visited the state more than four hundred and fifty years ago when Spanish explorer Hernando de Soto led his men across the Mississippi and through central Arkansas. A century and a half later, in 1686, the Frenchman Henri de Tonti established the first permanent settlement at Arkansas Post on the Arkansas River. The name of the state originates from the tribe of Indians in the area called Quapaws, pronounced by some redskins "oo-gaq-pa," recorded phonetically by the early French settlers. The state's first newspaper, *The Arkansas Gazette,* founded at Arkansas Post in 1819, single-handedly settled the spelling problem by dropping the "w" then affixed to the end of the word. But although the "Arkansaw" form soon disappeared, for years the citizens debated the proper pronunciation until finally, in 1881, the legislature decreed the correct way to say "Ark-an-saw." It was that session which gave rise to the famous speech that spoke to the rumor that the legislature was considering changing the state's name:

> Mr. Speaker, you blue-billed rascal! I have for the last thirty minutes been trying to get your attention, and each time I have caught your eye, you have wormed, twisted and squirmed like a dog with a flea in his eye, damn you! Gentlemen, you may tear down the honored pictures from the halls of the United States Senate, desecrate the grave of George Washington, haul down the Stars and Stripes, curse the Goddess of liberty, and knock down the tomb of U.S. Grant, but your crime would in no wise compare in enormity with what you propose to do when you would change the name of Arkansas! Change the name of Arkansas—Hell-fire, no! Compare the lily of the valley to the gorgeous sunrise; the discordant croak of the bull-frog to the melodious tones of a nightingale; the classic strains of Mozart to the bray of a Mexican mule; the puny arm of a Peruvian prince to the muscles of a Roman gladiator—but never change the name of Arkansas. Hell, no!

The crisis, if there ever really was one, passed, and Arkansas remained "Arkansas," "the natural state," as it calls itself. And, true to the nickname, in Arkansas you'll find natural,

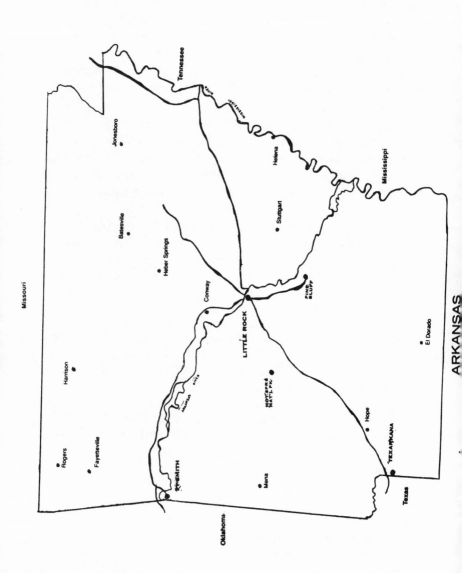

unspoiled people and landscapes. From the Ozark hills to the cotton and rice farms of the lowlands to the once Wild West areas lie a widely varied range of scenery and cultural and historical attractions that define one of the South's most diversified states.

Eastern Arkansas

Piggott—Old Davidsonville, Powhatan Courthouse and Other State Parks and Monuments—Stuttgart—Helena— Arkansas Post

Arkansas is a land of many facets, from diamond deposits to cold crystal-clear streams and hot springs located in varied regions that include Wild West towns, Ozark hill country and lowland cotton plantations. Although the state boasts well-known hot springs it's hardly a hotbed of literary production, so perhaps it's a bit surprising to learn that one of the twentieth century's most famous novels was in part written in the Arkansas town of Piggott. Tucked in the state's far northeastern corner, Piggott affords a good starting point for a tour of eastern Arkansas. It was in May of 1928 when Ernest Hemingway found himself in Piggott with his new wife, Pauline Pfeiffer Hemingway, who was visiting her parents in that Arkansas town. The writer had met Pauline in Paris three years before when Hemingway was living there with his first wife, Hadley. After divorcing Hadley the novelist married Pfeiffer in May 1927, and the following year, in Paris, he started *A Farewell to Arms.* Piggott would seem to be an unlikely place for Hemingway to write that famous book but, in fact, part of the novel was created in that remote corner of Arkansas. On May 31, 1928 Hemingway wrote his editor, Maxwell Perkins, from Piggott: "Am working steadily on the present novel and it seems to go well," and by July 23 the author, again from Piggott, advised Perkins: "Am now on page 486—it must average 180 words to a page." Hemingway-connected sights still survive in Piggott. The most important landmark of the famous novelist's presence there is the two-story barn-studio where the author worked on *A Farewell to Arms,* which he dedicated to Gus Pfeiffer, Pauline's uncle. Ernest and Pauline lived in the studio, which stands behind the gracious and spacious twelve-room Pfeiffer home at the corner of 18th and Cherry Streets. Hemingway took a fancy to the lovely old house, shaded by stately trees and graced by a delightful long front porch. After visiting President Roosevelt in Washington, the novelist wrote the Pfeiffers in August 1937: "I like the house in Piggott much better than the White House."

At the Piggott Public Library you can see signed copies of Hemingway's *Death in the Afternoon* and *A Farewell to Arms.* Pasted in the latter book is an old photo of Hemingway standing next to a strung-up fish he'd apparently just caught. A few blocks away, beyond the other side of the square, stands another reminder of Hemingway's time in Piggott, which he visited on various occasions until he and Pauline divorced in 1940. On Thornton Street, two blocks north of Main, stand a few weathered wooden buildings—one an unusual pagoda-type structure used to store cotton—where the Pfeiffer family operated their cotton company until they sold the business in 1962. Still today, more than half a century after Ernest Hemingway's presence in Piggott, a sign by the buildings reads "Pfeiffer Gin & Fertilizer"—a haunting memory of a famous American novelist's presence in a small Southern town a long time ago.

Scattered around northeast Arkansas are such hamlets, villages and towns as Success, Supply, Peach Orchard, Evening Star, Pocahontas and Clover Bend. A state with settlements bearing such endearing names can't be all bad. As you head west from Piggott toward Pocahontas you'll pass through Corning where one of the country's nearly hundred National Fish Hatcheries is located (open during business hours, free). Established in 1938, the Corning Hatchery includes thirty ponds where some three million largemouth bass, bluegill and other types of fish are cultivated every year to stock federally-owned or managed waters. In Randolph County, to the west, Arkansas's Delta farmland region, which lies near the Mississippi, meets the eastern edge of the Ozark highlands. Two pristine streams that flow through the county, the Eleven Point and the Current, offer "float trips"—canoe excursions down the scenic rivers. South of Pocahontas lies Old Davidsonville State Park, one of Arkansas's forty-four such areas, offering a wide variety of scenery, accommodations, history and recreational facilities. Although you'll find fishing and boating at Old Davidsonville, which nestles near the confluence of the Black, Eleven Point and Spring Rivers, the enclave is one of the state parks that emphasizes history. French settlers established Davidsonville, site of Arkansas's first courthouse and post office, in 1815. Around 1829 the town began to decline when the county seat was relocated and trade routes shifted from the Black River to the old Military Road, an overland route from St. Louis to Texas. Little remains of the settlement, apart from scattered traces excavated by the Arkansas archeological survey in the summers of 1979 and 1980 when pieces of plates, old tools, crumbled bricks, personal items and other materials were found.

Just to the south lie two other state parks—Lake Charles, featuring fishing and camping, and Powhatan Courthouse, a handsome cupola-crowned two-story red brick structure listed on the National Register, which served as seat of Lawrence County from 1888 to 1963. In the mid-nineteenth century Powhatan was a busy river port, from which shell

button blanks were shipped. The old courthouse now houses
area historical records and exhibits of north Arkansas. Yet
another state park, Crowley's Ridge off to the east, occupies
the former plantation of Benjamin Crowley, an early settler
whose name now designates the long narrow arc of rolling
hills that rises from the otherwise flat Delta area and extends
from upper Clay County in northeast Arkansas to the Mississippi River at Helena. Crowley reposes in a pioneer-era
cemetery at the park, where rustic log and stone structures
built in the 1930s by the Civilian Conservation Corps
offer accommodations and other facilities (for reservations:
501-573-6751). Just north of the park lies the town of
Paragould—named for a Mr. Paramore, president of the St.
Louis, Arkansas and Texas Railroad, and a Mr. Gould, president of the St. Louis, Iron Mountain and Southern line—
which bills itself as "Goldfish Capital of the World," a claim
that, no doubt, no other city has disputed. South of
Paragould is Jonesboro, the region's metropolis with more
than 30,000 inhabitants. The Arkansas State University Museum (M.-F., 9–12, 1–4; Sat., 1–4, free) contains a greatly
assorted series of displays on the region's history and culture,
including Indian artifacts, glass and china, and mounted birds
and animals. Jonesboro—home of Mrs. Hattie W. Caraway,
who in the 1930s was elected to two terms as U.S. senator—
also boasts a Riceland Foods plant, one of the firm's ten
such Arkansas facilities, believed to be the world's largest
rice-processing operation. Just off U.S. highway 49 near
Gibson, a few miles from Jonesboro, stretches what is supposedly the world's largest rice field.

Before heading east from Jonesboro it is worth swinging
out to the west to visit yet another state park at Jacksonport,
an old river settlement which, like Davidsonville, declined
when new transportation routes bypassed the place. Thanks
to its location near the confluence of the Black and White
rivers, the Jacksonport area evolved as a trade center, starting

in the late eighteenth century. After the town sprang up in 1833 the settlement developed into a bustling port, with steamboats carrying such local products as bear grease, cotton bales and wild game. During the Civil War five major generals from both the Confederate and Union armies used Jacksonport as headquarters. When the Iron Mountain and Southern Railroad built its track through Jackson County in the 1870s the line emplaced a bridge over the White River at Newport, six miles to the south, which eventually led to Jacksonport's decline, the mercantile houses, saloons and livery stables along Jefferson Street gradually shutting down. Remnants of the old town remaining today include a brick privy, originally walnut lined; a carriage house with four nineteenth-century vehicles on display; the 1880s-vintage "Mary Woods II" steamboat; and the 1869 brick courthouse, with period rooms containing history displays and, upstairs, the courtroom maintained as it was in the old days (April–Oct., Tu.–Sat., 8–5; Sun., 1–5; Nov.–March, Tu.–Sun, 1–5, free). At Weiner, south of Jonesboro, the annual Rice Festival—featuring more than four hundred rice dishes—takes place every October (for information: 501-684-2284); while off to the east of Jonesboro rises the Herman Davis Historical Monument, dedicated to Arkansas's most decorated World War I soldier, ranked fourth by General John J. Pershing on his list of a hundred heroes.

Nearby Blytheville boasts Mississippi County Community College, which operates what's supposedly the world's largest solar energy project and is the nation's only college campus designed to use solar energy exclusively. Osceola, to the south, is the hometown of Kemmons Wilson, founder of Holiday Inns, while the nearby town of Wilson, which sports an English Tudor-style square, was founded a century ago by Robert E. Lee Wilson, whose descendants still own in the area one of the world's largest cotton plantations. In Wilson is the Hampson Museum (Tu.–Sat., 9–5, adm.), a state-park facility that houses the archeological collection of Indian artifacts excavated by Dr. James K. Hampson, a physician, at Nodena, his family's plantation. Nearby to the west are Dyess, part of a colony established in 1933 to give Depression-era farmers a new start in life and one-time home of country singer Johnny Cash; Lepanto, where the Lepanto USA Museum (April 1–Nov. 1, Sat., 10–4; Sun., 1–4, free) contains an old-time general store, old-fashioned clothes and other relics of yesteryear; and Marked Tree, the world's only town with that name, so called from the oak that once indicated a short portage between the St. Francis and Little rivers, which flow in opposite directions, that saved Indians eight miles of paddling upstream.

From the northeast corner of Arkansas you can make your way farther south via the Wapanocca National Wildlife Refuge (open daylight hours, free), a link in the chain of natural habitats along the so-called Mississippi Flyway, the migration path birds travel on their trips north and south, and then West Memphis, home of Southland Park (open, April–Nov.), the nation's largest dog-racing facility. Off to the west, just south of Wynne, where Cross County Historical Museum contains displays on the Indian mound-builders and early French settlers in the area, lies Village Creek State Park, perched atop Crowley's Ridge. One of the park's trails follows the century-and-a-half-old Military Road, the first improved travel route between Memphis and Little Rock. Farther out to the southwest is the old railroad town of Brinkley, named for R. C. Brinkley, president of the Memphis and Little Rock line which opened in 1871. It's definitely worth a detour to dine or doze at the delightful 1915 Great Southern Hotel, the three-story brick successor to earlier hostelries there. Victorian-style couches and an old- fashioned cast-iron stove in the lobby recall the early days, while the dining room, with its high tin ceiling and quartet of hanging fans, will also take you back to a bygone era. Specialities of the house include pecan fried chicken, catfish and Mississippi Flyway duck, as well as such sweetly sinister desserts as praline pecan ice-cream pie and white chocolate cheesecake and Arkansas Derby pie (chocolate, coconut, pecans and brown sugar). Four of the hotel's original sixty-one rooms have been restored for overnight guests (501-734-4955; the dining room is open for lunch, M.–Sat., 11–2; dinner, Tu.–Sat., 5–9; and brunch, Sun., 11–2:30). At Des Arc, west of Brinkley, you'll find the Prairie County Museum, with exhibits on steamboating, commercial fishing, the White River pearl industry and Delta culture, as well as another old-time place to stay, the 5-B's bed and breakfast, installed in a National Register-listed eighty-year-old house (501-256-4789). Off to the west you can conveniently drop down to Clarendon, an early nineteenth-century White River settlement with a scattering of old structures sufficiently photogenic to have attracted to the town film crews who shot there parts of the 1983 movie *A Soldier's Story* and a 1984 TV production.

The hamlet of Holly Grove, just to the south, has recently undergone historic preservation, with the train station and Main Street storefronts restored to their original appearance. Before heading east to Helena, on the Mississippi River, it's worth continuing west to Stuttgart, center of the Grand Prairie rice-growing region. More bushels of rice are produced in Stuttgart than on any other acreage the same size anywhere else in the world. The industry began relatively late, in 1904, when an ex-Nebraskan named William H. Fuller planted seventy acres of rice that yielded a crop of nearly seventy-five bushels an acre. Before that, the Grand Prairie, an area some ninety by forty miles, was thought to be agriculturally valueless. But Fuller disproved this erroneous theory, and by the time he died in 1922 Arkansas was producing more than seven million bushels of rice a year. Stuttgart, headquarters of the huge Riceland Foods cooperative, the world's largest rice processor, pays homage to its principal crop with displays on the industry at the Agricultural Museum (Tu.–Sat., 10–12, 1–4; Sun., 1:30–4:30, free), which also contains displays on crop-dusting by air, wildlife dioramas and historical exhibits. The Producers Rice Mill in Stuttgart offers tours of a rice-milling facility (by appointment: 501-673-4444), and every year during Thanksgiving week the town hosts the World Championship Duck Calling Contest, with competitors sounding out flying, feeding and mating calls.

As you head east back toward Helena you'll pass near St. Charles, where the Civil War's most deadly single shot was fired when, on June 17, 1862, a Confederate cannonball hit the boiler of the Union warship "Mound City," causing a violent explosion that killed nearly one hundred and fifty Federal troops. Up to the north lies the Louisiana Purchase Historical Monument, a granite marker that indicates the base point established in 1815 for the survey of most of Arkansas, Missouri, Iowa, the Dakotas and Minnesota, which formed part of the 1803 Purchase. For more than a century the initial point remained unnoticed until 1921 when two men resurveying the Phillips and Lee county lines noticed a pair of large trees used as "witness trees" by the 1815 survey. The monument stands at the end of a three-hundred-yard long boardwalk that passes through an animal and foliage-filled swamp, a type of terrain rare in Arkansas since most such areas have been drained by land reclamation projects. At nearby Marianna throbs the five-million-gallon-per-minute W. G. Huxtable Pumping Station, said to be the largest such installation in the world, which controls the St. Francis River waters to protect farmland from flooding. Also at Marianna stands a memorial to John Patterson, believed to be the first European child born in Arkansas (1790). Patterson's self-composed epitaph (he died in 1886)—referring to France, Spain, the Louisiana Territory and

Arkansas—summarizes the state's history: "I was born in a Kingdom, raised in an Empire; Attained manhood in a Territory; Am now a citizen of a State; And have never been one hundred miles from where I live." Marianna is the gateway to St. Francis National Forest, one of the nation's smallest, where hardwood trees and wild orchids abound.

A backwoods road that cuts through the forest leads you to Helena, Arkansas's only truly "Old South"-type city. In *Life on the Mississippi* Mark Twain described Helena, named by an early settler for his daughter, as "occupying one of the prettiest situations on the river." With its Mississippi River location, Helena used to call itself "Arkansas's Only Seaport," but these days the city's slogan is "Long ago is not so far away." And it's true, for the old days linger in Helena, where you'll find memories of yesteryear at such places as the 1872 Almer Store, now an arts and crafts shop, built by Ulrich Almer from components of a flatboat he floated down the Mississippi; the half-acre Confederate Cemetery atop Crowley's Ridge where Dixie soldiers killed in the July 4, 1863, Battle of Helena repose; the early twentieth-century depot, which houses the new (1990) Delta Cultural Center, with regional exhibits, and the Phillips County Courthouse, both listed on the National Register; a monument commemorating de Soto's 1541 crossing of the Mississippi at a point south of Helena; and the four-block National Register-listed stretch of Cherry Street downtown. The Bank of Helena building (c. 1879) at 509 Cherry is the oldest structure, while 401-5 Cherry has a decorative pressed-tin facade with glazed brick and terra cotta detailing. The new Helena Reach River Park includes an elevated boardwalk with views of the Mississippi. Helena also once claimed the National River Academy where riverboat pilots were trained, and every fall the city hosts the King Biscuit Blues Festival named after the 1940s KFFA music show "King Biscuit Time." Although cotton, not the biscuit, was once "King" in Arkansas—in 1939 the nearly million and

a-half-bale crop produced half the state's total farm income—
today the fiber ranks merely as a lowly "Count." But the
many antebellum houses around Helena recall the era of cotton's rule, the city's two bed and breakfast mansions both
having been built by cotton businessmen: the Edelweiss, in
the 1901 Short-Bieri Home, listed on the National Register,
at 409 Bisco (501-338-3839) and the 1904 Edwardian Inn,
317 Bisco (501-338-9155).

Between Helena and the Louisiana line to the south lie
a few other places of historic or scenic interest. In the fall
of 1919 riots mounted by black sharecroppers terrorized the
village of Elaine, an incident that culminated in the 1923
U.S. Supreme Court case of *Moore* v. *Dempsey,* an opinion
written by Oliver Wendell Holmes that liberalized the ability
to attack a state conviction because of alleged violations of
a defendant's federal constitutional rights. Farther south, at
the now inaccessible point where the Arkansas flows into
the Mississippi, once stood the town of Napoleon, Desha
(pronounced "De-shay" by locals) County seat. Mark Twain
once surprised a riverboat captain by asking to be put ashore
at Napoleon, which by then had washed away: "Didn't leave
hide nor hair, shred nor shingle of it, except the fag-end
of a shanty and one brick chimney," the pilot informed
Twain. Before the river ended its reclamation project at Napoleon, L. W. Watson offered to donate five inland acres
of ground to the county, which moved its seat to what is
now the town of Watson.

Not far north of Watson lies the Arkansas Post National
Monument, which memorializes one of the state's most historic settlements. Founded in 1686 by the Frenchman Henri
de Tonti as a trading post, the village was supposedly the
first permanent European presence in the lower Mississippi
River Valley. During the colonial periods—the French controlled Arkansas until 1765 when the Spanish took over up

to 1800—and in the early part of the nineteenth century after the 1803 Louisiana Purchase, the Arkansas Post witnessed a never-ending series of new settlers, military expeditions, Indian trading and raiding parties and American pioneers. When Congress established the Arkansas Territory in 1819, the Post became the first capital, and in November of that year started *The Arkansas Gazette,* the oldest newspaper west of the Mississippi until it ceased publication in 1001. In 1821 the capital, the newspaper and many residents moved upriver to the newly established town of Little Rock and Arkansas Post began to decline. Little now remains of the old settlements in the area, but the visitor center (8–5, free) and historical markers there at Post Bend on the Arkansas River serve to recall the site's storied past. The Arkansas Post County Museum (March–Oct., W.–Sat., 9:30–4; Sun., 1–4; Nov.–Dec., F.–Sun; closed Jan.–Feb, free) contains other area historical displays, including a 1930s half-scale playhouse sized throughout for an eight-year-old girl.

To complete your tour of Arkansas's eastern edge, continue south via Dumas—where the Desha County Museum (Tu., Th., Sun., 2–4, free) offers historical artifacts—down to McGehee, a pleasant town with some attractive old houses. Just to the west snakes Bayou Bartholomew, the world's longest bayou (three hundred miles), while a few miles east lies Arkansas City, hometown of John N. Johnson, founder and publisher of *Ebony* and *Jet* magazines. At Arkansas City—which boasts one of Arkansas's oldest courthouses, a splended old building with bright white trim—runs the nation's longest levee. At Dermott, south of McGehee, you can see cotton processed from boll to bale at Arkansas's largest gin, the family-owned Lephiew Gin Company, established a century ago (tours available, Sep.–Nov., adm.; 501-538-5288). Oddly shaped Lake Chicot, a narrow arc of water by the Mississippi, once formed the great river's main

channel. A marker on eighteen-mile long Lake Shore Drive
recalls Charles A. Lindbergh's first night flight, made over
Lake Chicot in April 1923.

The area around Eudora, tucked away in the far southeastern corner of Arkansas, boasts some of the state's most pro-
ductive cotton-growing farms, which benefit from the more
than thousand-foot-deep rich alluvial soil (the world's average soil depth is a mere seven inches). It seems that
boosterism demands that every city worth its salt must boast
it's the "capital" of something. Since the state's seat of government resides in Little Rock, Eudora is reduced to claiming
a lesser honor: the town holds itself out as the "Catfish Capital of Arkansas." With such legendary Southern fiber and
fins as cotton and catfish, in this region you are now back
in the Deep South.

Southern Arkansas

Monticello—El Dorado—Texarkana—Crater of Diamonds and Old Washington State Parks

Although the first seat of Drew County, in eastern Arkansas near the south edge of the state, was called Rough and
Ready, the center of government now bears the more melodi-
ous name Monticello. But perhaps the former designation
more appropriately describes the rather rough-hewn, heavily
forested areas that dominate southern Arkansas. Great stands
of pine trees bristle from the landscape, a timber and logging
area harvested by Georgia-Pacific, International Paper and
other large forestry firms. The very eastern part of the region, near Monticello, consists of farmland similar to the
Delta area plantations toward the Mississippi, while west
of Monticello begin the forests. Monticello's Drew County

Historic Museum (Tu.–F., 1–5; Sat.–Sun., 2–5, free) occupies the 1907 Cavaness house, listed on the National Register, an imposing but not attractive boxy building made of molded cement blocks. The museum contains a richly varied display of historical items that provide a good introduction to the region. The Historic District on North Main Street includes a group of old houses, also listed on the Register. Just west of town is Warren, which holds the Pink Tomato Festival every year in June when produce buyers visit the tomato stands there and at the photogenic little town of Hermitage to the south. To the northwest of Monticello lie the Marks Mill Battleground Historical Monument, where Confederate troops captured a Union supply train in 1864, and the town of Rison, whose old log cabin, doctor's residence, blacksmith shop, mercantile establishment and 1867 Methodist church, listed on the National Register, comprise Pioneer Village (Tu.–Sat., 9–4; Sun., 1–4, adm.), a re-creation of a nineteenth-century south Arkansas settlement.

Through Cleveland County flows the scenic Saline River, on which you can take float trips. Nearby Fordyce boasts the world's first southern pine plywood plant, a Georgia-Pacific facility that pioneered manufacturing techniques. But the town's pride is that Alabama coach Paul "Bear" Bryant was born there; while nearby at Kingsland country singer Johnny Cash saw the light of day. In the spring Fordyce mounts a week-long "Fordyce on the Cotton Belt" festival commemorating the railroad's role in the town's development. Klappenbach's downtown sells great baked goods, while Register-listed Wynne Phillips House takes bed and breakfast guests. From Fordyce in 1960 was made the first direct-dial long distance telephone call.

The southern route out of Monticello takes you down to Crossett, near the Louisiana line, a one-time company town that a predecessor to Georgia-Pacific owned until 1946. The fifteen-acre Wilcoxon Demonstration Forest, developed by Georgia-Pacific, offers a hiking route certified as part of the National and the State Trail Systems; while to the west is another outdoor area, the Felsenthal National Wildlife Refuge, located in a bottomland area filled with bayous and lakes. Farther to the west lies El Dorado, the region's main city and the only major town in Arkansas not founded in connection with a river, road or railway line. Tradition has it that the settlement started after a wanderer named Matthew F. Rainey, whose wagon broke down there in 1843, was so impressed by the local farmers' eagerness to buy his possessions that he remained to open a store. But El Dorado lived up to its gilt-edged name only beginning in the 1920s when an oil strike brought to the area the riches of black gold, a development recalled at the Arkansas Oil and Brine Museum (M.–Sat., 9–5; Sun., 1–5, free) in the nearby town of Smackover. Around the many-columned (more than any other structure in Arkansas) Union County Courthouse in downtown El Dorado stands a group of restored commercial buildings, nine of which are listed on the National Register, as is the 1848 John Newton House (April–May, 10–4; or by appointment: 501-863-7102, adm.). Another restored El Dorado residence, 1926 Wilson Place, 520 East 8th Street (501-862-2530) offers bed and breakfast accommodations.

North of El Dorado, beyond Smackover, lies Camden, a town with martial memories. A Confederate cemetery and bullet holes in the walls of an upstairs room at the 1847 McCollum-Chidester House (April–Oct., 9–4, adm.) recall the Civil War era when the residence served in turn as headquarters for both Southern and Union generals. It was Camden native S. P. Morgan who supposedly fired the first shot of the Spanish-American War from Admiral George Dewey's flagship moored in Manila Bay. Antebellum homes along Washington Avenue also serve to bring back the nineteenth century in Camden. The road northwest out of Camden takes you to Poison Spring Battleground Historical

Monument on the site where Union soldiers poisoned the water in an attempt to halt a Confederate force marching from Camden, and then to Reader, home of the old-fashioned "Possum Trot Line" Reader Railroad, the nation's oldest standard gauge all-steam passenger train (June–Aug., Sat. 11 and 2; Sun., 2, adm.), powered by a wood-burning locomotive. Gurdon, farther north, glows with a ghostly brightness called the "Gurdon Light," which supposedly appears near where a railroad worker was killed next to the train tracks. In 1892 local lumbermen at Gurdon founded a trade group called the International Order of Hoo-Hoos.

If you're heading southwest from Camden, rather than northwest, the route to Magnolia—which passes by houses with oil wells in their yards—takes you to Logoly State Park, named from the first two letters of the Longino, Goode and Lyle families who donated the area, once frequented by people visiting there to drink the supposedly medicinal waters from eleven springs. Magnolia's magnolia-filled courthouse square presents a picture out of a Faulkner novel, for the square duplicates the one in the author's hometown of Oxford, Mississippi, which the writer described in some of his books. Around the square stand antique shops, one with fixtures from the old post office at nearby McNeil installed within. East of Magnolia is the village of Village—perhaps the state's most descriptive place-name—while to the west stands Stamps where author Maya Angelou, whose books include *I Know Why the Caged Bird Sings*, grew up. Stamp collectors from around the world send mail to be cancelled at Stamps, the nation's only town with that name, so called by the first postmaster in honor of her father, Hardy James Stamps. Southwest of Stamps, down near the Louisiana border, lies Conway Cemetery State Park where James Sevier Conway, Arkansas's first governor, and thirty-nine members of his family repose. From there it's fun to take the free ferry across the Red River, of cowboy and Western folklore fame, to continue north to Texarkana.

Texarkana is a bit of an oddity—two towns in one, or perhaps one town in two. The city straddles the Arkansas-Texas state line, a boundary indicated by a marker in front of the post office on descriptively named State Line Avenue where you can stand in Arkansas and Texas at the same time. Both of the states combine judicial and law enforcements agencies at the unique Bi-State Justice Center, said to be the world's only dual-jurisdiction office. But a few differences separate the twin towns: the Texas side is larger and drier (33,000 inhabitants and no alcohol publicly sold), the Arkansas section smaller and wetter (23,000 people and package liquor stores). Texarkana's name originates from not just two but fully three states. It's said that back in the 1870s railroad surveyor Gus Knobel posted a sign bearing the designation "TEX-ARK-ANA," the last trio of letters from the ending of "Louisiana." Sights in town (or the towns) include the 1924 Perot Theater, renamed for native son H. Ross Perot, founder of Electronic Data Systems Corporation, and an outdoor mural at Third and Main Streets honoring another local fellow who made good, ragtime composer Scott Joplin. The Texarkana Historical Museum (Tu.–F., 10–4; Sat., and Sun., 12–3, adm.) contains local history and Caddo Indian exhibits, and the 1885 Ace of Clubs House (W.–F., 10–3; Sat. and Sun., 1–3, adm.), built in a trefoil shape to recall the poker hand with which lumberman James Draugh won the funds to construct the residence, contains all the 1894-vintage furnishings of the second owner. To the north of Texarkana lies the curiously named town of DeQueen, so called for Jan Degolijen, a Dutchman who served as an official of the Kansas City Southern when the line extended through the area in the 1890s. The name of the town's newspaper, perhaps inevitably, is *The DeQueen Bee.*

To complete your tour of southern Arkansas, back to the

east you'll come to Hope, home of the world's largest watermelons, upwards of two hundred pounds. The third weekend of August Hope, whose motto is "A slice of the good
life," hosts the annual Watermelon Festival. Just north of
Hope lies Old Washington Historic State Park, one of
Arkansas's most evocative attractions. Much state history
haunts the houses, old official buildings and well-shaded
streets of the more than century-and-a-half-old settlement.
During the Civil War the 1836 Hempstead County Courthouse served as the state's Confederate Capitol, while the
Old Tavern Inn (the present version is a 1960 reconstruction
of the original, dating from the 1830s) was supposedly where
Sam Houston and others plotted the war to take over Texas
and where Davy Crockett and Jim Bowie stayed on their
way to the Alamo. The (reconstructed) blacksmith shop at
Washington is where metalworker James Black is said to
have forged for Bowie the world's first "Bowie knife," the
so-called "Arkansas toothpick," copies of which are on display at the Gun Museum, installed in a former bank building.
Old residences at Washington include the 1845 Royston
House, listed on the National Register; the 1832 Block-Catts
home, one of Arkansas's oldest two-story houses; the house
built in the mid-1840s by the father-in-law of Augustus Garland, governor, U.S. senator and U.S. attorney general; and
the Purdom House, which now contains a museum relating
the history of medicine in Arkansas. For breakfast or lunch
the Williams Tavern, an 1832 building housing a restaurant,
offers a delightful place to eat (7–2 daily, except Tu.), while
the Old Washington Jail Inn (501-983-2790) takes bed and
breakfast guests in a renovated 1872 jail house (open weekends only fall, winter and spring).

Arkansas's most unusual state park, and one unique in
the U.S., is Crater of Diamonds, north of Washington, the
nation's only public diamond field. Back in 1906 a farmer
named John Huddleson noticed a shiny stone roll away from

his plow as he tilled the land. Jewelers in Little Rock confirmed the find was a diamond, and eventually commercial mining operations started in the area. In 1952 the crater was opened to the public as a tourist attraction, and twenty years later Arkansas acquired the forty-acre field, which became a state park. Prospectors have unearthed more than seventy thousand diamonds, including the forty-carat "Uncle Sam" and thirty-four-carat "Star of Murfreesboro." Visitors recover an estimated one thousand diamonds a year at the park (March–Nov., 8–5; Dec.–Feb., 8–4:30, adm.), which attendants plow periodically to unearth fresh ground. In the spring of 1990 four mining companies, including one from Australia, did exploratory drilling to determine if Crater of Diamonds held commercial quantities of kimberlite "ore," which contains the gems. In December 1992 the consortium announced that the park contained one of the world's largest formations of diamond-bearing rock—78 million tons. Commercial development may diminish or eliminate the public's chance to prospect there. Of all the south's many attractions, Arkansas's Crater is truly a gem of a place—a description which, for once, is no exaggeration.

Central Arkansas

Little Rock—Pine Bluff—Heber Springs—Hot Springs—Mena—Russellville—Van Buren and Fort Smith

For more than a century and a half Little Rock has been the center of Arkansas. The capital and financial center stands in the middle of the state at a point where Arkansas's two major regions, the hill country to the northwest and the eastern flatlands, meet. You can actually see the transition point between the two regions as you drive from downtown Little Rock west up to such hillier neighborhoods as Pulaski Heights. In the early days travelers used a bare stone peak on the north side of the Arkansas River as a landmark. On the south bank two miles downstream from "Big Rock" rose a smaller outcropping referred to as "La Petite Roche." In the city's Riverfront Park a plaque marks the "Little Rock." Little Rock got off to a rocky start in more ways than one. Moses Austin, father of "Father of Texas" Stephen Austin, established a village near "La Petite Roche," only to learn that a speculator named William Russell claimed the terrain. Russell filed suit and in June 1821 the court upheld his claim to the land, whereupon Austin proceeded to remove his town, an unusual undertaking described by Thomas James in his 1847 *Three Years Among the Indians and New Mexicans:*

> As we approached Little Rock we beheld a scene of true western life and character that no other country could present. First, we saw a large wood and stone building in flames, and then about one hundred men, painted, masked, and disguised in almost every conceivable manner, engaged in removing the town. These men, with ropes and chains, would march off a frame house on wheels and logs, place it about three or four hundred yards from its former site, and then return and move off another in the same manner. . . . Such buildings as they could not move, they burned down. . . . In one day and night, Mr. Russell's land was disencumbered of the town of Little Rock.

Little Rock was thus perhaps the best-traveled town of the time. The best place to get a feel for those early days when Little Rock was established, then disestablished, and then reestablished, is at the Arkansas Territorial Restoration (9–5; Sun., from 1, adm.), a compound that contains a dozen or so restored nineteenth-century structures, including homes occupied by an early governor, by the founder of *The Arkansas Gazette,* and the late 1820s Hinderliter House, where the last Territorial Legislature assembled in 1835.

Some of the state's early history is traced in displays at the handsome Greek Revival Old State House (9–5; Sun., from 1, free) where the legislature of the new state (admitted in 1836) met until 1911 when the present capitol building was finished. Many of the leading early political figures, as well as later notables, ended in Little Rock's Mount Holly Cemetery, one of the few graveyards listed on the National Register, where ten governors, three Senators, five Confederate generals and John Gould Fletcher, Pulitzer Prize winner for poetry, repose. Old mansions that fill the Quapaw Quarter district of town give the flavor of Little Rock of a century and more ago. In the district are the Arkansas Museum of Science and History (9–4:30; Sun., from 1, adm.), installed in the former Little Rock Arsenal (1841), listed on the National Register, where General Douglas MacArthur was born in 1880; the Decorative Arts Museum (M.–F., 10–5; Sun., from 12, free); and the Arkansas Arts Center (10–5; Sun., from 12, free), with an exceptionally good collection of drawings. A lesser-known, more off-beat Little Rock collection is at the E.R.I. Museum—the initials stand for "Elderly Retired Instrument"—at 5702 West 12th (M.–F., 10–7; Sat., 10–6, free), with mandolins, banjos, an antique "New York Martin" guitar and other such old pieces that have found a comfortable place to retire at the museum.

Although central Arkansas's main attractions lie to the west of Little Rock (they are covered below), a few areas to the south and north are worth visiting if you're heading in one of those directions. Just south of Scott, where the Plantation Agricultural Museum recently opened, is Toltec Mounds State Park (Tu.–Sat., 8–5; Sun., 12–5, free), a National Historic Landmark where millennium-old mounds recall the Indians' presence in the area. The village of Wabbaseka, farther south, was the hometown of black activist Eldridge Cleaver, and Varner, even farther down, is the site of Arkansas's best-guarded public event—the Arkansas

Prison Rodeo, in which more than five hundred performers compete. Lincoln County seat, Star City, is named for its five surrounding hills which, when connected on a map, form the shape of a star. Cane Creek State Park is located four miles east.

Pine Bluff, the major city in the area and one of the oldest in the state, stretches alongside a deep bend of the Arkansas River. In early April 1861 Confederate troops fired a warning volley at Union ships steaming upriver to supply the Federal garrison at Fort Smith. This is said to have been the first shot of the Civil War, the more famous shelling of Fort Sumter at Charleston, South Carolina, taking place a few days later starting on April 12, 1861. Among the antique houses at Pine Bluff are the Victorian-era childhood home of Martha Mitchell (open by appointment: 501-535-4973), wife of Watergate Attorney General John N. Mitchell, and a trio of National Register-listed places: the Du Bocage House (by appointment: 501-541-8000), with period furniture and a graceful winding staircase; Margland II, a bed and breakfast establishment, 703 West 2nd (501-536-6000); and the 1860 Ben Pearson home (by appointment: 501-535-0462), formerly owned by the renowned archer and proprietor of the world's largest bow and arrow manufacturer. Nearby stands Register-listed Trinity Episcopal, the state's oldest church building (1837) in continuous use. "Engine 819," an oil-burning locomotive built in Pine Bluff in the mid-1940s, and other train memorabilia in the Arkansas Railroad Museum at the old Cotton Belt-line shops, recall railroading days of half a century ago.

If you leave Little Rock toward the opposite direction, to the north, you'll pass by Camp Joseph Robinson, a National Guard facility named for that triple-threat fellow who during one year (1913), served as governor, congressman and U.S. senator for Arkansas. Up at Conway rise two structures of yesteryear, the 1830 Daniel Greathouse home (April–Oct., M.–Sat., 9–4; Sun., 2–4, free), one of the state's finest old log houses, and the Cadron Blockhouse (6–10, free), replica of a two-century-old combination trading post, residence, stockade and gathering place. Just west of Conway, which boasts three colleges—University of Central Arkansas, Hendrix and Central Baptist—lies Toad Suck Park, near a former Arkansas River ferry crossing. A restored ferry tow recalls the days when rivermen would frequent a local tavern and suck on liquor bottles until the imbibers swelled up like toads, as the disapproving locals described them. Another log structure, the century-old one-room log cabin built by Martin Woolly, son of an early area pioneer, stands in Woolly Hollow State Park in the foothills of the Ozark Mountains. Farther north, a dam built in 1983 on the Little Red River created the forty-thousand-acre dragon-shaped Greers Ferry Lake, a resort area with excellent fishing, boating, swimming and other aquatic activities. A plaque and a bust mark the spot where President John F. Kennedy inaugurated the Greers Ferry Dam in October 1963, his last official dedication ceremony. Just below the dam is a National Fish Hatchery that produces rainbow trout, and on the west side of the dam is a Corps of Engineers visitor center and the starting point for dam tours. In 1992 the record brown trout, weighing more than forty pounds, was caught in the Little Red river at the base of the dam. Red Apple Resort (800-255-8900; in Arkansas, 800-482-8900) on Eden Isle is the area's most attractive hotel, designed by a student of Frank Lloyd Wright and built of wood and rock to blend with the surroundings. Heber Springs, the lake area's main town, offers a bed and breakfast establishment, Oak Tree Inn, highway 110 west (501-362-7731).

Batesville, to the northeast, was once Arkansas's leading city. Josiah H. Shinn, in *Pioneers and Makers of Arkansas,* recalls a stirring toast delivered at a Batesville Fourth of July celebration years ago: "May the hand wither and rot that plucks one feather from the tail of the Bird of Freedom to adorn the crown of royalty." Arkansas College, established in 1872, is supposedly the oldest private Christian college west of the Mississippi. A scattering of old homes line the streets of Batesville, while a marker north of town recalls the three Arkansas governors who lived in the area. Farther out, on highway 69 eight miles northwest of town, stands the 1867 Spring Mill, while to the southeast at Oil Trough, named for the bear oil shipped out in the old days on the White River, is the Hulsey Bend School, a restored one-room schoolhouse. From Batesville you can continue to Jacksonport State Park to the east or to the Ozark Folk Center at Mountain View to the northwest or you can return to Little Rock and proceed to the attractions in the western part of Arkansas.

Southwest of Little Rock lies the famous spa town of Hot Springs. On the way there you'll pass through Benton, near which was discovered in 1888 the nation's largest deposit of bauxite, used to make aluminum. The nearby town named Bauxite and Benton's Gann Building, the world's only baux-ite structure, constructed of piebald-hued blocks of the min-eral, recall the discovery. The 1853 Shoppach House and the 1836 Saline County Courthouse offer memories of nineteenth-century Benton, while a plaque on courthouse square memorializes Hernando de Soto's 1541 visit to the area and his discovery of the salt deposits which gave the county its name. The Spanish explorer was the first Euro-pean to come upon the "Valley of the Vapors," as the early Indians called the area watered by forty-seven thermal springs. Although it was 1921 when Congress designated the thermal enclave a National Park, the only one located within city limits, the reserve is in fact the oldest federally-owned land in the entire Park system, having been set aside as a "pleasuring ground" by the Jackson Administration in 1832, forty years before Congress acted to protect Yellow-stone, the first officially designated National Park. From early days Hot Springs was a popular resort area: locals built the first bathhouse in 1830. In 1902 H. I. Campbell opened an alligator farm, which still operates, and back then another entrepreneur ran an ostrich farm, while in 1906 a man named Simon Cooper opened a bathhouse for horses (it burned down in 1913). By 1927 sixteen companies were bottling and selling mineral water, and Bathhouse Row establishments attracted visitors from around the nation. In the 1920s the Ku Klux Klan tried to establish itself in Hot Springs, an effort that greatly alarmed the Catholic mayor, Lee McLaughlin, who called on a friend to help rid the city of the white supremacy group. The name of the mayor's friend was Al Capone.

Although Hot Springs started to decline and decay in the 1960s after the bathhouses began to shut down, in recent years a revival has taken place culminating in the 1989 restoration of Fordyce, the biggest and most elegant bathhouse, embellished with stained-glass skylights, etched-glass doors, marble benches, tile floors, mahogany dressing cubicles and a life-size statue of Hernando de Soto accepting an Indian maiden's offering of water. The old dowager of a place now serves as a museum and visitor center. Baths are available elsewhere, at the famous Arlington and Majestic resort hotels, at the Buckstaff bathhouse, and at a few other spas (baths cost about ten dollars). Hot Springs tends to be a bit tacky, with such attractions—or distractions—as a wax museum, the Educated Animal Zoo, the alligator farm, the Tiny Town display of mini-scenes and other such tourist come-ons or turn-offs.

Less commercialized sights include the splendid panorama viewed from the two hundred and sixteen-foot high Mountain Tower (March to mid-May, 9–6; mid-May to Labor Day, 9–9; Labor Day to Oct., 9–5, adm.) and the handsome gleaming white Mountain Valley Water headquarters building (Memorial Day to Labor Day, 10–6; Sun. from 1; other months, Tu.–Sat., 10–6, free), with displays on the famous mineral water—guzzled by presidents, senators, racehorses and other celebrities—whose bottling plant on highway 7 thirteen miles north of Hot Springs is also worth a visit (same hours as the headquarters). For accommodations in or near Hot Springs three places offer bed and breakfast: William House, an 1890 brownstone and brick Victorian-style structure listed on the National Register, 420 Quapaw Avenue (501-624-4275); Vintage Comfort, 303 Quapaw (501-623-3258), with four bedrooms named after the owner's children and the slogan "At fading light and fall of night beneath a starry dome / Oh ye shall find a warm and kind reminder of thy home"; and Stillmeadow Farm, in the country about ten miles south (501-525-9994). Another attractive place to stay is the lodge at De Grey State Park (501-865-4591) south of Hot Springs.

Beyond Hot Springs lie some additional attractions. Malvern, to the southeast, which calls itself the "Brick Capital of the World," celebrates its main industry with an annual "Brickfest" held the last weekend of June. At the hamlet of Caddo Gap west of Hot Springs stands a monument that marks the most western point Hernando de Soto reached during his 1541 explorations. Farther on, at Langley, is another bed and breakfast place, the Country School Inn (501-356-3091 or 289-5781). Mount Ida, north of Caddo Gap, calls itself the "Quartz Crystal Capital of the World." Rivals for the title are the island of Madagascar and a corner of Brazil, the only other areas in the world where the quartz crystal quality is high enough to warrant mining. At Wegner mine three miles south of town you can practice for the annual World's Championship Quartz Crystal Dig held in October, and at the Robins Mining Company Shop you can buy glittering specimens of the rock. On the way west to Mena you'll pass through Pine Ridge, originally called Waters but renamed for the mythical town referred to on the once-famous "Lum and Abner" radio show. Displays at the

"Jot 'Em Down Store" in Pine Ridge recall the famous comedy duo. Chester Lauck and Norris Goff, the original Lum
and Abner, were from nearby Mena, a railroad town founded
in 1896 when the Kansas City Southern tracks arrived there.

In Jannsen Park, listed on the National Register, stands
a structure predating the city, an 1851 log cabin where border
bandits and guerrillas used to gather in the 1860s and '70s
and where such notables as William Jennings Bryan, Carrie
Nation and Huey Long addressed public gatherings. In recent years Mena has developed as a center for Arabian horses
bred at several area stud farms. Rich Mountain, thirteen miles
north, is not idly named, for it contains in a single square
mile more species of wild plants, flowers and weeds in their
natural state than anywhere else in the world on a tract that
size. The twenty-seven-hundred-foot high peak, one of the
highest points between the Rockies and the Appalachians,
also boasts a mile-long scenic train said to be the nation's
loftiest miniature railroad. This route lies in Queen Wilhel-
mina State Park, originally a resort developed by the Kansas
City Southern and named in honor of the Dutch monarch,
since capital from Holland largely financed the railroad. The
first lodge, called "Castle in the Sky," as it crowned the
crest of Rich Mountain, burned in 1973, but a new thirty-
eight-room version of the old hotel was later built (for reservations: 501-395-2863). Through the park runs Talimena
Scenic Drive, a fifty-four-mile panoramic highway that winds
along the crests of the thickly wooded Ouachita ("good
hunting grounds" in Indian lingo) mountains, the nation's
only east-west range.

Such is the itinerary from Little Rock to the southwest.
The route northwest of Little Rock will take you to Fort
Smith via some scenic state parks and a few historical attractions. From the cone-shaped peak (reached by trails) of Pinnacle Mountain, in a state park only a short distance west
of Little Rock, spreads a panorama of the area extending

over some fifty miles. Farther on is another state park, Petit
Jean, named after a French girl who, legend has it, disguised
herself as a boy to accompany her fiance, a sailor, to America.
Rustic wood and stone-built Mather Lodge, along with
twelve cabin units, provides overnight accommodation (501-
727-5431), as do the thirteen modern old-style privately
owned cabins at Tanyard Springs (501-727-5200) near the
park. Each cabin carries out a different theme: in the Deer-
slayer a thirty-five-foot cedar tree trunk forms the staircase;
a nineteenth-century coach serves as a bed in the Stagecoach;
in the Cattle Rancher one bed occupies a wagon; the Settler
includes an "indoor outhouse"; and the Gambler sports a
five-card stud poker hand inlaid in the dining room table.
Also near the park is the Museum of Automobiles (10–5,
adm.), founded by Winthrop Rockefeller, the state's first
Republican governor (elected 1966) in ninety-two years, who
bought nearly a thousand acres at Petit John and established
there his Winrock Farms. At Pottsville, just outside
Russellville, stands Potts Tavern (Tu.–Sat., 10–5; Sun., from
1, adm.), a history-filled establishment built in 1850, which
served as a stagecoach stop on the Butterfield Overland mail
route between Memphis and Fort Smith. Kirkbride Potts,
who moved to Arkansas from Pennsylvania about 1828, financed the house by selling cattle to miners in the California
gold fields, to which he drove his herds three times. Stagecoach and river travelers stayed in the bedrooms on the first
floor, whose twelve-foot-wide central hall served as the mail
room. One of the four upstairs bedrooms now houses a
display of ladies' hats, said to be one of only two such collections in the country.

At Russellville the ARVAC (Arkansas River Valley Crafts)
shop offers an extensive selection of tasteful regional handmade items, including quilts, baskets, dolls, needlework,
rugs and pottery (April–Oct., 8:30–6; Nov. and Dec., M.–
Sat., 8:30–5; Jan.–March, M.–F., 8:30–5, free), and farther

west at Clarksville you'll find more homey local touches at May House, a bed and breakfast inn at 101 Railroad Avenue (501-754-6851) whose slogan is "treat your company like family and your family like company." The University of the Ozarks at Clarksville occupies an attractive tree-shaded campus, and at Subiaco to the south is another educational institution, the Subiaco Academy, a preparatory school run by the Benedictines, whose century-old buildings grace the grounds. The monks also operate Coury House, a lodge which takes overnight guests (501-934-4411). From the top of nearby Magazine Mountain, at 2,753 feet Arkansas's highest, you'll enjoy a wide panorama of the Boston Mountains and across Logan County, whose terrain is so rugged it needs two county seats, one to serve the north and another the south.

Altus, west of Clarksville, is Arkansas's wine town. Although Chateau Mouton-Rothschild has nothing to fear from the local products, the area's attractive hilly terrain nurtures grapes that the region's wineries convert into eminently drinkable vintages. Century-old Wiederkehr (M.–Sat., 9–4:30, free) nestles in a delightful little enclave of rustic wood and stone structures, including the National Register-listed original wine cellar, dug by Johann Wiederkehr in 1880, and now the Weinkeller Restaurant. Other wineries include Mount Bethel, tucked into a hillside, with 7,000-gallon redwood aging tanks; Post Familie, established in 1880 when German immigrant Jacob Post sold the first Altus wine to passengers on the Iron Mountain Railroad; and, at nearby Paris, Cowie Wine Cellars, where the barrelheads bear oil paintings picturing family and wine history.

Also at Altus, so named (from the Latin) as the site was the highest elevation on the 1870s rail line between Little Rock and Fort Smith, is St. Mary's Church, listed on the National Register, with paintings and ornate gold-leaf work; while at nearby Ozark stands a hydroelectric plant with the nation's largest inclined-axis turbines (tours by appointment:

501-667-2149). Through Franklin County flows the Mulberry River, designated a "Scenic River of the State of Arkansas" by the Arkansas legislature in 1985 and considered
one of the state's most challenging white-water canoeing
streams. Highway 71 to the north is a splendidly photogenic
route with such scenic spots as Mountainsburg, built on
a hillside, and Artists Point, with a view in all directions
of the Boston Mountains; while Winslow, a hamlet of under
four hundred people where Westerns have been filmed, offers
an unspoiled small-town rural Ozark atmosphere.

At the far western edge of the state Van Buren and Fort
Smith, which face each other across the Arkansas River,
bring to the supposedly Southern state a pronounced Western flavor. The old frontier and Wild West era seems to linger
in the area, whose wild reputation back in the nineteenth
century was summarized in the saying, "There is no Sunday
west of St. Louis and no God west of Fort Smith." The
main attraction in Van Buren is Main Street, a stretch of
more than seventy century-old buildings, many restored to
their original appearance. Main Street, a picture out of the
past, is anchored at one end by a turn-of-the-century train
depot, which houses a small railroad museum and a tourist
office, and at the other by the Crawford County Courthouse,
an 1841 structure later rebuilt, said to be the oldest such
building in continuous use west of the Mississippi. A marker
on the courthouse lawn commemorates the Butterfield Stage
route, which in the 1870s passed along Main Street on the
way to San Francisco. A fierce Civil War battle exploded
along Main, used more than a century later to film Civil
War scenes for "The Blue and the Gray" TV series. At
Fairview Cemetery repose the Confederate soldiers slain in
the battle (the real one, not the TV version), as well as steamboat captain Phillip Pennywit, after whom Phillip's Landing,
the outpost's original name, was called.

In 1871 the Federal District Court for the area was trans-

ferred from Van Buren to Fort Smith, which lies just across
the Arkansas River. At the National Historic Site downtown
(9–5, adm.) you can see the courtroom where Judge Isaac
Parker, the "hanging judge," meted out frontier justice.
Nearby stands a reproduction of the gallows, where as many
as six men at a time, and seventy-nine in all, were hanged.
Parker reposes at Fort Smith in the nation's oldest National
Cemetery, established in 1818 as part of the original frontier
post. The Old Fort Museum (Memorial Day to Labor Day,
M.–Sat., 9–5; Labor Day to Memorial Day, Tu.–Sun., 10–5,
adm.), adjacent to the Historic Site, exudes a certain musty
charm, with an oddly assorted series of displays that seem
like a miscellaneous accumulation of cast-offs from someone's attic. You'll find there such curios as Civil War uniforms and documents, Judge Parker's high-back leather
chair, and photos of legendary Wild West characters like
Wyatt Earp and Calamity Jane, as well as George Maledon,
the judge's hangman. Other museums at Fort Smith include
the Trolley Museum (Tu. 6–10; Sat., 8–5, free), with old
city transportation vehicles, and the Patent Model Museum
(M.–F., 8–5, free), featuring eighty-five mid-nineteenth-century models constructed by inventors to show how their
creations looked and worked. Before leaving Fort Smith it's
worth driving around the eleven-block Belle Grove Historic
District, listed on the National Register, filled with houses
occupied in the nineteenth century by the town's politicians,
emporium owners, steamboat captains and other such emi-
nent citizens. Some of them perhaps frequented Miss Laura's,
a high-class bordello that is the only house of ill repute listed
on the National Register. The establishment is still open—
these days as a restaurant only. But the atmosphere there
recalls the old days when Fort Smith was a rough, tough
shoot-'em-up town on America's far frontier, the last stop
before the Indian Territory out in the vast West.

Northern Arkansas and the Ozarks

*Eureka Springs—Rogers and Fayetteville—Highway 7 and
the Buffalo River—Mountain View—Hardy*

The Ozarks region occupies a fifty-five-thousand square-mile hill-country area that extends over the southern part of Missouri and the northern third of Arkansas. In all this extensive stretch of woodland, lakes, streams, villages, hills and hollows, the most original place is Eureka Springs, a town of two thousand people in northwestern Arkansas. The settlement spreads over hills and down a narrow valley in an eccentric way, such that none of the two hundred and thirty streets in town ever cross at right angles. Hundreds of feet separate the highest road from the lowest in Eureka Springs, where the free-form street system operates without traffic lights. One commercial structure, the Thomas Building opposite the Basin Park Hotel, bears different addresses on each of three floors: the bottom level fronts on Main Street, the second floor on Basin and the third on Spring. All seven of the Basin Park Hotel's floors are on a different ground floor. Many of the town's oddities featured in Robert Ripley's famous "Believe It or Not" cartoon.

Eureka Springs has attracted artisans and craftsmen—more than six hundred of them—like backwoodsmen are drawn to Ozark moonshine. Dozens of shops selling handmade folk items line the city's sinuous streets. The entire downtown shopping district is listed on the National Register, as is much of the town's residential quarter. There is no denying that Eureka Springs exudes a certain charm but, like many places that live from tourism, commercialism seems to be winning out over the town's underlying appeal. The local attractions

include the Ozark Mountain Hoe-Down and the Pine Mountain Jamboree shows, the Miles Musical Museum, the Heritage Village where you can "journey into where yesteryears
are alive," the Forgotten Treasure Doll and Toy Museum,
the Gay Nineties Button and Doll Museum, the Hammond
Museum of Bells, Frog Fantasies (figures of frogs), the Land
of Kong Dinosaur Park, as well as any number of gift shops,
snack shops, cafes and other places aimed at the tourist trade.
If you can look beyond these sorts of commercial establishments, Eureka Springs is a rather pleasant place with a few
more substantial attractions, among them: Hatchet Hall
(9–5, adm.), the home of temperance leader Carrie Nation
(born near Berea, Kentucky) with displays on the life of
the hatchet-wielding anti-alcohol crusader; the Eureka
Springs Bank, whose lobby is a meticulous reproduction
of a nineteenth-century bank, with an antique safe and vault,
a pot-belly stove, old candlestick-style phones and other
touches of yesteryear; the Historical Museum, installed in
the 1889 Calif Building, once the town's general store, with
furniture, photos, documents and other relics of the old
days; the 1880s Rosalie House (9–5, adm.), a restored Victorian-style residence, listed on the National Register; St.
Elizabeth's Catholic Church, entered through the bell tower;
and the Eureka Springs and North Arkansas Railway (April–
Oct., excursions on the hour, 10–4, adm.), an old-fashioned
steam train that runs through the Ozark countryside. At
the site of the Great Passion Play, with a cast of hundreds,
are the seven-story-tall Christ of the Ozarks statue, a Bible
Museum, the Inspirational Wood Carving Gallery, a Sacred
Arts Center and other such religious-oriented attractions.
Another such sight is the nondenominational Thorncrown
Chapel, an attractive modernistic wood-beam and glass
sanctuary west of town on highway 62.

For accommodations in Eureka Springs four venerable hotels offer comfortable rooms in an old-fashioned atmosphere:

the Basin Park (501-253-7837, outside Arkansas 800-643-
4972), the New Orleans (501-253-8630), and the Palace (501-
253-7474), all downtown; and the splendid Crescent which
crowns the crest of a hill overlooking town (501-253-9766).
Eureka is also the bed and breakfast capital of Arkansas,
if not of the entire South, with accommodations at such
places as Dairy Hollow House (501-253-7444), Eastcliff (501-
253-7324), the Queen Anne Mansion (501-253-6067), Magnolia Guest Cottage (501-253-9463), Tatman-Garrett House
(501-253-7617), Elmwood House (501-253-7227), Redbud
Manor (501-253-9649), the Heartstone Inn (501-253-8916),
Crescent Moon (501-253-9463) and Crescent Cottage Inn
(501-253-6022). The Bed and Breadfast Association of Eureka Springs offers a reservation service: 501-253-6657.

Among sites west of Eureka Springs Pea Ridge National Military Park (8–5, adm.) commemorates the largest Civil War
battle west of the Mississippi, an encounter that saved Missouri for the Union. A seven-mile driving tour with eleven
stops traces the ebb and flow of the battle, in which Federal
troops intercepted Confederate forces marching north on
their way to flank General Ulysses S. Grant's army. After
three days of fighting the Confederates fell back to the Boston Mountains to the south. At Bella Vista Village west
of Pea Ridge stands the Mildred B. Cooper Memorial Chapel
(9–5, free), a most striking new (1988) sanctuary graced with
glass walls and a web of curved wooden beams that form
a lacelike ceiling. Bentonville, to the south, is the home of
Wal-Mart stores; a Wal-Mart Visitors Center (Mon.-Sat. 9-5, Nov.-
Feb. closed Mon., free), in Sam Walton's original variety
store, recalls the history of the chain, started by him in nearby
Rogers in 1962. Rogers boasts not only that bit of Wal-Mart
history but also the Daisy Air Gun Museum, installed in
a room at the Daisy manufacturing plant on the south edge
of town. "Boy, it's a daisy!" exclaimed Lewis Hough, the
company's founder, when he saw a prototype of the rifle,

thus devising the product's name. Displays on the history of the famous "BB" gun include the earliest Daisy (1886), as well as nearly a hundred and fifty other non-powder weapons. The Poor Richard's Confectionary (National Register) includes a 1905 soda fountain. Bed and breadfast accommodations in Rogers are at Arkansas Discovery, 1801 highway 12 east (501-925-1744).

To the east, across Beaver Lake, stands War Eagle Mill (9–5, free), a reproduction of an 1873 grist mill, the third to stand at the site. An eighteen-foot waterwheel powers three sets of stone buhrs at the installation, the first grist mill built in Arkansas in nearly a century. A shop within sells handicrafts, while upstairs The Bean Palace (9–4; closed, Jan. 1–March 15) serves breakfast and lunch featuring waffles, biscuits, cornbread and other baked items made with mill-ground flour. Arkansas's largest crafts fair takes place at War Eagle in mid-October every year. At Springdale, between Rogers and Fayetteville, the Shiloh Museum (Tu.–Sat., 10–5; June–Oct., also Sun., 1–5, free) contains a large archive and exhibits on the history of northwest Arkansas. Springdale's Faubus House on Governor's Hill (800-737-2005) opened six rooms of the striking modern residence to bed and breakfast guests. At Fayetteville several old structures have survived the boom of recent years. The Old Post Office, a Georgian structure on the National Register, houses a restaurant and nightclub. The Walker-Stone House downtown, built in 1847 by David Walker, chairman of the Arkansas Secession Convention, was later occupied by architect Edward Durrell Stone, whose buildings include New York's Museum of Modern Art, the Kennedy Center in Washington, Chicago's Standard Oil (now Amoco), as well as the Arkansas University Fine Arts Center. Fulbright Scholarship legislation sponsor J. William Fulbright, onetime U.S. senator who grew up in Fayetteville, served as president of the University, whose most venerable building is 1874 Old Main, in front of which, inscribed with names of the first graduating class (1876), begins "Senior

Walk." The University Museum (9–5; Sun., from 1, free) contains a rather unwieldy selection of displays featuring such varied artifacts as fossils, Indian objects, textiles and Ozark crafts. The campus's 1930 Greek-style theater owes its existence to Chi Omega, which erected the building as a tribute to the founding of the sorority at the University in 1895. The Arkansas "razorbacks"—named after the now-extinct wild hogs believed to have descended from pigs brought to the area in 1541 by Hernando de Soto—play at a stadium whose enclosed boxes perched in the upper reaches are known as "Hog Heaven." Out at Drake Field, the airport, the Arkansas Air Museum (F.–Sun., 1–4; M.–Th., variable hours, free; for information: 501-521-4947) houses old planes in a hangar built of wood rather than steel because of wartime shortages, while other old transportation history is recalled with the new (1989) Eureka Springs and North Arkansas dinner and excursion train (departs 6:30, 501-442-7113) that travels to Winslow and back. Fayetteville offers bed and breakfast accommodations, at Mount Kessler Inn atop Kessler Mountain (501-442-6743), as does Siloam Springs to the west, at Washington Street Bed and Breakfast, 1001 South Washington (501-524-5669), a Victorian-era residence listed on the National Register. Southwest of Fayetteville lies Prairie Grove Battlefield State Park, where more than 18,000 Union and Confederate forces clashed on December 7, 1862, resulting in 2,500 dead, wounded and missing. The Hindman Museum (8–5, free) gives details of the engagement, while scattered about the battlefield are old buildings typical of a nineteenth-century hill-country community.

As you return east to the Eureka Springs area to begin an itinerary that will take you through the Arkansas Ozarks to the east, you'll pass across Madison and Carroll Counties. Six-time Arkansas governor Orval Faubus, who in 1957 temporarily blocked integration of Little Rock's Central High School, liked to recall, especially at election time, that he was born near Greasy Creek not far from the hamlet of Combs in the southwestern corner of Madison County. Late in life Faubus was reduced to taking a five-thousand-dollar-a-year job as a bank clerk in Huntsville, the county seat. Up in Carroll County a young man named George Washington Baines arrived in 1837 to homestead one hundred and sixty acres on Crooked Creek. In 1844 he moved to Louisiana and in 1850 settled in Texas where his great-grandson made a name for himself: Lyndon Baines Johnson. At Berryville, Carroll County seat, the 1880 courthouse contains a small display of pioneer history (M.–F., 9–4:30; open Sat. during summer, free), while the Saunders Memorial Museum (March 16–Oct., 15, 9–5, adm.), given by Colonel "Buck" Saunders, who appeared with Annie Oakley in Buffalo Bill's Wild West show, houses an extensive display of firearms, including weapons that belonged to such characters as Jesse James, Pancho Villa, Billy the Kid and Wild Bill Hickok.

Harrison, to the east, is a good place to pick up Arkansas highway 7, adjudged one of the nation's ten most scenic roads. The route winds and dips its way through splendid hills on which perch Ozark log cabins, their chimneys emitting wispy plumes of smoke. The road offers beguiling panoramas of the rustic countryside, especially alluring when spring blossoms or fall foliage add rich touches of color. At Dogpatch USA (June–Aug., 10–6; late May and Sept.–early Oct., Sat only, adm.), just south of Harrison, Al Capp's "Li'l Abner" comic-strip characters come alive in the theme park, featuring rides, shows and other entertainments. Nearby flows the Buffalo River, designated a "National River" in 1972 and among the country's least-spoiled waterways. One of mid-America's most popular float streams, the Buffalo meanders some hundred and forty miles through rugged country, past old logging and mining towns, with bluffs towering as much as five hundred feet above the water.

You can begin a float trip at many places. For information, contact the National Park Service: 501-741-5443 or 449-4311. It's fun to visit the general store at Gilbert, little changed from 1900 and on the National Register. Other attractions include the ghost town of Rush, a relic of zinc mining days; homes and fields of Boxley Valley are listed on the Register; Parker-Hickman Farmstead, also; and antebellum Beaver Jim Villines' home. Booger Hollow store has corny souvenirs.

East of Harrison are bed and breakfasts: Corn Cob Inn at Everton (501-429-6545) and Red Raven Inn (501-449-5168), on the Register, at Yellville (named for a politician). Near Mountain Home, a popular retirement area, are Bull Shoals and Norfolk Lakes, resorts with a full range of watersports. Mountain Village 1890 (April-Oct., 10-7, adm.) at Bull Shoals features nineteenth-century area buildings, one of them used by Herbert Hoover during an 1893 survey. At the town of Norfolk, south of the lake, stands the Wolf House, believed to be the state's oldest two-story log structure, which now contains a museum of nineteenth-century Ozark life. Beguilingly named Calico Rock nearby once boasted a mineral-streaked limestone bluff "presenting a diversity of color in squares, stripes, spots, or angles, all confusedly mixed and arranged according to the inimitable pencil of nature," so Henry Schoolcraft, an early traveler in the Ozarks, graphically described the unusual formation in 1819.

At Mountain View, just to the south, is the Ozark Folk Center, established in 1973 as a living museum of Ozark popular culture in an attempt to preserve examples of the traditional way of life in the back country. The area's isolation—no paved road reached Mountain View until the early 1950s—allowed Ozark music, arts and crafts to evolve relatively free of outside influences. The Center's twenty small wooden buildings house an array of craft workers who demonstrate their skills. Six nights a week the hill folk mount shows featuring old-time music, and on Saturday evenings fiddlers perform (free) in the courthouse square. The Ozark Folk Center, an Arkansas state park, is a noncommercial and tastefully operated facility which is probably the best single place in the state to get a feel for the Ozark backcountry way of life. The Center is open Friday, Saturday and Sunday in April and then daily (10–5) through October. For accommodations at the sixty-room lodge: 501-269-3871. The Commercial Hotel Bed and Bakery, a restored eight-room country inn listed on the National Register, offers bed and breakfast rooms in Mountain View: 501-269-4383. More fiddling around takes place at Salem, to the north near the Missouri line, where two groups called "Mountain Music Makers" give free musicals every Saturday night, one performance beginning at 7 and the other at 7:30. At Mammoth Spring State Park, to the east, just by the Missouri state line, one of the nation's largest springs gushes forth nearly ten million gallons an hour. You can't actually see the spring itself, which emerges below the pool, but the lake and beginnings of the Spring River, as well as a restored 1886 train depot, are on view at the park. Nashville, Tennessee's, famous Grand Ole Opry was first envisioned, or enaudioed, at the village of Mammoth Spring when George D. Hay, a cub reporter for the *Memphis Commercial Appeal,* traveled to the town to cover a war hero's funeral. After the service, locals invited the visitor to a hoedown, which inspired Hay to devise the Opry program later introduced on radio station WSM in Nashville.

Due south of Mammoth Spring lies the town of Hardy, whose downtown commercial district is listed on the National Register. But Hardy is more renowned for old folklore than for old buildings, as performances of the state's famous play *The Arkansaw Traveller* take place there (Memorial Day to Labor Day, Tu., F., Sat., dinner, 6–8; show, 8:15, 501-856-2256). Colonel Sanford Faulkner first recounted the story in the mid-nineteenth century, and in 1858 Edward

Payson Washburn, an Arkansas artist, illustrated the tale with a painting popularized by Currier and Ives. It seems that a stranger arrived one evening at the cabin of a settler in a remote part of the Ozarks. Asked where the road goes, the local replied, "Hit's never gone anywhar since I've lived here; hit's always thar when I git up in the mornin'." When the traveler asked if the hillbilly had any spirits, the fellow replied that he saw some spooking a nearby hollow and they like to scared him to death. The stranger inquired how far to the next house, to which the country bumpkin answered, "Dunno, I hain't never measured it, nor been thar." The local allowed that he's never fixed his leaky roof, as it's too wet to do the job when it rains and there's no need to repair the roof when the weather's dry. The woodsman finally asked the traveler, "Stranger, kin yew play the fiddul?" The outsider replied, "I can saw a little, sometimes," and he then proceeded to squeak out an entire tune, whereupon the delighted local broke into a dance and immediately warmed to the stranger, inviting him to stay, eat and drink. Such is Arkansas's most renowned folk tale, which for more than a century has amused locals and visitors alike. It has been a long round-about road from Piggott, toward the east, the town where Hemingway wrote *A Farewell to Arms,* to Hardy and the old-time *Arkansaw Traveller* tale, with which we can end our "Arkansaw" travels and bid farewell to Arkansas.

Bill Clinton's Arkansas

Hope-Hot Springs-Fayetteville-Little Rock

Bill Clinton's election as president of the United States was an extraordinary event for Arkansas. In some other states presidents are somewhat more common. Virginia, the "mother of presidents," produced five chief executives—Washington, Jefferson, Madison, Monroe and Tyler. With six holders of the top office, perhaps Ohio can be called the "father of presidents"—Hayes, Garfield, William Henry Harrison, McKinley, Taft and Harding. New York provided Van Buren, Fillmore, Arthur, Cleveland and the two Roosevelts, and from Massachusetts came the two Adams, Coolidge and Kennedy. Fully half of the nation's chief executives—twenty-one out of forty-two—originated from those four states. Many future presidents often lived in various states, which can thus claim some sort of connection with men who later reached the highest office in the land. Before Clinton, however, Zachary Taylor was the only president who ever lived in Arkansas. The twelfth president (1849-1850) served as military commander at Fort Smith from 1841 to 1844. For a century and a half thereafter Arkansas—unlike many other states—lacked even the slightest presidential connections. But in January 1993 Bill Clinton changed that.

Clinton's election focused national attention on Arkansas. Clinton has meant a lot to Arkansas; in turn, Arkansas has also meant a lot to him. The native son's roots run deep in Arkansas. Like Harry Truman and Lyndon Johnson, from the neighboring states of Missouri and Texas, Clinton is a president especially well grounded in the soil of his home state. When Clinton resigned as governor of Arkansas on December 12, 1992—a job he had held for twelve of the previous fourteen years—he noted in his farewell address:"For me, above everything else, this was an affair of the heart." Because Clinton is so closely identified with Arkansas—he was born there, grew up and received his early education in the state, lived his entire adult life (apart from his university years) there, taught at the state university, served for twelve years as governor—the state boasts a number of Clinton-related sights. These places—many of them simple and unprepossessing—enable visitors to get a feel for the influences and culture which helped to shape the forty-second president of the United States.

The president's story began in the small town of Hope (present population: 10,500) in southwestern Arkansas. Before Clinton's candidacy and election, Hope's main claim to fame was the city's annual watermelon festival. This event began in the 1920s when John S. Gibson, owner of Gibson Drugstores, began offering prizes for the largest watermelons grown in the area. The early festivals proved so popular that Hope was unable to handle the crowds and the town ended the event in the 1930s, and only in 1976 did the festival start up again. The largest watermelon grown in the Hope area to date tipped the scales at 260 pounds, a world record at the time.

Hope began in 1873 as a railroad stop on the Cairo and Fulton line. The area then started to develop as a cotton growing region, but since about 1920 other crops, along with poultry and cattle, have superceded cotton in importance. By now Hope is a rather typical middle American small town, with oak and magnolia trees garnishing the quiet residential streets lined with comfortable, unpretentious frame houses fronted by porches sporting old-fashioned swings. As in so many small American towns tucked away in remote corners of the continent, a certain sense of timelessness seems to envelop Hope. Invariably, vignettes of daily life in such a place appear unchanged: "Then we would make the slow walk back home in the dusk past the people sitting on their porches rocking slowly," wrote Willie Morris in *Good Old Boy: A Delta Boyhood.* Morris and Clinton were both southern small town boys who became Rhodes Scholars and, in time, entered the great wide world beyond the narrow confines of Hope and of Yazoo City, Mississippi, Morris's place of origin. In a kind of endless ritual, seasons come, seasons go there in those small southern settlements; the mild winters and bright springs, the long languid summers and then, once again, the autumn, a fall such as Morris recalled:

I absorbed all the smells of that autumn: the clean, crisp air, the wonderful delta earth. It was Indian summer, and everything—the earth and the trees, touched by the airy sunshine—was the lazy golden brown of that sad and lovely time; there was a faint presence of smoke eveywhere, and the smell of leaves burning, and sounds and their echoes carried a long, long way.

At such a typical small southern town, a town called Hope in Arkansas—about thirty miles northeast of Texarkana on the Texas-Arkansas border—Bill Clinton was born on August 19, 1946, and there he spent the first seven years of his life. A wooden sign at a vacant lot proclaims, "This is the birth spot of Bill Clinton." The sign stands on the site of the Chester Hospital, which burned down in 1991. From his birth to 1950, Clinton lived with his grandparents at 117 South Hervey Street while his mother attended nurse-anesthetist school in Louisiana. The city of Hope plans to buy and restore the house.

Clinton's father William Jefferson Blythe III died in an automobile accident in Missouri shortly before his son was born. Blythe and Clinton's maternal grandparents, Eldridge and Edith Cassidy, repose at the Rose Hill cemetery off Arkansas highway 29. Clinton's mother, Virginia Kelley, who died in 1994, is also buried there. Clinton's mother married Roger Clinton (the future president's name was then changed from William Jefferson Blythe IV to William Jefferson Clinton) and the family lived at 321 East 13th Street from 1950 to 1953. In the front yard of the modest one-story house stands a sign stating, "Boyhood Home of Bill Clinton." The present occupants also helpfully include a marker recommending where visitors should stand to take pictures of the residence.

Clinton's education began at Miss Mary Purkins School for Little Folks, where the boy attended kindergarten. The building, located at 601 East Second Street, now houses a hair salon. In 1952-1953 Clinton attended first grade at Brookwood School, 500 South Spruce Street, which these days serves as offices for local educational organizations.

The Union Pacific Railroad depot in downtown Hope featured in a video on Clinton's life presented at the July 1992 Democratic National Convention. The city plans to acquire the depot from Union Pacific and renovate the building to house a visitor center with a museum on Clinton's life in Hope and on local history. Meanwhile, materials on the town's past can be found at the three story 1903 Carrigan House, at the corner of Elm Street and Avenue C in the city's oldest residential area, headquarters of the Hempstead County Historical Society. Another area musem is the Klipsch Museum of Audio History, located in the village of Oakhaven not far from Hope. The collection includes loudspeakers and other items on the development of audio technology by the nearby Klipsch Company loudspeaker factory, established in 1948. For information about Clinton sites and other attractions in and near Hope: 501-777-6701.

In 1953—when young Bill was seven—the Clinton family moved to Hot Springs, now a city of 35,000, more than three times as large as Hope, which lies some eighty miles to the southwest. In Hot Springs the family lived at 1011 Park Avenue from 1954 to 1961, then from 1961 to 1964 occupied a one story brick house at 213 Scully. The boy was baptized at Park Place Baptist Church, 721 Park Avenue. Clinton attended St. John's Catholic School and Ramble Elementary School in Hot Springs and, later, Hot Springs High School, 215 Oak Street, which housed the school until 1968.

During Clinton's teenage years he frequented various Hot Springs hangouts, some still popular with local residents. The gang used to gather at the Malco Theater, 817 Central Avenue, to watch the latest movie. At the old Polar Bar, now Bailey's Dairy Treat, 510 Park Avenue, the youngster favored chili-cheeseburgers and Grapette soda. Ronnie Cecil, a friend of Clinton's step-father, owned the snack shop back then. The teenager also enjoyed the food at McClard's Barbecue, 505 Albert Pike, and he ate the grub at Magee's Cafe, 362 Central Avenue. At the eatery hangs a photo of Clinton, while behind the counter lies a stack of photos picturing the Magees with Virginia Kelley, Clinton's mother, who lived near Hot Springs until her death in January, 1994. At Magee's still plays George Gray, a musician who taught Clinton while he was performing in his high school years in a jazz trio called The Three Kings, also known as The Three Blind Mice for the dark sunglasses the boys wore. The trio, with Clinton on the saxophone, often played at weekend dances held at the YMCA-YWCA (now only the YWCA), 500 Quapaw Avenue.

Clinton majored in band at Hot Springs High School. While attending the school he was selected as delegate to Boys States, then later elected as Arkansas representative at Boys Nation in Washington, D.C. It was at that convention that he met President John F. Kennedy, an encounter Clinton later said influenced him to enter politics. After graduating from high school in 1964, Clinton left Hot Springs to attend college at Georgetown University in Washington. For information on Hot Springs and the Clinton sites there: 800-SPA-CITY or 501-321-2277.

Clinton remained away from Arkansas for some ten years, attending Georgetown, Oxford University in England as a Rhodes Scholar, and then Yale Law School. Finally, in the mid-1970s, he returned to his home state, settling for a time in Fayetteville where he taught at the University of Arkansas Law School, located at the corner of Maple and Garland Streets in "The Hill" area of the campus. Clinton taught at the Leflar Law Center—a 1950s (with later additions) modernistic structure sporting a distinctive large circular window—from 1973 to 1976, and Hillary Rodham, his fiance and then wife, taught at the law school from 1974 to 1976. In 1975 Clinton and Rodham bought the brick house at 930 California, where later that year they were married in the living room. Clinton sometimes dropped in to the Fayetteville Youth Center, across the street from the house, for a pick-up basketball game. Clinton began his political career in Fayetteville, with an unsuccessful campaign for the U.S. Congress. Campaign headquarters occupied the building at 824 North College Avenue. A later attempt—for Arkansas attorney general—proved successful, and in 1976 the Clintons moved to Little Rock, selling the house on California in 1983. For information on Fayetteville and its Clinton sites: 800-766-4626 or 501-521-1710.

Two years after Clinton won the attorney general's office he was elected governor of Arkansas at age thirty-two. Defeated for re-election by Republican Frank D. White in 1979, Clinton regained the office two years later. He remained governor until resigning in December 1992 after being elected president. The Clintons lived in Little Rock for sixteen years, twelve of them as Arkansas governor and first lady. A number of places in the capital recall the couple's presence in Little Rock, where the Clintons were active not only in politics but also in church and community affairs.

After the Clintons moved to Little Rock, on January, 5, 1977, the couple bought for $35,000 the one story brick house at 5419 L Street where they lived between 1977 and 1979 while Clinton served as attorney general. During that time Clinton occupied an office in the Justice Building, on the state capitol grounds. The 1958 Justice Building houses the Arkansas Supreme Court and the state's Court of Appeals, as well as other state legal facilities. The building's circular gallery includes a sculptured marble frieze depicting "Lawgivers of Antiquity," with Babylonian, Egyptian, Greek, Roman, Persian and other figures.

After Clinton became governor the couple occupied the Georgian colonial-style Governor's Mansion, 18th and Center Streets, in 1979 and 1980. The residence, built between 1947 and 1950, stands in the Quapaw Quarter, Little Rock's oldest neighborhood, filled with restored houses of various styles dating from about 1880 to 1920. One such structure, the Italianate Victorian-style Villa Marre, 1321 South Scott Street, built in 1881 by saloon keeper Angelo Marre, houses the headquarters of the Quapaw Quarter Association (501-371-0075). The Villa Marre, along with the governor's mansion and two other local houses, figure in the TV comedy series "Designing Women," produced by "FOB" (Friend of Bill) Harry Thomason, an Arkansas native, and his wife Linda Bloodworth-Thomason. The Thomasons served as TV advisers for the Clinton campaign. (The Calhoun County courthouse in Hampton, Arkansas, Thomason's home town, also occasionally appears on the show. The Thomasons also produce the CBS TV comedy show "Evening Shade," which at times includes scenes from the real Evening Shade, Arkansas, a hamlet of less than 400 residents on highway 167 about halfway between Hardy and Batesville. Established in 1847, the village is the state's smallest settlement with an official historic district.)

After being defeated by Frank White in the 1979 governor's race, Clinton and his wife bought the two story frame house at 816 Midland for $112,000. There the couple and their daughter, Chelsea Victoria Clinton, born February 27, 1980, lived until two years later when Clinton regained the governor's office and mansion, living there from 1981 to 1992. During most of the decade (from 1981 to 1992) Hillary Rodham worked at the Rose Law Firm, 120 East Fourth Street. She attended church at First United Methodist, 8th and Center Streets, while her husband went to Immanuel Baptist, 1000 Bishop Street, where he sang in the church choir. Chelsea attended school at Mann Magnet Junior High, 1000 East Roosevelt, a magnet school with an emphasis on math and science.

During Clinton's years as governor, 1979-1980 and 1981-1992, he occupied an office at the state capitol, a neo-classic building reminiscent of the United States capitol built for $2.5 million between 1899 and 1915 primarily of Batesville limestone quarried in Arkansas. On the east side of the capitol gleam six solid brass doors purchased from Tiffany's in New York, while the brass chandelier in the rotunda and chandeliers in the Senate and House chambers also came from Tiffany's. Clinton's polling place while he served as governor was the Dunbar Recreation Center, 1001 West 16th Street; here he cast his vote in the 1992 presidential election. Clinton worked out at the YMCA of Metropolitan Little Rock, 524 South Broadway. A block south stands the McDonald's where Clinton stopped frequently while on his daily jog through the streets of downtown Little Rock.

That McDonald's is probably the most famous of the eateries Clinton frequented while living in Little Rock, but he also supposedly ate at various other local establishments. Restaurants and cafes in Little Rock, and in Hot Springs, have become the Arkansas equivalent of "Washington slept here" claims by inns in the east.

Clinton seemingly sampled the fare at very nearly every fast food and diner eatery in those two towns. Most of the places where Clinton is said to have eaten are basic, down-home cafes typical of the area, and thus offer a good introduction to regional cuisine and the flavor of Arkansas life.

When Clinton ran on past McDonald's during his jog he would often then put in at the Community Bakery for coffee and a plain or cinnamon bagel. Clinton also favored the cinnamon rolls at Hungry's Cafe—an old-time place with a stamped tin ceiling, dark green walls flaked with chipped paint, and a worn linoleum floor— which features a plate lunch of one meat, two vegetables, bread, ice (spelled the Arkansas way, without the"d") tea, coffee or Kool-Aid, all for a price less than just the tax at fancier places. At Sims Bar-B-Q, a similarly old-fashioned place in a rundown little shack, Clinton supposedly liked such dishes as the sliced pork barbecue, sliced beef, baked beans, slaw, potato salad, and sweet potato pie. To pay a bet Clinton lost on an Arkansas-Georgia football game he sent Georgia governor Zell Miller some of Sims barbecue chicken. H.B. Barbecue, where Clinton might have eaten, features on Thursdays a Big Bun Day, with barbecue served up on an onion bun. Doe's Eat Place, a licensee of the half-century-old original Doe's in Greenville, Mississippi, specializes in steaks. Clinton also supposedly liked Mexican-type foods such as jalapeño cheeseburgers at the Band Box; a burrito called"Earthling Roll," at the Solar Cafe; and chicken enchiladas and the spinach dip at Trio's. At Juanita's, apparently Little Rock's only authentic Tex-Mex place, Clinton opted for chicken enchiladas, soft tacos and Clausthaler, a nonalcoholic German beer.

Little Rock"watering holes" associated with Clinton include the 1877 Capital Hotel (which hosted such guests as Ulysses S. Grant, Sarah Bernhardt, and other celebrities), with a bar and restaurant often frequented by political types, and the Excelsior Hotel. During the presidential primaries Gennifer Flowers claimed that she had previously met Clinton several times at the Excelsior bar. The Excelsior's Gas Hole retains the name of a colorful hole-in-the-wall political hangout formerly located in the basement of the old Marion Hotel, replaced by the Excelsior. Caricatures of Arkansas' movers and shakers decorate the new version of the Gas Hole, now updated, upstairs and upscale.

Clinton's race for the presidency began on October 3, 1991, at the Old State House, 300 West Markham, where the governor announced his candidacy. The central section of the Old State House, built between 1833 and 1842, opened in 1836. After completion of the new capitol in 1911, the elegant Greek Revival-style former state house served as a laboratory for the University of Arkansas medical department and as the state's War Memorial Building. In 1947 it became a museum on Arkansas history, featuring an archive, decorative arts, restored legislative chambers, period rooms, and a series of displays entitled "The Arkansas History Exhibits."

On election night, November 3, 1992, Clinton gave his victory speech from the Old State House.

Other campaign landmarks in Little Rock include the Statehouse Convention Center, Markham and Main Streets, the media center during election night and also the site of Clinton's gubernatorial inauguration balls, and the Clinton-Gore National Campaign Headquarters, 112 West Third Street. The headquarters occupied the 1908 *Arkansas Gazette* building, home of the state's oldest business (started in 1819), and the oldest newspaper west of the Mississippi until the paper was sold in 1991 to its competitor, the *Arkansas Democrat*. After Clinton's victory, his transition office was located on the third floor of the Atkins Building, Fifth and Louisiana Streets, while at the Joseph T. Robinson Center, Markham and Broadway, he met several hundred leading businessmen, academics and consultants for the December 1992 Clinton-Gore Economic Conference. The Robinson Center, built between 1937 and 1940, recalls an earlier national campaign involving Arkansas. United States Senator Joseph T. Robinson, whose name designates the facility, ran for vice president as a Democrat in 1928, the only Arkansan besides Clinton ever to appear on a presidential ticket.

(For information on Little Rock and its Clinton connected sites: 800-844-4781 or 501-376-4781.)

At the July 1992 Democratic Convention Clinton extended on national television an invitation to the nation to "come on down" to Arkansas. Those who accept the invitation will see the places and absorb the atmosphere of the culture which nurtured and nourished young Bill Clinton during his formative years. At Hope, Hot Springs, Fayetteville and Little Rock visitors can trace the life and career of the native son who rose from modest beginnings at "a place called Hope" to take the long journey on the road to the White House where he now serves as the forty-second president of the United States.

Arkansas Practical Information

For tourist information: Arkansas Department of Parks and Tourism, One Capitol Mall, Little Rock, AR 72201; 501-682-7777. Arkansas operates thirteen highway Tourist Information areas on roads entering the state. On the east side of the state: I-55 south of Blytheville; I-40 west, West Memphis; U.S. 49 bypass, Helena; U.S. 65-82, Lake Village. On the south: U.S. 167, El Dorado; I-30 east, Texarkana. On the west: U.S. 71 north, Red River; I-40 east, Fort Smith. On the north: U.S. 71 south, Bentonville; U.S. 65 south, Harrison; U.S. 63 north, Mammoth Spring; U.S. 67 south, Corning; U.S. 412, Siloam Springs.

Arkansas operates forty-four state parks, many with overnight accommodations at campsites, lodges and cabins. For information: 501-682-1191. Other useful numbers for outdoor attractions in Arkansas: Game and Fish Commission 501-223-6300; National Weather Service (central Arkansas) 501-834-0308; State Forestry Commission 501-664-2531.

Phone numbers of tourist offices in some of Arkansas's main cities are: Heart of Arkansas (Little Rock and surroundings), 501-376-4781; Helena, 501-338-8327; Hot Springs, 800-272-2081 (in Arkansas), 800-643-1570 (out of state); Eureka Springs, 501-253-8737, 800-643-3546; Fayetteville, 501-521-1710; Fort Smith, 501-783-6118; El Dorado, 501-863-6113.

The Arkansas and Ozarks Bed and Breakfast can book accommodations at nearly sixty rooms in north-central Arkansas: 501-297-8211 or 501-297-8764.

III

The Civil War
South

7. Civil War Sites in the Gulf and the Mississippi South States

Walt Whitman called the conflict "a strange and sad war," and the Southerners labeled it the War Between the States and "the Lost Cause." By whatever name, the Civil War—in which more Americans lost their lives (620,000 dead, plus nearly 1.1 million casualties) than during the two World Wars combined—was no doubt the nation's most traumatic, tragic and fascinating episode. Hundreds of reminders of the great conflict, which included an estimated 10,000 military encounters, survive—battlefields, historic buildings, displays, monuments, cemeteries, geographic features and other places which recall the bloody war. The following compilation lists the main Civil War sites in the South's Gulf and Mississippi River states, and also includes some of the lesser known or more unusual attractions.

Alabama

Athens

Founders Hall. The 1842 college building was spared from being burned by Union troops when a local resident produced a letter supposedly written by President Lincoln.

Sulfur Trestle Fort Site. Pesky Confederate general Nathan Bedford Forrest burned the seventy square yard Union outpost, southwest of town, during his raids in northern Alabama to disrupt Federal supply lines. In an experiment designed to free regular troops for front line duty, two companies of black troops—exslaves and free blacks—manned the position for the Union.

Auburn

A monument at the railroad station commemorates the occasion when Jefferson Davis, on his way to his inauguration in Montgomery, reviewed local troops on February 16, 1861.

Pine Hill Cemetery. Nearly 100 Confederate soldiers, honored by a monument, repose at the burial ground.

Bessemer

Tannehill Historical State Park. Union troops heavily damaged the furnaces here. One pre-War blast furnace which made iron for the Confederacy has been restored.

Thomas H. Owen House. The house was built in the 1830s by Owen, later a partner in a small forge which supplied iron to the Confederate army.

Bessemer Hall of History. Exhibits at the renovated Southern Railway depot include War artifacts.

Blakeley Park

Historic Blakeley Park, at the site of a town chartered in 1814 and once larger than Mobile, lies on the eastern edge of the Mobile Bay delta near the town of Spanish Fort, so named for the 1798 installation built there. A yellow fever epidemic and a bust after a boom depopulated Blakeley Park, where what was supposedly the War's last battle—after Lee's surrender—took place. *Harper's Weekly* noted in 1865 that "probably the last charge of the war, it was as gallant as any on record." Established as a state park in 1981, and supposedly the largest site east of the Mississippi listed on the National Register, the 3800 acre enclave includes old rifle pits, battery sites, the remains of earthen forts, and breastworks considered among the best preserved of the War.

Bon Secour

On the shores of Bon Secour Bay in Baldwin County at the southeast corner of Mobile Bay stands the Swift-Coles House.

Lumber magnate Charles A. Swift built the house, which his heirs sold to Nik Coles, who had often expressed a desire to own the elegant mansion. Local legend relates that a band of cavalrymen known as the"Baldwin Grays" would rally at the house, than sally forth to intercept Union forces engaged in pillaging salt and lumber in Bon Secour.

Cahaba

Now a ghost town with a few fragments of antebellum buildings, Cahaba served as the seat of Dallas County for nearly half a century, until 1866, and as state capital from 1818 to 1825. Yellow fever and area "Blue and Gray" encounters during the War reduced the town to a skeleton. In 1864 the Confederates established a prison in the town.

Citronville

On May 4, 1865 the last Confederate forces east of the Mississippi surrendered here.

Demopolis

Bluff Hall. The family of Francis Strother Lyon, a lawyer and cotton planter who served in both the U.S. and Confederate legislatures, built the house in 1832, adding the portico and back wing in 1850. During the War many Confederate political and military figures visited the mansion, named for the chalk bluff where the house stands above the Tombigbee River. In October 1863 Lyon entertained Jefferson Davis at Bluff Hall, whose other visitors included General Zachary Deas, who married a daughter of Lyon, and General Leonidas Polk, whose son married another Lyon daughter.

Double Springs

The Free State of Winston Festival recalls when Winston

County, whose seat is at Double Springs, considering seceding from the Confederate States of America.

Eufaula

Shorter Mansion. The neo-classic-style residence, now a museum, houses Confederate relics.

Florence

Popes Tavern and Museum. The one story structure, constructed by slave labor in 1811, served as a hospital during the War.

Peters Cemetery. A monument decorated with shells and figurines and bearing a reference to the Fourteenth Amendment honors slaves buried in the graveyard.

University of North Alabama. Sherman occupied 1855 Wesleyan Hall as his headquarters while on his way to reinforce Union units in Tennessee.

Fort Morgan

The pentagonal brick fort built between 1819 and 1834 occupies a spit of land at the entrance to Mobile Bay. On January 4, 1861, a week before Alabama seceded, Union forces were ousted from the fort by Confederate soldiers, who occupied the outpost during most of the War. The Southerners strung mines, then called torpedoes, across the channel to block the Union fleet, commanded by Admiral David Farragut, from entering the bay. During the Battle of Mobile Bay on August 4, 1864, guns at the fort damaged the *Tecumseh*, one of Farragut's fleet. As the ship sank, Farragut uttered his later famous war cry, "Damn the torpedoes. Full speed ahead!" The commander of the Confederate fleet, Admiral Franklin Buchanan, surrendered to the Federal navy, and by August 9 Union forces captured nearby Fort Gaines, an outpost on Dauphine Island which guarded the western approach to the bay. Like Fort Morgan, Fort Gaines is a five-sided brick structure; cannons and other relics of the War remain at the fortress. During the night of August 22 the North rained more than 3000 cannon-balls onto Fort Morgan, which surrendered the next afternoon. A ferry, which takes cars, travels between Dauphine Island and Fort Morgan.

Gadsden

A bas-relief recalls Emma Sansom, a fifteen year old who guided Nathan Bedford Forrest when the Confederate raider passed through Gadsden pursuing Federal troops.

Huntsville

At Huntsville lived two major Confederate figures: John Hunt Morgan, the "Thunderbolt of the Confederacy," so called for his lightning-like raids, born at 558 Franklin Street (see also the entry for Lexington, Kentucky), and Leroy Pope Walker, the Secretary of War who issued the orders to fire on Fort Sumter.

Marion

Judson College. By now one of the nation's oldest colleges for women, the school was the successor to the Judson Female Institute, organized in 1838. Nicola Marschall, who taught at the college, designed the Confederate flag. A monument at the Perry County courthouse honors her.

Marion Military Institute. The preparatory school and junior college, a successor to Howard College, established in 1842, maintains various Confederate-type traditions.

Mobile

Admiral Semmes House. Mobile citizens donated the house in 1871 as a residence for Admiral Raphael Semmes. A statue and a waterfront park in town also commemorate the Confederate officer.

Bragg-Mitchell Mansion. John Bragg, judge and U.S. Congressman, built the house in 1855. His brother, the renowned

Confederate general Braxton Bragg, once delivered an address from the iron balcony at the house. When the War began Judge Bragg moved the furnishings at the mansion to a plantation house, but Federal troops raided the country estate and burned the possessions Bragg had taken there for safekeeping. During the War Confederate soldiers cut down all the oaks on the grounds of the Bragg Mansion to open fields of fire for artillery. After the War, Judge Bragg started a new stand of oaks, using acorns he had salvaged from the original trees.

DeTonti Square Historic District. The nine block area just north of the downtown business district survives as Mobile's oldest residential district, with houses dating from the decade before the War. Admiral Franklin Buchanan, Confederate naval officer at the 1864 Battle of Mobile Bay, occupied the third floor of the large three story brick building at 250 St. Anthony Street.

Condé-Charlotte Street. The 1825 structure—built as the city's first official jail and in the 1840s converted into a residence—includes a Confederate Room, furnished as a Southern parlor at the time the War began.

City Museum. The museum, which occupies the 1872 Bernstein-Bush House, includes a War Room with uniforms, documents and weapons, among them Admiral Semmes' sword.

Magnolia National Cemetery. The burial ground, designated a national cemetery in 1866, includes the remains of Union soldiers killed in the April 9, 1865, attack on Fort Blakeley during the capture of Mobile. Also interred there are Confederate general Braxton Bragg and members of the crew of the C.S.S. *Hunley*, the world's first submarine.

Africatown U.S.A. State Park. The nation's first state park devoted to African-American history is at Prichard in eastern Mobile by the Mobile River. Sites in the area recall the *Clotilde*, the last known ship carrying a cargo of slaves to the U.S. At Plateau Cemetery repose many of the vessel's passengers, including Cudjoe Lewis, the last survivor of the last slave ship. A memorial to Lewis stands at the Union Baptist Church across the street.

Montevallo

At Brierfield Ironworks Park, seven miles southwest of town, remain ruins of a wartime iron producing furnace.

Montgomery

First White House of the Confederacy. The 1835 Italianate-style residence (moved from another location) houses antiques and personal possessions which belonged to Jefferson Davis and his wife when they occupied the mansion.

State Capitol. Known to some Southerners as the "Independence Hall of the Southern Confederacy," the 1851 Alabama state house holds many memories of the War years. On February 18, 1861, Davis took the oath of office as president of the Confederacy on the capitol portico. The Confederate States of America was formally established in the Senate chamber on February 4 by the Provisional Confederate Congress, representing seven Southern states. Davis's body lay in state in the former state Supreme Court chamber after his death. Three months after being established in Montgomery the Confederate capital was moved to Richmond, Virginia. A $28 million restoration of the capitol building, begun in 1976, was completed in 1992. On the grounds of the capitol across from the White House stands a memorial to Alabama servicemen who died in the War.

Alabama Archives and History Museum. Military history sections include War displays.

Murphy House. During Reconstruction the Union army occupied the house (now the city Waterworks Board) as headquarters.

St. John's. The Episcopal church retains the Davis family pew.

Other War related areas in Montgomery include the site of the Exchange Hotel, where the first Confederate cabinet met; the Gerald House, where Herman F. Arnold wrote the orchestral score for"Dixie"; the State Chamber of Commerce building, where in 1865 General James Wilson read the Emancipation Proclamation to a crowd of blacks; and the Winter Building, from where Secretary of War Leroy Pope Walker telegraphed to give authority for the shelling of Fort Sumter.

Mountain Creek

Confederate Memorial Park lies east of I-65 between Montgomery and Birmingham. An arch with cut-out white letters indicating "Confederate Cemetery" frames the entrance to this burial ground, one of the few where solely Confederate veterans repose. More than 200 Southern soldiers, and fifteen Confederate wives, are buried in two cemeteries at the site. One stone slab marker memorializes James Wildcat Carter, an Indian medicine man who died at age 105; the inscription describes him as "chief scout Gen. Forrest," referring to the famous Confederate raider, General Nathan Bedford Forrest of Tennessee. A log cabin at the park houses War artifacts as well as documents relating to the Confederate Soldiers Home, which operated in the area until closing in 1939. Although the buildings were razed, near the memorial plaque for the home survive cedar trees planted in the early years of the century by request of a widow, living in the expatriate Southern colony in Brazil, to honor her husband.

Point Clear

The present Grand Hotel, since 1981 a Marriott, opened in 1941 as the third version of the original Grand, constructed in 1847. The current building—centerpiece of the 550 acre resort garnished with moss-draped oak trees—includes heart of pine flooring and framing used in the first hotel. A fire in 1869 and then a hurricane in 1893 destroyed the two previous structures. During the War the nearby Gunnison House—built as part of the resort in the 1850s—served as a hospital for Confederate soldiers wounded at Vicksburg, Mississippi. In 1865 the 21st Alabama Regiment used the hotel grounds as an encampment site. The 1869 fire which destroyed the main hotel building also burned records of soldiers treated at the hospital. Lost were the identities of more than 300 men who were buried in a small plot near the present eighteenth tee of the resort's Azalea Golf Course.

Selma

During the War Selma served as an important military manufacturing center. The Brooke Cannon, a well known weapon, was developed and cast at the Selma Foundry, while an arsenal in town produced ammunition for the Confederacy. Shipyards on the Alabama River at Selma built the armored boat *Tennessee*. Few remnants of the War era remain, as 9,000 Union troops under General J.H. Wilson burned and looted Selma in the spring of 1865.

A monument recalls the arsenal, which covered three square blocks, while another marker indicates the site of the navy yard. At Old Live Oak Cemetery—filled with moss-draped oaks, dogwood, azaleas and other plantings—repose Confederate officers.

Tuscaloosa

Gorgas House. On the University of Alabama campus stands the 1829 building, one of the nation's oldest college structures, post-War residence of General Josiah B. Gorgas, Confederate chief of ordnance, who served as university president. The house contains nineteenth century silver and furniture. On the campus are a few War related markers.

Prewitt Slave Cemetery. War of 1812 veteran John Welsh Prewitt established the burial ground, where slaves and former slaves were interred before and after the War.

Tuscumbia

Ivy Green. Helen Keller's grandfather built the house in 1820. His wife Mary was Lee's second cousin. Captain Arthur Keller, a Confederate officer, brought his second wife to the house where in 1880 their daughter Helen was born.

St. John's. Federal troops stabled their horses in the Episcopal church.

Joe Wheeler Plantation

"Fighting" Joe Wheeler served as a Confederate cavalry general and later as a U.S. Congressman and as a major general in the Spanish-American War. He was the only Confederate general later to attain that rank in the U.S. Army. During the Civil War china now on display at the c. 1880 two story frame house was buried for safekeeping.

Mississippi

Aberdeen

Gregg-Hamilton House. The c. 1850 Greek Revival-style residence was the home of Confederate General John Gregg.

A number of antebellum buildings—including 1850 The Magnolias, open for tours—recall the affluent pre-War era when Aberdeen was a prosperous Tombigbee River port.

Biloxi

Beauvoir. Memories of the Confederacy abound at the seaside house occupied by Jefferson Davis in the last years of his life. In 1877, at age sixty-nine, the former president of the Confederacy settled at Beauvoir where he lived until his death in 1889. He spent three years while living there writing the two volume *The Rise and Fall of the Confederate Government.* After Davis died, his widow rejected a $100,000 offer for the property from a hotel developer, instead selling the estate to the Mississippi Confederate Veterans for use as a house for veterans, their families and former slaves. The property, which became a public attraction in 1940, includes a Davis family museum, a Confederate museum installed in the former hospital building, and a veterans' cemetery with more than 700 graves and the Tomb of the Unknown Confederate Soldier.

Fort Massachusetts. Excursion boats leave from the Biloxi area (and other points on the coast) to Ship Island, in the Gulf of Mexico twelve miles from the mainland. On the island survives the 1860s fort, one of the last masonry coastal fortifications in the U.S. During the War the installation served as a Federal prison, housing both military and civilian captives. One inmate was a woman—a New Orleans housewife who celebrated a Union defeat too ardently by telling her small children to spit on Yankee officers. The fort was started in the 1850s under the initiative of the then U.S Secretary of War—none other than Jefferson Davis. After the War broke out, his army briefly controlled the base, but in December 1861 General Benjamin Butler, the Union commander, took the fort over and named the installation—at which he planned the capture of New Orleans—for his home state.

Lighthouse. The sixty-five foot cast iron 1848 lighthouse, a Biloxi landmark, was painted black in mourning when Lincoln was assassinated.

The house at 1428 West Beach in Biloxi includes a date palm growing in the middle of the front steps and towering over the roof. According to tradition the tree occupies the spot where Father Abram Ryan, a Catholic priest, erected a large cross. Newly ordained at the outbreak of the War, the twenty-three year old Ryan, a staunch Confederate supporter, founded the *Banner of the South* and published a collection of patriotic Confederate poetry which he recited at meetings. Ryan, the so called"Poet of the Confederacy," was a frequent visitor at the Biloxi residence during the years 1870-1883 when he served as pastor of St. Mary's in Mobile, Alabama.

Brice's Crossroads National Battlefield Site

The majority of the 500 War encounters in Mississippi took place in the northern part of the state. One major encounter occurred on June 7, 1864, when Nathan Bedford Forrest's unit of some 3,500 Confederates defeated more than twice as many Northerners. The battle resulted when the Union attempted to bisect the South east of the Mississippi River. To thwart the attempt, Forrest decided to attack Sherman's supply line, a one track railroad line from Nashville to Chattanooga. When the Union tried to block Forrest's advance through northern Mississippi toward the line, the armies clashed at Brice's Crossroads. Graves at Bethany Cemetery, monuments, and also a log cabin museum housing relics from the battle at the town of Baldwyn recall the encounter. (See also the Tupelo entry.)

Canton

Sherman established a headquarters in a tent beneath a venerable tree locals dubbed "Sherman Oak." A monument in town honors freed slaves who served with the Confederacy. The Confederate Cemetery contains graves of fatalities from Shiloh and Corinth.

Columbus

Friendship Cemetery. The burial ground is claimed to be the site of the first Memorial Day, originating on April 25, 1866, when three local women decorated the graves of both Union and Confederate soldiers with flowers. Among those buried here are four Southern generals.

Blewett-Harrison-Lee House. One of the generals buried at Friendship Cemetery was Stephen D. Lee, who lived at this 1847 residence. Lee ordered the first shot at Fort Sumter which began the War. Lee served as the first president of Mississippi A & M, forerunner of Mississippi State University at Starkville, and was commander of the United Confederate Veterans. Now a museum, the house contains nineteenth century memorabilia and period items.

No major battles took place in Columbus, one of the few Mississippi cities never invaded. The town served as a medical center for both armies, with churches converted into hospitals, and the Confederacy operated an arsenal, where more than 1,000 people worked, in Columbus.

After Jackson, the state capital, fell to the North the Mississippi legislature met at the Lowndes County courthouse. The roof of First United Methodist Church was ripped off and the metal used to make canteens for Confederate soldiers. According to local lore, Jefferson Davis, while staying at Snowdoun, was roused from slumber and addressed a crowd from the balcony of the house dressed in his nightshirt.

Corinth

National Cemetery. Nearly 6,000 Union soldiers, some two-thirds of them unknown, repose at the twenty acre cemetery, located at the Corinth battlefield.

Battery Robinette. At this installation near downtown the most severe fighting took place, with Federal troops holding off the Southern assault, an attempt in 1862 to recapture the town the Confederates had abandoned the previous May in the face of an approaching Union force of nearly 130,000 men. Many other remnants of the battle—earthworks, rifle pits, battery sites, markers—are scattered around Corinth. One such site is a rifle pit, built by the Confederates in 1862, in an unusual circular design, about fifty feet in diameter.

Curlee House. The c. 1857 residence served as headquarters for various generals, including Confederates Braxton Bragg and Earl Van Dorn and Northerner Henry W. Halleck. Bragg and Halleck also used the building at 709 Jackson Street as a headquarters.

Northeast Mississippi Museum. The museum includes exhibits on and artifacts from the Battle of Corinth.

C. and D. Jarnagin Company in Corinth (601-287-4977) manufactures period uniforms and accessories used by re-enactors of War battles.

Edwards

The Battle of Champion Hill Site, outside of town, recalls the May 16, 1863, encounter, the most fierce of the Vicksburg Campaign and the direct prelude to the fall of Vicksburg. General John C. Pemberton led 20,000 of the 30,000 Confederate troops entrenched at Vicksburg out to meet Grant's advancing army of 30,000 men. The forces clashed at Champion Hill, a seventy foot ridge named for the nearby Champion family plantation. Pemberton was finally forced to retreat, allowing Grant to continue his advance toward Vicksburg. In the area stand a monument to Confederate general Lloyd Tilghman, killed during the battle, and Coker House, used by both sides as a hospital and as an artillery site.

Ellisville

According to tradition, many Jones County residents—who owned no slaves and resented supporting a "Planters'War"—seceded from the Confederacy, establishing their capital at Ellisville, near Laurel. The "Free State of Jones" citizens raided Confederate and Union supply bases for provisions and terrorized area settlers.

Friars Point

The museum at this remote town, which huddles below the Mississippi River levee contains some War relics.

At nearby Moon Lake a narrow channel called Yazoo Pass connected the lake with the Mississippi. When Grant sought a way to attack the Confederate stronghold at Vicksburg in 1863 he cut the Yazoo Pass levee and the Mississippi opened a navigation channel across Moon Lake and into the Coldwater River. Grant hoped the new canal would carry him to the Yazoo River so he could attack Vicksburg from behind, but the scheme failed.

Gautier

A few miles north of town David Farragut, in later life the

Gautier

A few miles north of town David Farragut, in later life the renowned Union admiral, lived as a boy. His father was a justice of the peace for the area.

Grand Gulf Military Monument Park

Confederate forces occupied the strategic area on the Mississippi River to defend Vicksburg, twenty miles north. Unable to take Vicksburg from the west, Grant decided to cross the river downstream. He targeted Grand Gulf as his landing point. Seven iron-clad gunboats supported the Union attempt to land at Grand Gulf, but the entrenched Confederates blocked the assault, forcing Grant to move farther south where his forces finally reached the east bank at Bruinsburg. The 400 acre park includes gun emplacements, War artifacts and other reminders of the role Grand Gulf played in Grant's campaign to capture Vicksburg.

Greenwood

The Cottonlandia Museum evokes the agriculture and cotton economy which dominated much of the South in the pre-War era. By 1860, on the eve of the War, America's cotton crop of nearly one billion pounds was some two-thirds of the world's production.

Fort Pemberton. Just west of Cottonlandia lies the site of this make-shift installation, thrown together with cotton bales and logs. In the nearby Tallahatchie River the Confederates sank the captured *Star of the West*—the Union ship fired on at Fort Sumter when War broke out—to block Grant's flotilla of gunboats from proceeding down the Mississippi to Vicksburg in early 1863. Although the *Star* still remains a fallen star, buried in the river, pieces from the boat are on display at Cottonlandia.

Greenwood Cemetery. At the graveyard repose some forty Confederate soldiers from the Battle of Fort Pemberton, including Lieutenant Arza Stoddard, who gave the orders to sink the *Star of the West*.

Grenada

The Grenada Historical Museum includes War relics.

Confederate generals John Pemberton and Sterling Price occupied houses in the town, where the Confederate Cemetery includes the graves of 160 unknown soldiers.

Hattiesburg

The Armed Forces Museum at Camp Shelby, twelve miles south of town, houses almost 2,000 items, from the Mexican War to Vietnam and including Civil War items.

Holly Springs

Holly Springs stood directly in the path of Union attempts to invade Mississippi from the north. The town suffered more than sixty raids by both sides and changed hands so often that residents checked every day to see which flag was flying. Much of the town, however, survived, including sixty or so antebellum houses, many of them evoking War episodes.

The c. 1850 Magnolias' front door bears a scar from a Federal bayonet; 1858 Wakefield belonged to Anne Dickens, who shocked townspeople by marrying a Union officer; 1858 Oakleigh was built by Judge J.W. Clapp, a member of the Confederate Congress who avoided capture by hiding in the capital of one of the mansion's Corinthian columns; Airliewood, occupied by Grant as his headquarters, suffered when his troops shot all the pickets off the iron fence. Walter Place, occupied by Grant's wife, Julia, fared better. Confederate troops refrained from entering the house while Mrs. Grant resided there. In return, the general put Walter Place off limits to Federal troops for the duration of the War. The house thus safely served as a meeting place for Confederate spies and soldiers.

Other reminders of the War at Holly Springs—"preserved rather than restored," notes one account—include 1837 Hillcrest Cemetery, called "Little Arlington," where thirteen Confederate generals along with other high ranking officers repose; Marshall County Historical Museum, in a former college building, with War items; Van Dorn Avenue, named for General Earl Van Dorn, who on December 20, 1862, led a successful raid on the town and a Federal supply depot there, which disrupted Grant's planning for the Vicksburg campaign. At Davis Mill, in Benton County just to the east, some 250 Union soldiers defeated some of the Confederate troops after the raid.

Iuka

The Battle of Iuka, fought on September 19, 1862, brought about heavy casualties, including Confederate general Henry Little. Many of the buildings in town served as hospitals. Shady Grove Cemetery includes the graves of some 300 Confederate soldiers; Union men, buried in trenches, were later disinterred for burial at the National Cemetery in Corinth.

Jackson

Old Capitol Museum. The 1838 former statehouse contains historical exhibits, including War displays. History haunts the halls: in 1861 the Ordinance of Secession was passed here; in 1865 delegates assembled for the first Constitutional Convention in the South held after the fall of the Confederacy; in 1884 Jefferson Davis addressed the Mississippi legislature at the capitol.

War Memorial Building. This museum, next to the Old Capitol, includes in a corner room the exhibit "Mississippi in the Confederacy."

Governor's Mansion. At the 1842 mansion—the nation's second oldest continuously occupied governor's mansion and one of only two designated a National Historic Landmark—Sherman hosted a victory dinner after the fall of Vicksburg.

Battlefield Park. Earthworks, trenches, and a remnant of the fortifications built to defend the city survive at the scene of encounters on May 14 and July 9-17, 1863, during the siege of Jackson.

Invaded by Federal forces four times, Jackson was burned by Sherman's men in 1863 and reduced to charred ruins nicknamed "Chimneyville." At Jackson Sherman supposedly uttered his famous comment, "War is hell."

City Hall. The 1847 structure was one of three public buildings which survived Sherman's burning. Other pre-War buildings include 1857 Manship House, a Gothic Revival cottage occupied by Charles Henry Manship, Jackson's War-time mayor, who surrendered the city to Sherman, and the Oaks, Jackson's oldest house (1846), the residence occupied by Sherman during the 1863 siege. At the Oaks is the sofa from Lincoln's law office in Springfield, Illinois.

Greenwood Cemetery includes Confederate graves.

Lake Washington

St. John's Episcopal Church. Although not damaged by shelling, the church—perched by the lake, located south of Greenville—fell victim to the War. After soldiers removed the windows so the lead frames could be melted down to make bullets, the elements entered the openings and the church eventually decayed.

Laureldale

The Laureldale Springs Confederate Cemetery contains War graves.

Meridian

Merrehope. The twenty room mansion is the only residence, and one of the fewer than a half a dozen buildings, which survived Sherman's February 1864 invasion of Meridian. Confederate general Leonidas Polk occupied the house as a headquarters.

Rose Hill Cemetery. A memorial commemorates Confederate soldiers killed in Meridian during the War. The Marion Confederate Cemetery, on Highway 45 north, also contains War graves.

Mound Bayou

At Davis Bend, on the Mississippi south of Vicksburg, Joseph Davis and his brother Jefferson, the Confederate president, owned extensive plantations which the Union confiscated during the War. The Freedman's Bureau established at the properties a model colony run by former slaves. Drought and floods eventually thwarted the project, so Isaiah Montgomery, son of the former leader at the colony, moved north to the Mississippi Delta area and established a new black settlement at Mound Bayou.

Natchez

Surrendering early in the War, Natchez escaped destruction and suffered only occupation by Federal troops. Nearly 500 antebellum structures survive in Natchez. Many of them recall War episodes.

Magnolia Hall. The last major mansion built before the War, the 1858 house was damaged in 1862 by shelling from the Union gunboat *Essex.* A shell from the boat struck a small child named Rosalie Beekman, the only known Natchez resident killed during the War.

Rosalie. The c. 1820 brick house on a bluff overlooking the Mississippi served as Union army headquarters. Grant visited the house.

The Briars. Jefferson Davis married Varina Anne Banks Howell here in February 1845.

Monmouth. A room in the slave quarters at the 1818 mansion houses a collection of War memorabilia, including weapons, maps, flags, and letters of Confederate leaders.

Longwood. Three years after construction began in 1858, the basement and basic structure of the octagonal Moorish-style mansion were completed at a cost of $100,000. When the War broke out, the northern artisans and carpenters abandoned their tools and utensils, which still remain as the fleeing Yankee workmen left them in 1861.

William Harris House. The 1835 residence—the first floor

built of brick, the upper level of wood—was constructed by the
father of Confederate general Nathaniel Harrison Harris.

Both the Natchez Cemetery and the Natchez National Cemetery
contain War graves.

Newton

Markers in town describe the 1863 attack by Union Colonel
Benjamin Grierson. More than 100 unknown Confederate soldiers
repose at the Doolittle Cemetery north of town.

Okolona

When Nathan Bedford Forrest recaptured the town for the
Confederates, his brother Jesse was fatally wounded by Union fire.
Some 1000 soldiers lie in the Confederate Cemetery.

Oxford

The University of Mississippi, chartered in 1844, held its first
session four years later. The Lyceum survives as the only structure
of the five original buildings, but the Old Chapel and the Barnard
Observatory date from before the War. Wounded from Shiloh and
Corinth were housed in university buildings. A small cemetery near
the campus contains graves of Southerners who died at Shiloh.
According to local legend, when Northerners occupied Oxford for
most of December 1862, Union soldiers rode horses through the
university's most elegant buildings. Three stained glass windows in
1889 Ventress Hall portray a mustering of the "Grays," a unit of
faculty and students which suffered nearly complete casualties at
Gettysburg.

Town Square. Oxford's square—described by local resident
William Faulkner in his novels, some of them laced with evocations
of the War—is one of the South's quintessential such spaces, with
its Confederate soldier statue and the "cotehouse," as residents call
the Lafayette County government building.

Lamar House. Lucius Quintus Cincinnatus Lamar, Confederate representative in Europe, lived at the house. He is buried at St. Peter's Cemetery, as is Faulkner.

College Hill Presbyterian Church. North of town, on College Hill Road, stands the antebellum Williamsburg-style church where Faulkner married. Union troops camped on the grounds when Sherman occupied the church as his headquarters in December 1862. The original pews and slave gallery doors in the church remain intact.

Pascagoula

Old Spanish Fort and Museum. The 1718 fort is one of the oldest buildings in the Mississippi Valley. Exhibits at the small museum include War memorabilia.

Pontotoc

The Pontotoc Cemetery includes Confederate graves.

Port Gibson

Grant spared Port Gibson as the town "too beautiful to burn." A driving tour of the area between Port Gibson and the Mississippi River to the west traces the route Grant followed after landing at Bruinsburg to begin his advance to Vicksburg. Markers recount the story of how Grant landed 30,000 men on April 30, 1863, gained a foothold on the eastern side of the Mississippi, then made his way north to capture Vicksburg on July 4.

Raymond

After defeating Confederate defenders near Port Gibson, Grant continued east to Raymond where on May 12, 1863, his forces encountered another Southern unit. The Hinds County courthouse and the St. Mark's Episcopal Church served as hospitals; blood stains on the sanctuary floor recall the wounded ministered to at the church. The Raymond Cemetery contain War graves.

Rodney

Remote Rodney, too small to appear on the official Mississippi highway map, once enjoyed prosperity as a thriving Mississippi River port. A cannonball from shelling by a Union boat disfigures the facade of Rodney Presbyterian Church. Confederate cavalry-men captured Union soldiers attending services in the church on September 15, 1863. A plaque on highway 552 indicates the site of a War encounter.

Sardis

At the 1851 Davis Chapel, built by slave labor, is still a slave gallery. A mass grave in the old cemetery contains the bodies of Union and Confederate dead. A slave gallery also may be seen at the 1842 Fredonia Church, the oldest in Panola County.

Senatobia

The Tate County Heritage Museum includes War items.

Tupelo

Tupelo National Battlefield. At the site the Confederate line formed to attack the Union defensive positions. Monuments, markers and artifacts recall the encounter. Sherman's northern Mississippi campaign focused on a single objective: to protect the rail supply line which brought food and ammunition to his army from Louisville through Nashville and Chattanooga. After the Union defeat at Brice's Cross Roads (see that entry), Sherman issued the order to pursue Forrest "to the death, if it costs 10,000 lives and breaks the Treasury." Federal forces left Memphis and crossed northern Mississippi to undefended Tupelo, which they occupied. On the morning of July 14, 1864, Forrest attacked. The Union repulsed the assault and managed to keep the Mobile and Ohio rail line secure until Sherman advanced past Atlanta and thus beyond the line. Although important, the encounters at Brice's Cross Roads and Tupelo were peripheral to Sherman's main campaign in the West and to Grant's clash with Lee in the East. Lincoln, recalling his rabbit hunting days, said of the side battles, "Those not skinning can hold a leg."

The Tupelo Museum houses artifacts from the Battle of Tupelo and a diorama of the battlefield.

Confederate Grave Sites. The thirteen unknown soldiers buried at the site, just off the Natchez Trace Parkway, were supposedly executed by General Braxton Bragg, their own commander, for various offenses.

Union

Boler's Inn. Built in 1835, the inn was one of the original stops on the stage coach line between Jackson, Mississippi, and Mobile, Alabama. In February 1864 Sherman spent the night here.

Vicksburg

Vicksburg National Military Park. A sixteen mile driving tour leads through the monument-filled battlefields, where trenches, earthworks and cannons indicate Confederate defensive positions. The visitor center contains exhibits on and artifacts from the forty-seven day Siege of Vicksburg. The park's northern section includes the U.S.S. *Cairo* gunboat, salvaged after a century under water. Artifacts from the boat evoke daily life in 1863. At the cemetery in the park three-quarters of the 17,000 graves bear the marking "Unknown." A lesser known burial area in town is the Soldiers Rest Confederate Cemetery on Sky Farm Avenue.

Old Court House Museum. War history haunts the 1858 building. Jefferson Davis—a resident of Warren County when he served as U.S. senator from Mississippi—launched his political career on the grounds, and from the tower Confederate generals observed the 1862 attack on Vicksburg. When Union prisoners were moved into the court room, Federal shelling of the building ceased. Northern troops raised the Stars and Stripes at the courthouse on July 4, 1863, and for more than a century thereafter citizens of Vicksburg refused to celebrate Independence Day. Exhibits at the museum include War memorabilia, Grant's chair, the tie Davis wore when inaugurated Confederate president, and many other era artifacts.

Antebellum mansions. War incidents occurred at many of Vicksburg's early-day houses. At McRaven, Confederates camped in the garden and as late as the 1950s a bomb squad removed a live shell from a wall. Balfour, Union headquarters after city fell, was the home of War diarist Emma Balfour and site of the 1862 Christmas ball interrupted by news of Union gunboats on the Mississippi. Duff Green housed a hospital. Davis spoke from the balcony of Anchuca. A Union cannonball remains embedded in a wall at Cedar Grove. The 1840s Willis-Cowan House served as headquarters for Confederate general John Pemberton during the siege.

"The Vanishing Glory." The thirty minute multi-media presentation dramatizes the campaign for and siege of Vicksburg.

Toys and Soldiers Museum. Displays include not only miniature soldiers but also War shells and other artifacts.

Christ Church. During the siege, daily services were held at the c. 1839 church, the oldest remaining public building in Vicksburg, in spite of heavy shelling.

Washington

Jefferson College. Jefferson Davis studied at the school, occupied by Union forces during the War.

West Point

Lenoir Plantation. Both Confederate and Union soldiers occupied the 1847 mansion, built by slave labor and located on a 2,000 acre property.

Winona

More than two dozen antebellum houses within a few square

blocks give the town a pre-War flavor. At the corner of Carrollton and Church Streets towers the oak under which Jefferson Davis addressed the townspeople.

Woodville

Rosemont Plantation. The parents of Jefferson Davis built the house, which contains many original furnishings, about 1810. Davis family members occupied the residence for eighty-five years. Jefferson, the youngest of ten children, was brought here at age two when the family moved from Kentucky. Five generations of the Davis clan repose at the cemetery.

Yazoo City

Triangle Cultural Center. The Yazoo Historical Museum at the Center includes War artifacts and a scale model of the ironclad ram *Arkansas*, built at the Confederate naval yard, its site indicated by a marker near the Yazoo River. The *Arkansas* helped fend off a July 1862 attack on Vicksburg by David Farragut. Yazoo City native Lieutenant Savvy Read, who served on the *Arkansas*, later helped capture a Union boat by using a wooden log painted to resemble a cannon. On the grounds of the Center stands a 1906 monument honoring the role of Mississippi women during the War. This is supposedly one of only two known memorials which commemorate women of the Confederacy.

Woodbine Mansion. The 1840s house, near Bentonia to the south of Yazoo City, boasts ghosts—so says local legend—including a spirited young woman who gazes out of the east window looking for her beau who never returned from the War. On one glass pane appear the young lovers' initials she scratched in the glass with her engagement ring.

Louisiana

Alexandria

Rosalie Sugar Mill. Union troops spared this c. 1852 house, south of town on Louisiana highway 1208-A off U.S. 71, as the owner was a friend of Sherman.

Pineville National Cemetery includes a monument to 1537 Union soldiers buried at the graveyard.

Bastorp

The Snyder Museum and Creative Art Center contains exhibits on the War and Reconstruction.

Baton Rouge

Old State Capitol. In January 1861 the Secession Convention met in the 1849 statehouse and voted for Louisiana to leave the Union. During the War Union soldiers used the building as a barracks and, briefly, as a prison for Confederate captives. On December 28, 1862, a fire caused by grease overheated when soldiers prepared supper gutted the capitol, later rebuilt and reopened in May 1882.

Pentagon Barracks. Confederate forces occupied the 1824 military facility until Federal troops entered Baton Rouge in the summer of 1862 to begin an occupation which lasted until 1879.

Louisiana State University. In the late 1850s none other than William Tecumseh Sherman, later the famous Union general, served as president of the Seminary of Learning, the early name for the institution which became L.S.U. All the students and teachers at the seminary joined the Confederate army, except for one who opted for the Union army and two who remained unaffiliated.

Mount Hope Plantation. Confederate troops used the property to rest and water their horses. A small War museum in the 1817 Creole-style house recalls the era.

Cemeteries. At the National Cemetery repose some 2,000 Union soldiers, and at Magnolia Cemetery occurred the August 1864 Battle of Baton Rouge. A monument at 330 South 19th Street marks the site of an August 5, 1862, battle, during which Confederate lieutenant Alexander H. Todd, Mary Todd Lincoln's half-brother, was killed.

West of the Mississippi lies Port Allen, named for General Henry W. Allen, based in Opelousas as governor of the Confederate part of Louisiana in 1864-5. Allen survived wounds he suffered during the Battle of Baton Rouge. His statue stands in front of the courthouse, while a monument on the grounds of the Old State Capitol (back on the east side of the river) marks Allen's grave site. Also west of the river is the West Baton Rouge Museum, with historical exhibits, including a reconstructed original slave cabin from Allendale Plantation, Allen's property, which was burned during the War.

Beggs

On the grounds of 1829 Homeplace (open to visitors) is the grave of an unknown Confederate soldier.

Belle Chasse

Bellechasse (spelled as one word) Plantation, established in 1808, was acquired in 1844 by Judah P. Benjamin, U.S. senator in the 1850s and later a member of the Confederate cabinet who served as Secretary of State, Secretary of War and Attorney General. After the War Benjamin fled to London where he established a new career as a leading member of the English bar. At the site of the now vanished plantation stands its 1848 bell, to which Benjamin— "to sweeten its tone"—added 200 silver dollars when the molten metal for the bell was being prepared.

Burnside

Houmas House. One of the famous antebellum plantation houses along the Mississippi, 1840 Houmas enjoyed a better fate during the War than many of the neighboring properties. When Union general Benjamin Butler arrived to occupy the plantation, owner John Burnside, an Irishman, argued that as a British subject his holdings should remain exempt from control by the U.S. Butler agreed, and withdrew, and the plantation was spared.

The Cabin Restaurant. The eatery occupies one of ten original slave houses, built a century and a half ago as part of the Monroe Plantation. Newspaper wall coverings to insulate the cabin, slave tools and other relics on display recall the pre-War era. Behind the main cabin stretches a two room slave dwelling from the Welham Plantation.

Cheneyville

Loyd Hall House. The residence, located outside town, was occupied by both Confederate and Union troops. A Union soldier is buried under the house.

Trinity Episcopal Church. The 1820s sanctuary retains its slave gallery and original furnishings.

Chopin

Much of the land in and around Chopin now comprises the 6,000 acre Little Eva Plantation, claimed to be the setting of Harriet Beecher Stowe's famous anti-slavery novel, *Uncle Tom's Cabin.* Local legend has it that plantation owner Robert B. McAlpin, portrayed in the book as Simon Legree, bought Uncle Tom at a sale in New Orleans and brought the slave back to the property. On the grounds stands a ramshackle shack of weathered wood, a replica of the original Uncle Tom's Cabin removed for display at the 1893 Chicago Exposition. A half mile or so beyond the cabin metal markers indicate the graves of McAlpin and "of the person said to be the character portrayed as Uncle Tom." (See the entry for Owensboro, Kentucky, which also claims Uncle Tom was a local character.)

Clinton

Clinton Confederate State Commemorative Area. The four acre cemetery contains the remains of some 150 Southern soldiers, about half of whom perished during the 1863 siege at Port Hudson. The Marston House and Silliman College in town both served as hospitals, which received the sick and wounded from nearby Port Hudson.

Delta

At various places in Mississippi (see the entry for Friars Point) and Louisiana (see the entry for Lake Providence) north of Vicksburg, Grant tried to devise a workable plan to by-pass that Confederate stronghold overlooking the Mississippi. At Delta, Grant dug a canal to change the river's course, an operation he also attempted at De Soto Point, opposite Vicksburg just to the north. None of Grant's schemes worked, so finally he crossed the Mississippi to Bruinsburg, south of Vicksburg.

Derry

Magnolia Plantation. The now restored brick mansion house at this working cotton plantation, dating from 1753, was burned during the War.

Destrehan Plantation

Believed to be the oldest plantation house in the Lower Mississippi Valley, the 1787 property was seized by Union forces and turned into a Freedman's Colony where newly liberated slaves took training in the economics of agriculture. More than 900 black freedmen were trained at Destrehan, returned after the War to its owners.

Donaldsonville

Northerners destroyed much of the town during the War, especially when they bombarded and burned Donaldsonville in

1862. The c. 1850 building on Railroad Avenue, now occupied by Ferris's Grocery, was used as a headquarters during the War. At nearby Port Barrow lurked guerrilla bands which harassed Federal troops after the occupation of New Orleans. In February 1863 the Union installed a log fort, attacked four months later by a small group of Confederates who captured the outpost. Union gunboats then shelled the Rebels, who soon retreated.

Fort Jackson

Built between 1822 to 1832 to protect the Lower Mississippi and New Orleans, the fort seemingly blocked a river approach to the city from the south. Military strategists believed that wooden ships would find it impossible to pass the fort, which bristled with armaments. In April 1862 Admiral David Farragut brought up the Mississippi a Federal fleet of twenty-four wooden gunboats and nineteen mortar schooners, which unleashed a four day bombardment on Fort Jackson and Fort St. Philip, located nearby on the east bank of the river. On the fifth day seventeen vessels managed to slip past the forts, and after a spirited encounter with Confederate gunboats and rams, the Union boats proceeded north towards New Orleans. Fort Jackson finally surrendered on April 28.

Fort Pike

At the outbreak of the War the Louisiana Militia captured the fort—built at the eastern edge of Lake Pontchartrain between 1818 and 1827—and held it until Federal forces took New Orleans on May 1, 1862. The Union occupied the fort as a base to protect New Orleans and for raids along the Gulf Coast. The Citadel, which the Confederates burned before their retreat, now houses historical exhibits.

Franklin

St. Mary's Parish Museum. Exhibits at the museum, which occupies the c. 1851 Grevemberg House, include War relics. In the spring of 1863 Confederate troops fought a delaying action against Union forces at Franklin.

Geismar

A few miles from town stands Belle Hélène, built in 1841 by Duncan F. Kenner and then named Ashland after Henry Clay's mansion in Lexington, Kentucky (see the entry for Ashland under that city). Jefferson Davis appointed Kenner Confederate minister plenipotentiary to Europe. After the War Federal authorities confiscated the property, which Kenner later recovered.

Grand Coteau

Academy of the Sacred Heart. The world's oldest Society of the Sacred Heart School (1821), the institution escaped damage during the War when General Nathaniel Banks, commander of the 20,000 Federal troops based in Grand Coteau in 1863, placed the school under his protection. At the time, his daughter was attending a Sacred Heart Academy in New York. Archives at the Academy include War era documents.

Hahnville

The town took its name from Michael Hahn, Union governor of Louisiana when the North occupied part of the state in 1864, after which Louisiana had two governors.

Near town lies the site of the old Fashion Plantation, owned by Confederate general Richard Taylor, son of President Zachary Taylor. A skirmish occurred on the property in August 1862 when Union troops defeated an attempt by Confederate forces to take cattle, horses, sheep, mules and slaves from the plantation.

Harrisonburg

Fort Beauregard. Now a park and amphitheater, the site—a natural formation of hills and ravines overlooking the downtown area—served as a Confederate stronghold established in 1862 to block Federal gunboats from ascending the Ouachita River.

Harrisonburg Methodist Church. Bullet holes from the War pock the walls of the church, frequented by soldiers for services.

Catahoula Parish Museum of Natural History. Installed in the courthouse, the museum includes War relics from area encounters.

Innis

On Louisiana highway 418 near Innis, on the grounds of St. Stephens Episcopal Church, stands a statue of a soldier, claimed to be the only monument in the South to an unknown soldier of the War (but see the entry for Beauvoir in Biloxi, Mississippi).

Jackson

Jackson Confederate State Commemorative Area. Although the cemetery here has no marked graves, the one acre site was established during the War to bury soldiers killed in an encounter at nearby Thompson's Creek. Adjacent to the burial ground is Centenary State Commemorative Area, with buildings from Centenary College, a Methodist school. Union troops occupied the Main Academic Building as a headquarters, while the school dorms served as a hospital.

Milbank. Union soldiers enjoyed especially lavish accommodations when they occupied as a barracks the elegant Milbank mansion, fronted by six thirty foot tall columns and a two level veranda.

Lake Providence

In the center of town remain traces of the canal Grant dug in a effort to allow Union gunboats to leave the Mississippi and, on a network of rivers and bayous, to bypass the heavily fortified bluffs at Vicksburg, Mississippi, downstream. (See also the entry for Delta, Louisiana.)

Grant supposedly stayed at 1841 Arlington, outside town. Union generals MacPherson, McMillan and MacArthur did use the house as a headquarters.

Lafayette

At the corner of Jefferson and Lee Streets stands a 1922 statue of Confederate general Alfred Mouton, son of Louisiana's first Cajun governor. Mouton lived in the nearby residence now housing the Lafayette Museum, which contains War items. He was killed at Mansfield (see the Mansfield State Commemorative Area entry) on April 8, 1864, and is buried in Lafayette.

Cathedral of St. John the Evangelist. During the War Union soldiers camped on the grounds, where a previous church then stood.

LaPlace

On the grounds of St. John the Baptist Parish offices, the Herbert Building, stands a cannon from the War.

Leesville

The Military Museum at Fort Polk, seven miles southeast of the Vernon Parish seat, includes War items.

At Burr Ferry Park (Louisiana highway 8, east bank of the Sabine River) west of town survive Confederate breastworks built late in the War to block an anticipated Union advance northward on the Sabine River.

LaSalle Parish

The LaSalle Museum Association, in the hamlet of Good Pine on U.S. 84, houses War weapons.

Mansfield State Commemorative Area

On the western edge of Louisiana occurred the South's last major victory of the War, when on April 8, 1864, fewer than 9,000

Confederate soldiers defeated 36,000 Union troops. A museum, monuments and library recall the encounter.

Battle of Pleasant Hill Park, in Sabine Parish not far south, commemorates another War encounter. At Keatchie, a village northwest of Mansfield, is a Confederate cemetery.

Marthaville

Rebel State Commemorative Area. The memorial area three miles northwest of town includes the site of an unknown Confederate soldier's grave. The soldier was killed April 1864 when wandering in the woods looking for his unit. The Barnhill family, local residents, buried the body and for nearly a century family members cared for the grave. As recently as 1962 a memorial was installed at the site, then designated a State Commemorative Area.

Napoleonville

Christ Episcopal Church. Leonidas Polk, the "fighting bishop of the Confederacy," dedicated the church, in which Union troops supposedly stabled their horses.

Natchitoches

Trinity Episcopal Church. In 1857 Polk laid the cornerstone of the church, construction of which was interrupted by the War.

Carroll House. The 1806 residence, also known as The Magnolia, served as the headquarters of Confederate general Richard Taylor, son of President Zachary Taylor.

Tante Hippe House. Slave quarters remain at the rear of the 1835 residence.

New Iberia

Shadows-on-the-Teche. The Union army made its headquarters in New Iberia during the 1864 Red River Campaign. Federal troops took control of the imposing 1834 "Shadows," centerpiece of an extensive sugar plantation established by planter David Weeks.

During the time Union forces occupied the manor house, Week's widow Mary, by then remarried, confined herself to the second floor where she died in 1863.

New Orleans

Confederate Museum. No less a figure than Jefferson Davis himself served on the planning committee for this museum, established in 1891. Although the former Confederate president died (1889) before the museum was completed, he returned post-mortem to the fanciful Romanesque-style structure two and a half years after his death when his body lay in state—after being disinterred from the Metairie Cemetery—prior to shipment to a cemetery in Richmond, Virginia. Exhibits at Memorial Hall, as the museum is called, include Davis family memorabilia, and such War items as uniforms, battle banners, photos, medical instruments, weapons, and paintings of Confederate generals. The book store-gift shop sells an interesting selection of items pertaining to the War.

P.G.T. Beauregard. Beauregard, a leading Southern general, served on the Confederate Museum's first board of directors. Various places in New Orleans recall his presence in the city. The 1826 Beauregard-Keyes House—named for him and for later resident novelist Francis Parkinson Keyes—was the general's residence for a time after the War. One room contains items which belonged to Beauregard and his family. In 1944 Keyes—whose book *Madame Castel's Lodger* tells of Beauregard's stay in the mansion—moved into the house. Beauregard (and his son) also lived after the War at 934 Royal Street, and he died on February 20, 1893, at 1631 Esplanade Avenue. An equestrian statue of Beauregard overlooks the Esplanade Avenue entrance to City Park. In June 1861 Beauregard sent part of a captured flagstaff from Fort Sumter—the general was in command when Confederates shelled the fort with the War's first shot—to New Orleans where the trophy was presented to the Orleans Guard at Gardette-Le Pretre House, 716 Dauphine. Before the War Beauregard served as engineer in charge when construction begun in 1848 at the Egyptian Revival-style Customs House, used by Union general Benjamin F. Butler when he occupied New Orleans. Locals nicknamed the reviled commander "Beast." It was "Beast" Butler who ordered carved on the base of the Jackson statue in Jackson Square the inscription, "The Union Must and Shall be Preserved."

Chalmette Battlefield. From 1880 to 1904 General Beauregard's son, Judge Réné Beauregard, occupied as a country residence the 1840 mansion at the Chalmette Battlefield, site of the 1815 Battle of New Orleans. The adjacent Chalmette National Cemetery was established in 1864 as a burial area for Union soldiers who died in Louisiana. A former powder magazine at the 1837 Jackson Barracks (occupied for a time by Confederate troops) a mile from the battlefield houses the Louisiana Military History and State Weapons Museum, with War items.

Museums. The Historic New Orleans Collection, housed in the restored 1792 Merieult House, includes items relating to the Federal occupation of the city during the War. Although New Orleans was occupied for fifteen years, starting in April 1862, plaques of the city's ruling governments in the bases of Canal Street light standards show New Orleans under "Confederate Domination, 1861-1865." In the colonnade of the Presbytere, part of the Louisiana State Museum, stands the *Pioneer*, launched by Confederates in the fall of 1861 as the world's first iron submarine. Built at a shipyard on Bayou St. John, the diminutive sub—six feet high and nineteen feet four inches long—required a crew of four. The ship, whose top speed was four miles per hour, never served in combat, completing only a trial run before Southerners sunk the vessel in Lake Ponchartrain to keep Federal troops from capturing the boat, later recovered as a relic of the War.

Monuments. At Lee Circle stands a bronze statue of Lee—looking north, as if on watch—perched atop a sixty foot shaft of Tennessee marble. Davis and Beauregard were present at the dedication in 1884. At 3400 Canal Street is a statue of Davis, who died in 1889 at the house of Judge Charles Fenner, 1134 First Street in the Garden District, after the Confederate leader, taken ill at Beauvoir, his house in Biloxi, Mississippi, was brought to New Orleans. Opposite the Davis statue is a monument to Charles Dreux, organizer of the Orleans Guards and the first New Orleans officer to die in the War. To the right of the entrance at Metairie Cemetery stands a statue of Confederate general Albert Sidney Johnston ("In His Honor, Impregnable; In His Simplicity, Divine," reads the inscription), killed at Shiloh on April 6, 1862. Beauregard and other Confederate soldiers are buried in the mausoleum beneath the statue. Atop a thirty-two foot granite shaft at the cemetery is a statue of "Stonewall" Jackson, while the mausoleum below contains the bodies of 2,500 men of the Army of Northern Virginia. A monument to Confederate dead at Greenwood Cemetery includes life-size busts of Jackson, Lee, Johnston and Leonidas Polk.

Hermann-Grima House. In 1850 Judge Felix Grima, whose family occupied the 1831 residence for five generations, bought the adjacent property for use as a stable, converted in 1881 to the Christian Woman's Exchange, established to raise money for impoverished widows of Confederate soldiers.

Nottoway

The huge house—supposedly the nation's largest plantation home—was spared during the War when a Union gunboat officer who had been a guest of sugar planter John Hampden Randolph, builder and owner of the mansion, decided not to shell it.

Opelousas

Governor's Mansion. When the Union occupied part of Louisiana Governor Henry W. Allen moved to Opelousas. Allen resided in the 1850 house of Homere Mouton, Louisiana's lieutenant governor in the late 1850s. Opposite the courthouse stood the LeCompte Hotel, Confederate capitol of Louisiana from May 1862 to January 1863.

Prudhomme House. The c. 1809 residence, the oldest structure in St. Landry Parish, was occupied by Union officers.

Jim Bowie Museum. The museum, installed in the tourist information center, includes War items.

Ray Homestead. The Confederate army used the house at the corner of Liberty and West Bellevue Streets as a medical facility. The owner of the property, Dr. George Hill, served as chief surgeon of the 2,000 man 9th Brigade Medical Department, headquartered at the house.

At Latwell, a village west of Opelousas, Matt's Museum includes a number of War related items.

Pineville

Mount Olivet Church. Union troops occupied the 1857 church as a barracks.

Alexandria National Cemetery. The burial ground, established in 1867, includes the graves of Confederate and Union troops.

Point Pleasant

In the cemetery lies General Paul O. Hebert, governor in the 1850s and the last commander of the Trans-Mississippi Department, which he surrendered after Lee's surrender at Appomattox.

Port Hudson State Commemorative Area

At a strategic point on the bluffs overlooking the Mississippi the Confederates established a fortification which served as the southern anchor of defenses along the river extending 150 miles north to Vicksburg. Reflecting Lincoln's observation that the Mississippi was the "key" to the Rebellion, the Union army targeted the Confederate strongholds at Vicksburg and Port Hudson. On May 23, 1863, some 30,000 Federal troops began a siege against 6,800 Rebels. On July 3 Lee's second invasion at Gettysburg was repelled, on July 4 Vicksburg fell, and on July 9—after a forty-eight day siege—Port Hudson finally succumbed, the last Confederate outpost on the Mississippi to surrender. Finally, the "key" was in the North's pocket. Six miles of trails, breastworks, a lookout tower at Fort Desperate, and a museum with interpretive displays recall the episode, a major factor in the Union's eventual victory.

St. Francisville

Locust Grove State Commemorative Area. This site, northeast of town, is a cemetery whose graves include that of Sarah Knox Taylor, Jefferson Davis's first wife. The burial ground is the only surviving part of Locust Grove Plantation, owned by the family of Davis's sister, Mrs. Anna E. Davis Smith. Davis brought his wife of three months (Zachary Taylor's daughter) to the plantation for a visit. Both contracted malaria, which proved fatal to Sarah, age twenty-one.

Grace Episcopal Church. In 1858 Leonidas Polk, the "fighting bishop of the Confederacy," laid the cornerstone of the church, severely damaged by shelling. Fighting was suspended for a day while Confederate and Union masons attended a last rites service for their fellow Mason, John E. Hart, captain of the Federal gunboat U.S.S. *Albatross*, whose shells had rained down on the church just before his death. The rector of the church Hart's boat damaged officiated at his burial.

Cottage Plantation. The main house and ten original outbuildings, constructed between 1795 and 1850, survive as one of the few complete antebellum plantation properties, strongholds of the South's culture prior to the War.

Mount Carmel Church. Completed in 1893, the church was built from plans drafted in 1871 by P.G.T. Beauregard, a leading Southern general (see entry for Beauregard under New Orleans).

Printer's Cottage. The c. 1814 house, now a bed and breakfast establishment, includes the Civil War Room, its beams damaged by an 1863 gunboat attack on St. Francisville.

St. Joseph

Christ Church Rectory. The building, moved to the site in 1881, bears bullet holes and shrapnel scars from shelling by Union forces.

St. Maurice

The 1840 St. Maurice Plantation, outside town off U.S. 84, survived the War, as Union troops were forced to retreat to the west of the Red River, but the main house burned in 1981. The grounds, however, include a number of original structures. The two story galleried house which burned, called the Prothro Mansion, served as headquarters for General Zachary Taylor during the Mexican-American War. Among his officers who visited here were Grant, Lee and Davis.

Shreveport

Confederate Monument. The statue, dedicated in 1906, includes busts of Lee, "Stonewall" Jackson, Beauregard and Henry W. Allen. At the site, in June 1865, the Confederate flag was lowered for the last time in Louisiana.

Courthouse Square. In May 1863 the old courthouse became the Confederate capitol of Louisiana. The present structure dates from the 1920s.

Fort Humbug. This was one of three forts built when General Nathaniel Banks' campaign threatened this last Confederate stronghold in Louisiana during the spring 1864 Red River Campaign. A shortage of cannons forced the use of charred logs as "artillery" designed to humbug the Union attackers.

Oakland Cemetery includes graves of Confederate veterans.

Slidell

The name of the town and John Slidell Park commemorate the man appointed as a Confederate emissary to England during the War.

Sunset

South of town lies Chretien Point Plantation, a splendidly restored 1831 Greek Revival-style mansion house. During the Red River Campaign some of the skirmishes occurred on the plantation, which was looted and ravaged. A bullet hole in one of the front doors recalls the fighting. A stairway and window of the house were used as models for Tara, the plantation in the movie "Gone with the Wind."

On the banks of Bayou Bourbeau near Sunset a band of Confederate soldiers blocked a Union advance headed for Texas.

Tangipahoa

Camp Moore State Commemorative Area. The four acre site includes a cemetery with graves of several hundred Confederate soldiers. The museum contains War artifacts and exhibits on Camp Moore, one of the South's largest training camps. The base was named for Governor Thomas O. Moore, whose house Mooreland, near Alexandria, was burned by Union soldiers in 1864,

Thibodaux

St. John's Church. In the yard of the sanctuary, built in 1844 by Leonidas Polk, first bishop of Louisiana, stands a memorial to Polk, later a Southern general known as the "fighting bishop of the Confederacy." A slave gallery, now a choir loft, was added in 1856 to the building, supposedly the oldest Episcopal church west of the Mississippi.

Magnolia Plantation. The 1858 house, on Louisiana highway 311 south of town, served as a hospital during area encounters between Federal general Nathaniel Banks and Confederate general Richard Taylor.

Chatchie Plantation. On Louisiana highway 308 southwest of town stands an 1867 raised cottage built to replace an earlier house, called Homeplace, used as a field hospital during the Battle of

Lafourche Crossing. The battle site, marked by a plaque, can be seen from highways 308 and 1.

Washington

Nicholson House of History. The nineteenth century house, built by the first mayor of Washington, served as a Confederate hospital.

Winnfield

The Free State of Winnfield Historical Museum at the tourist center recalls the occasion when—after Louisiana seceded from the Union—Winn Parish seceded from Louisiana. Nonetheless, most area residents rallied to the Southern cause.

Salisbury Bridge, outside town, is at the site where in 1864 a Confederate unit blocked Federal forces sent to destroy the nearby Drake Salt Works. Some of the soldiers killed in the encounter repose in Old Harmony Cemetery. The salt deposit took its name from Reuben Drake, whose nephew Edwin Drake drilled the world's first oil well in Pennsylvania in 1841. The innovative rotary drill Drake used for the well had been tested by his uncle Reuben while drilling for water at the salt works.

Winter Quarters State Commemorative Area.

Located south of Newellton, the long low-slung galleried house survived the War after Julia Nutt—whose Union sympathizing husband had fled to the North—crossed Federal lines to meet with Grant. She offered to feed and quarter Union troops if they refrained from destroying her home. Grant agreed, and although he burned all the other area plantation houses the Union general spared the Nutt house. The residence contains War weapons, uniforms, diaries and other items.

Kentucky

Augusta

In Augusta lived Senator Thornton F. Marshall, who cast the deciding vote which kept Kentucky in the Union. In May 1861 the state legislature decreed Kentucky's neutrality.

Joseph S. Tomlinson House. The house was built in 1823 as a residence for the president of Augusta College, the world's first Methodist college. Dr. Tomlinson was often visited here in the summer by his nephew, composer Stephen Foster, who wrote War era songs.

On September 27, 1862, a skirmish between Federal and Union troops in Augusta left twenty-one dead.

Barbourville

The first shot of the War in Kentucky was fired on Cumberland Avenue. On September 9, 1861, a skirmish took place at the Barbourville Bridge, north of town.

Bardstown

Civil War Museum. The museum at Old Bardstown Village, reproduction of a 1790 frontier community, includes a number of War artifacts.

The Mansion. The 1851 residence of William E. Johnson, Kentucky's first lieutenant governor and an acting governor, was the first place in the state to fly the Confederate flag, unfurled in 1861 before a crowd of some 5,000 onlookers. General John Hunt Morgan, known as the "Thunderbolt of the Confederacy" for his lightning-like raids, hid at The Mansion in 1863 after his escape from a Union prison. At the house lived Ben Johnson, a lawyer who defended members of Quantrill's Raiders, a Confederate guerrilla band.

Old Talbott Tavern. The Lincoln family, including young Abe, stayed at the 1779 tavern during a trial involving a title dispute over the family farm. After losing the case, the Lincolns left the property and moved to Indiana.

Gertrude H. Smith House. Built in the early nineteenth century by the ominously named Colonel Ben Doom, the house served as a hospital during the War.

Edgewood. The 1819 columned mansion was headquarters of Confederate officer Braxton Bragg before the Battle of Perryville (see the entry for Perryville).

Spalding Hall. The building, constructed in 1819 and once the home of St. Joseph College, housed a hospital during the War. The Hall now contains the Bardstown Historical Museum, which includes War artifacts and displays. The Hall also houses the Oscar Getz Museum of Whiskey History, where one exhibit shows a copy of Lincoln's liquor license for the New Salem, Illinois, tavern he ran in the mid 1830s.

Miniature Soldier Museum. The museum contains more than 10,000 items, including toy figures recalling the War.

"My Old Kentucky Home." The house recalls composer Stephen Foster, whose songs evoke the old South, as it was before the War.

By the courthouse stands a slave auction stone (moved there from elsewhere) used for sales of blacks.

Bonnieville

Glen Lily. The house, which stood by the Green River, was the birthplace of Simon Bolivar Buckner, who both surrendered to Grant at Donelson (see the Tennessee entry for Fort Donelson National Battlefield) and served as a pallbearer at Grant's funeral.

Bowling Green

Riverview-Hobson House. Construction of the mansion was halted during the War so the Confederate army could use the structure as an ammunition depot. Atwood, Hobson's oldest son, became the youngest colonel in the Union army.

Western Kentucky University. The museum, which emphasizes Kentucky history, includes War items. The university lies on a hill occupied during the War by a fort. Campus walkways follow the lines of the old trenches.

Bowling Green was Kentucky's Confederate capital. Although the border state did not secede from the Union, the Confederacy admitted Kentucky as the South's thirteenth state.

Burnside

The General Burnside State Park was named for Union officer A.E. Burnside, whose headquarters were located in 1863 at Port Isabel, head of navigation on what was then the Cumberland River (now Lake Cumberland). The general's hair style—beard and moustache with clean-shaven chin—became known as a "burnsider"; the lateral hair patches eventually came to be called "sideburns."

Columbus

Columbus-Belmont State Park. The park occupies one of the most splendid vantage points—and militarily strategic points—on the entire Mississippi. Here, in early September 1861, 19,000 Confederate troops under General Leonidas Polk occupied the bluffs above the river, establishing there a fortress bristling with arms. Polk also stretched a chain across the Mississippi to block navigation of the waterway by Union vessels. Challenged by this attempt to occupy Kentucky, ostensibly neutral, and to control the Mississippi, Grant inaugurated his first active campaign of the War in November by attacking Belmont, a Confederate base in Missouri just across the river. Grant was forced to withdraw, but by February 1862 he managed to outflank Columbus, which he occupied the following month. In the park survive artillery, the anchor which was attached to the chain, and other relics of the Confederate stronghold. Artifacts and a video presentation at the museum recall the episode.

Covington

On Riverside Drive, in the northeast corner of Covington by the confluence of the Ohio and Licking Rivers, survive some restored War era houses. A statue on Kennedy Street depicts James Bradley, a black abolitionist active in the Underground Railroad.

Federal forces fortified the hills behind Covington to defend Cincinnati, just across the Ohio River. When Confederate troops approached the area in September 1862 Union soldiers crossed the river on a bridge formed by coal barges and blocked the advance near Fort Mitchell.

Cumberland Gap

See the entry in the Tennessee section.

Cynthiana

Battle Grove Cemetery. Confederate dead killed in the June 1864 Battle of Cynthiana repose in the graveyard, site of the June 12 encounter when John Hunt Morgan's raiders were overwhelmed by Union forces.

Danville

Centre College. Among the school's graduates was John C. Breckenridge, the youngest U.S. vice president and later a Confederate general.

Eddyville

Lyon County Museum. Exhibits include part of a telegraph used by Grant.

Elizabethtown

Ben Hardin Helm, a Confederate cavalry officer, lived in the town. Helm married Mary Todd Lincoln's sister, Emily. President Lincoln offered him the post of Union paymaster, a position Helm declined. He was killed on September 20, 1863, at Chickamauga in Georgia.

On the main square stands a building where an embedded cannonball remains as a souvenir of John Hunt Morgan's raid on Elizabethtown.

Fairview

A 351-foot-high Washington Monument-type tower—the nation's third highest obelisk—commemorates the place where Jefferson Davis was born on June 3, 1808. Near the 1929 monument, which offers wide-ranging panoramas from the observation area at the top, stands a reproduction of the two room log house where Davis was born. By an odd coincidence, Lincoln was also born in the same region at about the same time, so both Civil War presidents were born within one year and 100 miles of one another.

Flemingsburg

At a room in the Fleming Hotel James J. Andrews, War soldier of fortune, plotted the "Great Train Robbery," during which he captured the Confederate locomotive "The General." (See also the entry for Chattanooga, Tennessee.)

Frankfort

Frankfort was the only state capital which remained loyal to the Union to be captured by Confederate forces, who occupied the town from September 3 to October 4, 1862.

The Kentucky Military History Museum. The museum includes War related displays.

Kentucky First Ladies in Miniature. A series of dolls clad in period garb includes wives of the War era governors.

The Museum of the Kentucky Historical Society. The museum houses War documents, official papers and artifacts.

Some antebellum houses in Frankfort recall the War. The 1854 Carneal-Watson House served as headquarters for the Military

Board of Kentucky during the War. The c. 1820 Vest-Lindsey House was the boyhood home of George Graham Vest, Confederate Congressman and later a U.S. Senator for thirty-five years. The house was also occupied by Daniel Weisiger Lindsey, a Union general. Confederate general Fayette Hewitt lived at the 1817 Rodman-Hewitt House.

Georgetown

Georgetown College. At Giddings Hall—the first building erected at the oldest Baptist college west of the Alleghenies (1829)—a riot broke out in 1861 when Southern sympathizers tried to raise the Confederate flag.

Georgetown Cemetery. At the graveyard reposes George W. Johnson, first governor of Confederate Kentucky, mortally wounded at Shiloh.

Glasgow

At the Barren County courthouse grounds stand markers recalling the Christmas 1862 War skirmish, for which Southern participants were awarded the Confederate Medal of Honor.

Greensburg

In the old courthouse square is a marker commemorating the two Union generals from Greensburg, E.H. Hobson and W.T. Ward. The Union military governor, General Stephen G. Burbridge, ordered six Confederate prisoners shot here on November 19, 1864, for their killing of two Union soldiers.

Harrodsburg

Old Fort Harrod State Park. The park includes the cabin (moved from elsewhere) where Lincoln's parents married on June 2, 1806.

St. Philips Church. Confederate general Leonidas Polk con-

ducted services at the Episcopal church before the Battle of Perryville.

Hawesville

At the 1822 Squire Pate House occurred Lincoln's first trial, in
which he defended himself against charges of operating an Ohio
River ferry without a license.

Hodgenville

Lincoln lore galore abounds in Hodgenville. A rather ponderous
neo-classic granite building at the Abraham Lincoln Birthplace
National Historic Site houses the supposed cabin in which the
future War president was born. The fifty-six steps outside the
granite building represent the number of years Lincoln lived.

Lincoln and his parents lived at nearby Knob Creek Farm for
some six years (1811-1816). A reconstructed log cabin evokes the
original residence.

The Lincoln Museum in Hodgenville contains twelve scenes
from Lincoln's life, including such War era vignettes as the president drafting the Emancipation Proclamation, the Gettysburg
Address, and the surrender at Appomattox. Exhibits and memorabilia upstairs at the museum also recall the man and the era.

Hopkinsville

Riverside Cemetery. Both Union and Confederate soldiers repose in the graveyard, where psychic Edgar Cayce is also buried.

Jackson

The Breathitt County Museum contains War artifacts.

Lebanon

The National Cemetery. Established in 1867, the burial ground
contains War graves. When Colonel Tom Morgan's forces attacked
Lebanon, located at the exact geographical center of Kentucky, on

July 5, 1863, Federal troops managed to delay his advance across the Ohio River.

Lexington

Mary Todd Lincoln House. Robert Todd—father of Mary Todd, Lincoln's wife—bought the c. 1806 residence in 1826. Mary lived there from age six to twenty-one when in 1839 she moved to Springfield, Illinois, to live with her sister. Some of her personal possessions are on display at the house.

Hunt-Morgan House. The c. 1814 Federal-style brick residence belonged to the famous Confederate general John Hunt Morgan. The Morgan Room contains displays of War memorabilia and exhibits on Morgan's Raiders, the unit led by the "Thunderbolt of the Confederacy," so called for his lightning-like raids. Morgan led his raiders farther north than any other unit in the Confederacy.

Bodley-Bullock House. The c. 1814 residence served as headquarters for both Union and Confederate forces.

Transylvania University. Old Morrison Hall (1833) on campus served as a prison and as a hospital for both sides during the War. John C. Breckinridge, born near Lexington and a law student at Translyvania, became the nation's youngest vice president (thirty-six), under James Buchanan, in 1857. He served as a general in the Confederate army and toward the end of the War became Secretary of State for the Confederacy. His statue stands in Cheapside Park. When Jefferson Davis attended Transylvania from 1821 to 1824 he roomed at the Ficklin House in Lexington. Other students at the school included Morgan and Albert Sidney Johnston, both Confederate generals.

Ashland. Three-time presidential candidate Henry Clay (1824, 1832, 1844) occupied the house from 1806 to his death in 1852. In his later years Clay, known as the "great compromiser," worked to preserve the Union.

Lexington Cemetery. The burial ground includes the graves of Clay, Morgan and members of Mary Todd's family.

Louisville

The Filson Club. The historical society, established in 1884, houses manuscripts and other items pertaining to the War.

Jefferson County Courthouse. The state legislature assembled here when Confederate forces occupied Frankfort in September 1862.

The Confederate monument at South Third and Shipp Streets belies the fact that Louisville remained a Union city, serving the north as a major supply base and medical center.

Maysville

Rand-Richeson Academy. The old boys school numbers among its graduates Grant, who lived in town for a time with his uncle, Peter Grant, now buried in the graveyard behind the library.

Mill Creek

The cemetery includes graves of Lincoln's relatives, among them Bersheba Lincoln, his grandmother, and Mary Lincoln (Crume) and Nancy Lincoln, his aunts.

Mill Springs

Located on the southeast side of Lake Cumberland, the mill here—which boasts one of the world's largest overshot water wheels—offers an audiovisual program on the area's War history. General Felix Zollicoffer and more than 100 other Confederate dead, killed in a January 19, 1862, battle, are buried in a mass grave at a cemetery near Nancy.

Morganfield

Bethal Baptist Church. Former slave Elisha W. Green founded the church, destroyed by fire in 1977, in 1845.

On the courthouse lawn Lincoln delivered the only political speech he gave in his native state.

The Union County Museum includes War items.

Morgantown

Butler County Courthouse. On the grounds stands a monument to both Confederate and Union soldiers, a rare example of a dual memorial honoring both sides.

Munfordville

Francis Asbury Smith House. Confederate general Braxton Bragg occupied the c. 1835 house as a headquarters. Bragg's forces used the 1830s Presbyterian church as a hospital. Across the street stands a one story house—originally two separate brick structures connected by a passageway—where nurses who worked at the hospital lived. A marker in town recalls the September 1862 Battle of Munfordville.

Newport

Taylor Mansion. The 1837 house formed a link in the Underground Railroad. Escaped slaves headed north hid in the basement.

Nicholasville

Some 3,000 Union soldiers repose at the Camp Nelson Cemetery. At Camp Dick Robinson, south of town, operated the first Union recruiting station south of the Ohio River.

Owensboro

At the former Riley Plantation on U.S. 60 (designated in this area the Josiah Henson Trail) stood the cabin of slave Josiah Henson, thought by some to have inspired Harriet Beecher Stowe's 1852 anti-slavery novel *Uncle Tom's Cabin.* In Owensboro during the summer of 1993 was held the premier of *Josiah!,* a musical based on Henson's life. (See the entry for Chopin, Louisiana, which also claims Uncle Tom as a local character.)

Paducah

Lloyd Tilghman House. The railroad builder and Confederate general occupied the house from 1852 to 1861. A statue on Fountain Avenue in Lang Park honors the West Point graduate, killed at the Battle of Vicksburg after being struck by a cannonball.

First Baptist Church. The original 1840 building served as a hospital for Union soldiers.

Market House. The 1850 second Market House, which preceded the present 1905 building, was used as a hospital when Federal troops occupied the area.

In response to the early September 1861 Confederate occupation of Columbus and Hickman, Kentucky towns on the Mississippi River not far west of Paducah, on September 6 Grant led 5,000 men into Paducah where they marched down Broadway to the levee on the Ohio river. Grant issued a proclamation to the citizens of Paducah, noting that the "strong arm of the government is here to protect its friends and punish its enemies." So began the Civil War in the west.

Perryville

Perryville Battlefield State Historic Site. Here occurred the most important of the 400 military encounters in Kentucky. Nearly 40,000 troops clashed on October 8, 1862, in what one Union general described as "the bloodiest battle of modern times." More than 7,500 casualties occurred during the battle, an episode in the Confederate attempt to gain control of central Kentucky. After securing the Union supply base in Louisville, General Don Carlos Buell advanced to engage the Southerners at Perryville. Following the encounter, Buell allowed the Confederates to retreat unhindered, a concession which led to his removal as Union commander. A museum contains artifacts, displays and a diorama of the battle.

The mansion now housing Elmwood Inn at Perryville, an attractive restaurant known for its bourbon-laced sauces, served after the battle as a hospital.

Pike County

In this county at the far eastern edge of Kentucky lived the McCoy clan, which engaged in a long feud with the Hatfield family of Mingo County in adjacent West Virginia. The feud originated during the War when Anderson "Devil Anse" Hatfield, leader of a guerrilla band during the conflict, was accused of killing Harmon McCoy, a Union sympathizer, on February 1, 1863. The dispute over this matter touched off the feud between the families, which supported opposing sides during the War. The mini Civil War between the Hatfields and the McCoys lasted for some thirty years, during which nearly forty members of the families were killed.

Pikeville. A marker in the city park indicates where future president James A. Garfield took the oath as a Union brigadier general in January 1862.

Richmond

Harris House. The 1813 residence was named for Dr. John McCord Harris, who treated wounded soldiers in the house after the August 29-30, 1862, Battle of Richmond.

Courthouse. The ornamental iron fence which once surrounded the grounds of the 1850 courthouse served to hold Union prisoners. Part of the fence is now at Richmond Cemetery, where Cassius M. Clay (see entry for White Hall) is buried.

Solomon Smith House. Union troops captured in August 1862 by General E. Kirby Smith's forces were paroled at the house.

McCreary House. The War officer and later U.S. Senator and two-time governor of Kentucky lived at the house.

The tourist office in Richmond offers a brochure and tape for a War battles driving tour from Richmond to Berea.

Russellville

A marker downtown recalls that the town served as the first capital of Kentucky after the Confederacy admitted the state in December 1861. Delegates from around the state met in

Russellville on November 18 to form a provisional Confederate government.

Bibb House. At the c. 1822 house lived Mayor Richard Bibb, a Revolutionary War veteran and early-day Abolitionist.

Springfield

The 1816 Washington County courthouse contains the 1806 marriage documents of Thomas Lincoln and Nancy Hanks, parents of the future president.

Lincoln Homestead State Park. Located five miles north of town, the park includes a replica of the 1782 cabin which belonged to Lincoln's father and the original cabin of his mother.

Vanceburg

The 1884 Union soldier statue on the courthouse lawn is claimed to be the only non-funerary monument south of the Ohio River to Federal troops killed in the War.

Versailles

The Versailles Historical Park memorializes eight War generals and also a Kentucky governor.

Washington

In the summer of 1833 Harriet Beecher (Stowe), while visiting her pupil Elizabeth Key, witnessed a slave auction at the block in front of the courthouse, a scene she evoked in *Uncle Tom's Cabin*, a novel which agitated anti-slavery sentiment and contributed to the mood which led to the War. Elizabeth, one of the six children of Colonel and Mrs. Marshall Key, lived with her family in the still existing 1807 house on Main Street.

Also on Main Street stands the c. 1800 house (now the visitor center) of lawyer and Abolitionist James A. Paxton, who hid runaway slaves under the stairwell at the adjacent Paxton Inn until they could continue north by the Underground Railroad.

In a c. 1797 house was born in 1803 Albert Sidney Johnston, Commander of the Confederate Army of the West and believed to be the highest ranking officer killed in action during the War. He died at Shiloh on April 6, 1862.

Water Valley

Camp Beauregard, the only Confederate training camp in Kentucky, was located east of the village.

White Hall

This estate—located in central Kentucky southeast of Louisville and south of Lexington—belonged to Cassius Clay, an outspoken opponent of slavery who became a national figure in the Abolitionist movement, published an Abolitionist newspaper, and served as a major general in the Union army. The colorful Clay fought his opponents not only with words but, on occasion, also with pistols, his hickory cane and a Bowie knife. The forty-four room three story brick c. 1799 mansion contains War era furnishings.

Wickliffe

Just south of town stood Fort Jefferson where—after Confederate forces seized nearby Columbus in September 1861—Union troops established a supply base on the Mississippi to serve the Western Theater.

Zollicoffer Park and Logan's Crossroads Cemetery

A 1911 monument at the site, nine miles west of Somerset, marks the January 1862 battle during which Confederate general Felix Zollicoffer was killed.

Tennessee

Ashland City

North of town, on Sycamore Creek, stood the 1835 Sycamore Powder Mill, which produced a huge amount of gunpowder for the Confederacy. At one time the DuPont Company operated the mill.

Beersheba Springs

When General Braxton Bragg withdrew from the area to fortify Chattanooga, the town was left outside Confederate lines and remained undefended. Marauders—some of them deserters from both sides—looted the hotel, now the United Methodist Assembly meeting area.

Bolivar

Union generals Grant, Sherman, Logan and McPherson occupied Magnolia Manor, now a bed and breakfast, as a headquarters.

Brentwood

At Windy Hill, an 1820s country house southeast of town, the owner hid valuables as well as horses and cows in the basement to protect them from Federal marauders during the War. (See also the entry for Franklin.)

Brownsville

College Hill Center houses a collection of books and memorabilia relating to Lincoln.

The Confederate monument at the courthouse honors not only the War dead but also the women of Haywood County.

Chattanooga

The Chickamauga and Chattanooga National Military Park,

mainly in Georgia south of Chattanooga, recalls a series of pivotal autumn 1863 encounters. The Battle of Chickamauga in September, one of the War's bloodiest encounters, resulted in nearly 4,000 dead and another 30,000 wounded and missing. The South's failure to pursue the defeated Yankee forces enabled them to regroup under Grant and defeat the Confederates at the Battles of Lookout Mountain and Missionary Ridge on November 23-25. The victory opened the so- called Gateway to the West, enabling Sherman to begin his devastating "March to the Sea" through Georgia.

Point Park (accessible only to pedestrians) at the north edge of Lookout Mountain, and Bragg's Reservation and Sherman's Reservation on Missionary Ridge at the eastern side of town, comprise areas where the encounters unfolded. Many of the private homes on Crest Drive on the top of Missionary Ridge display in their yards cannons and historical markers. The Ochs Museum and the Cravens House on Lookout contain War era displays. The Confederama at the bottom of Lookout offers a 480 square foot reproduction of the battle terrain, with a electronically controlled depiction of the fighting.

The 1863 National Cemetery and the 1865 Confederate Cemetery contain the graves of fallen troops. Buried at the National Cemetery are James J. Andrews and seven of his men, their graves marked by a replica of "The General," the Confederate steam locomotive they seized near Marietta, Georgia, in April 1862.

The six mile long steam train excursion from the Tennessee Valley Railroad Museum passes over a bridge and through a tunnel connected with the Battle of Chattanooga.

The Chattanooga Regional History Museum contains War exhibits.

The *Daily Rebel* began publication, at 523 Market Street, on August 2, 1862. At one time the newspaper was forced to publish in boxcars traveling with Confederate troops. The last issue appeared at Selma, Alabama, on April 11, 1865.

Clarksville

Greenwood Cemetery. A Confederate Monument—a soldier statue atop a column flanked below by other figures—honors War dead.

Emerald Hill. Gustavus A. Henry, Confederate senator and well known political orator, lived at the 1830s house.

The old Kennedy and Glenn's Bank, which stood on the west side of the town square, smuggled funds and securities to England for safekeeping during the War.

At nearby Fort Defiance by the Cumberland River survive well preserved earthen breastworks.

The Visitor Center and Museum at Fort Campbell, north of town, include a few War relics.

Columbia

Advance and Retreat. At this country house three miles south of town Army of Tennessee commander John Bell Hood established his headquarters on November 24, 1864. A month later an order for the Army's retreat was issued from the house.

At Chapel Hill, east of Columbia, a monument indicates the site of the cabin where Nathan Bedford Forrest, the pesky Confederate general, was born on July 13, 1821.

Cumberland Gap National Historical Park

The Pinnacle, the high point in the park, was the site of War trenches. To defend the Gap, which changed hands several times during the War, the Confederates emplaced "Long Tom," then the largest kind of gun in use, in the lowlands. Three months after Federal troops captured the Gap on June 17, 1862, they were forced to retreat, only to recapture the strategic pass on September 9, 1863.

Elizabethton

Andrew Johnson, Lincoln's successor (see the entry for

Greeneville), died in 1875 at the home of his daughter, Mary Johnson Stover, located north of the Watauga River outside town.

Nathan Bedford Forrest State Historic Area

The site commemorates the place where in November 1864 the Confederate general's forces secured a commanding artillery vantage point over the Tennessee River at Pilot Knob. From the height the Southerners shelled a Federal supply and munitions depot below, and also fired on a supply convoy. This attack resulted in the first defeat in history of a naval force by a cavalry unit.

Fort Donelson National Battlefield

At Fort Donelson the Union, its forces led by Grant, won its first major victory of the War. The loss of the fort after a four day battle in February 1862 proved devastating to the Confederate cause. With the victory the North gained control of the Cumberland and Tennessee Rivers, thus breaking the Southern defense line from the Alleghenies to the Mississippi. This opened the way for the invasion of the South.

Sights at the park include a Confederate Monument, a National Cemetery with 655 Union dead, the Dover Hotel where General Simon B. Buckner surrendered the fort and 13,000 men to Grant, and the riverside battery which on February 14 saw an exchange of "iron valentines."

When Buckner asked his opponent the surrender terms, Grant replied, "No terms except an unconditional and immediate surrender can be accepted." With the capture of Fort Donelson and, on February 6, the nearby Fort Henry on the Tennessee River fifteen miles to the west, the Union won key victories and found a new hero—U.S. ("Unconditional Surrender") Grant. The six and a half mile Fort Henry Road at Land Between the Lakes passes a turnoff to hiking trails which follow the retreat route of Southern forces from Fort Henry to Fort Donelson.

Fort Pillow State Historical Area

Original breastworks and a reconstructed fort recall the outpost, built to help the South control the Mississippi River. In the early summer of 1862 shelling by Federal gunboats forced the evacuation of the fort by the Confederates, who recaptured it in April 1864 with an attack led by Nathan Bedford Forrest.

Franklin

In and around the picturesque town swirled War clashes. For four years Federal troops who occupied the area were garrisoned at 1863 Fort Granger—where traces of trenches, gun replacements and walls remain—overlooking the town. On November 30, 1864, Confederate general John Bell Hood attacked General John Scholfield's Federal forces in the Battle of Franklin. The North lost 2,000 men, the South three times as many, including five generals taken to Carnton, a nearby 1826 country estate. They were buried elsewhere, but at Carnton repose nearly 1,500 soldiers at the nation's only privately owned and maintained War cemetery.

Carter House. Bullet holes in the walls recall that the residence changed hands several times during the battle. Displays at the house include War artifacts.

St. Paul's. The state's oldest Episcopal church (1834) served as a hospital. Soldiers took its furnishings to use as firewood.

Gant House. Sally Ewin Gant used a trap door in the roof of the house to spy on Union activities.

Between Franklin and Brentwood to the north lie Creekside, whose still bloodstained floors recall that the house was used as a hospital after the Battle of Franklin; Green Pastures, where Forrest and his men camped before the Battle of Nashville; and Mooreland, used by both sides as a hospital. At Century Oaks, northeast of Franklin, the owners supposedly blindfolded their horses and led them up a circular staircase to the third floor ballroom to hide the animals from Federal raiders.

Gatlinburg

Near the town was born on October 18, 1818, John H. Reagan, Postmaster General and Acting Treasury Secretary of the Confederacy.

Greeneville

Courthouse. The yard is one of the few places with monuments honoring both Confederate and Union soldiers. This recalls how the region suffered from divided loyalties. Union sympathizers met in Greeneville in 1861 in an attempt to make East Tennessee a separate state. One marker memorializes General John Hunt Morgan, "The Thunderbolt of the Confederacy," killed September 4, 1864, after a Union sympathizer revealed his whereabouts.

Cumberland Presbyterian Church. A cannonball from a War shelling remains embedded in the wall of the sanctuary.

Andrew Johnson. Lincoln's successor, North Carolina native Andrew Johnson, came to Greeneville in the 1820s at age seventeen and began his political career there. Johnson's tailor shop and his solid looking brick house—the family home from 1851 to 1875— recall the seventeenth president's time in Greeneville. Johnson and members of his family are buried in the Andrew Johnson National Cemetery where an urn-decorated monument topped by an eagle marks his grave.

Harrogate

Lincoln Memorial University. The Lincoln Museum on the campus of the school contains an extensive collection of materials relating to the president and the War. The holdings include not only displays but also books, manuscripts, photos, paintings and artifacts. Lincoln's friend, General O.O. Howard, established the university in 1897 in the area designated by the president during an 1863 meeting between the two men.

Hendersonville

Monthaven Bed and Breakfast House was used as a hospital during the War.

Henning

The childhood home (1921-1929) of Alex Haley, author of *Roots*, Henning developed after the War. But Bethlehem Methodist church (1830), established a mile east of the present town, housed wounded brought to the sanctuary after the battle at Fort Pillow, on the Mississippi to the west. Those who died were buried in the 1840 Bethlehem Cemetery, which now includes the Haley family plot. Haley himself is buried in the yard of his childhood house.

Jackson

James S. Lyons House. During the weeks preceding the April 1862 Battle of Shiloh, Grant occupied the residence, which stood at 512 East Main Street, as a headquarters.

Riverside Cemetery includes graves of unknown Confederate soldiers.

Near Britton's Lane, south of town, a monument to soldiers killed in a September 1, 1862, encounter honors the combatants, some buried here.

Johnson City

A monument at Lamont and Tennessee Streets marks the site of the 1861 Confederate training camp.

Knoxville

Confederate Memorial Hall. The antebellum mansion, also known as "Bleak House" (for the popular Charles Dickens novel of the time), was used by Confederate general James Longstreet as his headquarters during the November 1863 siege of Knoxville. The house contains war era artifacts and furniture.

Speedwell Manor. Built c. 1830 by slave labor in Tazewell,

Tennessee, the house—moved to its present location—includes a window sill with an inscription written by a Confederate soldier as he watched the burning of Tazewell.

Volunteer State Veterans Hall of Honor. The shrine includes both Union and Confederate artifacts, a reminder of the divided loyalties in East Tennessee.

Three burial grounds in Knoxville—Confederate, National and Old Gray Cemeteries—contain War graves.

Various markers around Knoxville indicate points of interest relating to the November 1863 siege when Confederate troops tried unsuccessfully to recapture the city they had evacuated in August. Fort Byington, which stood near the main entrance to the University of Tennessee and Fort Sanders on the campus, along with Forts Dickerson and Stanley near present day Chapman Highway south of the Tennessee River, served as the Union's main defensive points. Confederate forces camped during the siege at the site of Knoxville College, while Union general Ambrose Burnside occupied as his headquarters the J.H. Crozier House, on the site of the old Farragut Hotel, now the First Tennessee Bank Building.

LaGrange

This unspoiled nineteenth century hamlet fifty miles east of Memphis includes such time haunted houses as 1834 Twin Gables, occupied by various Union officers; 1850 Hancock Hall, used by Grant as a headquarters in 1862; Woodlawn, a hospital and a headquarters for Sherman; and Westover of Woodstock, where Lucy Holcombe (Pickens) grew up. Known as the "Queen of the Confederacy," she was the only woman whose portrait appeared on the Confederacy currency. Holcombe became the third wife of Francis Wilkinson Pickens, U.S. Congressman from 1834 to 1843 and governor of South Carolina, which seceded on December 18, 1860, two days after he took office.

Immanuel Episcopal Church. The pews of the 1832 church

were made into coffins for Union dead. The church served as a hospital and barracks.

Lebanon

Cedar Grove Cemetery. The 1899 Confederate monument bears an unusual inscription enumerating the number of soldiers, fatalities, prisoners and the public debt involved with the War.

Memphis

Confederate Park. The park, which overlooks the Mississippi, offered a vantage point for Memphis citizens who watched as Union gunboats sank six of the seven defending Southern vessels on June 6, 1862. After a brief (ninety minutes) encounter the Northerners demanded the surrender of Memphis, to which Mayor John Park responded, "The city is in your hands." On the south side of the park is a plaque summarizing the Confederate history of Memphis. Facing Front Street stands a statue of Jefferson Davis who worked in Memphis in the insurance business after the War. A plaque at 129 Court Avenue marks the site where Davis lived from 1867 to 1875. The original Confederate cannons which stood in the park were taken in 1942 in a scrap metal drive during a later war.

Malmo Building. The 1842 office building, the city's oldest commercial structure, was used during the War as a hospital for Union troops awaiting passage north on Mississippi River boats.

Gayoso Hotel. At the 1842 hotel, which stood on Front Street, William Forrest, brother of General Nathan Bedford Forrest, supposedly rode his horse into the lobby on August 21, 1864, looking for Union commander Stephen A. Hurlbut. The general died on October 27, 1877, in the Memphis home of another brother, Colonel Jesse Forrest, who lived at 693 Union Avenue. An equestrian statue in Forrest Park marks the grave of Nathan and his wife Mary.

Elmwood Cemetery. Confederate soldiers, along with many

Memphis notables, repose in the city's most historical burial ground.

Leonidas Polk and, later, Grant occupied the house which stood at 533 Beale Street.

From the old Union Planters Bank building on Madison the press and type of the *Memphis Daily Appeal* were removed on June 6, 1862—the day before the city was occupied—for shipment to Grenada and later Jackson, Mississippi, eventually going to Columbus, Georgia, as the paper continued to publish until Union troops finally destroyed the equipment and scattered the type. Called a "moving *Appeal*" by Sherman's troops, the paper resumed publication in Memphis on November 5, 1865.

Murfreesboro

Stones River National Battlefield. The 350 acre park recalls the three day battle, which started December 31, 1862, involving more than 80,000 soldiers and resulting in 23,000 casualties. A self-guided driving tour includes what is supposedly the nation's earliest War monument, the boxy looking stone block 1863 Hazen Brigade Monument. An audio-visual presentation at the museum explains the battle. The National Cemetery contains the graves of 6,100 Union soldiers.

Courthouse. The 1859 Rutherford County Courthouse and the Federal garrison in town were targets of a July 1862 dawn raid by Confederate cavalry under Forrest.

Fortress Rosecrans. Located west of town at Stones River, this was the largest earthworks fort built by the Union during the War. The installation originally covered 200 acres and included a huge supply base which provisioned troops for the attack on Chattanooga. Some of the earthworks, which averaged fifteen feet high, remain.

In a house which stood on East Main Street, General Leonidas Polk, the "Fighting Bishop of the Confederacy," officiated at the December 14, 1862, marriage of John Hunt Morgan, the "Thunderbolt of the Confederacy." Groomsmen included Generals Braxton Bragg and John C. Breckinridge, former U.S. vice president.

Evergreen Cemetery. Unknown Confederate soldiers killed in the Battle of Murfreesboro are buried here.

Nashville

Capitol. At the state capitol stands a statue of Sam Davis, executed in November 1863 as a Confederate spy (see the entry for Smyrna).

Tennessee State Museum. The museum opened a new wing in the early 1980s to display War materials. Photos, drawings and artifacts recall the War in Tennessee.

Belle Meade. The elegant mansion—once the centerpiece of a 5,300 acre plantation and horse farm—served as headquarters for the Confederate general James R. Chalmers during the December 15-16, 1864, Battle of Nashville, the last major encounter in the state.

Travellers' Rest. At the 1779 house, residence of John Overton, a friend and political advisor to Andrew Jackson, Confederate general John B. Hood made his headquarters. A key encounter during the Battle of Nashville—the Battle of Peach Orchard Hill—occurred on the grounds of the property.

Vanderbilt. On campus survive breastworks which formed part of the seven mile long defensive lines that ran southwest across the city. At Shy's Hill, where the Confederates made one of their last stands, the earthworks are still visible.

Opposite the entrance to The Hermitage, Jackson's house, lies the Confederate Cemetery. Most of the 483 soldiers buried here died at the Confederates Soldiers' Home, which stood about one mile to the north.

Downtown Presbyterian Church. Union soldiers used the church as a hospital.

At a house at 511 5th Avenue South lived Captain William Driver, a mariner who in 1831 dubbed an American flag he received as a present "Old Glory"; by 1850 the name had become common for the flag in general. When he lived in Nashville during the War, Driver concealed the flag by making it into a quilt. Union troops flew the flag at the capitol when they took the city.

Puluski

Sam Davis Museum. The museum, which houses War memorabilia, occupies the site where the "Boy Hero of the Confederacy" was executed as a spy on November 27, 1862 (see the entry for Smyrna). In courthouse square stands a monument to Davis. A plaque on the old law office of Judge Thomas Jones notes that the Ku Klux Klan was founded in Pulaski on December 24, 1865.

Rogersville

Hale Springs Inn. On the town square stands the state's oldest hostelry in continuous operation—since 1824, except during the War when Union soldiers used the inn as a headquarters.

Savannah

Cherry Mansion. The house, in the western outskirts of town, was used as a headquarters by Union commander C.F. Smith, who died here. His successor was Major General Ulysses S. Grant, who breakfasted at the house just as gunfire broke out at Pittsburg Landing—prelude to the imminent encounter at Shiloh.

Sewanee

At the secluded college town repose Southern officers Kirby Smith and Jack Eggleston, the last full Confederate general and last naval officer, both of whom died at Sewanee. In October 1860 at the University of the South, Leonidas Polk laid the main building's cornerstone, which Union soldiers later broke into pieces as souvenirs.

Shiloh National Military Park

More military encounters (over 800) took place in Tennessee—the last state to secede and the first to be readmitted to the Union after the War—than in any state other than Virginia. Shiloh is one of the state's four War related National Military Parks.

After Confederate general Albert S. Johnston attacked Grant's forces encamped on the Tennessee River on April 6, 1862, the Northerners counterattacked the following day and forced the Southern army to retreat to Corinth, Mississippi. Johnston, who Jefferson Davis considered the finest officer in the War, bled to death after a rifle ball severed an artery in his leg. Monuments, graves (the National Cemetery overlooks Pittsburg Landing and the Tennessee River) and a museum recall the famous battle. During the fighting about one-quarter of the 100,000 combatants were killed, wounded or captured—more casualties than of the Revolutionary War, War of 1812 and Mexican-American War combined. The encounter at Shiloh shattered the illusions of both sides that victory would be easy. After Shiloh, Grant said, "I gave up all ideas of saving the Union, except by complete conquest."

Smyrna

Sam Davis Home. The 1810 house commemorates the twenty-one year old Confederate soldier captured behind Union lines on November 19, 1863, while carrying secret papers to General Braxton Bragg, then near Chattanooga. Federal authorities tried Davis as a spy and sentenced him to death. Davis rode to the gallows in Pulaski (see the entry for that city) on November 27 perched atop the coffin used to bury him.

Tiptonville

A marker at the Lake County courthouse recalls the battle for the Island Number 10 in the Mississippi and the capture of Tiptonville by Union Forces in April 1862.

Tullahoma

The Army of Tennessee made its headquarters in Tullahoma during the first half of 1863. At a Confederate cemetery repose more than 400 Southern soldiers.

Union City

Dixie Gun Works. On display is a firearms collection with some 1,500 antique revolvers and rifles, many dating from the nineteenth century and earlier.

The Confederate Cemetery includes graves of soldiers killed during Forrest's December 23, 1862, raid. A Confederate monument in the town square bears an unusual inscription, memorializing Southern soldiers "killed in battle...[or] starved in Federal prison" who preserved the South's "Anglo-Saxon civilization."

Winchester

Citizens meeting at the Franklin County courthouse voted on February 24, 1861, to secede from Tennessee. The group petitioned the state of Alabama to annex the country. This attempt to join the Confederacy became unnecessary after Tennessee seceded on June 24.

Arkansas

Arkansas Post

Arkansas Post National Memorial. In 1686 French explorers carved an outpost out of the wilderness and established near the confluence of the Mississippi and the Arkansas Rivers the first European settlement in the lower Mississippi valley. The frontier town prospered, then declined when the state capital was moved to Little Rock in 1821. The area enjoyed—or suffered from—one last moment of gory glory when 5,000 Confederate soldiers defended Fort Hindman, built near the old town on the banks of the

Arkansas, during a January 10 and 11, 1863, attack by Federal gunboats and 30,000 Union soldiers under General John A. McClernand. The bombardment severely damaged the fort and destroyed many of the old buildings of the Arkansas Post settlement, which eventually disappeared. A visitor center with history displays and walkways through the site recall the early day town.

Arkansas Post County Museum. The museum (located on the main highway outside the National Memorial) includes War items, such as a copy of the July 2, 1863 *Vicksburg Daily Citizen* printed on wallpaper due to the lack of newsprint.

Benton

Shoppach House. Both sides occupied the small 1853 brick residence, which now houses antiques and history displays.

Berryville

Saunders Memorial Museum. The extensive gun collection includes War era weapons, among them firearms belonging to Jesse James, desperado and guerrilla of the time.

Cabot

Camp Nelson Confederate Cemetery. At the burial ground repose some 500 Southern soldiers from Texas and Arkansas who died during a measles epidemic while stationed at a nearby base. A rough-hewn stone monument, installed in 1905, commemorates the unknown deceased.

Camden

McCollum-Chidester House. Confederate general Sterling Price and Union general Frederick Steele both, in turn, occupied the eleven room 1847 house as a headquarters at the time of the Battle of Poison Spring (see the entry for Poison Spring). Bullet holes in upstairs walls supposedly originated during a Confederate attack. The house contains original furniture of the era used when the Chidester family lived there.

Confederate Cemetery. Seven rows of gravestones around a tall marble shaft indicate the last resting place of more than 200 Confederate soldiers, some of them killed at Poison Spring and Jenkins' Ferry (see those entries).

Fort Lookout. Confederate general Edmund Kirby Smith built earthen fortifications to defend Camden. Rifle trenches and cannon pits remain on the bluff overlooking the Ouachita River.

Cypress Bend

Henry M. Stanley. The hamlet of Cypress Bend, once located on the Arkansas River a few miles upstream from Arkansas Post, disappeared in the 1860s when flood waters washed the settlement away. At Cypress Bend lived Henry M. Stanley, who as a boy worked as a storekeeper for his foster father, Louis Altshul, until the War began. Stanley then joined the Arkansas Volunteers, and was later captured at Shiloh. After his release, Stanley enlisted in the Union army, then later served in the Union navy. After the War Stanley became famous as the journalist who located explorer David Livingston in Africa.

Dardanelle

Dardanelle Rock. From atop the sheer rocky formation overlooking the Arkansas River Confederate soldiers spied on Federal activities in the area.

Doddridge

After the Emancipation Proclamation, former slaves homesteaded the East Kiblah community at Doddridge, located in the far southwestern corner of Arkansas. During the War, when the community was known as "The Bend," Union and Confederate soldiers took refuge there. The former Kiblah school now serves as a community center.

Fayetteville

Headquarters House. Both sides at various times occupied the restored residence, built in 1853 by Judge Jonas Tebbetts, a strong Union supporter. The Union command used the house as a headquarters during the April 1863 Battle of Fayetteville.

Walker Stone House. Judge David Walker, chairman of the Arkansas Secession Convention, lived in the house. The "Stone" refers not to the structure's building material, which is brick, but to a later occupant—Edward Durrell Stone, the world famous architect.

Confederate Cemetery. At the burial ground, located by the base of Mt. Sequoyah, repose Southern soldiers from Arkansas, Missouri, Texas and Louisiana.

Fort Smith

National Cemetery. The nation's oldest national cemetery—established in 1818 as part of the original military post—includes War graves, among them that of Confederate general James B. McIntosh. Some 1,600 Union soldiers repose at the cemetery.

Old Fort Museum. Displays of the area's military history between 1817 and 1970 include War relics.

Sebastian County Courthouse. On the grounds stands a Confederate monument, installed here rather than at the national cemetery as Federal officials objected that the monument's inscription failed to include a reference to Union soldiers buried at the cemetery.

Harrison

Boone County Heritage Museum. Displays at the museum include War medical instruments.

Robinson Museum. The museum, on highway 65 southeast of Harrison, includes War items.

Helena

War Markers. Markers around town recall episodes in the July 4, 1863, Battle of Helena.

Fort Curtis. One marker on Perry Street indicates the site of Fort Curtis, erected in August 1862 by Union forces as the centerpiece of the city's five fortified Federal positions. With the help of the gunboat *Tyler*, the 4,129-strong Union forces successfully defended against 7,646 Confederate attackers, who hoped to occupy Helena and then relieve the Federal siege at Vicksburg. The same day that the Battle of Helena occurred proved disastrous for the South elsewhere; on July 4, Vicksburg fell to Grant and Lee withdrew in defeat at Gettysburg.

Granny Holmes. Confederate soldiers at Helena nicknamed their aged commander, Theophilus Holmes, "Granny" as the feeble old man scarcely presented a commanding appearance. While defending Arkansas Post to the south the previous January, "Granny" ordered his forces to "hold the place until every man is dead," a do-or-die attitude received rather unenthusiastically in the ranks.

Confederate Cemetery. On a steep hillside tucked away at the back of Maple Hill Cemetery nestles a small Confederate graveyard, with moss-bearded markers in a shadowed grove. A pillar topped by a soldier statue memorializes unknown Confederate dead. Helena was the home of seven Southern generals, several of them buried at the cemetery.

Phillips County Museum. The collection includes War artifacts.

Jacksonport State Park.

In the late eighteenth century the town of Jacksonport developed near the confluence of the Black and White Rivers. The settlement began as a trading center, and later became a steamboat port and the county seat. Thanks—or no thanks—to its strategic location by the rivers, the town was occupied by both armies, with five generals using Jacksonport as a headquarters at various times. On June 5, 1865, General Jeff Thompson, called the "Swamp Fox of the Confederacy," surrendered 6,000 troops to Union lieutenant colonel C.W. Davis at the steamboat landing. After the railroad line bypassed Jacksonport on the 1870s the town declined. In 1963 restoration began, and two years later the old settlement became a state park, with a few nineteenth century structures and some period items which evoke the early days at Jacksonport.

Jenkins' Ferry Civil War Battle Site

The Red River Campaign. At Jenkins' Ferry occurred the third and last of the three major episodes in the Red River Campaign in Arkansas. After the War broke out, a shortage of cotton developed in the north. To remedy the deficiency, the Union devised a plan to enter the Red River in Louisiana and, along with a unit pushing south from Little Rock, to invade Texas where cotton could be grown to supply northern textile mills. Only in 1864 was the plan finally activated. On March 23 General Frederick Steele's troops left Little Rock to rendezvous with General Nathaniel Banks' forces in the Red River region of Louisiana to begin the invasion of Texas. Steele encountered Confederate resistance at Prairie De Ann, at Camden, at Poison Spring on April 18, and at Marks' Mill on April 25 (see the entries for those four places) before finally beginning his retreat toward Little Rock, on April 30 crossing the Saline River at Jenkins' Ferry.

Jenkins' Ferry. After losing most of his supplies at Poison Spring and Marks' Mill, Steele decided to retreat to Little Rock. His troops left Camden on April 26 and three days later reached Leola (then called Sandy Springs). Heavy rains had swollen the Saline River, which Steele's forces crossed on a rubber pontoon bridge. The morning of April 30 the Confederates attacked along the Federal line. Steele defended as his men crossed the river, then his troops continued on to Little Rock, arriving there on May 3. The unsuccessful Red River Campaign proved costly; Steele lost 635 wagons,

2,500 horses and mules, and suffered 2,750 casualties. Of the 4,000 men at Jenkins' Ferry, some 800 were killed or wounded. Exhibits and explanatory plaques at the site recall the episode, while a monument honors Confederate soldiers who died "for the cause."

Lake Village

Ditch Bayou. In a early June 1864 Confederate soldiers defended their positions against some 10,000 Union attackers, sent to remove the pesky Southerners who harassed Northern boats on the Mississippi River.

Little Rock

Old State House. A series of displays entitled "The Arkansas History Exhibits" in the elegant 1836 classic-style former capitol (parts of it were completed later) includes a section on "The Devastation of the Civil War and Reconstruction." The Arkansas secession convention met in May 1861 at the Old State House, from which the state's Confederate government fled when Union troops arrived to occupy Little Rock in September 1863.

Mount Holly Cemetery. Many Arkansas notables, including five Confederate generals, repose at the burial ground. At one grave lies David O. Dodd, a seventeen year old Arkansas youth hanged as a spy by Union military authorities in January 1864. Known as the "Boy Martyr of the Confederacy," Dodd refused an offer to live if he would reveal the identity of the person who had described to him the Union defenses in Little Rock.

Philander Smith College. Founded in 1877, the school was established to provide educational opportunities for freed slaves.

MacArthur Park. The 1838 Old Arsenal Building, in which General Douglas MacArthur was born, now houses the Museum of Science and History. The park occupies land acquired in 1836 by the U.S. government for a military post. The Confederates seized the base when the War broke out, and when they abandoned

Little Rock in 1863 the Southerners tried to burn the arsenal, which survived the attempt.

Lonoke

Courthouse. On the grounds of the 1926 red brick Lonoke County Courthouse stands a monument to Lee and a vintage cannon.

Marianna

Marianna-Lee County Museum. The museum houses War relics.

Marshall

Searcy County Museum. The museum, which occupies the 1902 former city jail, includes War artifacts.

Marks' Mill Battle Site

At Marks' Mill, located near the village of New Edinburg, occurred the second of three major encounters during the Red River Campaign in Arkansas. On April 25 a Confederate force of 2,500 men attacked a Union wagon train of 240 vehicles and some 1,600 men. During the five hour battle, the Southerners captured the entire convoy, along with most of the enemy soldiers and 1,500 horses and mules. Deprived of food and ammunition after the attacks on Union supply convoys at Poison Spring and Marks' Mill, Steele's forces were forced to retreat back toward Little Rock.

Monticello

The last known military action of the War occurred near Monticello on May 24, 1865, more than six weeks after Lee's surrender at Appomattox on April 9.

North Little Rock

Old Mill. The re-created old-time water powered grist mill was filmed for the opening scene of the movie *Gone with the Wind*, the War era epic.

Old Washington Historic State Park

Hempstead County Courthouse. Following the capture of Little Rock on September 10, 1863, the Confederates moved the seat of government to the 1863 courthouse, where on October 2, 1864, the Arkansas Confederate state government held its last General Assembly session. Meanwhile, back in Little Rock, Isaac Murphy, who cast the lone dissenting note at the secession convention, was elected to serve as the state's Union governor.

Royston House. At the 1846 residence lived lawyer and planter Grandison D. Royston, who was a member of the Confederate House of Representatives.

B.W. Edwards Weapons Museum. A c. 1925 former bank building houses the collection which includes War era firearms and Bowie knives, nicknamed the "Arkansas toothpick." A reconstructed blacksmith shop in the park recalls the original shop where James Black supposedly forged the very first Bowie knife for James Bowie, who designed the weapon.

Pea Ridge National Military Park

More than 750 military encounters occurred in Arkansas. Although most of them involved only skirmishes, ambushes and minor incidents, the March 7-8, 1862, clash at Pea Ridge, with some 26,000 combatants, was the largest battle fought west of the Mississippi. The Union victory at Pea Ridge enabled the North to retain control of Missouri. On March 4 General Earl Van Dorn's 16,000-man force started north from the Fayetteville area with the intention of invading Missouri and capturing St. Louis. In the Pea Ridge area Van Dorn encountered 10,500 Union troops under General Samuel Curtis. Van Dorn mounted a two-pronged attack, during which two of his generals were killed. Southern forces included three regiments of 1,000 Cherokees from the Indian

Territory, now Oklahoma. Pea Ridge was the War's only major battle which included Indian combatants. On the morning of March 8 Curtis counter-attacked, forcing Van Dorn to retreat.

The 4,300 acre park includes a visitor center and twelve viewing points and other sites on a seven mile driving tour around the battlefield area.

Pea Ridge—the largest battlefield west of the Mississippi and the first one west of the river to be designated as a national park—is the most important War site in Arkansas. The state of Arkansas is surveying some lesser known War sites, as yet undeveloped. These sites (not listed in this section) include: Bayou Fourche in Pulaski County; Hill's Plantation in Woodruff County; Canehill in Washington County; Devil's Backbone in Sebastian County; Old River Lake in Chicot County; and Elkins' Ferry in Clark County. For further information: 501-682-1191.

Piggott

Chalk Bluff. War trenches remain at this area east of town.

Pine Bluff

Pine Bluff/Jefferson County Museum. Installed in the restored train depot, the museum includes War exhibits.

University of Arkansas at Pine Bluff. The "Persistence of the Spirit" exhibit traces the history of black Arkansas residents from 1803 to 1986. Photos and memorabilia recall the War era.

The First Shot. Pine Bluff claims that the War's very first shot was fired in the city and not at Charleston, South Carolina. A few days before the shelling of Fort Sumter on April 12, 1861, two Confederate militia companies at Pine Bluff fired a warning shot at a steamboat carrying supplies up the Arkansas River to Federal troops garrisoned at Fort Smith.

Poison Spring Battleground Historic Monument

At the Spring—named after Union soldiers poisoned the water

in an attempt to deter a Confederate force advancing from Camden—occurred the first of three major encounters of the Red River Campaign in Arkansas (for a summary of the campaign, see the entry for Jenkins' Ferry Civil War Battle Site). General Frederick Steele's army included 13,000 soldiers, 9,000 horses and mules, 800 wagons and thirty artillery pieces. To supply this force required an extensive logistical support system. At Poison Spring, about ten miles west of Camden, some 3,100 Confederate troops on April 18, 1864, attacked a Federal supply train of 198 wagons. The Southerners captured 170 of the wagons, burned the others and routed the Union units.

Prairie De Ann

Earthen embankments recall the early April 1864 encounter when General Frederick Steele, advancing from Little Rock to join General Nathaniel Banks for the invasion of Texas, spent a day and a half overcoming a Confederate defensive unit.

Prairie Grove Battlefield State Park

On December 7, 1862, General Thomas C. Hindman led 11,000 Arkansas Confederate troops into combat against some 7,000 Union soldiers near Prairie Grove Church. After Union troops withdrew, the Confederates, short of ammunition, also retired, leaving the outcome of the encounter indecisive. Federal forces, however, soon took control of northern Arkansas.

Hindman Hall Museum houses a diorama of the battle, War artifacts, and displays on the life of a soldier, while a driving tour and a one mile trail take visitors through the 130 acre park, which includes a nineteenth century museum village. Among the buildings is the Morrow House (moved to the park from Cove Creek), where Confederate General Sterling Price stayed prior to the Battle of Pea Ridge and where Hindman stayed the night before the Battle of Prairie Grove. The residence now houses an exhibit on the effect of the War on Ozark culture.

Prescott

Nevada County Depot Museum. The old train depot houses a museum which includes War relics from the Prairie De Ann battlefield.

Scott

Plantation Agricultural Museum. The museum recalls the antebellum way of life which the South fought to preserve. Exhibits trace the story of cotton growing and the plantation culture in Arkansas from the pre-War years, starting in 1836, up to World War II.

Sheridan

Grant County Museum. Located in a one story wood building with a porch front like an old general store, the museum houses War relics from the battlefield at Jenkins' Ferry.

Both Grant County, formed during the Reconstruction era, and the county seat of Sheridan were named for Union generals—Ulysses S. Grant and Phillip Sheridan. Area residents seeking their own county thought their petition would stand a better chance of approval by Federal authorities with Union heroes' names for the county and its seat.

Springdale

Shiloh Museum. The museum, established by the city in 1965 and named for the mid-nineteenth century settlement which became Springdale, includes extensive archives on regional history and the historical collections of six counties. A new facility houses some of the materials. The museum sponsors War encampments and re-enactments of battles.

St. Charles

On June 17, 1862, at St. Charles occurred the War's single most destructive shot when a Confederate cannonball hit a boiler of the

Mound City on the White River and touched off a massive explosion which killed nearly 150 Union soldiers. A sign outside town bears a cannon image, which alludes to the episode.

Texarkana

Confederate Monument. The memorial statue, carved in Italy and installed in 1918, commemorates not only Confederate soldiers but also their mothers.

Van Buren

Main Street. Troops of the Blue and of the Gray fought along the street and at the waterfront in the warehouse district, which burned to the ground during the encounter. The Union unleashed the attack in an attempt to block Confederate access to Indian allies in the area. More recently, the turn-of-the-century buildings lining Main Street served to portray Gettysburg and Vicksburg in the TV mini-series "The Blue and the Gray."

Fairview Cemetery. Confederate soldiers killed during the Van Buren battle repose in the burial ground.

War Eagle Mill

A latter-day (1973) reproduction of an 1873 water-powered grist mill recall the site's earlier mill (c. 1840), which a Confederate general burned to prevent its capture and use by Federal forces.

White Oak Lake State Park

Near this area General Frederick Steele's troops camped prior to occupying Camden.

Index

Index

Index

Index